MULTINATIONALS andEMPLOYMENT

THE GLOBAL ECONOMY OF THE 1990s

Edited by Paul Bailey,
Aurelio Parisotto
and Geoffrey Renshaw

INTERNATIONAL LABOUR OFFICE   GENEVA

Bailey, P., Parisotto, A. and Renshaw, G.
Multinationals and employment: The global economy of the 1990s
Geneva, International Labour Office, 1993
/Employment/, /Multinational enterprise/, /Developed country/, /Developing country/. 13.01.3
ISBN 92-2-107105-7

ILO Cataloguing in Publication Data

ILO publications can be obtained through major booksellers or ILO local offices in many countries, or direct from ILO Publications, International Labour Office, CH-1211 Geneva 22, Switzerland. A catalogue or list of new publications will be sent free of charge from the above address.

Printed in Switzerland   HEL

Preface

The social and labour aspects of the activities of multinational enterprises have been a matter of special concern to the ILO ever since the internationalization of the economy began to take firm root in the early 1960s.

The Organization's principal response to the concerns of its constituents was the adoption, in 1977, of the Tripartite Declaration of Principles concerning Multinational Enterprises and Social Policy. This universal voluntary "instrument" provides guidance to governments, employers and workers in adopting policies and taking measures within multinational enterprises that would minimize conflict and promote cooperation. As a complement to action at national levels, the ILO's Multinational Enterprises Programme carries out a series of activities designed to give meaning to the provisions of the Tripartite Declaration in the fields of employment, training, conditions of work and life and industrial relations.

The research component of the Office's work in this area has been primarily in the field of employment – of which this book is the latest example.

Much of the controversy which characterized discussions on multinational enterprises (MNEs) in previous years is now being replaced by constructive dialogue and pragmatic approaches in the search for solutions. At the same time, the sustained pace of globalization, in which multinational enterprises in both industrialized and developing countries play active roles, is affecting economies and labour and social practices worldwide.

Within the context of growing economic interdependence, the importance of voluntary regulatory instruments like the Tripartite Declaration, in providing guidelines to solving the problems that arise, naturally comes to the fore.

It should be underlined that any attempt to look at the activities of MNEs completely separated from those of national enterprises can only show part of the overall picture. Besides, the Tripartite Declaration is in substance equally applicable to both, since the labour and social practices of one are bound to influence the other.

We hope this publication will be useful in clearly identifying the issues involved, and provide the tripartite partners, including national and multinational enterprises, a sound basis for dialogue that will help to overcome the obstacles to more and better employment and higher standards of living.

Abebe Abate,
Chief, Multinational Enterprises Branch,
Industrial Relations and
Labour Administration Department.

Contents

List of tables

List of figures

List of boxes

Abreviations

ABB	Asea-Brown Boveri
AMT	Advanced manufacturing technology
ASEAN	Association of South-East Asian Nations
BA	British Airways
BEA	(US Department of Commerce) Bureau of Economic Analysis
BIAC	Business and Industry Advisory Committee
BIP	Border Industrialization Programme
BIS	Bank of International Settlements
BKPM	Badan Koordinasi Penanaman Modal (Indonesia)
BLEU	Belgium and Luxembourg Economic Union
BOC	British Oxygen Company
CAD/CAM	Computer-aided design and manufacture
CEOs	Chief executive officers
CIS	Commonwealth of Independent States
CNC	Computer numerical control
COLEF	El Colegio de la Frontera Norte (Mexico)
CPEs	Centrally Planned Economies
CSFR	Czech and Slovak Federal Republic
DCs	Developing countries
EC	European Communities
ECU	European Currency Unit
EFTA	European Free Trade Association
EIBJ	Export and Import Bank of Japan
EPZs	Export processing zones
ESPRIT	European strategic programme on research in information technology
EUREKA	European Research Coordination Agency
FDI	Foreign direct investment
FMCG	Fast-moving consumer goods
FTA	Free Trade Agreement
FY	Fiscal year
GATT	General Agreement on Tariffs and Trade
GATS	General Agreement on Trade in Services
GDP	Gross domestic product
GDR	German Democratic Republic
GE	General Electric
GM	General Motors
GNP	Gross national product
HQ	Headquarters
IBM	International Business Machines
ICFTU	International Confederation of Free Trade Unions

IMMM	Institute for Manufacturing and Materials Management
INEGI	Instituto Nacional de Estadística, Geografía e Informática
INTUG	International Telecommunication User Group
ISIC	International Standard Industrial Classification
JETRO	Japan Exterior Trade Research Organization; Japan External Trade Organization
JIT	Just-in-time
JV(s)	Joint venture(s)
MAAs	Mergers, acquisitions and alliances
M&As	Mergers and acquisitions
MITI	Ministry of International Trade and Industry (Japan)
MNE(s)	Multinational enterprise(s)
NAFTA	North American Free Trade Agreement
NASDAQ	National Association of Security Dealears Automated Quotation (system)
NIEs	Newly Industrializing Economies
NMUK	Nissan Manufacturing of United Kingdom
NUMMI	New United Motors Manufacturing Inc.
ODI	Overseas direct investment
OECD	Organisation for Economic Co-operation and Development
QC	Quality control
R&D	Research and development
SCB	(US Department of Commerce) Survey of Current Business
SITC	Standard International Trade Classification
SMEs	Small and medium-sized enterprises
TEP	Thai Engineering Products Co.
TQC	Total quality control
UK	United Kingdom
UNCTC	United Nations Center on Transnational Corporations
UNCTAD	United Nations Conference on Trade and Development
UN/ECE	United Nations Economic Commission for Europe
US	United States
USGAO	United States Government Accounting Office
USITC	United States International Trade Commission
UTEP	University of Texas at El Paso
VANs	Value added networks

About the authors

Tito Alegria
Research Associate at the Colegio de la Frontera Norte, Tijuana, Baja California, Mexico.

Jeffery T. Brannon
Associate Professor of Economics, University of Texas, El Paso, United States.

Duncan Campbell
Senior Research Officer, New Industrial Organization Programme, International Institute for Labour Studies, Geneva, Switzerland.

Noe Aron Fuentes
Research Associate at the Colegio de la Frontera Norte, Tijuana, Baja California, Mexico.

James Hamill
Senior Lecturer in International Business and International Marketing at the Strathclyde Business Unit, University of Strathclyde, Glasgow, Scotland.

Hal Hill
Senior Fellow in Economics, and Head, Indonesia Project, Research Fellow of Pacific Studies, Australian National University, Canberra.

Dirk Holtbrügge
Research Assistant at the Chair of Management, University of Dortmund, Germany.

Dilmus D. James
Professor of Economics, University of Texas, El Paso, United States.

Rolf Jungnickel
Head of the Research Group on International Capital and Enterprises, HWWA Institute for International Economics, Hamburg, Germany.

William G. Lucker
Associate Professor of Industrial/Organizational Psychology, University of Texas, El Paso, United States.

Aurelio Parisotto
Research Officer, Multinational Enterprises Branch, International Labour Office, Geneva, Switzerland.

Geoffrey Renshaw
Lecturer, Department of Economics, University of Warwick, Coventry, United Kingdom.

Ana T. Romero
Technical and Programme Officer, Multinational Enterprises Branch, International Labour Office, Geneva, Switzerland.

Susumu Watanabe
Professor of Economics, Tokyo International University, Kawagoe, Japan.

Acknowledgements

In addition to the authors, the editors would like to thank several colleagues at the ILO for their helpful comments on all or part of the manuscript. Special thanks, in particular, are due to Gijsbert van Liemt and John Myers for their extensive advice. An invaluable contribution was provided by Geoffrey Hamilton of the UN/ECE, who also contributed box 4.1. Box 2.3 was prepared by Paul Bailey.

Introduction

Over the years the ILO has commissioned and published many working papers and books addressing the main questions of concern to the ILO in the field of multinational enterprises and social policy, primarily on the direct and indirect effects of MNEs, in both industrialized and developing countries, on employment, wages, working conditions, occupational health and safety, training and technology transfer.

In the early 1980s the ILO published two volumes which surveyed more comprehensively the employment effects of MNEs – one volume dealing with industrialized and the other with developing countries. The present book has its genesis in a relatively modest proposal to update these two works. However, as thoughts crystallized there was a perception that a fresh approach was required. In the 1980s there were many fundamental changes both in the behaviour of MNEs and in the world economic environment. Among the behavioural changes may be mentioned, first, that there were sharp swings in multinational activity: a phase of massive retrenchment in the early 1980s was followed by a huge expansion in foreign direct investment (FDI) in the second half of the decade. Second, the characteristics and underlying motivation of FDI changed quite fundamentally: whereas in the 1970s such investment had been predominantly aimed at establishing new productive capacity, in the 1980s it overwhelmingly took the form of mergers and acquisitions which were aimed at rationalizing and reducing capacity. This development clearly had profound implications for employment. Third, there were important changes in the relative importance of countries and regions both as sources of, and hosts to, FDI. Among these may be mentioned the declining importance of the United States as a source, but its increasing importance as a host; the emergence of Japan as a major source of FDI; the beginnings of FDI emanating from some of the Newly Industrializing Economies of Asia and Latin America; the declining relative importance of developing countries (particularly in Africa) as hosts to FDI; and increased FDI activity in Western Europe.

At the same time, and in ways which may be considered as being both causes and consequences of these changes, the world economic environment changed too. Regional and global economic integration proceeded rapidly, driven by advances in communications and information processing, the quest for market expansion, and political developments of which the most conspicuous was the movement towards the Single European Market. The decade also saw quite visible cumulative effects of long-term shifts in the balance of economic strength between countries and regions, which was marked particularly by the ending of the long postwar period of US economic dominance and its replacement by an uneasy balance between a "triad" of economic powers – Japan, North America and Western Europe. Finally, the end of the decade saw the liberalization of Central and Eastern Europe and this opened a new chapter in world economic history.

In view of these fundamental changes in the 1980s, it was clear that a wider and deeper analysis of MNEs' behaviour was necessary if their current and future implications for employment and other areas of ILO concern were to be understood. However, it also had to be recognized that a single volume could only aspire to being a partial analysis of immensely complex and truly global developments, the conclusions of which would be no more than tentative. This book, consisting of studies specially commissioned from authorities in their respective fields, therefore focuses on a selection of the more salient issues and is offered to the reader as one contribution to a burgeoning literature.[1]

Part 1 of this book is concerned with global trends in MNE activity in the 1980s, the analysis of MNE behaviour which underlies these trends, and their implications for employment, mainly in industrialized countries. Part 2 examines, by means of case studies, the employment effects of MNEs in developing countries and in Central and Eastern Europe. Finally, Part 3 tends to look towards the future, considering the growth of MNE activity in the service sector, and some of the broader economic and social implications of MNEs' "globalization" strategies. The final chapter briefly summarizes each author's contribution, draws together some of the strands of the data and arguments, fills in where possible some of the lacunae which are inevitable in any multi-authored work, and offers some evaluative comments and tentative conclusions.

[1] The reader is referred for example to the works of M. E. Porter (ed.): *Competition in global industries* (Boston, Massachussetts, Harvard Business School Press, 1986); P. Dicken: *The global shift: Industrial change in a turbulent world* (Manchester, Paul Chapman Publishing, 1988); E.M. Graham and P.R. Krugman: *Foreign direct investment in the United States* (Washington, DC, Institute for International Economics, 1989); J. DeAnne: *Global companies and public policy: The growing challenge of foreign direct investment* (London, The Royal Institute of International Affairs, 1990); R. Reich: *The work of nations: Preparing ourselves for 21st-century capitalism* (New York, Alfred A. Knopf, 1991); and G. van Liemt (ed.): *Industry on the move* (Geneva, ILO, 1992).

Part 1

Global trends

1

Recent trends in foreign direct investment

Rolf Jungnickel

1. Introduction

Multinational enterprises (MNEs) enjoyed a period of rapid expansion throughout the 1980s. Foreign direct investment (FDI) flows grew to the level of some US$ 222 billion of outflows in 1990. The worldwide stock of FDI tripled from an estimated value of US$ 500 billion in 1980 to over US$ 1,500 billion in 1990.

FDI flows reflect only loans and equity investments made by parent corporations in their affiliates and therefore do not take into consideration the full range of the activities of MNEs. They do not, for example, take account of the rapid growth of international strategic alliances and other non-equity arrangements between MNEs in the 1980s nor the considerable activities of these firms which are financed locally from loans and local shareholders. Often, reinvested profits are not included either. None the less, albeit partially, FDI flows do convey the rapid increase in MNE activities which have occurred in international markets in recent years, while stock data highlight the structural developments in the longer run (see box 1.1).

The aim of this chapter is to describe the nature and structure of MNE activities during the 1980s through an analysis of recent trends in FDI. A number of regional, sectoral and strategic aspects are touched upon only briefly, as they are discussed in detail in Chapters 5, 8 and 9 (on Japan, Central and Eastern Europe and services respectively). Section 2 analyses FDI flows and stocks in the 1980s in relation to a number of key economic variables to show the growing internationalization of the world economy and the increasing role played by the MNE as an agent of economic integration between countries. Section 3 describes the regional and country composition of FDI flows and the changes which have occurred. Section 4 describes the sectoral and industrial distribution of FDI. A distinctive feature of MNE investment strategies in the 1980s, the growth of mergers and acquisitions, is briefly discussed in section 5. Finally, the conclusion looks at how far these changes constitute a new structure in MNE activities.

Box 1.1. FDI as an indicator of internationalization

For the benefit of the non-specialist reader, it may be helpful to point out that the magnitude of FDI may be assessed by reference to either annual flows or accumulated stocks. Flow data may be collected by looking either at outflows from "source" countries or at inflows into "host" countries. Similarly stocks may be measured by looking either at "outward stocks" of countries (that is, stocks of capital located abroad which are owned by companies located in those countries); or at "inward stocks" of countries (that is, stocks of capital in those countries which are owned by companies located abroad).

Although FDI data are widely used in the literature on multinational enterprises and international production, there are some limits in the information provided by such data, as well as in their comparability across countries. Statistics on FDI are collected on a national basis, generally in accordance with a set of definitions by the OECD and the IMF. However, discrepancies remain in the various national sources. These relate mainly to the coverage of reinvested profits or investment funds taken up abroad, the treatment of offshore centres, the valuation of investments and disinvestments, as well as to basic definitions: e.g. as concerns stock at a certain time v. annual or cumulated flow data; actual v. notified v. approved investments; FDI v. portfolio investments (see Turner, 1991, pp. 109 ff.; Cantwell, 1990; UNCTC, 1989). Considering these (and other) differences, it is not surprising that the figures on global inward and outward FDI flows do not match. In the past five years the world ran FDI surpluses with itself to the order of up to 27 per cent of the capital outflow (1990). More important, FDI includes total funds of the home-country investor used for buying or increasing a controlling interest or for setting up and operating a foreign affiliate, including payments for trademarks, company goodwill and other assets, and purely financial transactions. But it does not include local financing, which can constitute an important component of the activity of an affiliate.

FDI data should then be interpreted as an order of magnitude only. They are more informative in their development over time than as absolute values. Neither stocks nor flows indicate the market value of foreign subsidiaries/branches. They specify part of the financing (from the home country) of foreign subsidiaries/branches or the book value, which can be much less than the market value, particularly in the case of long existing investments.

In order to assess fully the relevance of MNEs for the economic development of a country or on a global scale, one should consider performance of MNE indicators such as sales, value added, employment, foreign trade, R&D, etc. Unfortunately, such data are available only for a few countries, so that FDI has to be used as a second best solution.

2. The relative importance of the activities of MNEs in the world economy

During the 1970s and the early 1980s, growth in foreign direct investment and domestic output tended to occur at similar rates, while exports of goods and services, on average, expanded more strongly. From the mid-1980s, however, the rate of growth of FDI well outpaced the other economic indicators. As a result, the stock of FDI outflows increased from 5 per cent of world output in 1980 to over 8 per cent in 1990, with the strongest growth occurring in the second half of the decade (see figure 1.1). During the 1985-90 period, global FDI grew almost three times as fast as domestic output (gross domestic product) and world exports. For this period average annual growth rates for FDI outflows were 33 per cent, for current GDP 12 per cent, and for exports 13 per cent.

This growth in FDI outflows and in trade illustrates the speed at which economies were becoming international. Growth in FDI, however, outpaced growth

Figure 1.1.   FDI in the world economy, 1980-90

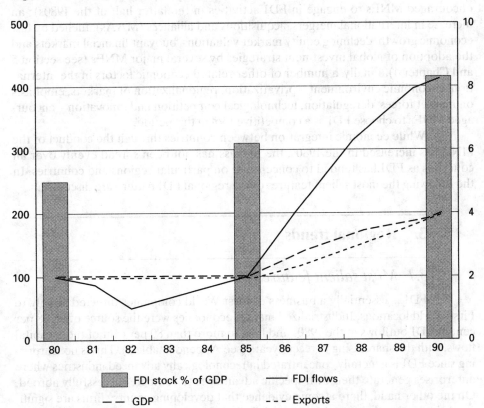

Source: Calculated from IMF: *Balance of payments statistics and economic outlook*, various years.

in trade. Global sales of foreign affiliates are now as important as exports in delivering goods and services to foreign markets. By 1989, for example, it was estimated that worldwide sales of foreign affiliates were over US$4 trillion (UNCTC, 1992); roughly the same order of magnitude of the volume of the world exports of goods and services. Considering that an estimated 25 per cent of world trade and the bulk of licensed international technology transfer take place as intra-company transactions (UNCTC, 1992 and Jungnickel, 1989), and that international strategic alliances are booming, it appears that world economic integration is increasingly being driven by MNEs and international production as well as by international trading relationships.

Reflecting the growth of FDI in the world economy, MNEs have become increasingly important to the economies of individual host countries. Prior to the 1980s, foreign-owned corporations accounted for relatively moderate shares in all economic activities in host countries, although they were particularly important in specific industrial segments. However from the 1980s and particularly the mid-1980s the importance of FDI in the economic activities of most developing and industrialized countries grew appreciably with increases being most marked in the latter.

Several factors lie behind this increase in MNE activities: favourable economic conditions (FDI tends to be pro-cyclical and prospects of increased returns encouraged MNEs to engage in FDI activities in the latter half of the 1980s); an increase in international mergers, acquisitions and alliances (MAAs), fuelled by fast economic growth, declining equity market valuations, buoyant financial markets and the adoption of global investment strategies by several major MNEs (see section 5 and Chapter 4). Finally, a number of other related economic factors in the international economic environment – privatization, regionalization of markets, emphasis on market forces, deregulation, technological competition and innovation – encouraged MNEs to choose FDI as a competitive tool in this period.

While economic integration between countries through the conduct of the MNE has increased in the 1980s, the process has not been spread evenly over all countries as FDI has tended to concentrate on particular regions and countries. In the following the most salient features of the regional FDI pattern are discussed.

3. Regional trends

3.1 Most salient features

FDI is essentially a business of First World companies directed largely to First World locations. Industrialized market economies were the source of 95-98 per cent of FDI outflows in the 1980s and host to more than 80 per cent of these capital flows, with the share rising in recent years (see Appendix table 1). This is not surprising since FDI is generally concentrated in technologically advanced industries where enterprises generate their own specific advantages to compete successfully abroad. On the other hand, there is some evidence that developing country firms are significantly increasing their activities abroad. Still, their share of global outward FDI stock remained below 2 per cent in 1990.

Figure 1.2. FDI flows^a in the 1980s: Developing countries' share

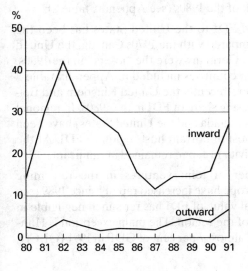

^a Corrected for financial US-FDI in the Netherlands Antilles. Estimates of BIS (1992); for 1990, BIS and IMF slightly diverging.

Source: IMF, BIS (1992).

Figure 1.3. FDI stock in percentage of GDP, 1980-90

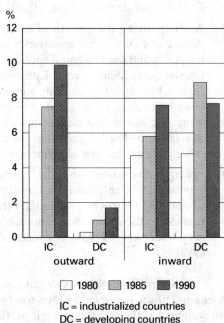

IC = industrialized countries
DC = developing countries

Source: Appendix table 1.

In general, the regional distribution of FDI did not change fundamentally in the 1980s. The attractiveness of developing countries to foreign investors has generally diminished over the decade although this trend was reversed slightly in 1990 and 1991 (see figure 1.2). The concentration of FDI in industrialized host economies largely reflects their economic predominance. In relative terms, the ratio of inward FDI to domestic output (GDP) was approximately the same for industrialized and developing countries in both 1980 and 1990 (see figure 1.3).

In contrast the position of individual countries as homes and hosts of FDI changed considerably:

■ While the *United States* has lost ground as the dominant home country of MNEs, it has acquired a position as a major host country to FDI. About 27 per cent of the world FDI stock was invested there in 1990 compared with 17 per cent at the beginning of the decade (Appendix table 1). The United States has become the most important host for investing firms of virtually all other countries. It now records a roughly balanced investment position.

■ In the late 1980s Japan and the United Kingdom assumed the mantle of the world's leading foreign investors. In addition investors from Australia, Finland, France, Belgium/Luxembourg, Italy and Sweden registered above-average increases in their direct investments abroad, though from a much lower level. On the other hand, along with the United States, FDIs from the Netherlands and Canada have declined in the latter half of the 1980s (see Appendix table 2).

■ Accompanying the growth of *inward* FDI to the United States has been the decline of FDI to other countries. Compared with the 1970s Canada, the United Kingdom and the Federal Republic of Germany were the "losers" in the 1980s. On the other hand, several European countries included in Appendix table 2 (Spain, Portugal, France, Italy and more recently the United Kingdom and Belgium/Luxembourg) attracted an increasing share of FDI in the 1980s. In regional terms, the North American countries (Canada and the United States) have been overtaken by the EC region as the most important host region to FDI. At the other extreme, foreign investment activity in Japan remained insignificant.

■ Foreign investment and the number of joint ventures in the reforming economies of Central and Eastern Europe have increased rapidly since 1989 (see Chapter 8). However, to date the total value of FDI has remained negligible in relation to the size of the economies of the region. The main exception is Hungary, where inward FDI stock reached almost 7 per cent of GDP in 1991 (OECD, 1992).

All in all, the 1980s showed a certain diversification of international FDI stocks and flows. In outward FDI a triad structure has developed with not too different weights for the three core regions, the United States, EC (excluding intra-EC investment, see below, part 3.3) and Japan. On the other hand, in inward FDI the concentration on the United States and the EC has left room only recently for a modest diversification.

With the regional diversification of outward FDI and the concentration of inward FDI on the United States and the EC there is now a tendency towards:

■ more balanced national FDI positions; and

■ a regional FDI structure more in line with national economic potentials.

Both should help to reduce conflicts arising from one-sided FDI positions.

3.2 The American challenge reversed?

The rapid expansion of inward investment leading to a turnaround of the American FDI position can be regarded as the most significant feature of the international investment scene in the 1980s. From the beginning of the decade, FDI inflows surpassed outflows. The stock of inward investment has caught up rapidly with the outward stock although in the recession years of 1990 and 1991, inward FDI flows declined rapidly (table 1.1).

Although the source countries of inward investment have changed, the concentration of FDI in a few countries remains (table 1.2). While the MNEs of most of the important home countries have invested at least 25 per cent of their FDI stock in the United States and often place over 50 per cent of the FDI outflows there, the

Table 1.1.   Shift in the United States FDI position,[a] 1980-91 (US$ billion)

Flows (annual average)	1980-84	1985-88	1989	1990	1991
(1) Inward	17	43	66	41	13
(2) Outward	7	15	25	28	27
(3) Balance (1)-(2)	10	28	41	13	-14
Stocks (end of period)	1980	1985	1989	1990	1991
(4) Inward	74	169	355	379	392
(5) Outward	198	225	341	387	411
(6) Balance (4)-(5)	-124	-56	14	-8	-19

[a] FDI to and from "other Western Hemisphere" and Panama is excluded.

Sources: US Department of Commerce: *Survey of current business*, various issues; author's calculations.

aggregate share of the top four investing countries remained at around 70 per cent. British firms now command the largest stock while Canadian, Dutch and German investors have declined relatively. In contrast, Japanese investment has more than quadrupled within five years and has taken the position of the Netherlands as the number two investor in the United States. Strong expansion rates have also been recorded for other European countries. French companies for example tripled their annual investment outlays in the United States in 1990 making France the biggest investor in the manufacturing sector in that year (SCB, May 1991).

Several factors influenced MNE decisions to invest in the US, including US political stability, liberal stance towards inward FDI, fear of trade barriers or, at times, a low dollar value. However, the main reasons seem to result from changes in the international competitive environment. First, non-United States firms have caught up with the United States counterparts in terms of technological, organizational and marketing know-how and they have developed the financial capacity to make large investments abroad. Second, the internationalization of competition has led to an increased interdependence between the companies in different countries. There is growing pressure to achieve more efficient R&D, production and marketing structures worldwide and to establish a strong presence in the largest and most dynamic markets. For these reasons, the United States has become a highly attractive location for MNEs.

While until the 1960s or early 1970s some European politicians (and others, especially from developing countries) felt their economic, technological and hence political sovereignty was being challenged by the massive invasion of the United States firms (Servan-Schreiber, 1968), fears have been raised in the United States of an overtly strong dominance by foreign-controlled firms of the United States economy. In particular, several notable acquisitions (including "national symbols" such as the Rockefeller Center, Columbia Pictures and MCA with Universal Studios) by Japanese investors have generated considerable debate.

However, from both a theoretical and empirical point of view, such concern is no better founded now in the United States than it was 20 years ago in Europe:

Table 1.2. Sources of inward, directions of outward FDI of the United States, 1980-91 [a]

Country	Inward FDI (%)			Outward FDI (%)			Balance (inward-outward) ($bn)		
	1980	1985	1991	1980	1985	1991	1980	1985	1991
Canada	16	10	8	20	18	15	-33	-30	-39
Europe	72	70	65	44	46	49	-42	15	34
United Kingdom	18	26	27	13	13	15	-15	10	38
Netherlands	25	21	16	4	5	5	11	29	39
Denmark	10	8	7	7	6	7	-8	-2	-5
France	5	4	6	4	4	5	-6	-2	2
Sweden	2	2	–	–	–	–			
Switzerland	7	6	4	5	6	5	-6	-5	-9
Japan	6	11	22	3	4	5	-2	10	66
Developing countries	6	7	5	26	30	25	-53	-63	-93
Total percentage	100	100	100	100	100	100			
($ bn)	(76)	(172)	(400)	(211)	(251)	(454)	(-136)	(-77)	(-54)

[a] FDI stock corrected for financial investment in the Netherlands Antilles.

Sources: US Department of Commerce: *Survey of current business*, various issues; author's calculations.

■ The involvement of foreign-owned firms in the United States has to be set against the foreign involvement of American MNEs. With a roughly balanced FDI position, there is hardly any reason for general concern. Bilateral balances are of course larger. But table 1.2 reveals that the greater part of the shift in the FDI position has taken place (until now) with the United Kingdom and the Netherlands, i.e. with countries that are at the same time among the main destinations of American outward investment and which can hardly be considered politically unfriendly or economically "too" strong. Only the Japanese involvement in the United States stands out, with four times the stock of the American investment in Japan.

■ Even the "real" investment balance with Japan is far from being one-sided, as can be seen from table 1.3. The Japanese lead in sales is the result of traditionally large involvements in the wholesale sector and not from manufacturing, which is more at the centre of the current political debate.

■ Foreign-owned firms accounted for 4 per cent of total paid employment in the United States in 1989 (see Chapter 2, table 2.9). In the manufacturing sector the share was 11 per cent with chemicals reaching 29 per cent and electronics 14 per cent. In the tertiary sector the United States affiliates of foreign firms account for less than 3 per cent of the total United States employment. These shares have doubled since 1980. Nevertheless, from the limited evidence available (see Chapter 2) the United States economy is less international than other major industrialized market economies and most developing countries.

■ Quite independent of the balance of FDI flows and stocks, it is by no means clear that inward investment is detrimental to the host country's economy. According to the "eclectic theory" (Dunning, 1981), increased inward FDI can be viewed as an indicator of the (improved) quality of locations in the host country (United States) and/or increased competitive advantages of the investing (non-American) firms. The inflow of superior production factors can, and does, as Graham and Krugman (1989) have argued, increase competition and lead to productivity growth, thus furthering structural change and the income level.

Table 1.3. United States-Japan FDI balance, 1989-91[a]

Involvement	FDI $ billion	Total assets $ billion	Employment (1'000)	Sales $ billion
United States in Japan				
Total	23	134	392	165
Manufacturing	10	59	240	85[b]
Japan in the United States				
Total	89	328	504	267
Manufacturing	19	44	242	n.a.

[a] FDI: 1991; other variables 1989. [b] 1988.

Source: US Department of Commerce: *Survey of current business*, various issues.

3.3 Multinational investment in the European internal market

Changed investment conditions

The EC 1992 programme aims to improve the international competitiveness of EC firms, to abolish border controls and other technical and administrative barriers, to open up public procurement to foreigners, and to reduce government-imposed trade and entry barriers. EC firms will therefore have to be prepared for stiffer competition both at home and abroad. In addition, it is hoped that individual countries, regions and companies will, in this more liberal framework, be able to generate and exploit their competitive advantages better.

All this has implications for the FDI decisions of both EC and third country firms:

- For EC firms, there is on the one hand better market access for exports, hence less pressure for FDI. On the other hand, with reduced government-imposed barriers to international trade and investment, there may be more reasons for firms to reorganize their existing pattern of international production, sourcing, and distribution according to locational advantages and reduced transaction costs. The prospect of increased competition can also induce firms into "offensive" FDI in order to capture "first mover" advantages or offset competitors' moves.

- For non-EC firms the process of integration makes the EC an attractive investment location. This holds true in particular if the non-EC companies are in those global industries where being active in a large, dynamic market is a prerequisite for competitive success.

- In addition, third country firms are directly affected by trade barriers (such as those raised against the import of Japanese cars) and by strict anti-dumping policies, all of which create uncertainty about future market access, and encourage enterprises to invest behind such trade barriers.

In response to such developments created by this process of integration, table 1.4 shows that since the mid-1980s the EC attracted substantially increasing shares of worldwide inward FDI, reaching nearly 50 per cent in 1990.

With the exception of Germany, all the major EC-host countries recorded above-average increases, with the United Kingdom by far the largest beneficiary (with 36 per cent of the total EC inflow).

This upsurge in FDI has tended to take the form of intra-EC flows. French MNEs have considerably increased their total outflows in the region (table 1.5). In the majority of the EC countries, investment from EC MNEs has come close to or even surpassed third country investment (table 1.6), which had traditionally predominated. The main exception is the United Kingdom (26 per cent) followed by Germany (35 per cent). The table also shows the limited weight of Japanese investment in the region so far.

Table 1.4. Inflow of FDI to the EC, 1985-91

Host country/region	1985	1986	1987	1988	1989	1990	1991	(1980-90)
	Percentage of worldwide FDI inflows							
EC (12)	29	26	30	36	39	49	43	36
	Percentage of EC inflows							
Belgium/Luxembourg	7	4	7	10	9	10	–	9
Denmark	5	5	5	2	9	2	–	5
France	18	16	14	16	14	15	–	15
Netherlands	10	18	8	9	12	9	–	11
Spain	14	17	13	13	11	16	–	13
United Kingdom	33	37	39	34	37	37	–	36

Sources: IMF: Balance of payments statistics; author's calculations.

Table 1.5. FDI in the EC by country of origin, 1985-90

Home country	Share of EC in FDI stock 1990		Share of EC in FDI flows p.a. (%)				Flows to EC 1989-90 1985-86 (%)
	$ bn	%	1985-87	1988	1989	1990	
France	59	60	41	63	62	68	980
Germany	70	45	32	36	63	68	218
Japan[a]	55	18	17	18	21	23	428
Netherlands	48	46	46	24	51	58	197
Sweden	18[b]	50[b]	31	46	52	70	768
Switzerland	32	48	42	69	24	51	79
United Kingdom	54	24	17	26	27	55	142
United States	178	42	38	54	58	28	95

[a] Notification based, cumulated flows.   [b] 1989.   [c] Calculated in national currency.

Source: National statistics of home countries.

Table 1.6. Sources of inward investment in EC countries[a] (percentage of total national inward FDI stock)

	US	Japan	EC	BLEU[b]	France	Germany	Netherlands	UK
Host country								
BLEU[b]	44	3	41	1	10	11	11	7
Denmark	28	1	36	2	2	9	8	14
France	16	2	54	8	–	12	11	16
Germany	33	7	35	2	6	–	13	10
Ireland	38	–	45	9	–	9	–	–
Italy	15	1	54	8	11	9	13	12
Netherlands	25	3	40	3	5	8	–	19
Portugal	16	2	48	3	11	8	4	21
Spain	13	3	61	3	12	12	17	12
United Kingdom	47	4	26	2	4	4	13	–

[a] Year not specified in source, probably 1988-89. Because of substantial differences in the national FDI statistics, the shares can only be interpreted across rather than down. They give orders of magnitude. No recent data are available for Greece.   [b] BLEU = Belgium and Luxembourg Economic Union.

Source: Thomsen and Nicolaides 1991, host country statistics.

This growth in intra-EC investment is often seen as being part of a regional rationalization of EC business activities (UNCTC, 1990). While this can be observed frequently in the distribution and logistics functions, there are fewer examples of investments, whose motivation is locational rationalization of the production system (Jungnickel, 1989). True, lower transaction costs can lead to a lesser number of highly specialized plants. However, given:

- the similar locational conditions in the core EC countries;

- the high degree of openness of markets (both for trade and FDI); and

- the advantages of a local presence in terms of better adjustment to local needs;

the companies often appear to be following market-oriented strategies, expanding into EC countries in order to strengthen their market position. Thereby they reduce both the uncertainties and adverse consequences of the intensified competition which is – or is expected to be – brought about by 1992.

It seems that MNEs from non-EC countries follow similar strategies:

- By their free trade arrangements, the EFTA countries enjoy privileged access to the EC markets. Yet they have built up a strong investment position, with around half of their outward FDI in the EC. Swiss and Swedish MNEs employ 430,000 and more than 300,000 people respectively in the EC. While the EC involvement of Swiss firms has fallen back recently, Swedish MNEs have stepped up their activities, often through mergers and acquisitions. They have been among the most active buyers recently, and placed about 70 per cent of their FDI in 1990 in the EC.

- American MNEs have reinforced their traditionally strong position inside the EC. With 2.4 million employees, their affiliates had sales of over US$ 500 billion in 1987 – eight times the value of the American exports. In manufacturing, the ratio was 5:1. The American affiliates had a "European content" of more than 90 per cent (US Department of Commerce, June 1989). Despite this insider position, American firms have expanded further their investments in the EC relative to other regions. Over 40 per cent of American FDI stock was invested there at the end of 1991, an increase of 8 percentage points since 1985 (US Department of Commerce, August 1992).

- Japanese MNEs have generally followed export strategies in the EC with a local production/exports ratio in the range of 1:4 to 1:5 in 1989 (the exact opposite of the ratio for the American MNEs). However, in the late 1980s they have been among the most dynamic elements in the EC's inward investment. Within three years their FDI stock more than trebled – four times the growth rate of the EC investments of the American MNEs (which still is almost four times as large). While the Japanese have invested relatively more than the American firms in the services sector particularly in financial services, American and Japanese firms tend to choose the same EC countries as the location for their investment (Thomsen and Nicolaides, 1991). The United Kingdom is the most important; with the Netherlands and Germany figuring at the top of the host country rankings.

3.4 New investors from the Far East

The unprecedented growth of Japanese FDI is one of the most remarkable features of international FDI in the later 1980s, and this is discussed in detail in Chapter 5. Of great importance too have been the investments made by companies from other Asian countries and areas.

Emerging Asian investors

Although evidence is limited and less reliable it seems to be clear that FDI by Asian NIEs and China already plays an important role in Asia-Pacific integration:

- Hong Kong has a long-standing tradition as a host to foreign MNEs that have established production bases or regional financial and trade centres there, often as a gateway to mainland China. But Hong Kong is also considered the No. 2 investor (after Japan) in the Asia-Pacific region. The stock of Hong Kong's FDI can be estimated at over US$ 20 billion in 1991 (estimate based upon Ramstetter 1991; Borrmann and Jungnickel, 1992). Hong Kong MNEs have spread their activities over a large number of countries, including industrialized ones (United States). However, most of the FDI is in the Asia-Pacific region, with a clear focus on the neighbouring Guangdong Province of China. Up to 3 million people are working there for Hong Kong investors, manufacturing simple consumer goods at about one-sixth of wages in Hong Kong. Even if one takes into account that an unknown share is indirect investment by third countries or areas, the Hong Kong economy can be regarded as extremely internationalized.

- Taiwan (China) shows the highest growth of FDI in the late 1980s. With outflows of US$ 7 billion and 5.5 billion in 1989 and 1990 respectively the stock of Taiwanese FDI could have reached the level of Hong Kong's. While a few large investors have developed technological competence and, on that basis, invest in industrialized countries (e.g. the United States), a large number of smaller firms invest in the Asia-Pacific region primarily in order to exploit an abundant supply of cheap labour. While FDI in the ASEAN countries has reached a significant level, with Malaysia and Thailand in the top ranks, mainland China has increasingly attracted Taiwanese investment, estimated at up to US$ 3.5 billion, most of which has been invested via Hong Kong for political reasons (and thus counted twice, as Hong Kong and Taiwanese FDI).

- The multinationalization of firms from the Republic of Korea intensified after FDI was liberalized in 1987. However, FDI has not yet reached the level of Taiwan and Hong Kong, although the dominant "Chaebols" seem to have achieved technical competence and management know-how that could serve as a basis for enhanced FDI outflows in the future. From an FDI stock of about US$ 3 billion (1990), most has been invested in manufacturing (40 per cent) and mining (25 per cent) industries. A typical feature of Korean FDI is the concentration on North America (42 per cent) and ASEAN countries (25 per cent, with Indonesia ranking top).

■ Despite a liberal policy, Singapore's outward FDI is probably the smallest of the NIEs and has expanded at lower rates. This can partly be attributed to the singular dominance of foreign-owned firms in the Singaporean economy. At the end of 1989 the Department of Statistics calculated the stock of industrial outward FDI at S\$5.3 billion (US\$2.8 billion) as against S\$2.4 billion in 1981, one-third of which was undertaken by foreign-owned investors. The bulk of Singapore's FDI still is in labour-intensive processing activities in Thailand, Malaysia and Hong Kong. However, FDI in industrialized countries is on the increase (20 per cent in 1989 compared with 10 per cent in 1981).

■ China has emerged as a leading Third World investor from the mid-1980s – second only to Taiwan (China) and Hong Kong. While statistics on Chinese FDI are poor, FDI seems to be concentrating on Hong Kong. Estimates of cumulated FDI flows from China to Hong Kong ranged around US\$9 billion in 1989 (Hong Kong and Shanghai Banking Corporation, 1991). These investments will of course (as well as Hong Kong's FDI in China) no longer be counted as FDI after 1997.

Asianization of FDI in the Asia-Pacific region

With the rapid increase of Japanese and NIEs' FDI and with their strong orientation towards the Asia-Pacific region (AP region), an "Asianization" of the regional FDI is taking place. While the intra-NIEs' FDI linkages are still limited, the Asianization is visible in the ASEAN region and China. In all countries, except for Singapore, most of the recent FDI is from within the region, as can be seen from figure 1.4.

The NIEs as a group – with Hong Kong and Taiwan (China) at the top – have outstripped Japan as the main source of new FDI in China, Malaysia, Indonesia and the Philippines.

The "new wave" of intra-regional FDI (Borrmann and Jungnickel, 1992) was not only caused by rapid market growth but also by economic progress and structural change in Japan and the NIEs. What could no longer be produced profitably in the home country was relocated to "cheaper" AP locations. Rapidly increasing wages and revalued exchange rates served as triggers to this development, which was further promoted by more liberal investment conditions in virtually all economies of the region. Also, cultural, ethnic and family ties within the Chinese community around the Asia-Pacific region (the "Chinese connection") help reduce the "foreignness" of FDI. In fact, it often seems hard to differentiate the home and host countries or areas of Chinese FDI since "... many Asian family businesses are now really Pacific-Rim ones: the patriarch lives in Hong Kong or Taipei; some of the factories are in Malaysia or Thailand; but the research and development, the marketing and (often) the brightest children are in California, Seattle or Vancouver" (*The Economist*, 14 Sep. 1991).

Production networks

The Asianization of FDI in the AP region has – beyond its quantitative aspects – a qualitative dimension. The MNEs have built regional production networks, thereby realizing economies of scale, exploiting the comparative advantages of different locations, and improving the access to the markets involved (UNCTC,

Figure 1.4. Foreign direct investment in the Asia-Pacific region, by origin, 1989-90

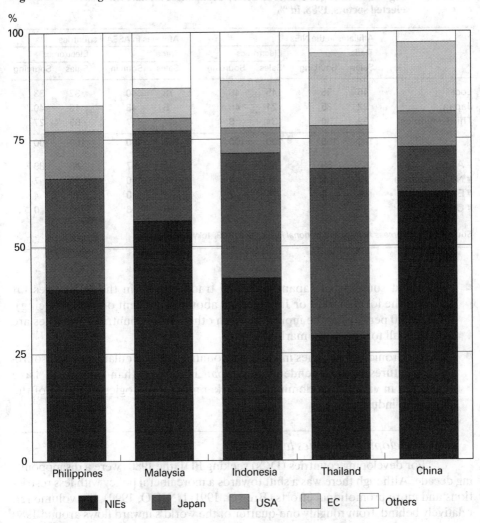

Indonesia: Average volume 1989-91.
China: EC, including some non-EC investments.
Source: National statistics of host countries.

1991; Borrmann and Jungnickel, 1992). This leads to increased intra-firm trade in inputs and final products. As "industrial linkage creators" (UNIDO, 1990), MNEs are an important element of de facto integration in the region even when formal integration is limited.

While Japanese MNEs (along with some American and European firms) have pioneered this development, the NIEs are now following in a similar pattern. An illustration of the way Japanese production and trading subsidiaries have integrated themselves into a regional or even worldwide division of labour is given in table 1.7.

Table 1.7.   Regional sourcing and sales structure of Japanese affiliates in Asia – selected sectors, 1988, in %

	Affiliates in the NIEs				Affiliates in ASEAN countries			
	Trade		Electronics		Trade		Electronics	
	Sales	Sourcing	Sales	Sourcing	Sales	Sourcing	Sales	Sourcing
Local	46	35	45	46	78	40	32	33
Japan	22	35	21	46	5	43	13	40
Third countries	32	30	34	8	17	17	55	27
	100	100	100	100	100	100	100	100
# Asia	43	89	45	97	13	97	48	89
# North America	37	2	35	1	86	0	30	7
# Europe	6	2	11	2	1	0	17	4
# Other	14	7	9	0	0	3	5	0

Source: MITI, *Overseas Activities of National Firms*, No. 18-19, Tokyo, 1990.

■ The input sourcing of Japanese-owned trading firms in the NIEs goes far beyond the local market or Japan (each about 35 per cent of total sourcing). Almost 30 per cent of the inputs are from other Asian countries. The sales are virtually all for the world market.

■ The electronics subsidiaries in ASEAN countries show similar sales and sourcing structures. The dependence on Japan is far less than one might have expected in view of the dominating market and technological position of the Japanese industry.

Developing countries left aside?

For developing countries (DCs) seeking FDI, the 1980s were a disapppointing decade. Although there was a shift towards a more liberal policy with less restrictions and more promotional efforts (Brewer, 1991; UNIDO, 1990), the volume fell relatively behind, from roughly one-quarter of the world's inward flows around 1980 to a mere 12 per cent in 1987. At times, in the early and mid-1980s, it even fell in absolute figures. Since 1989, a modest recovery seems to have begun. In 1989-90, FDI reached a new peak with inflows of over US$ 28 billion, although this was only 16 per cent of the worldwide inflows as recorded by the IMF. Preliminary estimates for 1991, however, indicate a strong increase, particularly in Asia (Appendix table 4).

The bulk of FDI in developing countries is invested in a few host countries and originates from a handful of leading source countries or areas. With varying weights, the United States, Japan and the United Kingdom supply over 60 per cent of the annual outflows to developing countries. Japan has reached the weight of the former leader, the United States. Other sources follow far behind these three, with the areas of Taiwan (China) and Hong Kong having recently graduated to the next rank, well ahead of certain industrialized countries.

Table 1.8.   FDI in developing countries by country of origin,[a] 1980-91 (percentage of total outward FDI)

Home country	Outward stocks			Outward flows		
	1980	1985	1990	1989	1990	1991
Germany	17	13	10	5	3	4
France	27[b]	24[b]	9[b]	6	3	6
Japan	53	45	24	18	17	20
Netherlands	12[c]	10[c]	8[c]	14[c]	7[c]	11[c]
United Kingdom	17[d]	17[e]	11	8	n.a.	n.a.
United States	19	22	17	17	26	31

[a] Caribbean tax havens and Panama excluded as far as possible.   [b] Cumulated flows to non-OECD countries; tax havens could not be excluded.   [c] Netherlands Antilles only excluded.   [d] 1981.   [e] 1984.

Source: Calculated from national statistics.

The declining share of FDI invested in developing countries (before 1991) is a feature common to virtually all of the six leading industrialized countries (see table 1.8). Only as host countries to American MNEs could developing countries generally maintain or even slightly improve their position (non-manufacturing in the mid-1980s (Langhammer, 1991)).

MNEs from the other industralized home countries included showed a clear swing towards OECD locations. Of course, this is largely a consequence of the rapid increase of FDI in the United States and the EC which drives down the share of other regions. In particular, French and German MNEs have engaged very little in developing countries recently.

Return of the runaway plants?

In the early 1980s fears were raised (Rada, 1980) that the tendency of developing countries to fall behind as a host to FDI was to be permanent, and that production which had been relocated to the South would return to the North. This "return hypothesis" was based on the assumption that "new" technologies (such as microelectronics, new materials and biotechnology) would bring about such a reduction in direct labour costs and increases in productivity that the North would regain its competitive advantage in the manufacture of formerly labour-intensive goods.

While a number of such relocations took place (Frobel et al., 1986; Jungnickel, 1990), the return hypothesis, as a general rule, neither seems to be theoretically conclusive nor has it been supported by general statistical evidence in recent years.

The main criticism of this thesis is its underlying assumption that the latest technologies are widely utilized in the North but not at all in the South. Both assumptions are doubtful. There are numerous factors preventing a widespread use of new technologies in the North (e.g. lack of finance, technological restrictions in labour-intensive production, risk considerations), and the experience of the NIEs shows a clear technological upgrading (Ernst and O'Connor, 1989; Jungnickel, 1990). In addition, evidence on FDI shows that export-oriented investment projects have increased in the dynamic South-East Asian economies and also in the northern Mexico *Maquiladoras* in recent years (see Chapter 6).

Latin America, Africa and the Middle East were the regions most affected by the decline in FDI inflows to developing countries in the 1980s. Since 1990, however, there were signs of a revival of foreign investment in Latin America, as the liberalization of trade and FDI policies and macroeconomic stabilization may have contributed to a more favourable climate for foreign investors in the region (see Appendix table 4).

Overall, success in attracting FDI in a developing country is likely to depend on country-specific factors. The winners in the locational competition are countries with:

- large and growing markets;
- a good supply of skilled but low-cost labour;
- supporting industries and infrastructure available;
- a stable and predictable environment (in terms of political stability, administrative efficiency, level of regulation) offering good prospects for profitable operations (UNIDO, 1990; UNCTC, 1988; Brewer, 1991).

Furthermore, economic proximity seems to play a crucial role (UNCTC, 1991). The three poles of the US, Japan and the EC (as well as the Asian NIEs) have traditionally concentrated their Third World investment on a limited number of nearby countries – nearby in terms of geography, culture, language, political links (such as post-colonial ties), transport, etc.

4. Sectoral and industrial distribution of FDI

4.1 Industrial countries

The sectoral composition of the outward stock of FDI by major home countries at the end of the 1980s is shown in table 1.9. The rapid increase in investment flows in the 1980s was accompanied by a shift in the sectoral composition of both flows and stocks towards services. For Japan and Germany, the services sector became the single largest sector, and reached, for outward investment, about two-thirds of the stock of Japan. Services accounted for about 40 per cent of the stock in the other countries.

The general shift in FDI towards services reflects long-term structural changes in national economies (see Chapter 9). Mainly, it was fuelled by deregulation in national services markets, increased outsourcing of services by MNEs, growing trade-related transactions which provide opportunities for business abroad, and development of firm-specific competititive advantages in service activities.

Manufacturing, however, remains the traditional core of FDI and accounts for the largest share of MNE employment and production in most home and host countries (see Chapter 2, tables 2.3 and 2.8 and UNCTC, 1992).

FDI in manufacturing is concentrated in industries characterized by: complex technologies and high R&D outlays; high marketing costs; vertical integration

Table 1.9. Sectoral composition of the stock of outward FDI, 1980-90 (percentage share)

Home country	Sector of investment				
	Year	Raw materials[b]	Manufacturing	Services	Total
Canada	1980	32	46	22	100
	1984	20	47	33	100
	1989	15	48	38	100
Germany[a]	1980	4	51	45	100
	1985	4	47	49	100
	1990	2	42	56	100
Japan[a]	1980	24	38	39	100
	1985	16	33	51	100
	1990	6	29	65	100
Netherlands[a]	1980	c	84	16	100
	1985	c	68	32	100
	1990	c	57	43	100
United Kingdom	1984	33	32	35	100
	1987	27	34	39	100
United States[a]	1980	25	48	28	100
	1985	27	44	30	100
	1990	16	45	39	100

[a] Excludes FDI in Caribbean offshore centres.   [b] US: petroleum only; UK: agriculture, energy; Germany: mining including petroleum.   [c] Included in manufacturing.

Source: Calculated from national statistics.

of production; and marked interdependence of the leading firms. The chemical and pharmaceuticals, electrical and mechanical engineering, electronics, automobile and food and drink industries are indeed those in which FDI is generally clustered. This pattern is common to the major investor countries and has not changed substantially in the last decade. The main changes can be observed in Japan (electronics), France (electronics, automobiles and food and drink) and the United Kingdom (food and drink) (see table 1.10).

4.2 Developing countries

Taking the recent data for three large source countries and excluding the Caribbean offshore centres and Panama, the following sectoral picture emerges (table 1.11).

■ Investments in natural resources increased in the early 1980s but lost ground in the second half of the decade.

■ In services, American, German and particularly Japanese MNEs increased their investments.

Table 1.10. FDI in manufacturing by leading investor countries and industry, 1980-90 (percentage of total outward FDI stock in manufacturing)

United States	1980	1985	1990	Japan	1980	1985	1990
Chemicals	21	21	23	Electrical machinery			
Mechanical machinery	18	20	17	and electronics	13	15	25
Transport equipment	14	12	14	Chemicals	21	16	13
Food, drink, tobacco	9	10	10	Transport equipment	8	14	13
Electrical machinery				Metals	21	21	13
and electronics	8	9	8	Textiles	13	9	5
Total	71	73	72	Total	75	75	69

Germany	1980	1985	1990	Netherlands	1980	1985	1990
Chemicals	37	39	38	Chemicals[a]	63	64	59
Electrical machinery				Electrical machinery			
and electronics	15	17	17	and electronics,			
Transport equipment	15	14	13	plus metals	24	21	23
Mechanical machinery	9	9	9	Food, drink, tobacco	10	12	13
Iron and steel products	5	3	2				
Total	81	83	80	Total	97	97	96

France	FDI flows 1984-87		1988-90	United Kingdom	1980	1985	1990
Chemicals	22		20	Chemicals	28	29	27
Electrical machinery				Food, drink, tobacco	27	19	20
and electronics	31		14	Electrical machinery			
Transport equipment	14		6	and electronics	10	10	11
Non-metallic products	6		8	Paper	6	4	8
Food, drink, tobacco	17		24	Mechanical machinery	6	8	5
Total	89		71	Total	77	70	71

[a] Includes mining, quarrying, oil and chemicals.

Source: Calculated from national statistics.

- In manufacturing, developing country locations lost attractiveness for Japanese and to a lesser extent German investors, but not for American firms.

- Generally, there were larger changes in the share of developing countries for Japanese FDI while the American pattern remained fairly stable. Since Japanese investors traditionally have high commitments in developing countries, the total FDI of the First World in the Third World largely followed the changes in the Japanese pattern.

The sectoral investment pattern shows a clear trend only for Japan with a shift from natural resources and manufacturing to services. Services accounted for more than 60 per cent of Japanese FDI flows (notifications) to developing countries in the late 1980s. In American and German FDI, services also gained in importance

Table 1.11. Japanese, American and German FDI[a] in developing countries, 1980-90, by sector (percentage)

Source countries		I. Share of DCs in total outward FDI			II. Share of sectors in FDI in DCs		
		Natural resources	Manufacturing	Services	Natural resources	Manufacturing	Services
United States	1980	17[b]	20	19	23	49	28
	1985	27[b]	20	21	32	39	29
	1990	25[b]	20	17	20	46	34
Japan	1980	66	68	28	29	47	20
	1985	74	55	27	28	41	31
	1990	55	31	17	14	38	47
Germany	1980	18	24	8	9	70	19
	1985	40	19	8	11	67	22
	1990	34	14	5	8	67	24

[a] Stock of FDI; excluding Caribbean offshore centres and Panama. Sectoral breakdown of Japanese FDI in these countries was estimated (services: 90 per cent; manufacturing: 5 per cent; natural resources: 5 per cent); for Germany it was fully allocated to services.   [b] Petroleum only.

Source: Computed from national statistics.

during the entire 1980s, whereas neither natural resources nor manufacturing showed any uniform trend. There were only small changes in the importance of investments in manufacturing.

5.   Strategic changes: Mergers and acquisitions

The second half of the 1980s was characterized by a "boom" in the number and value of national and transnational mergers and acquisitions (M&As). Although the data on M&As cannot be fully compared with FDI data, it is clear from table 1.12 that the expansion of international investment in the late 1980s was largely carried out through cross-border M&As. These, in fact, more than tripled between 1986 and 1989, reaching a peak value of US$131 billion in 1989. Their main features reflected the general patterns in FDI discussed above, with US companies being the main target of M&As and most other operations taking place within the EC.

Several environmental pressures and strategic considerations by MNEs explain the decision to "go global" through cross-border M&As, as it will be discussed in detail in other chapters of this book, particularly Chapter 4. Suffice it here to say that the wave of M&As has registered a decline in 1990 and 1991, linked partly to economic recession, and that according to some investigations M&As may not necessarily meet the expectations of the companies which embarked on such operations (Jacquemin, 1989). Nevertheless, the number and volume of M&As and the size of the companies involved accounted for a rapid reshuffling of ownership patterns and brought about considerable restructuring, changes in market shares and shaking or reinforcing national and international oligopolies in a number of industries, with long-lasting implications.

Table 1.12. Value of cross-border mergers and acquisitions, 1986-91 (percentage shares by country/area)

	1986	1987	1988	1989	1990	1991[a]
Target country/area						
North America	74	74	62	53	46	35
Japan	0	0	0	0	0	0
United Kingdom	15	10	14	21	18	21
Continental Europe	8	14	14	19	23	32
Rest of the world	3	2	9	7	13	11
Total	100	100	100	100	100	100
Bidder country/area						
North America	13	11	14	21	18	17
Japan	4	5	9	11	16	11
United Kingdom	42	51	39	18	18	7
Continential Europe	29	26	30	37	43	55
Rest of the world	12	8	8	11	7	10
Total	100	100	100	100	100	100
Memorandum (US$ billion):						
Total value of M&As	39	71	110	131	114	25
FDI – outflow from industrialized countries	91	138	164	206	221	n.a.

[a] First quarter

Sources: Turner, 1991: KPMG: Deal watch (for 1989-91 data); IMF: BoP statistics.

6. Conclusions

During the 1980s the integration of the world economy via FDI has increased substantially. This process was neither continuous nor did it affect all countries equally. While FDI stagnated in the early 1980s, there was an "explosion" in the international investment activities of MNEs in the second half of the decade. Developing countries, with the exception of the dynamic economies of South-East Asia, suffered a setback as a result of unfavourable political and economic conditions, but for practically every industrialized country the importance of both inward and outward foreign direct investment increased considerably. Concerning outward investment, a substantial share in this period has been generated by non-US MNEs, particularly from Japan, which was increasingly active in the United States and in the EC.

As we have seen, there have been several economic events and environmental factors which might account for this growth. However, as FDI has always been a competitive tool of internationally active firms, it can be argued that the growth of FDI in the 1980s was part of a catching-up process by non-US MNEs, especially Japanese companies, to the positions of their US counterparts and to levels more commensurate with the size of their economy and its technological competitiveness. To a certain extent too, the decline in FDI to developing countries over this same period reflected the greater importance MNEs were giving to compete in the most strategic, i.e. developed market economies, while the rise of international mergers and acquisitions was also attributable to the way it allowed firms a convenient and rapid – even if in the long term not always successful – route to win market share in these competitive encounters.

The speed and success of this exercise has been such that by the end of the 1980s Japanese, US and European MNEs have achieved a certain degree of parity as to the size of their outward investments.

Since 1990, there has been a significant fall in total FDI (in 1991 the total was estimated by the Bank for International Settlements at $ 177 billion in comparison to $ 222 billion for 1990), a rapid decline in mergers and acquisitions and a notable drop in overseas investment by Japanese MNEs, especially in the United States. These developments mainly reflect the slow-down in economic activity worldwide and the lack of dynamism in the economies of a number of important home and host countries. Reflecting this new stage has been a shift in FDI flows from industrialized to developing countries (according to the BIS, the share of total FDI of developing countries in 1991 was around 27 per cent compared with 17 per cent in 1990), with Asia and Latin America as the major beneficiaries.

The recent decline in FDI by no means suggests a decline in the degree of influence of MNEs in international markets. Having established their new operations, MNEs are binding these together across borders, furthering the process of integration between countries. In addition, MNEs continue to use non-equity forms of investment, e.g. strategic alliances, particularly in high-technology industries, to permit them to continue to be internationally active without requiring them to make new FDIs. In such operations, MNEs therefore remain highly significant actors and employers in marketplaces around the globe.

The assessment of future FDI trends is necessarily a speculative exercise. While it will be unlikely that FDI will enjoy the same rate of increase as in the late 1980s, there are some arguments to support the view that FDI will remain one of the most dynamic elements in the world economy.

Despite the general increase in FDI in the 1980s, the degree of internationalization in a number of countries, Japan in particular, is still limited by international standards. There is growth potential for FDI, which could be activated by a recovery in economic activity worldwide. Internationalization in the services sector has just begun and it is much below the levels which have been reached in manufacturing. Further liberalization in services could then provide additional scope for the expansion of FDI. Privatization worldwide, the continuing opening up of Central and Eastern Europe to FDI and the emergence of regional trading blocs in North America, Latin America and the Asian Pacific Rim could help keep strong the pace of overseas investment. Finally, the pressure on firms to exploit technological and other firm-specific assets on a large (i.e. international) scale is likely to persist, e.g. the need to amortize rapidly the huge budgets for R&D and the introduction of innovations, and to be present in the centres of technological excellence. FDI will hardly be substituted by non-equity arrangements such as the strategic alliances, which are now quite common in high-tech industries. Rather, a number of such alliances may eventually result in international mergers or acquisitions and hence in FDI.

Bibliography

Bank for International Settlements (BIS): *62nd Annual Report*, Basle, 1992.

Borrmann, A.; Jungnickel, R.: *Die Position ausländischer Investoren im asiatisch-pazifischen Integrationsprozess*, HWWA, Report No. 102, Hamburg, 1992.

Brewer, T.L.: *Foreign direct investment in developing countries*, WPS No. 712, World Bank, Washington, DC, 1990.

Cantwell, J.: *The methodological problems raised by the collection of foreign direct investment data*, Reading, United Kingdom, University of Reading Discussion Paper, Series B, No. 147, 1990.

Dunning, J.H.: *International production and the multinational enterprise*, London, George Allen and Unwin, 1981.

The Economist: "A flirtation with the Pacific", 14 Sep. 1991.

Ernst, D.; O'Connor, D.: *Technology and global competition: The challenge ahead for newly industrialising economies*, OECD, Paris, 1989.

Frobel, F., et al.: *Umbruch in der Weltwirtschaft*, Hamburg, Reinbek, 1986.

Graham, E.M.; Krugman, P.J.: *Foreign direct investment in the United States*, Washington, DC, Institute for International Economics, 1989.

Hong Kong and Shanghai Banking Corporation: *Economic Report*, Feb. 1991.

IMF: *Balance of payments statistics*, Washington, DC, various years.

—: *Economic outlook*, Washington, DC, various years.

Jacquemin, A.: "Multinational strategic behaviour", in *Kyklos*, Vol. 42, 1989.

Jungnickel, R.: "Weltwirtschaft und internationale Unternehmung", in *Handwarterbuch Export und Internationale Unternehmung*, Stuttgart, Poeschel, 1989.

—: *Neue Technologien und Produktionsverlagerung*, Hamburg, Weltarchiv, 1990.

KPMG (Krijnveld Peat & Marwick Group): *Deal Watch*, London, various issues.

Langhammer, Rolf: "Competition among developing countries for foreign investment in the 1980s – Whom did OECD investors prefer?", in *Weltwirtschaftliches Archiv*, No. 2, 1991.

OECD: "Foreign direct investment flows: Recent developments and prospects", in *Financial market trends*, Paris, No. 52, 1992.

Rada, J.F.: *The impact of microelectronics – A tentative appraisal of information technology*, Geneva, ILO, 1980.

Ramstetter, Eric D.: *Foreign direct investment in Asia and the Pacific in the 1990s: Potential policies and issues*, paper for round table on "FDI in Asia and the Pacific in the 1990s", Honolulu, pp. 26-28, 1991.

Servan-Schreiber, J.J.: *The American challenge*, Atheneum, New York, 1968.

Thomsen, S.; Nicolaides, P.: *The evolution of Japanese direct investment in Europe: Death of a transistor salesman*, Hemel Hempstead, Hertfordshire, Harvester Wheatsheaf, 1991.

Turner, P.: *Capital flows in the 1980s: A survey of major trends*, Bank for International Settlements (BIS), Basle, 1991.

UNCTC: *Transnational corporations in world development: Trends and prospects*, New York, United Nations, 1988.

—: *Foreign direct investment and transnational corporations in services*, New York, United Nations, 1989.

—: *Transnational corporations, services and the Uruguay Round*, New York, United Nations, 1990.

—: *World Investment Report, 1991*, New York, United Nations, 1991.

—: *World Investment Report, 1992*, New York, United Nations, 1992.

UNIDO: *Foreign direct investment flows to developing countries: Recent trends, major determinants and policy implications*, Vienna, 10 July 1990.

US Department of Commerce: *Survey of current business*, Washington, DC, various years.

Appendix table 1. Stock of outward and inward foreign direct investment, 1980-90

Country	Outward			Inward		
	1980	1985	1990	1980	1985	1990
A. Values in US$ billion						
United States[a]	220	251	423	83	185	404
Canada	23	36	73	52	59	109
Germany[b]	43	60	155	37	37	94
United Kingdom	79	107	249	63	63	206
Netherlands	40	50	195	20	25	66
France	14	19	100	16	20	78
Italy	7	18	64	9	19	61
Switzerland	22	24	66	9	11	18
Japan	20	44	202	3	5	15
Total nine countries	470	610	1 440	290	420	1 010
Other industrialized[c]	25	40	140	70	80	200
Developing[c]	8	20	60	120	185	270
World	510	670	1 640	480	685	1 520
B. Regional structure (%)						
United States[a]	43	37	26	17	27	27
Canada	5	5	4	11	9	7
Germany[b]	8	9	9	8	5	6
United Kingdom	15	16	15	13	9	14
Netherlands	8	7	6	4	4	4
France[d]	3	3	6	3	3	5
Italy	1	3	4	2	3	4
Switzerland	4	4	4	2	2	1
Japan	4	7	12	1	1	1
Total nine countries	92	91	88	61	61	69
Other industrialized[c]	5	6	9	14	12	13
Developing[c]	2	3	4	25	27	18
World	100	100	100	100	100	100
C. Significance (% of GDP)						
United States[a]	8	6	8	3	5	7
Canada	8	10	13	20	17	19
Germany[b]	5	10	10	5	6	6
United Kingdom	15	24	26	12	13	21
Netherlands	24	39	37	12	20	24
France[d]	2	4	9	2	4	7
Italy	2	4	6	2	5	6
Switzerland	22	26	29	9	12	8
Japan	2	3	7	–	–	1
Total nine countries	7	8	10	4	5	7
Other industrialized[c]	3	5	7	8	10	10
Developing[c]	–	1	2	5	9	8
World	5	6	8	5	6	8

[a] The United States outward FDI corrected for financial FDI in the Netherlands Antilles. [b] Inward FDI without indirect investment. [c] Other industrialized and developing countries and areas as well as some national 1990 inward stocks calculated from the shares in FDI flows since 1970, developing countries and areas data include estimates for Taiwan and Hong Kong, based on Ramstetter (1991, p. 3) and Lall (1991). Developing countries include former centrally planned economies.

Sources: Calculated from national sources; UNCTC, IMF.

Appendix table 2. National position in foreign direct investment flows, 1971-90 (in % of total)

	Outward investment				Inward investment			
	1971-79	1980-85	1986-89	1990	1971-79	1980-85	1986-89	1990
United States[a]	44.6	26.7	14.5	13.7	26.3	50.8	47.9	24.6
United Kingdom	17.4	20.1	20.9	7.8	20.3	14.0	14.6	21.6
Austria	0.2	0.3	0.3	0.8	0.8	0.7	0.5	0.7
Belgium/Luxembourg	1.2	0.4	2.6	3.2	5.1	3.2	3.3	5.7
Denmark	0.3	0.3	0.7	0.7	1.0	0.2	0.4	0.8
France	4.3	5.8	8.3	16.5	9.1	6.4	5.9	8.7
Germany	7.6	7.9	7.7	10.6	9.0	1.9	2.3	0.9
Italy	1.1	3.2	2.1	3.3	3.4	2.6	2.9	4.2
Netherlands	8.6	8.8	5.9	5.6	5.7	4.4	4.3	5.6
Norway	0.3	1.0	0.8	0.6	2.0	0.4	0.6	0.5
Sweden	1.6	2.6	4.3	6.7	0.4	0.5	1.0	1.5
Switzerland	2.2	2.7	3.3	3.0	1.8	1.6	1.7	3.3
Canada	3.0	7.6	3.9	0.5	3.3	-0.8	2.9	3.9
Japan	6.2	9.7	19.3	22.7	0.8	0.9	0.0	1.2
Finland	0.2	0.5	1.0	1.7	0.2	0.1	0.4	0.6
Greece	–	–	–	–	–	1.4	0.6	0.7
Iceland	–	–	0.0	0.0	–	0.1	0.0	0.0
Ireland	–	–	–	–	0.9	0.5	0.0	0.1
Portugal	–	0.0	0.0	0.1	0.3	0.5	0.7	1.4
Spain	0.4	0.6	0.7	1.4	3.7	4.7	5.1	9.1
Australia	0.8	1.9	2.9	1.0	6.3	5.3	4.7	4.7
New Zealand	–	0.1	0.4	0.1	–	0.8	0.4	0.2
Total industrialized countries	100.0	100.0	100.0	100.0	100.0	100.0	100.0	100.0
US$ billion (cumulated flows)	253	288	583	212	150	223	464	151

[a] Corrected for financial US-FDI in the Netherlands Antilles.

Source: Calculated on the basis of IMF: *Balance of payments statistics*, various years.

Appendix table 3. Foreign direct investment flows in the industrialized economies, 1980-90 (in % of GDP)

	Outward investment			Inward investment		
	1980-85	1986-89	1990	1980-85	1986-89	1990
United States[a]	0.4	0.4	0.5	0.6	1.2	0.7
United Kingdom	2.0	4.2	1.7	1.1	2.3	3.3
Austria	0.2	0.4	1.1	0.4	0.5	0.6
Belgium/Luxembourg	0.2	2.5	3.3	1.2	2.6	4.2
Denmark	0.3	1.0	1.1	0.1	0.5	0.9
France	0.5	1.4	2.9	0.4	0.8	1.1
Germany	0.6	1.0	1.5	0.1	0.2	0.1
Italy	0.4	0.4	0.6	0.2	0.4	0.6
Netherlands	3.1	4.1	4.3	1.2	2.4	3.0
Norway	0.9	1.4	1.3	0.3	0.9	0.8
Sweden	1.2	3.8	6.2	0.3	0.7	1.0
Switzerland	1.3	2.9	2.8	0.6	1.2	2.2
Canada	1.2	1.2	0.2	-0.1	0.7	1.0
Japan	0.4	1.1	1.6	0.2	0.0	0.1
Finland	0.5	2.0	2.6	0.2	0.4	0.7
Greece	–	–	–	1.4	1.5	1.5
Iceland	–	0.1	0.2	0.7	-0.2	0.1
Ireland	–	–	–	1.1	0.2	0.2
Portugal	0.1	0.1	0.1	0.8	2.2	3.5
Spain	0.2	0.3	0.6	1.0	1.9	2.8
Australia	0.6	1.9	0.7	1.2	2.4	2.4
New Zealand	0.0	1.3	0.4	1.2	1.1	0.5
Total industrialized countries	0.6	1.1	1.3	0.5	0.9	0.9

[a] Corrected for financial US-FDI in the Netherlands Antilles.

Source: IMF: *Balance of payments statstics*, various years.

**Appendix table 4. Global pattern of foreign direct investment, 1975-91
(in billions of US dollars, annual averages)**

	1975-79	1980-84	1985-89	1990	1991*
Total outflows	35.3	42.4	134.9	222.4	177.3
Industrialized countries	34.7	41.0	128.4	209.5	165.5
of which: United States	15.9	9.6	22.8	33.4	29.5
Japan	2.1	4.3	23.8	48.0	30.7
European Community	14.2	20.9	59.4	97.5	80.5
Developing countries	0.6	1.4	6.5	12.9	11.8
of which: Asia	0.3	0.8	5.6	11.2	10.3
Latin America	0.1	0.2	0.4	1.1	1.0
Total inflows	26.9	52.6	117.6	179.6	157.9
Industrialized countries	19.9	36.2	98.1	148.7	115.2
of which: United States	6.1	18.6	48.2	37.2	22.2
Japan	0.1	0.3	0.1	1.8	1.4
European Community	11.4	14.2	38.4	85.9	67.7
Developing countries	7.0	16.4	19.5	30.9	42.7
of which: Asia	1.9	4.7	10.8	19.9	25.7
Eastern Europe	0.0	0.1	0.1	0.5	2.3
Latin America	3.6	5.4	5.7	7.8	12.0

* Partly estimated.

Source: BIS (1992).

2

Direct employment in multinational enterprises in industrialized and developing countries in the 1980s: Main characteristics and recent trends

Aurelio Parisotto

1. Introduction

By any standard or definition, multinational enterprises (MNEs) are major employers. Over 70 million workers, accounting for about 20 per cent of paid employment in non-agricultural activities in OECD countries, are employed world-wide by MNEs.[1] Although this represents only 2 to 3 per cent of the world's economically active population, these MNE employees belong to the core workforce in modern, technologically advanced, capital- and marketing-intensive industries.

This chapter provides an overview of direct employment in multinational enterprises (MNEs) in industrialized and developing countries and reviews the main trends in the 1980s, presenting data collected by the ILO from questionnaires sent to governments, employers' and workers' organizations. Over 500 questionnaires were sent in total and 36 governments, 36 employers' organizations and 91 workers' organizations from a total of 76 countries supplied information, while 28 governments replied that they did not possess the information requested. Information on the largest MNEs is taken from companies' own figures. This statistical information is supplemented by several ILO country studies on the employment impact of multinationals.

MNE direct employment is a useful indicator for several reasons. First, it provides a stock-indicator of MNE activities in home and host countries which is not influ-

---

[1] Incomplete data prevents an exact appraisal of the total number of people directly employed in the home country and in subsidiaries and affiliates abroad. MNEs are broadly defined as enterprises under private, mixed or public ownership, which own or control production, distribution, services or other facilities outside the country in which they are headquartered. Following OECD definitions, an enterprise receiving foreign direct investment is defined as one in which a single foreign investor either controls at least 10 per cent of the ordinary shares or voting power, or has an effective voice in the management of the enterprise. These include: subsidiaries (where the foreign investor directly or indirectly controls more than 50 per cent of the voting shares or has the right to appoint or remove a majority of the members of the board of the enterprise); affiliates (where the foreign investor directly or indirectly controls at least 10 per cent and no more than 50 per cent of the voting shares or has an effective voice in the management of the enterprise); and branches (which are unincorporated enterprises in the host countries directly owned by a foreign investor). For brevity's sake, the term "affiliate" will be used throughout to indicate the above three categories.

enced by inflation and currency fluctuations, unlike figures on MNE output or foreign direct investment (FDI). Second, MNE employment is easily measurable, statistics being collected at a national level – albeit not homogeneously – in various countries.

The chapter is organized as follows: section 2 reviews the empirical evidence available from home-country sources on the major features of direct employment; section 3 focuses on recent trends; section 4 draws on host-country sources to investigate patterns of employment in national affiliates of foreign-based MNEs. Various labour market issues raised by the presence of foreign investors are discussed in section 5.

2. The main characteristics of direct employment in MNEs

2.1 Overall estimates

The first attempts to measure the magnitude of MNE direct employment date back to the early 1970s. In 1972, a Harvard-CEI project estimated that the 400 largest MNEs in manufacturing alone employed some 30 million people throughout the world (ILO, 1981a). In 1973, the EC conducted a survey of 5,105 MNEs operating in various economic sectors and estimated overall employment as being in the region of 46 million. However, it was not until the appearance of two ILO studies (1981a, 1981b) that a more comprehensive picture emerged. These studies estimated MNE employment at over 40 million in the mid-1970s. In the mid-1980s, according to further ILO research, around 65 million were employed by MNEs worldwide and of these 43 million were in their respective home countries. Thus, 22 million were employed outside the home country of the parent, of which only 7 million in developing countries (ILO, 1988). In addition, multinational banks accounted for about 5 million employees, one in ten employed in an entity abroad (ILO, 1991b).

This section restates and updates some major aspects to be considered when evaluating the employment impact of MNEs in industrialized and developing countries, but does not attempt to derive comparable estimates for the most recent years. Basically, as will be shown in section 3, the global "quantitative" picture has remained unchanged with respect to the estimates for the mid-1980s. An indeterminate increase in the number employed by MNEs has occurred because of the multinationalization of several service activities; the operations of enterprises, particularly from the Far East, which had not engaged in international production before; and the rapid growth in employment in a few successful EPZs in developing countries. On the whole, however, the upsurge in FDI which was registered in the late 1980s mainly took the form of a reshuffling of ownership patterns of existing multinationals through major mergers and acquisitions, and thus had an "employment-acquiring" rather than an "employment-creating" impact. Employment growth in EPZs, moreover, partially supplanted employment in labour-intensive production in industrialized regions.[2]

---

[2] The employment consequences of the new strategies and organizational forms of MNEs which have emerged in the 1980s will be discussed in other chapters.

The efforts to derive accurate empirical evidence – and particularly to make comparisons over time – are hampered by the lack of precise figures. Exact data on total direct MNE employment (at home and abroad) are available only for two major home countries: the United States and Japan. In both countries, specific annual surveys provide complete sets of financial and operating data on home-based multinationals and national affiliates of foreign-based multinationals, which constitutes a unique and invaluable source of information on MNE employment. The 1989 benchmark survey of US direct investment abroad by the US Department of Commerce took into consideration over 2,000 non-bank MNEs headquartered in the **United States** and estimated that they employed 25.3 million people worldwide, 56 per cent of whom were in manufacturing. The same number of employees was registered in an earlier benchmark survey in 1982. In March 1990, according to the Ministry of International Trade and Industry (MITI) of **Japan**, 1,360 non-bank Japanese MNEs accounted for over 4 million employees – about 80 per cent of whom were in manufacturing companies – and an increase from the 3.1 million registered in 1980.[3]

Distinct aggregate figures do not exist on employment in MNEs headquartered in other countries. In general, FDI statistics concentrate on overseas activity of national or foreign economic entities, and labour market statistics do not distinguish MNEs from domestic firms. Thus, we must rely on estimates or derive samples of leading MNEs for which consolidated employment figures are available. In various years, conservative estimates of employment at home and abroad in MNEs from the other major industrialized countries were around 5 million for **Germany** and the **United Kingdom**, about 4 million for **France** and between 1 and 2 million for **Canada**, the **Netherlands**, **Switzerland**, **Italy** and **Sweden** (see table 2.1). In comparison to total domestic paid employment, the percentage share of worldwide employment in home-based MNEs ranged from 8 per cent in Japan and Italy to more than 30 per cent in Sweden, Switzerland and the Netherlands, although this figure would be much higher if the manufacturing sector – where MNEs are particularly active – was taken alone.

Home-based MNEs account for a large portion of domestic manufacturing paid employment in the countries with a tradition of foreign investment – the United Kingdom, Germany, France, Switzerland, the Netherlands, the United States – and in Sweden and Finland, where multinationalization is more recent. At the other end of the spectrum, Japanese and Italian MNEs' share of domestic employment is small, although their indirect impact is probably greater due to their more extensive reliance on subcontractors.[4]

For Japan and Italy too, the number of employees abroad compared with domestic manufacturing employment is low relative to the other major industrialized countries, which may indicate room for further expansion of production abroad. In

---

[3] In both countries, the data account for a thorough coverage of home-based MNEs. In the survey for Japan, however, the voluntary nature of the replies and the fluctuations in the number of companies surveyed each year are more likely to curtail completeness and comparability of the data over time (for more details, see Chapter 5).

[4] The relative share of MNE employment in Japan and Italy declines further if compared to total employment and not, as in figure 2.1, to paid employment only. In fact, self-employment in manufacturing in both countries is unusually high with respect to industrialized countries' averages.

Table 2.1.   Worldwide direct employment in MNEs by country of origin of parent; selected OECD countries, latest available year

Country (ranked by GNP)	Number of parent companies or groups	Number of employees at home and abroad ('000)	As a share of domestic paid employment (%)	Year	Type of source
United States[a]	2 167	25 342	23	1989	CS
Japan[a]	1 360	4 064	9	1989	CS
Germany, Fed. Rep. of	87	4 459	18	1989	SS
France	100	3 680	20	1990	SS
Italy[b]	211	(1 100)	8	1987	IE
United Kingdom	100	5 484	24	1990	SS
Canada	n.a.	(1 764)	18	1984	IE
Australia	34	846	14	1989	SS
Netherlands	n.a.	(1 454)	33	1980	IE
Switzerland	100	1 095	31[c]	1988	SS
Sweden	702	1 110	28	1987	CS
Belgium	15	266	9	1989	SS
Austria	764[d]	270	9	1986	CS

CS = comprehensive survey; IE = ILO estimate; SS = sample survey.

[a] Excluding banks.   [b] Parents whose main activity is in manufacturing only.   [c] The share is calculated over civilian employment.   [d] Including 122 foreign-owned firms which are based in Austria and have subsidiaries abroad.

Sources: *United States*: government reply to the ILO questionnaire, based on data from the US Department of Commerce; *Japan*: government reply to the ILO questionnaire, based on data from MITI; *Germany, Fed. Rep. of*: sample of 87 leading MNEs, based on *Die Zeit, Frankfurter Allgemeine Zeitung*, and UNCTC; *France*: sample of 100 leading MNEs, based on the *French Company Handbook: 1991* and *Expansion*; *Italy*: ILO estimate based on *Mondo Economico* and a comprehensive survey of Italian-based MNEs (CNEL, 1989); *United Kingdom*: sample of 100 leading MNEs, based on the *Financial Times* and UNCTC (according to the UK Central Statistical Office there were in 1989 approximately 2,000 UK company groups which had foreign affiliates); *Canada*: ILO (1988); *Australia*: sample of 34 leading MNEs, based on UNCTC BDC; *Netherlands*: ILO (1988); *Switzerland*: sample of 100 leading MNEs, based on the *Schweizerische Handelszeitung* and the government reply to the ILO questionnaire; *Sweden*: government reply to the ILO questionnaire; *Belgium*: sample of 15 leading MNEs, based on UNCTC BDC; *Austria*: government reply to the ILO questionnaire, based on data from the Austrian National Bank.

fact, the proportion of MNE employment abroad compared with the total domestic workforce in manufacturing in industrialized countries ranges from about 20 per cent for Germany and the United States to over 80 per cent for Switzerland.

These comparisons, although approximate, clearly show the importance of international production for manufacturing companies from the major industrialized countries and the full direct exposure of national labour markets to international economic developments and FDI trends. If the presence of foreign MNEs is also taken into account, the "multinationalization" of manufacturing and the limited importance of non-MNE employment are even more evident. Similar comparisons are not available for other economic sectors. Overall, despite a recent increase in some specific service activities, MNE activities remain limited outside manufacturing and mining.

Figure 2.1. Paid employment in manufacturing firms in selected industrialized countries by ownership, latest available year

(a) Million employees

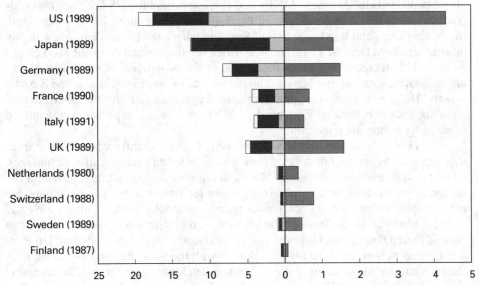

(b) Share of domestic paid employment

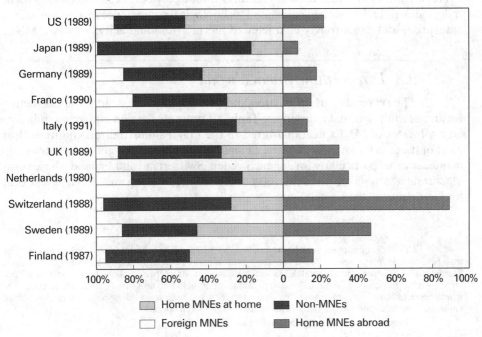

2.2 Direct employment at home

Generally, employment in parent companies and affiliates in the country of origin accounts for a considerable proportion of total MNE direct employment: about two-thirds for Japanese MNEs and three-quarters for US MNEs. This holds true for most other industrialized countries, the only exceptions being Switzerland, the Netherlands and to a lesser extent Sweden, where the presence of a few highly internationalized large MNEs is coupled with a relatively small domestic market.

The degree of multinationalization, or the proportion of employees in foreign affiliates, varies across MNEs. The prevalence of employment at home is partly due to MNEs which maintain an international presence but produce goods or services mainly within their national borders. MNEs in services, in particular, are indeed more likely to operate nationally.[5]

However, in general, MNEs are rooted in the country where they started their operations and first developed their own firm-specific comparative advantages. Even the well-established leading MNEs maintain a strong national base and the largest share of their total employment at home. Truly "stateless" companies are rare, despite a few cases of companies whose national identity cannot be clearly defined, not even on the basis of the location of the central headquarters – e.g. the British/Dutch companies Unilever and Royal Dutch/Shell, US/Canadian Du Pont and the recent merger of the Swedish ASEA with the Swiss Brown Boveri. No matter how international the operations are, top level management and the company board of most leading MNEs are generally nationals from the home country.[6] While it is open to question whether considerations of economic nationalism affect actual strategies and operations, national features imbue corporate culture, management style, industrial relations and cumulated technological competence of a multinational enterprise, and can strongly characterize the international activities of an MNE.

2.3 Direct employment abroad

The ownership of production and other facilities abroad is the distinctive feature of multinational enterprises. Table 2.2 presents data on employment in foreign affiliates of MNEs headquartered in the major industrialized countries. For most of these main investor countries, employment abroad is highly concentrated in manufacturing, particularly for Japan, Sweden, Switzerland and Finland where manufacturing accounts for more than 80 per cent of the total, against about 70 per cent for Germany and the United States.

---

[5] In 1988, employment at home in US MNEs in services accounted for 84 per cent of their worldwide employment, against 70 per cent for MNEs in manufacturing (US Department of Commerce). For the size of the domestic market, the US services sector is characterized by large firms, some with a relatively strong propensity to multinational expansion, unparalleled in most other industrialized countries, where services industries are more often characterized by a large number of small and medium-sized enterprises, by international standards, with limited international operations.

[6] Relevant examples are provided by Holstein (1990).

Table 2.2. Employment in the largest industrial multinational enterprises by country of origin and industry of parent, 1989 (thousands of employees)

Country (ranked by GNP)	Number of companies	Extractive industries	Food and beverages	Textiles and clothing	Paper and printing	Chemicals	Metals	Metal products	Machinery and equipment	Electronics	Transport equipment	Building materials	TOTAL
United States	182	638	1 155	232	351	1 421	216	18	1 254	1 565	1 524	261	9 637
Japan	86	10	76	76	20	183	32	128	354	1 097	524	13	2 512
Germany, F.R.	46	282	—	—	48	669	350	198	627	41	854	46	3 116
France	38	151	90	—	—	317	72	131	160	203	433	263	1 820
United Kingdom[a]	65	466	1 148	84	—	394	189	37	179	315	286	342	3 439
Italy	8	83	45	21	181	69	416	—	—	57	18	—	977
Canada	17	—	69	—	—	26	96	—	15	48	17	—	452
Netherlands[b]	8	—	171	—	15	100	28	—	—	308	107	—	639
Switzerland[c]	11	—	197	—	—	193	27	47	107	18	—	25	566
Sweden	18	—	—	—	90	65	—	—	466	—	128	56	879
Finland	10	—	—	—	84	16	26	—	38	41	—	—	180
Other industrialized countries	29	79	320	—	78	88	154	111	33	—	45	22	930
Developing countries	16	1 108	19	32	—	—	—	52	—	177	96	—	1 484
TOTAL	534	2 816	3 289	445	868	3 542	1 656	669	3 235	3 870	5 212	1 029	26 630

a Including Unilever PLC. b Including Unilever NV, excluding Royal Dutch Shell. c Including ASEA Brown Boveri.

Source: ILO-MULTI database (based on the UNCTC Billion Dollar Club and *Fortune*).

**Box 2.1.   Statistics on employment in foreign affiliates
of home-based MNEs**

In addition to the US and Japan, some evidence could be derived on overseas activity and employment of multinational enterprises based in Germany, Italy,
Switzerland, Sweden, Austria, Finland and Norway. For most of these countries, classification of MNE employment abroad by industry is in accordance with the specialization of the foreign affiliate. For the US, the data are also organized according to the
primary activity of the parent company at home. This allows us to assess the discrepancy due to differences in classification. In fact, the share of manufacturing goes from
64 per cent to 70 per cent of total US MNE employment abroad when employees are
classified according to the industry of the US parent company as opposed to the classification by industry of the foreign affiliate. That is, US MNEs primarily engaged in
manufacturing have affiliates abroad whose main line of business is outside manufacturing, mainly in wholesale trade and in business services. Consumer-oriented industries dominated by MNEs — like food and beverages, chemicals, office and computing
equipment — show the largest increases. Accordingly, the absolute numbers of those
employed abroad by US MNEs primarily engaged in wholesale trade and business services is considerably lower than the number of workers in US affiliates abroad whose
main activity is in wholesale trade or other services. Or to take it the other way round,
US insurance and holding companies often appear to have foreign affiliates primarily
active in the non-financial sector. (cf. US Department of Commerce "US Direct
Investment Abroad", various years, tables 12 and 15). Additional complications arise
from the fact that affiliates can be broadly diversified but data are commonly collected
at consolidated affiliate level. Employees or sales, including those generated by establishments (plants) in secondary activities, are classified according to the affiliate's primary activity, yet. Data on employment in foreign affiliates at establishment level are
rarely collected. The US are, again, the exception. Here, the number of employees on
the payroll of manufacturing plants of US affiliates of foreign MNEs is generally 12-15
per cent lower than the number of employees in those affiliates whose primary activity
is in manufacturing (Bezirganian, 1991, tables 2 and 5).

Overseas investment in the primary sector is marginal as regards MNE
direct employment abroad. In the tertiary sector, employment is strongly concentrated in affiliates in the distributive trades: 68 per cent of total employment abroad
in services for Germany, and (excluding banking) 60 per cent for the US and 75 per
cent for Japan in 1988. Business services and non-bank finance and insurance mainly
account for the remaining share. This distribution supports the view that investment
abroad in services remains directly or indirectly dependent on the international activities of the leading industrial MNEs.

The main features of employment abroad are influenced by the structure of
parent companies. Large, well-established MNEs are in general more likely than
smaller enterprises to be engaged directly in productive activities abroad. In Germany, for example, in 1989 more than 40 per cent of employees abroad were concentrated in just 20 leading MNEs. Such concentration is even higher in other smaller
industrialized countries. In Italy, Switzerland, Sweden and Finland respectively 8, 10,

Table 2.3. Employees in MNEs' subsidiaries and affiliates abroad by country of origin and sector of parent; selected OECD countries, latest available year

Country (ranked by GNP)	All sectors A. Number of employees ('000)	Manufacturing B. Number of employees ('000)	A/B (%)	Type of source (%)	Year
United States[a]	6621	4189	67	CS	1989
Japan[a]	1600	1300	80	CS	1989
Germany, Federal Rep. of	2154	1511	70	CS	1989
France	791	n.a.	–	IE	1981
Italy	n.a.	511	–	CS	1991
United Kingdom	1390	n.a.	–	SS	1981
Spain	231	n.a.	–	CS	1977
Netherlands	1071	n.a.	–	CS	1981
Switzerland	971	779[b]	80	CS	1990
Sweden	488	416	85	CS	1988
Belgium	182	n.a.	–	CS	1975
Austria	65	35[b]	54	CS	1986
Finland	139	123	88	CS	1989
Norway	50	29	58	CS	1982

CS = comprehensive survey; SS = sample survey; IE = ILO estimate.

[a] Excluding banks. [b] Industry.

Sources: *United States*: see table 2.1; *Japan*: see Chapter 5 by Watanabe; *Germany*: government reply to the ILO questionnaire, based on data from the Bundesbank; *France*: Savary (1983); *Italy*: CNEL (1992); *United Kingdom*: IRM Directory, based on a sample of 67 leading UK multinationals; *Spain*: IRM Directory; *Netherlands*: IRM Directory; *Switzerland*: government reply to the ILO questionnaire, based on data from the Swiss National Bank; *Sweden*: government reply to the ILO questionnaire, based on Swedish Ministry of Industry (1990); *Belgium*: IRM Directory; *Austria*: see table 2.1; *Finland*: government reply to the ILO questionnaire based on data from the Bank of Finland; *Norway*: government reply to the ILO questionnaire based on data from the Bank of Norway.

17 and 20 leading MNEs accounted alone for 80 per cent, 55 per cent, 70 per cent and 90 per cent of employment abroad in recent years.

MNEs also differ in their geographical spread and focus. Large groups are usually keener than smaller enterprises on investing in developing countries, since they can better face the risks involved. Small and medium-sized MNEs reveal a stronger tendency than large MNEs to invest in nearby developed countries (Fujita, 1990). Similarly in the case of Sweden smaller MNEs concentrated their employment abroad in the Nordic area and in the EC (50 per cent and 30 per cent of employment abroad respectively), with only a negligible presence in developing countries (Ministry of Industry, Sweden, 1990).

Table 2.3 presents aggregate data on employment abroad by MNEs headquartered in seven home countries where employment figures for recent years were broken down according to geographic areas. The sample probably represents half of global MNE employment abroad, with the first three countries – United States, Germany and Japan – accounting for a significant proportion.

Around 30 per cent of the employees in US, German and Italian subsidiaries abroad are in developing countries. This was precisely the same figure for an earlier study on French MNEs (Savary, 1983) and it is safe to assume that, if the data were available, there would be a similar breakdown for all other countries. The smaller countries in the sample – Sweden, Switzerland and Finland – tend to concentrate more in industrialized countries (especially the EC). One country which stands out is Japan, whose employment pattern is the opposite of the majority of the other industrialized countries. Here only 38 per cent of the employees abroad are in industrialized countries while 62 per cent are in developing countries, largely in nearby Asia.

The geographical distribution of employees in foreign affiliates in services does not seem to follow that of manufacturing. Where a comparison can be made, e.g. for the US and Switzerland, there is a tendency for investment to be concentrated in manufacturing in developing countries, while employees in affiliates in services are overwhelmingly (over 80 per cent) in developed areas.

2.4 Large, well-established MNEs

A considerable amount of MNE employment is concentrated in huge, well-established industrial MNEs headquartered in the major industrialized countries. These enterprises are characterized by the gigantic scale of their operations, their geographical and product diversity, their considerable financial resources and large research budgets. Possessing intangible assets, such as brand names, proprietary technology, cumulated technological and organizational competence and skills, they tend to be found in capital- and marketing-intensive or science-based industries like chemicals, soaps and cosmetics, pharmaceutical products, brand-name food and drinks products, automobiles, electronics, electrical and non-electrical machinery and equipment. In such industries, competition is between large, oligopolistic multi-national enterprises throughout the world.[7]

Table 2.4 shows worldwide employment in 534 leading MNEs by industry and country/region of origin of the parent.[8] The United States accounts for the

[7] Individual figures on employment in the leading parent MNEs and in their consolidated affiliates abroad can be obtained from various sources, mainly company directories and lists compiled by the business press, e.g. *Fortune* magazine, *Financial Times*, etc. These sources are usually based on company reports and exclude corporations which are privately owned or which do not have any obligation to make their financial and operating statements available to the public. Consolidation principles are country-specific. In general, only majority-owned subsidiaries are consolidated, e.g. in the US, the United Kingdom and Sweden. As long as minority-owned affiliates are excluded, aggregate data derived from individual company sources may underestimate the volume of MNE employment in comparison with estimates derived from national statistics which adopt the OECD definition of control. Examples of analyses of MNE performances, including employment, based on various samples of leading MNEs, are provided by Stopford and Dunning (1983) and Dunning and Pierce (1985).

[8] The source of data is the UNCTC Billion Dollar Club (BDC) database. It contains financial and non-financial information on major corporations in the manufacturing or extractive sectors which have one or more foreign affiliates and whose annual total sales exceed 1 billion dollars; 534 such large corporations accounted in 1989 for around 26 million employees, of whom about 20 million were employed by a core group of 343 companies for which employment data is available over a ten-year period. BDC firms are estimated to account for roughly one-fifth of world value added. For a description of the database, see Simon, Fraga and Marulli-Koenig (1989).

Table 2.4. Distribution of employment in subsidiaries and affiliates abroad of MNEs from selected countries by host region; all sectors, latest available year (percentage)

Heading	United States 1989	Germany (FRG) 1989	Japan 1988	Italy[a] 1991	Switzerland 1990	Sweden 1988	Finland[a] 1987	Total number of employees Thousands	%
Industrialized countries	68	72	38	67	83	81	95	7 914	67
North America	14	22	24	11	19	17	16	2 017	17
EC	39	34	10	49	46	42	44	4 217	36
Other Europe	2	11	7	7	12	16	36	604	5
Other industrialized countries	12	5	3	–	6	6	–	1 076	9
Developing countries	32	28	62	17	17	19	5	3 865	33
Latin America	20	19	11	19	...	11	...	2 051	17
Africa	1	2	1	5	...	–	...	173	2
Asia and Middle East	11	7	50	9	...	8	...	1 640	14
(OPEC)	(3)	(2)	(6)	–	(1)	–	(3)	(335)	(3)
Total	100	100	100	100	100	100	100		100
Total number of employees abroad (thousands)	6 621	2 154	1 316	510	971	488	108	11 808	

[a] Manufacturing only.

Source: ILO-MULTI database. Calculated from a variety of national sources.

largest number of companies and the largest volume of employment. US MNEs are also found in practically all the main industries, while for the other countries (or groups of countries) MNE employment is not so evenly distributed across industries. In the table, the distribution of employment by industry is only indicative, as some companies are broadly diversified and the employees in their consolidated subsidiaries in secondary activities are classified according to the primary line of business (in terms of sales) of the parent company. However, national patterns of specialization or the prevalence of one nation's MNEs in specific industries can be distinguished. Large Japanese MNEs, for example, are found primarily in electronics and transport equipment; German MNEs are prominent in chemicals, machinery and automobiles; British MNEs in food and chemicals; Swedish MNEs in machinery and equipment; Finnish and Canadian MNEs in forest products.

For the US and Japan, it is possible to compare the volume of employment in the leading MNEs to the total number of employees in all home-based MNEs: 182 leading US industrial MNEs had 9.6 million employees in 1989, about 40 per cent of total US MNE employment and 70 per cent of employment in manufacturing MNEs; in Japan, 86 industrial MNEs accounted in 1989 for 62 per cent of total employment at home and abroad by the non-bank MNEs surveyed by MITI (see tables 2.1 and 2.4).

2.5 Non-conventional MNEs

A group of firms falling under the label of "non-conventional" MNEs, and attracting interest particularly for their employment-creating role in developing countries, are small and medium-sized MNEs and MNEs from developing countries. In general, small and medium-sized enterprises (defined here as those enterprises with fewer than 500 employees) account for a marginal share of FDI, as their limited financial resources restrict them from establishing manufacturing operations abroad. Even so, recent statistics from the US and the UK show that the number of SMEs with FDI is large, although overall the magnitude of their assets and, presumably, the number of their employees abroad, is negligible (Fujita, 1990). Employment-specific evidence on Swedish MNEs reveals that only 5 per cent of the workforce abroad is accounted for by companies with fewer than 1,000 workers. In Italy this percentage rises to 9 per cent (CNEL, 1989) and is probably even higher in Japan, where SMEs accounted for approximately 15 per cent of total outflows over the period 1984-86 (Fujita, 1990).

Existing statistics on FDI and international production are likely to underestimate the international operations of small and medium-sized enterprises since small investments – precisely those most likely to be done by SMEs – are usually excluded from most surveys. However, even if the number of investors which are excluded can be fairly high, the volume of their assets (and employment) may not be. The 1989 US Benchmark survey, for instance, considered 12,913 fully consolidated US affiliates of foreign companies in 1987. Only 8,577 were over the threshold and had to report financial and operating data for the census; yet, according to the Department of Commerce, these accounted for virtually all the value of the investment.

In fact, small and medium-sized multinational enterprises are likely to follow traditional and risk-averse paths of expansion abroad. They may establish agencies to provide commercial support to their sales abroad before starting international production (Buckley et al., 1978), or prefer to arrange joint ventures, non-majority participation, collaboration and alliances. In low-tech, labour-intensive industries like textiles, offshore manufacturing could provide SMEs with an option to cut labour costs; but, in general, it is the highly specialized or high-technology SMEs which are more liable to take advantage of international production opportunities to strengthen their competitive position in their particular "niches". Litvak (1990) monitored the performance during the 1970s and the 1980s of 29 high-technology Canadian SMEs which went international. Most oriented their international investments to the adjacent US market. Of the companies which did not fail or were not acquired by competitors, specialization was identified as the key factor explaining their success in competing with larger companies.

A special situation is likely to exist in those countries where SMEs play an important role in the industrial structure, i.e. Japan and Italy. In Italy, multinationalization lags far behind the other major industrialized countries, except for two groups of companies: a few leading corporations and a handful of small enterprises (CNEL, 1992).[9] The nature of corporate relationships and corporate hierarchy within the two countries also accounts for different patterns of foreign investment by SMEs. In Japan, small subcontractors often follow their primary contractor abroad. In fact, overseas investment by small Japanese subcontractors in nearby Asian countries and in the US has increased in recent years following the expansion abroad by major Japanese corporations. In contrast, the fragmentary, decentralized Italian industrial structure tends to produce SMEs capable of autonomously expanding abroad in specialized niches. Nevertheless, in both countries the SMEs which have invested abroad are only a minority of the galaxy of small, domestic enterprises and the volume of employment they are able to generate abroad remains, on the whole, limited.

A recent development which is hard to register is the expansion of multinational enterprises from developing countries. Most MNEs from developing countries are large conglomerates, often state-owned, which are leaders in their national market and whose (usually limited) overseas investments are concentrated in low technology, resource-based activities, frequently in neighbouring or historically related developing countries (Cantwell and Tolentino, 1990). Although the breakdown at home and abroad is not available, according to data collected by the United Nations Centre on Transnational Corporations (UNCTC) and *Fortune* magazine, it appears that about 1.5 million people were employed in 1989 by 16 large Third World MNEs, which primarily include state-owned mining, steel and oil companies and a few large private conglomerates from the Republic of Korea and Turkey (see table 2.2). Increasingly however, as we shall see below, direct investment by dynamic companies from Asian and Latin American NIEs is taking place in industrialized and developing countries.

---

[9] The evidence on Italian MNEs also clearly showed that the preference for controlling foreign affiliates through majority participation increases in parallel with the increase in the size of the investor: the bigger an MNE, the higher the proportion of wholly or majority-owned affiliates.

3. Evolution and recent trends

Viewed from the perspective of the previous four decades, it can be said that MNE expansion was at its height during the "Golden Age", the long expansionary period which characterized industrialized economies from the end of the Second World War up to the oil crisis of the 1970s. Rapid and enduring growth of manufacturing employment was paralleled by expansion of MNEs and international production and employment, with large industrial companies from the US first, in the 1950s and the 1960s, and from Europe and Japan later at the forefront of multinationalization. The "Golden Age" ended in the 1970s when a marked decline in the rate of growth of MNE employment occurred followed by a downturn in the 1977-82 period (see table 2.5).

MNE employment is subject to cyclical fluctuations, shifts in output composition and differential regional and country growth. Sluggish economic growth in industrialized countries, excepting Japan, and large restructuring were the main causes of the reversal in the growth of MNE employment in the early 1980s. The downturn was particularly evident for the largest leading MNEs. It affected MNEs from all the major countries and was felt particularly in the oil, steel and automotive industries. This decline was followed by an increase in 1986 and 1989, albeit not to the absolute level of 1980 (see figure 2.2 for a group of 343 MNEs).

A series of factors specifically affected employment in these MNEs: cost reduction through rationalization and cutting employment; introduction of labour-saving technology; and the spread of national and international subcontracting arrangements. Rationalization, automation and subcontracting were particularly common among the leading MNEs. Indeed, large firms can afford fast rates of automation and technological change. Also, they have a greater capability to weaken trade unions, which are likely to be stronger in large firms, by decentralization of production and dispersion of labour to smaller satellite units (Cantwell and Randaccio, 1989). This decentralization mostly affected "routine producers", un- or semi-skilled

Table 2.5. **Rate of growth of employment in the leading MNEs, selected periods (per cent)**

Period	Dunning and Pierce[a]	UNCTC[b]
1962-67	23	
1967-72	14	
1972-77	5	
1977-82	-0.4	
1980-83		-8
1983-86		2
1986-89		4

[a] Sample of leading MNEs for which employment data were available at the start and at the end of each quinquennium. Sample size varies from almost 500 to more than 800 companes. [b] Constant sample of 343 leading MNEs, accounting for about 20 million employees.

Sources: Dunning and Pierce, 1985; UNCTC Billion Dollar Club.

Figure 2.2. Employment in 343 leading industrial multinational enterprises, 1980-89

(a) by country of origin, selected years

Million employees

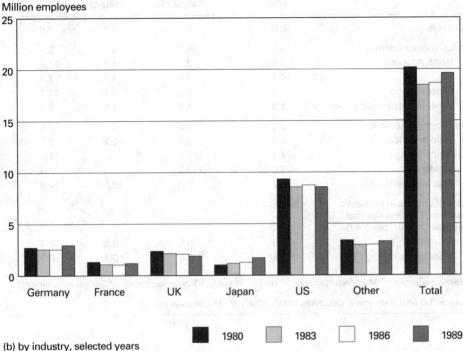

Germany · France · UK · Japan · US · Other · Total

■ 1980   ▨ 1983   □ 1986   ▨ 1989

(b) by industry, selected years

Million employees

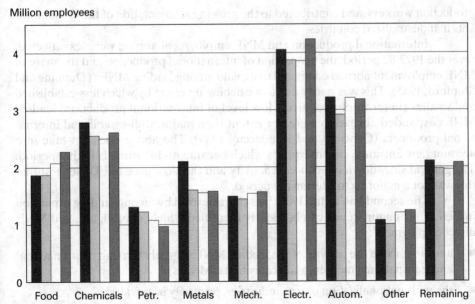

Food · Chemicals · Petr. · Metals · Mech. · Electr. · Autom. · Other · Remaining

Table 2.6.   Rate of change in employment in subsidiaries and affiliates abroad of MNEs based in the United States, Germany, Sweden and Switzerland by host region; all sectors (annual average growth, selected periods, in per cent)

	United States[a] (1982-89)	Germany (1982-89)	Sweden[b] 1982-87)	Switzerland (1985-90)
All areas	-0.0	3.5	5.7	8.6
Industrialized countries	0.1	4.0	6.0	9.2
North America	0.5	3.4	11.1	11.2
EC	-0.4	4.4	4.8	7.1
Other Europe	1.8	5.2	9.7[c]	14.9
Other industrialized countries	1.3	1.2	-2.5	9.7
Developing countries	-0.3	2.5	4.7	5.8
Latin America	-0.5	3.7	-0.2	1.1
Africa	-4.8	-12.5	...	11.8
Middle East	-5.8	-113.3	...	n.a.
Asia and the Pacific	2.2	2.8	16.2	14.9
Rate of change in domestic paid employment (annual average growth, per cent)				
All sectors[d]	2.8	0.5	0.3	2.3[e]
Manufacturing[d]	0.5	0.0	-0.1	0.9[e]

[a] Excluding banks.   [b] Manufacturing only.   [c] Nordic area only.   [d] Including banks.   [e] Civilian employment.

Source: ILO-MULTI database. Calculated from a variety of national sources.

production workers, and contributed to the growing segmentation of the labour markets in industrialized countries.

International production and MNE employment abroad were less affected. Over the 1977-82 period, the proportion of international production and the share of MNE employment abroad continued to expand among leading MNEs (Dunning and Stopford, 1985). This was partly due to a catching up effect by which less-established and smaller (in terms of a relatively low level of international production) leading MNEs expanded abroad to a greater extent than major, well-established international producers (Cantwell and Randaccio, 1989). The above does not take into account new entrants, i.e. enterprises which became multinationals in that period. The general slow-down of economic activity and the slow pace of FDI suggest that this was not a major factor during the period.

The second half of the 1980s was characterized by an outstanding expansion in FDI. Four major trends can be clearly identified which, overall, affected MNE direct employment:

■   a resurgence in the activity of the leading MNEs, largely through major national and transnational mergers and acquisitions (M&As);

■   the multinationalization of new industries, primarily in services;

- the emergence of new MNEs, with new entrants coming mainly from Japan and the Asian NIEs.

- the decline of foreign investment and MNE activities in developing countries, with the exception of assembly-type operations in EPZs.

Before examining in detail these main trends, we can take a closer look at trends in MNE employment abroad. The expansion of FDI points to an indeterminate increase in the proportion of the workforce employed abroad, particularly among industrialized countries. Table 2.6 shows the average annual growth of employment in recent years in all the subsidiaries and affiliates abroad for four major investor countries. A decrease is to be noted for the United States in Latin America, Africa, the Middle East and the EC, against an increase nearly everywhere for Germany, Sweden and Switzerland. With the exception of the United States, employment abroad appeared more dynamic than domestic paid employment, particularly in manufacturing. A similar trend has occurred in several other industrialized countries which are homes of MNEs, and may have accelerated recently. The expansion of Japanese outward investment accounts for a spectacular rise in employment in Japanese subsidiaries abroad, particularly in industrialized countries.

On the whole however, while multinational enterprises have increased their international activities, direct employment levels have not increased at the same rate. There is thus no evidence that the recent increase in the absolute level of MNE direct employment will halt its long-term decline as a proportion of the global labour force.[10]

The declining importance of MNEs as direct employers does not imply any diminution in these companies' economic and social role. Those who are directly employed by MNEs constitute only a fraction of the number of people whose employment situation is significantly affected by MNEs. To account for the full range of employment effects by MNEs we should consider indirect or external employment which arises because of subcontracting and various other backward and forward linkages as well as employment in non-MNE firms connected to multinational enterprises through non-equity links (licensing, franchising, management contracts, alliances and cooperative agreements, etc.). The increase in these new relationships and their impact on employment were important features of labour market development in the 1980s, which, due to serious methodological and data problems, cannot be assessed properly, but should be borne in mind when considering the total employment impact of MNEs.

---

[10] The 400 largest industrial MNEs accounted for about 40 million employees in the early 1970s (ILO, 1981a). In 1989, the 400 largest industrial MNEs in the Billion Dollar Club accounted for 23.4 million employees. This rough comparison can give an idea of the restructuring processes which have occurred over the last two decades. Global employment trends in the 1980s included increases in employment in industrialized countries, mainly among small and medium-sized enterprises and in the services sector, coupled with the strong tendency to cut the workforce in large firms in manufacturing (largely overlapping with MNE direct employment) and the expansion of "less than fully stable" forms of employment: self-employment, part-time, temporary and marginal employment. Likewise, in most developing countries the economic and debt crisis induced a halt in the growth of formal employment and an upsurge of employment in the informal sector.

3.1 Employment in the leading MNEs

In the 1980s, large MNEs tended to rationalize employment in the work-place, to concentrate on core activities, to divest peripheral assets, to contract out production and – especially in some industries – to cut costs through worldwide economies of scale and the adoption of "global" strategies. Economic recovery was a key factor in the recovery of employment levels in the second half of the decade. However, the leading MNEs increasingly resorted to major transnational and national mergers and acquisitions in order to obtain rapid increases in their market shares and to respond adequately to the emerging patterns of international competition and the opportunities opened up in industry and services by the wave of liberalization and regional integration policies. This produced an intricate reshuffling of transnational and national ownership patterns, which was partly "internal" to MNEs in highly "multinationalized" industries. Overall, with the exception of Japanese investments in Europe and North America, "greenfield" investments were rare.

MNE expansion efforts abroad were oriented particularly to the US and within the EC (see Chapter 1). Well-established leading MNEs were by far the most dynamic overseas investors in Finland, France, Germany, Italy, Japan, New Zealand, Sweden and Switzerland. In Sweden, large-scale "market-share acquisitions" carried out by a single group accounted for a large part of the rapid increase in employment abroad (Swedish Ministry of Industry, 1990). Detailed data on FDI in manufacturing by 350 German companies over the 1985-89 period show that the majority of transactions (602) involved acquisitions and led to an increase of 258,000 employees abroad, over 70 per cent of which accrued to only 13 MNEs. The 216 remaining transactions involved the establishment of new affiliates, but only generated 11,000 new jobs (FAST, 1990).

3.2 Foreign direct investment in services

Expansion of FDI in services has traditionally followed MNEs' activities abroad in manufacturing, subject to the constraints of a generally higher pattern of protection of domestic markets. The increased "service-intensity" of production (e.g. as concerns distribution, product development, customer assistance) and the contracting out of supporting service activities which were previously internal to industrial firms contributed to FDI growth in services over the 1980s. However, this growth also had a more autonomous nature. Increasingly, companies in finance and banking, insurance, fast food services, hotels and tourism, and telecommunications expanded their overseas activities, yet, on the whole, FDI growth occurred mainly in "capital-intensive" industries: banking, insurance, property, publishing, airlines, or sophisticated services like accounting, advertising, or computer software. The increase in the number of newly created or transferred (high-quality) jobs was far less than the rapid increase in the value of investment.

Data on changes in employment abroad by industry are only available for the US and Germany. They show that over the 1980s employees in foreign affiliates primarily engaged in the tertiary sector remained a minor proportion of total employ-

Table 2.7. **Employees in foreign affiliates of MNEs headquartered in the United States and the Federal Republic of Germany by sector, latest available year (thousands and per cent)**

Sector	United States[a]		Federal Republic of Germany	
	Number of employees abroad in 1989	Per cent change over 1982	Number of employees abroad in 1988	Per cent change over 1982
Primary sector	467	-29	16	33
Secondary sector	4 189	-5	1 391	10
Tertiary sector[b]	1 966	26	561	34
of which:				
Distributive trades	1 162	23	382	40
Banking, finance and insurance	160	36	49	44
Other services[b]	644	30	130	17
Total	6 621	-0.1	1 968	16

[a] Excluding banks.   [b] Including construction.

Sources: US Department of Commerce: *US direct investment abroad: Preliminary 1989 estimates*; Deutsche Bundesbank: *Statistical supplement to the monthly report*, Series 3, No. 4, Apr. 1990.

Box 2.2. National statistics on employment in foreign firms

The following countries published – more or less regularly – statistics on the number of employees in domestic affiliates and subsidiaries of foreign enterprises: Argentina, Australia, Austria, Barbados, Botswana, Canada, former Czechoslovakia, Denmark, Finland, Germany, Indonesia, Ireland, Jamaica, Japan, New Zealand, Norway, Malaysia, Mexico, Panama, Poland, Portugal, the Republic of Korea, Rwanda, Singapore, Sweden, Tunisia, the UK and the US. "Ad hoc" surveys or official estimates are available for other countries, e.g. Bangladesh, China, Egypt, Italy, Jordan, Romania and the Philippines. Zambia and the Philippines are undertaking a survey of foreign investors' activities, the results of which should be ready soon. Coverage, collection methods, definition of foreign ownership and consolidation procedures may, however, differ across the various countries. Most countries apply OECD criteria to define control of an affiliate (see note 1). For Finland, France, the United Kingdom and (since September 1989) Germany, the floor proportion increases to 20 per cent; for Australia, Japan and New Zealand to 25 per cent; for Denmark to 50 per cent. Lacking an international effort to promote a proper harmonization, "differences in definitions and standards will remain a fact of life with which analysts must live" (Graham and Krugman, 1989). However, in practice control is associated with ownership shares in excess of 50 per cent, so that the above differences disturb but do not hinder cross-country comparisons. In fact, with respect to the Benchmark Survey on foreign firms in the US Graham and Krugman note that "preliminary calculations done by the BEA staff suggest that raising the classifying criterion from 10 to 20 per cent or even 50 per cent has a minor impact" (ibid. p. 10).

ment abroad, although employment in this sector registered the highest increase (table 2.7). More comprehensive data can be obtained from host country sources. Out of a sample of nine industrialized countries for which figures were available on the sectoral distribution of employment in foreign firms, six registered an increase in the share of the tertiary sector in recent years, i.e. the United States, Japan, Germany, Canada, Norway and New Zealand (table 2.8).

3.3 New multinationals

Investments by the newly industrializing economies of South-East Asia are emerging as a special case, representing a group of increasingly dynamic international firms.

In Hong Kong, the Republic of Korea, Singapore and Taiwan, China, pressures on domestic labour costs are pushing firms in labour-intensive industries such as textiles, clothing, toys and low-level consumer electronics to produce "offshore" in the export-processing zones of nearby Asian countries (e.g. China, Malaysia and Thailand), Africa (Mauritius) and the Caribbean. According to a 1989 survey, out of a sample of about 2,000 Hong Kong enterprises in manufacturing, 532 were found to have established production facilities abroad – in 90 per cent of the cases in the nearby areas of China – and 353 had plans for expansion abroad – again mainly in nearby China (Hong Kong Government, 1990a). It is estimated that Hong Kong's investment activities in China may have generated 2 million jobs by the end of 1989 (World Bank, 1989).

Increasingly, investments are also taking place in industrialized countries to safeguard access to markets for exports from protectionist pressures or to acquire technology and brand names. Examples include the establishment of manufacturing affiliates in Silicon Valley, the acquisition of brand names like Singer and Sansui, or the take-over of small high-tech companies by investors from the Republic of Korea, Hong Kong and Taiwan, China. There is fragmentary evidence that the enterprises from these countries are rapidly gaining the status of established and active international producers, at present mainly in labour-intensive production, but potentially with the capacity and the resources to move up-market. Some of these enterprises, in fact, are accumulating and starting to export their own technological capabilities by themselves.[11]

Similar cases are less frequent in the other developing countries. However, Brazilian firms already constitute the fourth largest group of foreign investors in Portugal and some leading Brazilian and Mexican industrial companies are also active in the United States. In Brazil, Mexico and Colombia, large media private conglomerates have emerged which broadcast or produce for the international market and which own affiliates in industrialized countries.[12]

[11] For a discussion see Cantwell and Tolentino (1990) and Hill and Pang Eng Fong (1991). The growth of Asian NIEs in recent years has been such that now they can hardly be properly termed developing. The Republic of Korea's GDP is higher than that of the Netherlands and per capita income levels are close to those of Portugal. GNP per capita in Singapore and Hong Kong is higher than in Spain.

[12] For Brazil, see Wells (1988) and Marcovich (1991).

Table 2.8. **Distribution of employees in affiliates of foreign-based MNEs in selected host countries by sector; circa 1980 and 1988 or latest available year (per cent)**

Country	Primary	Secondary	Distributive trades	Other tertiary	Total	Year	Type of source
OECD COUNTRIES							
United States[a]	3	47	25	25	100	1990	CS
	3	61	27	10	100	1980	
Japan	–	78	17	5	100	1988	CS
	–	83	14	3	100	1983	
Germany, Fed. Rep. of	1	73	14	12	100	1989	CS
	1	76	12	11	100	1980	
Canada	4	51	21	25	100	1986	CS
	5	56	24	15	100	1978	
Sweden	4	60	22	15	100	1989	CS
	2	49	35	15	100	1980	
Austria	–	65	17	18	100	1985	CS
	–	65	15	20	100	1979	
Finland	–	45	35	21	100	1988	CS
	–	40	38	22	100	1982	
Norway	4	33	24	39	100	1987	CS
	1	44	31	24	100	1980	
Portugal	1	67	16	16	100	1989	CS
	1	64	13	22	100	1982	
New Zealand	0	41	28	31	100	1990	CS
	0	47	20	33	100	1986	
EASTERN EUROPE							
Poland	–	84	0	16	100	1989	CS
	–	87	1	13	100	1983	
Czechoslovakia	4	64	0	32	100	1989	CS
LATIN AMERICA AND THE CARIBBEAN							
Mexico	1	67	6	26	100	1988	CS
Peru	4	79	13	5	100	1986	IE
Uruguay	–	64	–	35	100	1988	CS
Panama	71	18	5	6	100	1988	CS
Jamaica	34	41	8	16	100	1988	CS
AFRICA							
Côte d'Ivoire	9	48	n.a.	43	100	1984	IE
Senegal	12	63	8	17	100	1984	IE
Rwanda	–	32	35	33	100	1989	CS
Botswana	29	17	8	46	100	1989	CS
ASIA							
Malaysia	19	62	7	12	100	1984	CS
Singapore	–	72	14	14	100	1988	CS

CS = comprehensive survey; IE = ILO estimate; IRM = IRM Director   [a] Preliminary.

Source: ILO-MULTI. Based on a variety of national sources.

4. MNE direct employment levels in host countries

4.1 Industrialized countries

A massive presence of firms with foreign participation is a standard feature of most industrialized countries. The portion of total domestic employment which is directly accounted for by affiliates of foreign MNEs is not large with respect to total employment, but it increases considerably in the manufacturing sector, particularly in science-based industries or in those industries where brand names and a strong local marketing base constitute a specific competitive advantage.

In both the United States and the EC as a whole, the share of employment by foreign firms in total paid employment was approximately 3 per cent in all sectors and about 10 per cent in manufacturing (table 2.9).[13]

The foreign presence in Japan is barely visible, but for several other major OECD countries the share of foreign firms in manufacturing employment ranges from 10 to 20 per cent. The proportion is well above 20 per cent in Ireland, Canada, Austria, Australia and New Zealand. Despite national differences, chemicals and allied products and electrical equipment are almost invariably the two-digit industries where foreign presence is higher, followed by food and beverages, rubber products, motor vehicles and non-metallic products.

In looking at the main trends in the 1980s, a marked increase in the share of foreign firms in manufacturing employment is visible in the US, Sweden and Finland – where the share almost doubled from the early 1980s to 1988 – and to a lesser extent in Ireland, Norway and New Zealand (table 2.9). Apart from Ireland, in these latter countries foreign penetration was rather low at the start. During the 1980s, in all other OECD countries for which figures are available, only marginal changes occurred in the share of employment in foreign firms.[14]

4.2 Developing countries

The influence of multinational enterprises on the labour market in host developing countries appears to be marginal when compared to the large number employed or underemployed in agriculture, in the informal sector or in small-scale

[13] The share for the EC is calculated on the basis of data on employment in EC affiliates of multinationals from the United States, Japan, Switzerland, Sweden and Finland, plus estimates for the other industrialized and developing countries.

[14] This pattern requires further explanation. First, the latest available employment data generally refer to 1988 and thus do not yet fully reflect the impact of the expansion in FDI, particularly of the recent major cross-border M&As. Secondly, as already mentioned, throughout the 1980s MNEs engaged in employment rationalization in their operations at home and abroad. Thirdly, in analysing the employment performances of foreign firms, the changes in the firm-size composition of industrial structure and employment should be taken into account, and employment growth partitioned by groups of firms. An ILO study on Canada found that over the 1976-86 period the volume of employment accounted for by foreign MNEs increased relative to similarly large Canadian firms but diminished with respect to Canadian SMEs, so that the employment share of foreign firms in total manufacturing employment in Canada declined (Ray, 1990). A similar phenomenon has probably been at work in several OECD countries.

Table 2.9. Employees in affiliates of foreign-based MNEs by host country and affiliates' primary activity; all sectors and manufacturing, circa 1980 and 1989 (thousands and per cent of domestic paid employment)

Country (ranked by GDP)	All sectors		Manufacturing		Year	Type of source
	No. of employees	%	No. of employees	%		
OECD COUNTRIES						
United States	4 735	4	2 221	12	1990	CS
	2 034	2	1 103	5	1980	
EC	3 500	3		9	1988	IE
Japan	169	0	132	1	1988	CS
	140	0			1983	
Germany, Fed. Rep. of	→1 768	7	1 058	16	1989	CS
	1 636	6	1 240	14	1980	
France			—	20	1982	IRM
Italy			509	12	1991	CS
			475	12	1985	
United Kingdom			—	15	1989	CS
			858	14	1981	
Canada	1 329	13	704	36	1986	CS
	1 344	15	791	41	1978	
Spain			—	48	1977	IRM
Australia			248	24	1986-87	CS
			265	26	1982-83	
Switzerland	130	4	35	4	1988	IE
Sweden	202	5	122	13	1989	CS
	114	3	56	6	1980	
Belgium				33	1975	IRM
Austria	—	20	—	33	1989	CS
	—	20	—	27	1979	
Finland	60	3	28	6	1988	CS
	45	2	18	3	1982	
Norway	107	6	36	11	1987	CS
	77	5	33	9	1980	
Denmark			45	9	1986	CS
			31	6	1976	
Portugal	175	6	117	12	1989	CS
	171	6	117	13	1982	
New Zealand	144	12	60	23	1990	CS
	117	10	55	18	1986	
Ireland			84	43	1987	CS
			77	37	1983	
EASTERN EUROPE						
Soviet Union	130	0			1990	CS
Poland	109	1	91	3	1989	CS
	21	0	18	1	1983	
Czechoslovakia	2	0	1	0	1989	CS

CS = comprehensive survey; IE = ILO estimate; IRM = IRM Directory.

Source: ILO-MULTI. Based on a variety of national sources.

Table 2.10. Employees in affiliates of foreign-based MNEs by host developing country/area; all sectors and manufacturing, latest available year (thousands and per cent of domestic labour force (EAP) and paid employment)

Country/area (ranked by GDP)	All sectors			Manufacturing			Year	Type of source
	No. of employees in foreign firms ('000)	(A) Share of EAP (%)	(B) Share of paid employment (%)	No. of employees in foreign firms ('000)	(C) Share of EAP (%)	(D) Share of paid employment (%)		
LATIN AMERICA AND THE CARIBBEAN								
Brazil				909	14		1977	IRM
Mexico	756[a]	2	12	516[a]	8	21	1988	CS
Argentina				185	32[b]		1984	CS
Colombia				81	16[c]		1981	IRM
Uruguay	24	2		15	7[d]		1988	CS
Panama	24		3	4	6		1988	CS
Jamaica	87	10	12	36	26		1988	CS
Barbados				3	19	31	1989	CS
AFRICA								
Cameroon	35	1	10[e]	34			1984	IE
Côte d'Ivoire	61	1	14[e]	34			1984	IE
Zaire	67	1	30[e]	44			1984	IE
Senegal	41	1		26			1984	IE
Rwanda	6	n.a.		2	14		1989	CS
Botswana	35	8		6		36[e]	1989	CS
Mauritius				35	26	33	1990	OE
ASIA								
China	2 700	n.a.					1989	OE
Republic of Korea	315	2		288	9	15[f]	1978	CS
Indonesia			1	400	7	24[g]	1985	IE
Thailand				183	9	15	1986	IE
Hong Kong				100	12	14	1989	CS
Philippines	156	1		124	5	20[c]	1988	CS
Malaysia	215[h]	4		134	16	27[f]	1984	CS
Singapore	270	21	26	193	52	58[i]	1988	CS
Sri Lanka				71[j]	8	40[k]	1989	OE

CS = comprehensive survey; IE = ILO estimate; IRM = IRM Directory; OE = official estimate.

[a] Instituto Mexicano del Seguro Social. [b] Firms with 300 or more workers. [c] Firms with ten or more workers. [d] 1987 Censo Economico Nacional. [e] Modern sector. [f] Firms with five or more workers. [g] Firms with 20 or more workers. [h] Majority-owned foreign limited companies. [i] Private sector firms with ten or more workers. [j] Foreign firms in Greater Colombo over 1986, paid employment in firms with five or more workers.

Note: Unless otherwise specified, EAP and paid employment totals for the columns (A), (B), (C) and (D) are taken from the ILO *Year Book of Labour Statistics*, tables 1A, 3A, 2A and 5B respectively.

craft activities. However, it can be fairly high in the extractive sector and in modern manufacturing activities and in services like advertising, accounting, consulting, car rental or advanced telecommunications.

Based on available sources, data and estimates on the number of employees in foreign firms for several developing countries are shown in table 2.10. Some problems relate to the definition of control.[15] Cross-country comparisons, moreover, are hindered by the lack of homogeneous statistics on employment (in the table, the number of employees in foreign firms is shown as a percentage of the economically active population and paid employment throughout the economy and in manufacturing). The foreign presence can be considerable for small economies (in terms of population) like Jamaica, Botswana or Singapore, but in general, employees in foreign firms hardly constitute more than 2 per cent of the economically active population (EAP) in most developing countries. In manufacturing, however, the share rises considerably when related to paid employment in large and medium-sized establishments (by developing country standards). Argentina, Côte d'Ivoire, Indonesia, Mexico, Malaysia and Sri Lanka provide relevant examples.

In spite of employing only a limited number of people, MNEs are nevertheless major economic actors in developing countries. They play a decisive role in the strategically important primary resource sector, particularly through their influence over the marketing and processing of raw materials, and are typically active in these countries' most dynamic economic activities. Their productive, technological and financial assets are huge in comparison to those of the host country. As an essential component of the modern private sector, their importance to a country's industrial structure is often crucial because of the pervasiveness of state-owned enterprises, the lack of dynamic small and medium-sized enterprises, and the weak indigenous technological and management resources which generally characterize developing countries. Thus, even though small in number, their skilled labour and managerial capacities can make a decisive contribution to these countries' prospects for economic development. Together with state-owned enterprises, MNE affiliates are also major actors in the establishment and development of the rules of the game in the formal labour market.

Time series data on the evolution in MNE employment over the 1980s are available only for a few developing economies. Some registered an increase in the number of employees in foreign firms and in the proportion over total employment: Hong Kong, Singapore and the Republic of Korea. Absolute increases were also recorded in Mexico, Jamaica, Panama and several Asian countries, mainly linked to the provision of successful "offshore" facilities. On the other hand, Barbados and the debt-burdened Philippines saw a decline.

Scarce foreign capital was available to finance new or existing productive activities by MNEs in the other developing regions in the 1980s. Latin America and developing Africa – where FDI declined in real terms over the 1970-89 period (World

---

[15] In contrast to industrialized countries, where a rather positive overall attitude to foreign investment prevails – at least in sectors not considered strategic by host country governments – the enforcement of restrictive regulations has hindered the establishment of fully owned foreign firms in several developing countries and favoured the constitution of joint ventures, often with the participation of the host government. In this latter case, foreign participation does not provide a clear indication of control, but foreign inputs may characterize the behaviour and performance of such ventures.

Bank, 1991, p. 96) – were largely peripheral to the wave of investments that was taking place elsewhere. As foreign investors in these regions have in the past oriented production mainly to the home market, it is no surprise that MNE affiliates particularly suffered from the shrinking of domestic markets and GNP decline in host economies. The scarcity of the data does not allow comprehensive comparisons over time. However, considering investor countries' data from table 2.6, the decline in the number of MNE employees in the 1980s was dramatic for Africa, the Caribbean and the Middle East, and considerable for US subsidiaries in Latin America (excluding Mexico), even when compared to the poor employment performances of the countries of these regions.

4.3 Export processing zones (EPZs) in developing countries

Export-oriented investment in EPZs presents a special case. Not only has EPZ growth been spectacular in some countries, but their significance for MNE employment in developing countries is substantial when one considers that, excluding China, over 2 million are employed in EPZs and that the vast majority of new MNE employment in developing countries is most likely to be in EPZs. Such employment depends mainly on the expansion and the openness of industrialized countries' markets for traditional, labour-intensive products with a high value to volume ratio: primarily textiles and clothing, electronics, electrical appliances and toys, but also automobile parts (in Mexico) and data processing (e.g. in Jamaica and Barbados).

Not all investment in EPZs is by MNEs. Much of it – depending on the zone – can be domestic or joint ventures with local entrepreneurs. Foreign equity participation varies considerably across the various zones.[16] Even in the absence of equity ties, however, EPZ expansion may depend significantly on non-equity links involving MNEs, such as international subcontracting and supply relations. MNE (and non-MNE) producers and retailers in industrialized countries can contract out production to small enterprises in EPZs, while keeping a firm control on product design, marketing, quality control and distribution.

Today, over 200 EPZs exist in approximately 60 developing countries. EPZs are planned or being introduced in at least another 20 countries. The zones themselves, as well as the numbers of people employed and the quantity of goods produced, are distributed to varying degrees amongst the different countries and regions of the world.

In Africa, only three countries – Egypt, Mauritius and Tunisia – have EPZs with any significant levels of activity.[17] In a number of other African countries – Ghana, Kenya, Lesotho, Liberia, Morocco, Senegal, Togo and others – EPZs have been set up as well without, however, reaching a significant level of industrial production.

---

[16] Foreign-owned firms are estimated to account for about 30 per cent of all EPZ firms in Mauritius, 63 per cent of EPZ firms in the Philippines, 77 per cent in South Korea, and over 80 per cent in the Dominican Republic, Sri Lanka, Jamaica and the Mexican *Maquiladora* (cf. US Department of Labor, 1988-90, Chapter 6, in this volume; and the reply by the Mauritius Employers' Federation to the ILO questionnaire).

[17] Tunisia does not have formal EPZs nor free ports, but exporting companies may operate as if they were located in foreign trade zones.

Table 2.11. Employment in export processing zones and other special zones in developing countries/territories: 1990 (or latest available year)

Country or area	Number of EPZs in operation	People employed
AFRICA		230 648
Botswana	1	13 000
Egypt	7	25 000
Ghana	1	2 600
Lesotho	1	...
Liberia	1	...
Mauritius	1	90 000
Morocco	1	1 500
Senegal	1	1 200
South Africa	1	...
Swaziland	1	...
Togo	1	3 971
Tunisia[a]	–	93 377[b]
ASIA AND THE PACIFIC		2 648 759
Bahrain	2	4 600
Bangladesh	1	10 000
China	7	2 200 000
Fiji[a]	–	...
India	6	30 000
Jordan	1	...
Korea (Republic of)	2	21 910[b]
Macao	4	60 000
Malaysia	10	98 900
Pakistan	3	2 000
Philippines	5	43 211[b]
Sri Lanka	2	71 358
Syrian Arab Republic	6	...
Thailand	1	27 990
Tonga	1	...
Turkey	7	...
United Arab Emirates	2	5 500
Yemen	1	...
Taiwan (China)	3	70 700
LATIN AMERICA AND THE CARIBBEAN		1 073 700
Antigua and Barbuda	1	...
Argentina	1	...
Aruba	2	800
Bahamas	2	8 000
Barbados[a]	–	20 000
Belize	1	600
Brazil	1	137 000
Chile	1	8 500

Country or area	Number of EPZs in operation	People employed
Colombia	8	7 000
Costa Rica	4	6 000
Dominica	1	...
Dominican Republic	18	150 000
El Salvador	1	5 890
Grenada	1	...
Guatemala	1	55 000
Haiti	2	43 000
Honduras	3	3 000
Jamaica	4	18 000
Mexico	23	460 000
Netherlands Antilles	1	300
Nicaragua	1	...
Panama	1	6 476
Puerto Rico	2	155 000
St. Kitts and Nevis	1	583
St. Lucia	2	1 500
St. Vincent	1	400
Trinidad and Tobago	1	400
TOTAL		3 967 156

[a] There are no geographically demarcated EPZs, but exporting enterprises which enjoy conditions similar to those generally granted in EPZs.   [b] 1991.

Source: ILO-MULTI database, based on Starnberg Institute and other sources.

In West Asia, EPZs have been set up in several countries, but the activities in the EPZs in this region have remained relatively insignificant so far. The developments in South-East Asia are of a quite different nature. Over the last two decades, the most important EPZs are to be found in four newly industrializing economies (Hong Kong, the Republic of Korea, Singapore and Taiwan, China) as well as in three other countries in the region (Malaysia, the Philippines and Sri Lanka). The export processing activities in other South-East Asian countries (Bangladesh, India, Indonesia, Pakistan and Thailand) have remained rather limited with, however, some significant offshore activities in this group of countries. In China, special economic zones (SEZs) have been in operation since 1980 and have expanded steadily.

The picture in Latin America and the Caribbean is highly varied. In some economies in Central America and the Caribbean there are a number of relatively successful EPZs (Barbados, the Dominican Republic, Guatemala, Haiti, Jamaica, Mexico and Puerto Rico). In others (Belize, St. Kitts and Nevis and St. Lucia), EPZs are either expanding or being built. In a third group (the Bahamas, Costa Rica, El Salvador, Honduras, Trinidad and Tobago, among others) export production activities have remained rather restricted. Two countries in South America – Brazil and Colombia – have large processing zones; however, the Manaus zone produces mostly for the domestic market. In other countries (Chile, Ecuador, Panama and Venezuela) EPZs have been set up without attracting any significant industrial activity to date.

In terms of EPZ employment, all host countries are dwarfed by China, since it is estimated that more than 2 million are employed in manufacturing and assembly plants in China's southern provinces (largely subcontracted by Hong Kong-based companies). Next come: Mexico (446,200 *maquila* employees), Puerto Rico (155,000), the Dominican Republic (150,000), Brazil (between 75,000 and 137,000 according to different sources), Malaysia (98,900), Tunisia (93,000), Mauritius (90,000), Taiwan, China (70,700), Sri Lanka (71,000) and Guatemala (55,000). These ten economies accounted for over 80 per cent of all EPZ employment in developing economies (see table 2.11, which gives the number of EPZs in operation and their individual employment figures where available).

EPZ employment increased rapidly over the last 15 years. Overall, according to the Starnberg Institute, EPZ employment grew annually by 9 per cent between 1975 and 1986 and by more than 14 per cent between 1986 and 1990. In comparison the annual growth rate of manufacturing employment in the developing market economies was 2.9 per cent for the period between 1975 and 1986.[18] Behind these overall average rates are to be found more or less stagnating (and in a few cases even declining) EPZ employment figures in some countries, and even more rapidly increasing growth rates in others. The former category includes countries or areas like Egypt, the Philippines, the Republic of Korea and Taiwan, China, and the latter includes countries like China, the Dominican Republic, Guatemala, Mauritius, Mexico, Sri Lanka and Tunisia.

As revealed by several studies (a comprehensive one is ILO/UNCTC 1988), the employment pattern in the majority of the EPZs is still characterized by the concentration of production in two branches: textiles and clothing on the one hand, and electrical engineering and electronics on the other. Over three-quarters of the employees working in EPZs in Costa Rica, Jamaica, Mauritius, Pakistan and Sri Lanka produce textiles and clothing. Conversely the majority of employees in Malaysia and Taiwan, China, work in the electrical engineering and electronics industries. The male/female ratio in employment appears to be related to the product mix: women make up around 70 per cent or more of employees in both cases.

From an economic point of view, EPZs – where they are well run – are capable of offering several advantages which are of interest to the ILO's constituents: technology, increased productivity, management techniques, employment creation, export earnings, etc. On the social policy side, despite providing jobs, EPZs have come under fire *if* and *when* the benefits and conditions of work they offer are less favourable than those provided by comparable domestic employers, diverge from the norms subscribed to by the country in question (including international ones aspired to by virtue of ratification of international Conventions), or involve violations of trade union recognition or of the right to negotiate or bargain collectively. In fact, organized labour and enforcement of protective labour legislation can be weak, so that in addition to cheap labour MNEs can find opportunities to maximize profits which are ruled out in their home countries by the different organization of the labour market.

---

[18] Starnberg Institute (1991). For China, the calculation by Starnberg takes into account only employment in the Shenzhen and Dongguan zones.

Box 2.3. Industrial relations in EPZs

Although the whole gamut of issues subsumed under the heading of industrial relations is of paramount importance for EPZs, it is perhaps the least studied of all to date. Two bodies have recently devoted attention to this, the ICFTU (1991) and the United States Department of Labor (1989-90). The interest of the ICFTU in the issue is obvious and needs no commentary. Under the Omnibus Trade and Competitiveness Act of 1988, which requires the Secretary of Labor to submit a biennial report to Congress on internationally recognized worker rights, the US Department of Labor carried out a study on workers' rights in EPZs and visited 11 countries with EPZs.

One of the major questions which arises is whether workers are free to join trade unions. While the US Department of Labor's field missions did not find, in general, "special laws or regulations concerning freedom of association", a few exceptions may be noted. First of all, by virtue of the fact that most governments constitute an EPZ authority to manage day-to-day affairs in the zone, the temptation may exist to impinge upon national labour legislation. This, for example, is the case in Pakistan, where the Government "entirely exempted all export processing zones from the scope of the Industrial Relations Ordinance, whilst section 4 of the Export Processing Zone (Control of Employment) Rules, 1982, deprived workers of the right to strike or to take other forms of industrial action". The ILO Committee of Experts in 1989 considered these provisions to be inconsistent with the Freedom of Association and Protection of the Right to Organize Convention, 1948 (No. 87). Another subtle infringement is the request for and granting of initial "honeymoon periods" during which workers are forbidden to strike (e.g. in Turkey) or trade unions would not be set up — a practice reportedly widespread in the Caribbean in the late 1970s and early 1980s (see in particular, ILO, 1992).

Lack of a formal prohibition of trade unions does not mean, on the other hand, that unionization rates are high. The US Department of Labor study did find that high union activity in a country as a whole did not always imply a high unionization rate among EPZ workers.

Thus, Jamaica's labour laws, for example, apply equally to EPZ and non-EPZ operations. And yet, while many domestic Jamaican firms are unionized, the US Department of Labor team identified only one of 16 firms in the Kingston Free Zone with union representation. Similarly, while 20 per cent of Sri Lanka's non-EPZ workers are represented by unions, not a single EPZ firm is unionized. Mexico's nearly 400,000 *maquiladora* workers have the same legal right to form and join unions as other Mexican workers, but only 10-20 per cent belong to unions compared to over 90 per cent of workers in similar non-*maquiladora* industrial enterprises.

While concerted organizing campaigns may lead to high membership in some zones, on the whole low union membership rates in EPZs also reflect the industry, age and sex of the workforce. The ICFTU also reports similar discrepancies. While previous ILO research and the US Department of Labor suggest that low rates of unionization may relate to a number of factors such as the type of industry, period that the plant has been in operation, lack of previous employment and the fact that most employees are young girls — who are hard to unionize — the existence of a consistent pattern suggests that other factors are also at work.

Despite the overall proviso that most governments did not have special labour laws for EPZs, the US Department of Labor team did find examples of legal efforts to restrict or discourage unions in Bangladesh and the Republic of Korea. In addition, in a number of countries the US Department of Labor team found that governments and/or employers engage in restrictive practices which have the effect of limiting the ability of EPZ workers and unions to organize and bargain collectively. They found, for example, that many governments and EPZ authorities (e.g. the Dominican Republic, Jamaica and Sri Lanka) do not permit union officials to enter EPZs for the purpose of organizing, distributing union literature, or holding meetings with workers. Union access to EPZ workers, therefore, can usually only take place outside of the zones before or after work. Other examples of restrictive practices cited include Malaysia, where government policy restricts the scope of collective bargaining in companies accorded "pioneer status" (including those in EPZs); India, which classified its EPZs as "public utilities", making strikes more difficult; and the Dominican Republic, where there are widespread allegations of collusion between the Secretariat of Labor and EPZ employers to ensure a union-free environment in the zones.

5. MNE impact on labour markets in host countries: A few remarks

In general, foreign MNEs introduce a varied package of productive resources in a host economy, including capital, technology, know-how, management and marketing skills, and links with world markets. The overall impact depends on the quantity and quality of this package and on the extent to which the host economy is capable of capturing the potential beneficial effects. Employment creation is but one of the many aspects which are related to inward foreign direct investment, although it is passionately debated. The discussion is complicated by the complexity of the issue, because FDI may have direct and indirect as well as quantitative and qualitative effects on employment, each of which may be positive or negative.[19]

This warns against the danger of generalizations. The direction and magnitude of the employment impact are likely to be highly industry- and country-specific. A broad range of factors is at work, which includes:

- size, resource endowments and development levels of the host economy, including the regulatory framework and the effectiveness of local institutions in maintaining competitive conditions and avoiding restrictive practices;

- the motivations for FDI, the mode of entry by foreign firms and the way in which subsidiaries fit into parent companies' global strategies;

- the differences between foreign firms and national firms, as regards size and market power, production methods, technology, sourcing decisions, practices in labour policies and industrial relations;

- the competitiveness of the local industries which are directly and indirectly affected by foreign investment and their capacity to catch up.

[19] See for instance the discussion on the employment effects of foreign multinationals in the United States by Campbell and McElrath (1990).

At the aggregate level, it can be observed that, while FDI or MNE affili-ates' activities stimulate (depress) the overall level of economic activity and help to release (reinforce) foreign exchange or other constraints to growth and full employ-ment policies, they also provide increased (reduced) employment opportunities throughout the economy of the host country. In principle, net employment creation and economic growth are likely to result when the investments by foreign MNEs constitute a net addition to domestic investment in a situation in which domestic capital, technology, management and skills are scarce relative to investment oppor-tunities in the host country.

The employment impact of MNEs is not confined to their effects on direct employment. MNE affiliates naturally engage in an intricate network of economic interlinkages with local units. Therefore, their activity implicitly accounts for a broad array of potentially significant indirect employment effects, going from conventional effects or linkages (job creation through local purchases and job destruction through competition) to forward linkages which encompass distribution and servicing, to remote and sophisticated second- or third-order effects. On the whole, the sum of these indirect employment effects can have an impact equal to or even higher than the direct creation of jobs in MNE affiliates.

The possibilities indirectly opened up by MNEs for employment genera-tion can be better observed at the level of individual companies. A number of stud-ies have been carried out for the ILO which have developed rough estimates of MNE indirect employment for individual MNE subsidiaries in some developing countries (ILO, 1984). After consideration is given to all backward and forward linkages and to the displaced jobs, the overall assessment was that on the whole, the number of jobs indirectly generated by an MNE subsidiary was, at a minimum, at least equal to the number directly employed. However, the results were affected by MNEs' choices and by the policy and structural features of the host country, and depended strongly on the industry concerned. For instance, the automobile and food processing industries seem marked by comparatively high indirect effects on employment, while textile and clothing, electronics and mechanical engineering show weaker effects. In general, the intricacy of the various linkages is such that the attempts at measuring or predicting indirect employment effects in a precise and unambiguous way are doomed to fall short of the expectations (for an overview, see Jéquier, cf. p. 27, 1989).

Often, in the literature on multinational enterprises, the focus is on sourcing decisions by MNE affiliates concerning foreign or local procurement. Most studies underline MNE preference for imported inputs, at least in the initial stages. As long as production by foreign firms simply substitutes for production by local enterprises, this can have macroeconomic repercussions through a worsened trade deficit and a somewhat higher rate of unemployment, at least in the short term. Still, in the long term, local procurement may increase, as affiliates take root in the host economy and local suppliers improve their capacity to service them.

Restructuring, shifts in employment and changes in skill requirements occur even though the "macroeconomic" employment impact is small. In fact, some regard changes in skill requirements as the major effect of FDI on employment (Graham and Krugman, 1989, p. 49). The mismatch between workers and jobs, which follows shifts in employment associated with foreign MNEs, could make labour market clearing in the host economy less smooth and stress the capacity of the host work-force to adjust to rapid industrial change. Some segments of the labour force could be particularly affected. In a typical sequence, for instance, MNEs from industrialized countries transfer low-skill, low-wage activities to the host country, keeping "good" jobs at home. On the other end, technology-driven FDI could lead to more R&D being done abroad.

In addition to quantitative direct and indirect employment effects, efficiency gains of a micro-economic type are often considered a primary result of FDI. The range of spill-over effects which follow inward foreign investment is quite extensive and impinges upon economic, social and cultural activities. Because of their nature, these effects are difficult to evaluate and measure. Nevertheless they could represent an important benefit to a country, to the extent that they act as catalysts in bringing about long-term structural transformations in the host economy, for instance, by pro-viding a spur to R&D and innovation, introducing technological and managerial advances, setting up technical standards, creating links with world markets or helping to build up a market mentality.

The view that these benefits are considerable – primarily with regard to R&D, work organization and product innovation in industrialized countries and transfer of skills and low-level technology in developing countries – partly explain the more liberal attitude of many governments towards multinationals and foreign investment in recent years. However, in general, benefits do not trickle down per se, but require proper market conditions, an adequate institutional framework and per-haps policy interventions to bring them about. Quite naturally, MNEs do not let their proprietary technology and managerial resources leak out. The learning process results indirectly because of competitive pressures within a dynamic and reactive economic environment. FDI may foster or revive technological capacities in a host economy, but in certain circumstances the dominance of foreign-based MNE affili-ates in a specific industry could undermine the domestic potential for product and technological innovation and therefore thwart expansion of output and exports in key areas. Nor is inward FDI a necessary condition for endogenous accumulation and import of technology. Aggressive export orientation and barriers to FDI may have the same impact, as shown in the case of Japan.

In the labour market, "qualitative" gains accrue to the host country primar-ily through higher wages, training of workers and managers, and the introduction of new attitudes with regard to work organization, industrial relations and working con-ditions. Emulation by domestic firms and mobility of skilled labour are among the main channels by which these efficiency gains can be incorporated. Here again, no systematic patterns emerge, but a variety of sometimes contradictory trends. The acquisition of management skills is considered a major gain from MNE participation (e.g. in the tourism industry in Thailand, see ESCAP/UNCTC, 1989), but the contri-bution to training by MNEs can be quite poor and local mobility of MNE managers very low (e.g. in Kenya, see Gershenberg, 1987). MNEs usually pay higher wages rel-ative to national firms, but in some cases they can still maintain less than satisfactory working conditions, by international standards, or deprive local firms of skilled-labour resources, which are particularly valuable in a developing country. MNEs can assist in the introduction of a modern system of labour relations or they may simply not export their normal labour practices.

To sum up, net employment creation or improvement in the conditions and the quality of the labour force are likely to result from the operations of MNEs, but they do not necessarily and automatically accrue to the host economy in all cases.

6. Conclusions

This overview of MNE direct employment at home and abroad has shown that MNE employees account for a small proportion of world employment, albeit a qualitatively important one. In particular, manufacturing activities and employment in the major industrialized countries are concentrated to a large extent in MNEs, primarily in large, well-established companies which are at the centre of extensive global networks of production and distribution. In developing countries, MNE employees constitute a small proportion of domestic employment; however, technological and managerial capacities are often mainly concentrated in the affiliates of large foreign MNEs.

Overall, the upsurge of FDI in the late 1980s mainly had an employment-acquiring rather than an employment-creating impact. In the first half of the 1980s, the largest well-established MNEs undertook intensive rationalization of employment. It is only in the second half of the 1980s that these leading companies increasingly resorted to major national and cross-border mergers and acquisitions. This produced an intricate reshuffling of transnational and national ownership patterns, which was mainly "internal" to MNEs in highly "multinationalized" industries. Overall, global MNE networks of production and distribution expanded, as indicated by a general increase in employment in affiliates abroad; but total direct employment at the end of the 1980s – at least in a large sample of leading industrial MNEs – remained lower than in 1980. Still, significant implications for employment and labour institutions derived from the new strategies and organizational forms which were increasingly adopted by MNEs during the period, as will be discussed elsewhere in this book.

Over the decade, a growing number of workers have been exposed to new multinational patterns of production and management because of two other major components in the growth of FDI: (a) the emergence of new multinational investors from Japan and East Asian NIEs, which exported their own original productive and organizational patterns; and (b) the multinationalization of several activities in services, which were previously mainly conducted nationally. Both trends may increase in importance in the future.

The growing economic integration through FDI and MNE activities mainly affected the industrialized countries and the fast-growing economies of East Asia. The other developing regions, Latin America and Africa in particular, were marginal to this process and registered a decline in MNE investment and employment. The only exception was the impressive growth of employment in a few successful export processing zones in some countries.

Bibliography

Australian Bureau of Statistics: *Foreign ownership and control of the manufacturing industry: 1986-87*, Canberra, Dec. 1990.

Bezirganian, S.D.: "US affiliates of foreign companies: Operations in 1989" in *Survey of Current Business*, Washington, DC, US Department of Commerce, July 1991.

Buckley, P.J., et al.: *Going international: The foreign direct investment behaviour of smaller United Kingdom firms*, Reading, Berkshire, University of Reading Discussion Paper No. 41, July 1978.

Campbell, D.C.; McElrath, R.G.: *The employment effects of multinational enterprises in the United States and of American multinationals abroad*, Multinational Enterprises Programme Working Paper No. 64, Geneva, ILO, 1990.

Cantwell, J.; Randaccio, F.S.: *Catching up amongst the world's largest multinationals*, Reading, Berkshire, University of Reading Discussion Paper No. 125, 1989.

Cantwell, J.; Tolentino, P.E.: *Technological accumulation and Third World multinationals*, Reading, University of Reading Discussion Paper No. 139, 1990.

CEPAL (United Nations Economic Commission for Latin America): *Nuevas formas de inversión de las empresas extranjeras en la industria Argentina*, Documento de Trabajo No. 33, Buenos Aires, 1989.

CNEL (Consiglio Nazionale dell'Economia e del Lavoro): *Italia Multinazionale*, Milano, ETAS, 1989.

Deutsche Bundesbank: *Statistische Beihefte zu den Monatsberichten*, Reihe 3, Zahlungsbilanzstatistik, Apr., various years.

Dunning, J.H.; Cantwell, J.: *IRM Directory of Statistics of International Investment and Production*, London, Macmillan, 1987.

Dunning, J.H.; Pearce, R.D.: *The world's largest industrial enterprises, 1962-83*, New York, St. Martin's Press, 1985.

ESCAP/UNCTC: "Transnational corporation participation in the international tourism industry in Thailand with special reference to the transnational hotel chains", in *Asia Pacific TNC Review*, Series A, No. 6, Bangkok, ESCAP, 1989.

FAST (Forschungsgemeinschaft für Aussenwirtschaft Struktur und Technologiepolitik): *Internationaler Investitions Monitor 1990*, Berlin, 1990.

Fujita, M.: "Small- and medium-sized TNCs", in *The CTC Reporter*, United Nations, New York, No. 30, Autumn 1990, p. 17.

Gershenberg, I.: "The training and spread of managerial know-how: A comparative analysis of multinational and other firms in Kenya", in *World Development*, Vol. 15, No. 7, pp. 931-937, 1987.

Graham, E.M.; Krugman, P.R.: *Foreign direct investment in the United States*, Washington, DC, Institute for International Economics, 1989.

Hill, H.; Pang Eng Fong: "Technology exports from a small, very open NIC: The case of Singapore", in *World Development*, Vol. 19, No. 5, 1991.

Holstein, S.J., et al.: "The stateless corporation: Forget multinationals – Today's giants are really leaping boundaries", in *Business Week*, 14 May 1990, p. 52.

Hong Kong Government, Department of Industry: *The 1990 Survey of Overseas Investment in Hong Kong's Manufacturing Industries* (1990a).

—: *Survey of Hong Kong Manufacturing Industries, 1990* (1990b).

ICFTU: *Annual Survey on Violations of Trade Union Rights, 1991*, Brussels, ICFTU, 1991.

ILO: *Employment effects of multinational enterprises in industrialized countries*, Geneva (1981a).

—: *Employment effects of multinational enterprises in industrialized countries*, Geneva (1981b).

—: *Les entreprises multinationales et l'emploi en Afrique francophone: Données recentes sur le Cameroun, le Congo, la Côte d'Ivoire, le Gabon, le Sénégal et le Zaïre*, Geneva, 1988.

—: *Technology choice and employment generation in multinational enterprises in developing countries*, Geneva, 1984.

—: *General Report*, Food and Drink Industries Committee, Second Session, Geneva, 1991a.

—: *Multinational banks and their social and labour practices*, Geneva, 1991b.

—: *Proceedings of the UNCTC/ILO Training Workshop on Export Processing Zones for Government Officials in Latin America and the Caribbean,* Geneva, 1992.

ILO/UNCTC: *Economic and social effects of multinational enterprises in export processing zones*, Geneva, 1988.

Jéquier, N.: *Measuring the indirect employment effects of multinational enterprises: Some suggestions for a research framework*, Multinational Enterprises Working Paper No. 56, Geneva, ILO, 1989.

Kreye, O., et al.: *Multinational enterprises and employment*, Multinational Enterprises Programme Working Paper No. 55, Geneva, ILO, 1988.

Litwak, I.A.: "Instant international: Strategic reality for small high-technology firms in Canada", in *Multinational Business*, No. 2, 1990.

Marcovitch, J.: "Industrial and technological modernisation in Brazil: Stagnation and prosperity", in *Labour and Society*, Vol. 16, No. 3, Geneva, IILS, 1991.

Marrel, C.: "Les investissements directs Suisses à l'étranger en 1990", in Banque Nationale Suisse, *Monnaie et Conjoncture*, No. 4, 1991.

Ministry of Industry, Sweden: *Swedish industry and industrial policy*, Uppsala, 1990.

Ray, M.: *Standardising employment growth rates of foreign multinationals and domestic firms in Canada: From shift-share to multifactor partitioning*, Multinational Enterprises Programme Working Paper No. 62, Geneva, ILO, 1990.

Savary, J.: *Les effets des entreprises multinationales sur l'emploi: Le cas de la France*, Multinational Enterprises Programme Working Paper No. 24, Geneva, ILO, 1983.

Simon, J.; Fraga, J.; Marulli-Koenig, L.: "UNCTC's Billion Dollar Club database", in *The CTC Reporter* (New York, United Nations), No. 28, Autumn 1989, p. 59.

Starnberg Institute: *Employment and working conditions in export processing zones*, mimeo., Geneva, ILO, 1991.

Stopford, J.M.; Dunning, J.H.: *Multinationals: Company performance and global trends*, London, Macmillan, 1983.

UNCTC: *Transnational corporations in world development: Trends and prospects*, New York, United Nations, 1988.

UNCTC/ECE: *Dimensions and structures of foreign direct investments and transnational corporation activities in developed market economy countries*, ECE/UNCTC Publication Series No. 4, Geneva, United Nations, 1985.

United States Department of Commerce: *US direct investment abroad: Operations of US parent companies and their foreign affiliates*, Washington, DC, Bureau of Economic Analysis, various issues.

—: *Foreign direct investment in the United States: Operations of US affiliates of foreign companies*, Washington, DC, Bureau of Economic Analysis, various issues.

United States Department of Labor: *Workers' rights in export processing zones*, Department of International Labor Affairs, Vols. I and II, Washington, DC, US Department of Labor, 1989-90.

Wells, C.: "Brazilian multinationals", in *Columbia Journal of World Business*, Winter 1988.

World Bank: *Foreign direct investment from the newly industrialized economies*, Industry Series Paper No. 22, Washington, DC, World Bank, 1989.

—: *World Development Report 1991*, Washington, DC, World Bank, 1991.

3

Employment effects of the changing strategies of multinational enterprises

James Hamill

1. Introduction

This is the first of two chapters which examine the employment and related effects of changing multinational enterprises (MNEs) strategies during the last decade. Here, we examine the broad changes which took place in MNE strategies in the 1980s and their effects on employment. The effects of one specific feature of these strategies in the 1980s – international takeovers and strategic alliances – will be discussed in Chapter 4. It should be emphasized that the two chapters do not seek to provide a formal macro-analysis of MNE employment impact. Rather, the focus is on strategic change at the level of individual firms and industries. The underlying theme of these chapters is that changes are taking place in the nature of MNE strategies with potentially significant employment effects – especially concerning job creation and job displacement effects.

Viewed from the perspective of the early 1990s, a number of distinct phases in the evolution of MNE strategy over the last four decades can be identified (see figure 3.1). The initial phase of MNE expansion in the 1950s and 1960s was characterized by the establishment of clone-like subsidiaries in each new country of operation. Such subsidiaries typically supplied the local market and were mostly miniature replicas of the parent company. There was usually little central coordination of their operations. This period of MNE expansion was replaced by one of retrenchment during the 1970s. During this decade, major job losses as a consequence of large-scale MNE divestments, rationalizations and plant closures, occurred in response to the world economic crisis, increased international competition and rapid technological change.

In the 1980s, one of the main factors behind MNE strategies was the development of global competition. Creating a sustainable competitive advantage in global markets became one of the dominant strategic concerns of the decade. As a consequence, many MNEs adapted their traditional strategies accordingly and created closer coordination, specialization and integration of their geographically dispersed activities. This trend towards more coordinated global strategies was reinforced by the closer economic integration of countries, especially on a regional level. The latter years of the decade, in particular, were characterized by changing

Figure 3.1. Evolution of MNE strategy: 1950-1990s

Period	Strategy
1950s/1960s	Multinational expansion through the establishment of miniature replica subsidiaries abroad. Predominance of multi-domestic strategies, with largely autonomous foreign subsidiaries supplying local/regional markets. Limited global coordination or integration of geographically dispersed operations.
1970s	Multinationals in retreat: MNE divestment, rationalization and plant closures.
1980s	Shift towards coordinated and integrated global strategies by established MNEs; focus on global competitiveness and use of global scope as a competitive weapon in global industries involving plan specialization and interdependency. Strategies for the Single European Market (late 1980s onwards). Shift from export based to FDI strategies by emerging MNEs.
1990s	Transnational strategies. MNE networks.

Source: The author.

Figure 3.2. Employment and related effects of changing MNE strategies: 1980s and beyond

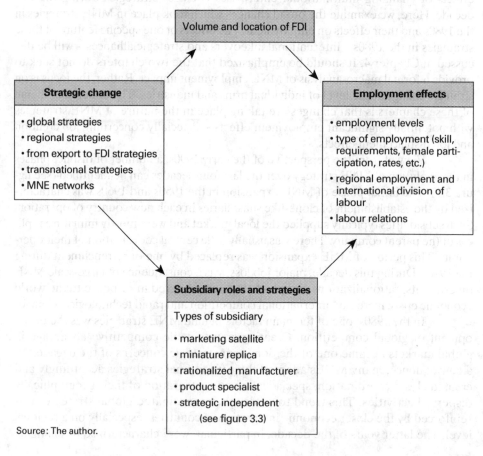

Source: The author.

MNE strategies in Europe in the run-up to "1992" and the establishment of the Single European Market. Accompanying the trend towards global or regionally coordinated strategies, the decade of the 1980s also witnessed the emergence of "new" MNEs – a consequence of the shift from export-based strategies to strategies involving greater FDI by Japanese and other Far East Asian companies, and by US companies in new industries such as information technology.

This chapter examines the employment and related effects of these three major aspects of MNE strategy during the 1980s: the shift towards global strategies; the strategic response of MNEs to "1992"; and the shift from export-based to foreign direct investment (FDI) strategies by emerging MNEs. It also looks ahead by examining two of the most likely future directions in MNE strategy during the 1990s, namely transnationality and MNE network strategies.

This chapter focuses on strategic change at the level of the MNE's global or regional operations. The employment and related effects are a function of both the volume and location of FDI and the type of subsidiary established abroad (see figure 3.2). Important subsidiary characteristics with potentially significant employment effects include: the nature of activity – whether a manufacturing or assembly plant or sales/marketing subsidiary; plant/subsidiary roles in terms of product specialization and geographical markets supplied; inter-plant relationships, especially the extent of cross-border coordination and integration of activity; the location of R&D; and issues relating to subsidiary autonomy and the centralization/decentralization of decision-making. There is an important link, therefore, between global strategic change and the role and strategy of foreign subsidiaries. White and Poynter (1984), for example, have developed a typology of MNE subsidiary strategies which is particularly useful to this chapter and is summarized in figure 3.3.

2. From multi-domestic to global strategies

The dominant strategic concern of many MNEs during the 1970s was corporate survival. During the 1980s this changed to a concern with creating and sustaining global competitive advantage. The three major driving forces behind this change were the globalization of markets; the emergence of global competition; and rapid technological change which required global marketing to amortize R&D costs.[1]

The "globalization hypothesis" has often been exaggerated with many industries remaining national or, at best, regional in scope. None the less, in many industries in the 1980s it became accepted that success depended on building an international or global presence. The characteristics of global strategies vary by company and industry. Their essential feature, however, is the use of the MNE's global scope as a key competitive weapon through the coordination and integration of geographically dispersed operations.[2] Both Doz (1986) and Porter (1986a and 1986b), for example, developed typologies of MNE strategy according to the extent

---

[1] There is an extensive literature on the globalization of markets and global strategy. For a synthesis see Hamill, J.: "Global marketing", in Baker (1991).

[2] ibid.

of global coordination and integration of activity. In Doz, a distinction was made between multinational integration, national responsiveness, and multi-focal strategies. Multinational integration was defined as the specialization of plants across countries into an integrated production and distribution network involving substantial cross-border flows of components or products. National responsiveness, by contrast, involves subsidiaries acting as local companies responsive to local market needs and host country demands. Finally, multi-focal strategies represent an intermediate situation where companies seek both the benefits of integration and the flexibility of responsiveness, depending on prevailing circumstances (e.g. government policy). This may imply integration at a regional rather than global level, an issue which is examined in more detail in section 3.

The two main dimensions of Porter's model of international strategy are the configuration and coordination of value-chain activities. Configuration refers to the geographical location of value-added activities throughout the world, with options ranging from concentrated configuration (performing an activity in one location serving world markets) and dispersed configuration (geographical dispersion of value-chain activities). Coordination refers to the extent of central coordination and control of value-chain activities globally, with options ranging from high coordination, implying tight central control, to low coordination, implying substantial subsidiary decision-making autonomy. The combination of different configuration and coordination options gives rise to Porter's four-fold classifications of international strategies as shown in figure 3.4. Apart from the country-centred (multi-domestic) strategy in the bottom left-hand quadrant, all the other strategies represent forms of global strategy which Porter defines as one in which a firm seeks to gain "a competitive advantage from its international presence through either concentrating configuration, coordination among dispersed activities or both". These competitive advantages derive mainly from the economies of scale, cost savings and greater efficiency available through global specialization and coordination.

2.1 Employment effects

The typologies of MNE strategy discussed above have important implications concerning strategy in foreign subsidiaries and hence for the employment and related effects of MNEs. The three types of subsidiary strategy most relevant to a discussion of multi-domestic and global strategies are the "miniature replica", "rationalized manufacturer" and "product specialist". The employment effects of each type of subsidiary are summarized in figure 3.5 in relation to the impact on employment levels; employment type; job security; the regional distribution of employment; and labour relations issues. Clearly, from a host country perspective, "product specialists" with enhanced product and market responsibilities are preferable to "miniature replicas" or "rationalized manufacturers".

Figure 3.5 is essentially static in nature since it refers to the employment effects deriving from the establishment of one or other of the three subsidiary types. What is more important in the context of this chapter is the employment and related effects of a change from multi-domestic to global strategies. These are likely to include:

Figure 3.3. Classification of foreign subsidiaries' strategies

Type	Strategy
Marketing satellite	Marketing/sales subsidiaries which sell products manufactured centrally on the local market; associated mainly with export based or pure global strategies.
Miniature replica	Subsidiaries which produce and market all or part of the parent's product line mainly for the local market; miniature replica subsidiaries may be "new" operations established as part of a shift from export to FDI strategies or "mature" subsidiaries associated with multi-domestic strategies.
Rationalized manufacturer	Subsidiaries which produce parts or components as part of a vertically integrated global strategy; alternatively the plant may be a final assembly operation.
Product specialist	Subsidiaries which develop, manufacture and market a limited product line for global or regional markets; associated with horizontally integrated global strategies.
Strategic independent	A subsidiary is granted autonomy to develop lines of business for global/regional markets; associated with transnational strategies.

Source: Adapted from White and Poynter (1984).

Figure 3.4. Porter's model of international strategies

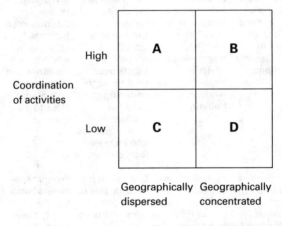

Note:

A = Strategy of high FDI with extensive coordination among subsidiaries, i.e. geographically dispersed, but highly coordinated operations.

B = Purest global strategy, i.e. concentration of activity in a few countries which act as global platforms.

C = Country-centred or multi-domestic strategy, i.e. geographically dispersed, nationally responsive, uncoordinated operations.

D = Export-based strategy with decentralized marketing, i.e. production concentrated at home, and decentralized sales/marketing subsidiaries.

Source: Adapted from Porter (1986).

Figure 3.5.   Subsidiary strategy and the employment effects of MNEs on host countries

Subsidiary strategy	Employment effects				
	Employment levels	Employment type	Job security	Regional/inter-national division of labour	Labour rela-tions
Miniature replica	Employment creation through import substi-tution and multiplier effects; restricted long-term employment growth prospects due to limited product/mar-ket role of the subsidiary.	Low-medium skill content; limited R&D.	Depends on market share and market growth; in the longer term, job security in miniature replicas is threatened by shift to global/ regional strategies.	Miniature replicas locate in close prox-imity to major markets and centres of population; adds to regional imbalances.	Host country industrial rela-tions prac-tices.
Rationalized manufacturers	Employment creating effects limited by restrictive plant role and high import content in final assembly operations.	Low skill con-tent; routine assembly work "screw-driver opera-tions"; limited functional responsibility or R&D; limited workforce training.	Plant status dependent on international factor cost movements; but possible upgrading of assembly plants over time through widening product/ market responsibilities and increased local content.	Reinforces international division of labour through inter-national sourcing in low-cost countries and location of final assembly close to major markets.	Anti-union practices to reduce threats to coordinated and integrated global produc-tion system.
Product spe-cialists	Major positive effect through wide prod-uct/market role of plant.	High skill con-tent and decentraliza-tion of R&D and other functional activities.	Long-term job security due to enhanced plant status.	Product spe-cialists located mainly in highly devel-oped coun-tries or regions; access to skilled labour.	Transfer of parent com-pany indus-trial relations practices.

Source: The author.

- a major reduction in employment levels as a consequence of the rationalization and specialization of international production. One of the main rules of globalization according to Savary (1991) is "do whatever seems best wherever it seems best, even if people ... lose jobs or responsibilities";

- a significant reallocation of subsidiary roles and responsibilities, which will have a major impact on employment quality. Some subsidiaries will be closed altogether or become assembly operations with limited skill content or responsibilities in R&D, marketing, etc. Others, however, may be reallocated as product specialists, implying a higher quality of employment;

- the shift to global strategies will have a major adverse effect on job security not only because of the overall reduction in employment levels (as above) but also because of the greater in-built flexibility for transferring production between countries in response to market, costs and labour relation factors and government incentives;

- global strategies will exacerbate inequalities in the regional and international division of labour. Low-cost countries or regions within countries will be utilized for part and component sourcing or for routine assembly operations. R&D, marketing, manufacturing, etc., will move towards already prosperous regions due to market size or availability of skilled personnel;

- the adoption of global strategies will have a major impact on labour relations within MNEs. On the face of it, strategies of global coordination and integration would enhance the bargaining position of trade unions, since an industrial dispute at one subsidiary could have a major adverse impact on the whole integrated system. It is not surprising, therefore, that many MNEs operating globally integrated strategies (e.g. in the electronics industry) refuse to recognize or negotiate with unions. Similarly, the shift from a multi-domestic strategy to a coordinated global strategy will normally be accompanied by the introduction of radically new working practices designed to maximize the benefits to be derived from international integration.

2.2 Case examples

There are significant variations in the extent to which MNEs have adopted globally coordinated and integrated strategies. Some companies, such as Ford or IBM, have long operated integrated networks of large plants specializing in specific components or final assembly. Japanese MNEs, too, are highly integrated on a global basis, especially in electronics and automobiles.[3] By contrast, the extent of global coordination and integration is considerably lower in many European MNEs. There is evidence, however, of a shift towards more integrated strategies in a number of companies including Electrolux, Thomson, Ciba-Geigy, Jacobs-Suchard, BSN, Saint Gobain, Renault and Philips.[4] The four brief case studies below present

[3] See Jatusripitak, Fahey and Kotler (1985).
[4] Savary (1991).

examples of MNEs at different stages in the shift towards global coordination and integration and associated employment effects.

Caterpillar: Two main phases can be identified in Caterpillar's attempt, during the 1980s, to coordinate and integrate its global production and logistics system. In 1981, for the first time in its history, Caterpillar experienced severe financial problems as a consequence of the collapse in the world construction equipment market and the emergence of a powerful global competitor in the form of Komatsu of Japan. In response to its deteriorating financial position, Caterpillar embarked on a massive five-year rationalization programme between 1981 and 1986 aimed at reducing costs by 20 per cent and establishing the company as the lowest cost producer in the industry. This required a major shift from the company's traditional country-by-country approach to production and marketing, and towards a global strategy, the three key elements of which were the global standardization of parts and components; global sourcing of parts and components in low-cost areas; and the consolidation of production into fewer, larger and more cost-efficient plants.

The latter element was reinforced in the second phase of global restructuring in the "Plant With a Future (PWAF)" programme announced in 1986. This involved massive capital expenditure of more than $1 billion aimed at improving efficiency in remaining plants through new technology (flexible manufacturing systems, just-in-time, etc.) and increased coordination between plants.

The employment and related effects of Caterpillar's strategic shift towards greater global coordination and plant specialization were profound (table 3.1). A total of nine plants were closed in the period 1980 to 1987 with an overall reduction in the company's workforce of more than 30,000 employees. One of the most controversial of these plant closures was the Uddingston facility near Glasgow, Scotland. Although total employment at this plant had fallen from 2,000 in 1981 to 1,200 by 1986, the plant's future appeared secure with the announcement in 1986 that

Table 3.1.   Worldwide employment at Caterpillar, Philips, Renault and Toyota, 1980-91

Year	Caterpillar	Philips	Renault	Toyota
1980	86 350	373 000	223 450	47 064
1981	83 455	348 000	215 844	48 757
1982	73 249	336 000	214 000	51 034
1983	58 402	343 000	219 805	57 034
1984	61 624	344 000	213 725	57 846
1985	53 616	346 000	196 414	59 467
1986	53 731	344 000	182 448	79 901
1987	54 463	337 000	188 936	84 207
1988	57 954	310 000	181 715	86 082
1989	60 784	305 000	174 573	91 790
1990	59 662	273 000	157 378	96 849
1991	53 636	240 000	147 195	102 423

Source: Annual reports.

Uddingston was to be a "PWAF". A total of £62 million was to be invested in upgrading the plant which was to become a major location for new products and components manufacturing. Less than a year after the granting of PWAF status to Uddingston, the complete closure of the plant was announced.

To achieve the full benefits of PWAF, a radical change in working practices was required at Caterpillar aimed at improving worker flexibility and mobility. The company negotiated a new labour agreement with the United Automobile Workers and the International Association of Machinists, and with nationally based unions, which significantly reduced the number of worker grades and job classifications and the rules for assigning workers to jobs.

Philips: While Caterpillar's attempt to consolidate its global operations dates back to the early 1980s, Philips' shift towards a global strategy is much more recent and ongoing. Although operating on a global scale with a large number of geographically dispersed subsidiaries, Philips has traditionally adopted a multi-domestic strategy. National subsidiaries have mainly been responsible for their own domestic markets, with only limited global coordination of activity. In 1989, however, the company announced a major change in its corporate mission and strategy for the next decade. The principal change was the adoption of a global orientation with the objective of becoming a leading global electronics company with strengths in each of the main markets – Europe, North America and Japan. The adoption of a global philosophy and the reorientation of strategy towards global markets has been brought about by a number of factors currently affecting the world electronics industry, including the globalization of markets and of competition; technology developments leading to a stream of new product developments and the greater convergence between consumer and professional electronics; changes in production processes (e.g. computer-aided design and manufacture) which are becoming less labour intensive; and new patterns of cooperation through strategic alliances. As a consequence of these changes, Philips has established three strategic imperatives to achieve global competitiveness:

- technological expertise;

- global sales to achieve economies of scale and learning curve effects, spread R&D costs, justify new product developments, etc.;

- the strategic location of production centres to supply global products to global markets.

It is the last of these which is particularly important from an employment perspective. Philips is currently attempting to restructure its geographically dispersed production plants by shifting from local production for local markets to highly efficient factories for large volume production for global markets. This will be achieved through the establishment of International Production Centres which will become Product Specialists with global market responsibilities for specific lines of business. As a consequence, a large number of plants are to be closed or substantially run down with an additional loss of 60,000 jobs from a workforce which has already been significantly streamlined in recent years (table 3.1).

Toyota: The highly coordinated and integrated global strategies of many Japanese MNEs, especially in the electronics and automobile industries, are by now well known.[5] A typical pattern of vertical integration between plants located in Japan, developing and industrialized countries is shown in figure 3.6. The aim of such integration is the strategic location of plants throughout the world to obtain the lowest costs of production and distribution.

One company which has established a highly coordinated and integrated global production and distribution network is Toyota. The company operates 12 plants in Japan. Of these, five are responsible for the assembly/manufacture of trucks, buses and passenger cars. The remaining seven plants specialize in part and component production for both Japan and overseas assembly operations (engines, chassis parts, exhausts, electronics, etc.). In addition, there are three technical/research centres, together with six centres responsible for warehousing and shipping.

In terms of overseas operations, Toyota has established subsidiary or affiliate companies in more than 25 countries. These fall into one of three categories: First, assembly operations – most of which rely on complete or semi knock-down kits supplied from Japan – established in developing countries aimed at supplying local markets, in Brazil, India, Indonesia, Peru, the Philippines, Thailand, Venezuela and Taiwan, China; second, sales, marketing and financing subsidiaries established in the major industrialized country markets of North America and Europe; and third and more recently, the establishment of assembly or manufacturing operations in industrialized country markets mainly in response to the continued appreciation of the yen and real or threatened import restrictions.

To date, Toyota's main overseas subsidiary operation in an industrialized country market has been the joint venture in the United States with General Motors established in 1984 (New United Motor Manufacturing Inc.) to manufacture the Prizm and Corolla vehicle ranges. As part of a general strategy of increasing overseas production, however, the company announced in 1990 the establishment of a major manufacturing centre in the United Kingdom. The new plant will have an annual production volume of 200,000 cars which will be sold both in the UK and exported to Continental Europe. Like many other Japanese companies in the UK, the new plant will operate under a single union, no strike agreement. A second UK plant, at Swansea in Wales, is to be constructed to produce engines. The employment effects of Japanese automobile transplants in Europe have aroused considerable controversy in recent years and are examined in more detail in a later section of this chapter.

Renault:[6] In contrast to Toyota's geographically dispersed operations, Renault's production centres are more highly concentrated in fewer countries, especially France, Belgium, Spain and Portugal, but also in Yugoslavia, Turkey and Mexico. Like Toyota, however, the manufacturing system is highly coordinated and integrated with plants specializing in components, body-building or final assembly. This integration is mainly European based rather than global, although the Mexican plant supplies engines to the European operations. In 1989, Renault operated 17 plants in

---

[5] Jatusripitak, Fahey and Kotler, op. cit.

[6] This section is based on Savary (1991).

Figure 3.6. Global marketing network: Japanese MNEs

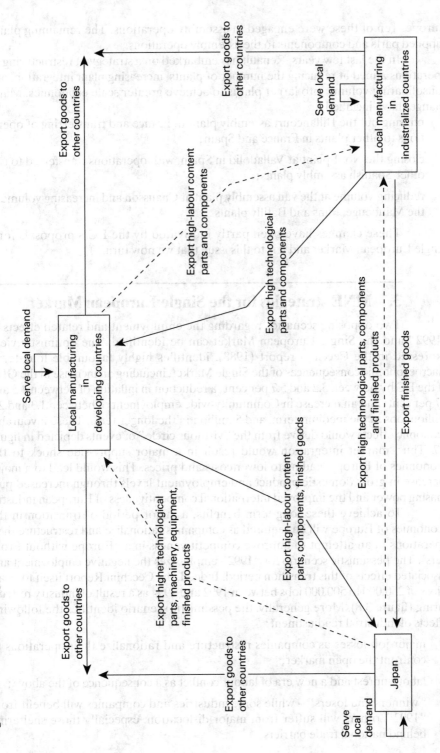

Source: Jatusripitak, Fahey and Kotler (1986), p. 50.

Europe. Ten of these were engaged in assembly operations. The remaining plants supplied parts and components to the assembly operations.

In the last few years, Renault has embarked on a strategy of restructuring its operations aimed at reducing the number of plants, increasing plant integration, and consolidating volume into larger plants to achieve greater scale economies. Major changes have included:

■ phasing out the Billancourt assembly plant in France and transferring of operations to other plants in France and Spain;

■ closing the No. 1 plant at Valladolid in Spain, with operations transferred to two other Spanish assembly plants;

■ reducing volume at the van assembly plant at Chausson and increasing volume at the Maubeuge, Flins and Batilly plants.

These changes have been partly motivated by the EC's proposals for a Single European Market and it is to this issue that we now turn.

3. MNE strategies for the Single European Market

Two opposing scenarios regarding the employment and related effects of "1992" and the Single European Market can be identified. The optimistic view, expressed in the Cecchini report (1988), identifies highly favourable long-term, macroeconomic consequences of the Single Market, including an increase in the GDP of the EC by between 3.2 and 5.7 per cent; a reduction in inflation of between 4.5 and 7.7 per cent; and an increase in Community-wide employment of between 1.3 and 2.3 million jobs in the medium term, and 5 million in the longer term. These favourable economic effects would derive from the "virtuous circle" of events depicted in figure 3.7. Thus, market integration would result in a major supply-side shock to the economies of Europe leading to lower costs and prices. This would lead to a major increase in gross domestic product and employment levels through increased purchasing power and the improved international competitiveness of European industry.

To achieve these long-term benefits, a major period of transition in the economies of Europe will be required as companies rationalize and restructure their operations in an attempt to improve competitiveness in a "Europe without Frontiers". The pessimistic scenario for "1992" emphasizes the negative employment and associated effects of this transition period. Indeed, the Cecchini Report itself forecast a loss of 250,000 to 500,000 jobs between 1992 and 1994 as a result of industry restructuring (figure 3.8). More generally, the pessimistic scenario identifies the following effects of industrial readjustment:

■ major job losses as companies restructure and rationalize their operations to confront the open market;

■ labour unrest and a new era of labour conflict as a consequence of the above;

■ "winners and losers" – while some industries and companies will benefit from "1992", others will suffer from major dislocation, especially those sheltering behind national trade barriers;

Figure 3.7. The "virtuous circle": Principal macroeconomic mechanisms activated in the course of completing the international market

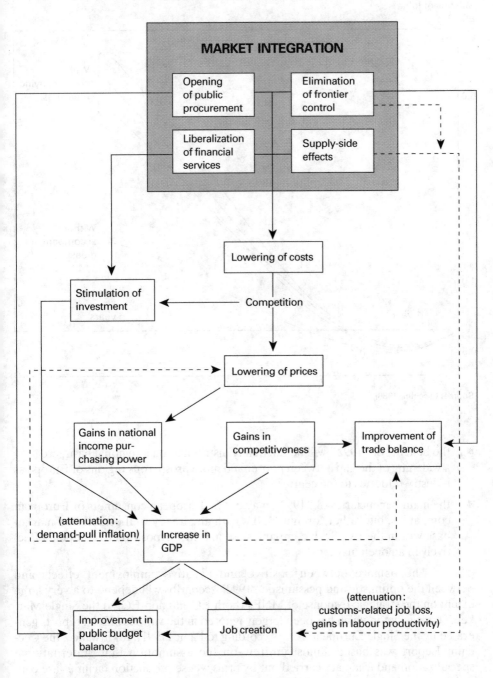

Source: Cecchini (1988).

Figure 3.8.   Illustrative profile of evolution of employment

Millions of jobs
EC 12

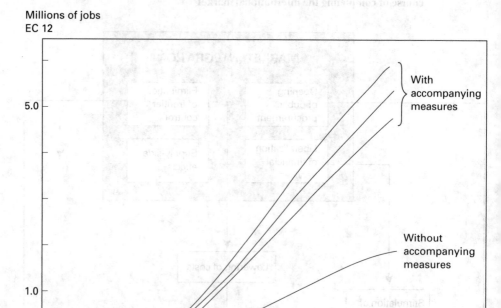

Source: Cecchini (1988).

- the benefits of "1992" will be unequally distributed on a regional basis, creating a widening of the gap between poorer and more prosperous regions of Europe as industry relocates to the centre;

- the main beneficiaries of "1992" may not be European consumers or European companies, but rather foreign MNEs with an already well-established market base within the EC. Such companies are in a strong position to compete effectively in an open market.

The balance between positive and negative employment effects and between the optimistic and pessimistic "1992" scenarios will depend to a very large extent on the strategic response of MNEs (both EC and non-EC) to the Single Market. This is a factor which has been largely ignored in the various official reports generated by the Single European Act. According to Panić (1991), for instance, the Cecchini Report was based almost entirely on the assumption that "international specialization and trade are carried out by firms whose production facilities are confined to a single country".

3.1 Employment effects

There are two main aspects of MNE strategy which are particularly important in the context of the employment effects of "1992". First, the impact of "1992" on FDI flows both into and within Europe; and second, the impact of MNE restructuring. In both of these areas, major adverse employment effects can be expected, at least in the short-to-medium term.

In terms of the first of these issues, recent years have witnessed a significant increase in FDI flows into the EC, especially by American and Japanese MNEs, motivated mainly by the fear of "Fortress Europe". Unlike the initial phase of foreign MNE expansion in Europe during the 1950s and 1960s, however, the employment effects of current FDI inflows will be significantly less favourable. This is the case for at least three main reasons. First, a very high proportion of the current inflow of FDI is in the form of mergers and acquisitions, rather than the establishment of greenfield subsidiaries. This poses major questions about both the increased level of foreign ownership of key European industries and, more specifically, the possible adverse employment effects of post-acquisition rationalization (see Chapter 4). Second, much of the current wave of greenfield FDI in Europe, especially by Japanese companies, is in routine assembly operations designed to circumvent real or threatened import restrictions (i.e. the so-called "screwdriver operations"). This raises important concerns regarding local content and the high import propensity of such plants, although there is some evidence of higher local content over time (e.g. Nissan in the UK). Third, much of the current wave of FDI in Europe is occurring in industries already suffering from over-capacity or growth constraints, e.g. automobiles. As a result, fears have been expressed concerning the possible adverse employment effects of the new wave of FDI on indigenous European companies and the large-scale job losses which may result from industrial restructuring and rationalization.

The second main aspect of MNE strategy important from the perspective of "1992" and employment effects is restructuring. The removal of internal trade barriers and closer economic integration within Europe will reduce the need for a market-by-market approach to plant location. As a consequence, many MNEs may be expected to rationalize their European production networks by consolidating activity into fewer, larger plants serving multi-country markets. Section 3.2 presents industries in which MNE restructuring is taking place in Europe in the run-up to "1992".

3.2 Industry cases

Automobiles: "1992" will have a profound effect on this industry, which is Europe's largest industry and employer. A major competitive shake-out is expected before the mid-1990s with the loss of thousands of jobs. This will be a consequence of four related problems facing the industry. First, the Single Market will lead to much more open competition among European manufacturers and the abolition of subsidies paid to "national champions". Second, despite major productivity improvements during the 1980s and the introduction of new technology, major inefficiencies remain in the production base in Europe, especially compared to Japan. Third, as in other

Figure 3.9. Japanese automobile transplants in Europe

Company	Plant location	Plant role
Hino	Dublin, Ireland	Small volume truck assembly
IBC vehicles	Luton, UK	Joint venture between GM (60%) and Isuzu (40%) to produce Isuzu and Suzuki vans
Nissan	Sunderland, UK	Output of 200,000 cars per year for both UK and export markets (Bluebird and Miora models)
Nissan	Greece	Small-scale assembly of Nissan cars and pick-ups
Nissan	Barcelona, Spain	Commercial vehicles, vans, trucks, four-wheel drive and leisure/utility vehicles
Honda	Birmingham, UK	Alliance with Rover to produce 40,000 Honda Concertos a year at Longbridge plant
Honda	Swindon, UK	Car engine production from autumn 1989
Toyota	Derby, UK	200,000 cars a year (1.8 litre models) from mid-1980s
Toyota	Swansea, UK	Car engine plant
Toyota	Hanover, Germany	Licensing agreement with Volkswagen to produce 15,000 pick-up trucks per annum
Suzuki	Spain	Joint venture, producing Suzuki four-wheel drive and future production of at least 120,000 cars per year
Isuzu, Mazda, Mitsubishi, Toyota, Hino	Portugal	Several locally owned small-scale assembly operations

Source: The author.

regions of the world, Europe is suffering severely from over-capacity. Five consecutive years of market growth between 1984 and 1989 encouraged most of the major European producers to increase capacity significantly. When the downturn came in the early 1990s, there was massive over-production. Finally, and most serious of all, the wave of Japanese direct investment (figure 3.9) means that by the mid-1990s, total production capacity of Japanese automobile transplants in Europe is expected to reach 1.3 million vehicles per year, or about 10 per cent of the total market. The extent to which this will contribute to over-capacity and competitive shake-out will clearly depend on whether European production replaces, or adds to, exports from Japan, and how well European producers compete with the Japanese. Various estimates of the employment effects of Japanese auto transplants in Europe have been suggested, the worst scenario being the demise of several European manufacturers and a loss of 300,000 jobs.

Regardless of the direct effects of Japanese auto transplants, employment in the European automobile industry will decline significantly during the early 1990s as a consequence of changing MNE strategies in response to the Single Market and import competition. Two main aspects of such strategic change are particularly important from an employment perspective. First, as in many other industries, the last few years have witnessed a wave of mergers, acquisitions and strategic alliances in the automobile sector, raising concerns regarding the adverse employment effects of post-MAA rationalization. Second, automobile producers have been attempting to improve efficiency, productivity and competitiveness through restructuring their European production and logistics systems. This has involved the closure of smaller, inefficient plants and the consolidation of production into fewer, larger and more economic facilities, as in the case of Renault discussed earlier. Similarly, in 1989 Ford of Europe announced a major restructuring of its operations with the aim of becoming the lowest cost producer in Western Europe by the early 1990s. One of the most significant changes introduced was the ending of production of the Sierra (then Europe's best selling medium-sized car) at the Dagenham plant in the UK with the loss of 500 jobs and the transfer of production to the Genk plant in Belgium, which will also become the single European production source for Ford's new range of cars to replace the Sierra in Europe and the North American Tempo and Mercury Topaz ranges from 1992/93. These changes have been accompanied by the introduction of radically new working practices designed to achieve greater labour flexibility at all plants. The most recent reduction in employment at Ford of Europe follows a total payroll reduction of 50,000 employees during the 1980s.

This restructuring and rationalization of the automobile industry in the early 1990s will be paralleled in the automotive components industry, which is highly fragmented into numerous sub-scale operations and suffers from underinvestment in R&D, product design and engineering. This will make it difficult for European-based firms to compete after the expected arrival of Japanese and other Far East Asian component suppliers to service Japanese automobile companies in Europe.

Telecommunications: In Europe, this industry has traditionally been highly fragmented, with strong domestic companies protected from foreign competition as a consequence of different national telecommunications systems and government procurement policies. As in the case of automobiles, the Single Market will result in a much more open and competitive industry in Europe as a result of attempts to standardize network systems and the liberalization of government procurement. The move towards pan-European competition will result in a significant consolidation of the industry into fewer, but much larger telecommunications companies through mergers, acquisitions and alliances and the possible demise of several small-to-medium sized companies. These trends will be compounded by the entry of American and Japanese manufacturers, attracted by market size and growth prospects in Europe. Currently, there are six major telecommunications companies in Europe – Alcatel (France); AT&T/Italtel (US/Italy); Ericsson (Sweden); Northern Telecom (Canada); Siemens (Germany); and GEC (UK). Industry observers believe that only three of the most competitive of these manufacturers will survive by the end of the 1990s. Already there have been significant redundancies announced in the industry including 1,500 jobs lost at the GEC/Siemens telecommunications joint-venture GPT.

Food and drink: This industry, too, has long been fragmented on a national basis, with domestic producers being protected from foreign competition by trade barriers (e.g. food content, labelling, etc.) and real or perceived differences in consumer tastes between countries. Even MNEs which operate across Europe in terms of market coverage have adopted country-by-country (multi-domestic) production and marketing strategies.

The progressive removal of trade barriers in the run-up to "1992" and the closer coverage of consumer tastes as a result of "Europeanization" is forcing the leading multinational food and drink companies to consider pan-European marketing strategies. Competitiveness in the food and drink industry in the Single Market will depend on three important criteria: product strength in terms of a strong portfolio of brands; extended geographical market coverage within Europe, if not globally; and an efficient and low cost production and distribution system to support Euro-brand strategies. Multinational food and drink companies positioned to gain most from the advent of the Single Market are those with strong brands across most European countries supported by a coordinated production and logistics network.

The trend towards pan-European strategies has a number of important consequences for employment in the industry. First, as in many other sectors, recent years have witnessed a wave of MAAs, as MNEs attempted to strengthen products (brands) or extend geographical market coverage prior to "1992", and may be expected to lead to significant job losses. Second, massive redundancies may be expected in small-to-medium sized companies lacking pan-European competitiveness. Third, to support pan-European marketing strategies several food and drink MNEs, including Unilever, BSN and Jacobs-Suchard are actively considering restructuring their manufacturing and logistics systems to reduce costs and improve efficiency. This will involve plant closures and consolidation of previously fragmented operations into fewer, more cost-effective plants to achieve economies of scale in both production and distribution.

Fast-moving consumer goods (FMCG): Similar developments to those in food and drink are being experienced, and the move towards more standardized Euro-products has allowed FMCG companies such as Procter & Gamble to restructure and consolidate their European production and distribution systems in order to reduce costs through greater plant specialization. Seven plants were involved in the restructuring of P & G's European activities – Manchester and London (UK); Greven and Worms (Germany); Amiens and Marseille (France) and Pomeria.[7] The main changes introduced included:

- the complete closure of the Greven plant;
- the transfer of detergent production from Greven to Amiens in France;
- the transfer of fabric softener production from Marseille to Worms;
- the transfer of detergent production from Marseille to Amiens;
- the transfer of the production of toiletries from Manchester to Amiens.

In addition to the jobs lost as a result of such changes, an important feature of P & G's restructuring is that the measures introduced favour those plants located close to the European core (Amiens and Worms) to the detriment of peripheral sites (Manchester, Marseille and Greven).

[7] Savary (1991).

3.3 *Summary*

The above analysis and industry studies cast serious doubt on the optimism of the Cecchini Report about the employment effects of "1992", because the macro-economic model used by Cecchini considerably underestimates the negative employment effects of MNE strategic restructuring in response to the Single Market. The 1990s will witness a major employment shake-out in many European industries as a consequence of MNE rationalization and the increase in inward direct investment in industries already suffering from over-capacity. The optimistic scenario is further undermined in the long run, by the process of industry consolidation and oligopolistic interdependence as a consequence of the wave of mergers, acquisitions and strategic alliances sweeping across Europe (see Chapter 4).

4. **Export-based to FDI strategies**

A third important aspect of MNE strategic change during the decade was the shift from export-based to FDI strategies by Japanese and other Far East Asian companies, and by American MNEs in "newer" industries such as information technology. There was also a rapid increase in FDI by European MNEs, especially in the US, but as most of this took the form of acquisitions rather than the establishment of greenfield subsidiaries, this will be discussed in Chapter 4.

In analysing the economic effects of the "new wave" of FDI during the 1980s, comparisons are naturally drawn with the earlier period of MNE expansion during the 1950s and 1960s, which was characterised mainly by American FDI in Europe. This evoked initial concerns regarding the possible "colonization" of Europe by American MNEs summarized in Servan-Schreiber (1968), in which he warned of the major threats posed to the social, economic, political and technological future of Europe by the growing American industrial presence. Similar concerns are now being expressed regarding the increase in Japanese (and other Far East Asian) FDI in both the US and Europe.

In his book *Trojan horse*, James (1989) presents a critical analysis of the growing shift of Japan's productive capacity to the US and Europe, warning that Japan will be the only winner. By using Japanese-made equipment to assemble components created, designed, developed and manufactured in Japan with low-skilled low-cost Western labour, Japanese firms, argues James, can evade increasing protectionism and the high value of the yen, while maintaining access to Western consumers. Paraphrasing the opening remarks in Servan-Schreiber's much earlier book, James states that —

> Twelve years from now it is quite possible that the world's fourth and fifth largest industrial powers behind the US, Japan and the EEC will not be Russia and China, but Japanese industry in the US and in the EEC.

In terms of the employment effects of Japanese FDI, James argues that any job-creating effects of new plants being established will be more than offset by corresponding job losses in indigenous companies, and that the quality of employment in Japanese transplants is often "in low-skilled automated and routine assembly operations and metal bashing".

James's concerns, however, are mainly responses to short-term developments, largely ignoring the evidence of how the status of plants evolves over time. Taking American FDI in Europe as a historical parallel, the evidence strongly suggests that over time US subsidiaries evolve from "branch plants" to more thoroughly European companies involving widening product and market roles, localized R&D, greater transfer of managerial skills and technology and closer integration with local suppliers.[8] Indeed, the "new wave" of American FDI in the European information technology industry has largely taken this form, conferring greater local responsibilities for product strategies within the EC and increasing local R&D. Important examples include:

- IBM's decision to transfer worldwide responsibility for its Communications Systems division to Europe (see later);

- Apple Computer Inc.'s major expansion of its manufacturing facility at Cork;

- Compaq's further expansion of its Erskine manufacturing plant in Scotland which will lead to over 60 per cent of the company's rapidly growing international sales being produced in Scotland;

- Motorola's announcement of a new manufacturing and headquarters facility in Swindon.

There is evidence, too, of the evolution in plant roles and status among Japanese MNEs in Europe. In a fairly short period, for example, the Nissan car plant in the North of England has evolved from routine assembly of car kits for the UK market to higher local value-added and local content, accompanied by a broadening of market coverage to include exports to Continental Europe. This has been accompanied by a doubling of total employment at the plant.

5.   Towards transnationality: A strategy for the 1990s ?

So far in this chapter we have looked at changing MNE strategies during the 1980s. Now we examine likely developments in MNE strategy in the 1990s, focusing in particular on the shift towards transnationality and MNE network strategies.

5.1 Transnationality

As stated earlier, a major driving force underlying MNE strategy during the 1980s was the globalization of markets. According to some authors such as Bartlett and Goshal,[9] the globalization concept has already become dated, being superseded by the concept of transnationality. While there are few, if any, MNEs which could be described as truly transnational (as defined below),[10] the decade of the 1990s is likely to see a further evolution in MNE strategy in this direction, which will have a number of important implications for employment.

[8] See Young, Hood and Hamill (1988).

[9] Bartlett and Goshal (1989 and 1990).

[10] It should be noted that this section uses the term transnational as defined by Bartlett and Goshal – which differs significantly from the use of the term in UNCTC publications.

Bartlett and Goshal distinguish between three main types of generic strategy in international business: (a) multinational companies which manage a portfolio of multiple national entities, with strategy and organization being very sensitive and responsive to different national environments, i.e. a multi-domestic strategy as defined in previous sections; (b) global companies which strive to achieve cost advantages through centralized global-scale operations, i.e. globally coordinated and integrated strategies; and (c) international companies which rely mainly on export-based strategies and the international transfer of parent company knowledge and expertise to foreign markets.

The importance of this distinction is the strategic capability which the firm attempts to exploit in global or international markets – national responsiveness in the case of multinational companies; global efficiency in global companies; and the worldwide diffusion of knowledge in international companies. According to Bartlett and Goshal, however, the focus on a single strategic approach has become inappropriate because of the rapid changes in the global business environment of the late 1980s and early 1990s. These new challenges create a need for a new solution different from the single focus approach of multinational, global or international strategies. What is now required according to these authors is a multi-dimensional or transnational philosophy which emphasizes national responsiveness, global competitiveness and global learning simultaneously.

The shift towards transnationalization would have important implications for the organizational characteristics of MNEs, especially for the roles of overseas subsidiaries and the development and diffusion of knowledge within the enterprise. In multinational companies, the role of overseas subsidiaries is to exploit local market opportunities; in global companies, overseas subsidiaries implement global strategies; and in international companies, subsidiaries adapt parent company knowledge to local needs. In terms of knowledge development and diffusion, both global and international companies centralize the innovation process, while multinational companies rely mainly on local innovations.

Transnational firms in contrast give their subsidiaries greater flexibility and more knowledge and information to respond to local constraints (e.g. government regulation) and the specific challenges they face in these locations. Certain subsidiaries may be limited to adapting parent company products and technology to local markets; while others may have a much more important strategic role to play. Four main types of national organization are identified depending on the strategic importance of the subsidiary and its level of resources and capabilities (see figure 3.10). Particularly important, in this respect, is the strategic leader – a national subsidiary located in a strategically important market with a high level of local competence. Such strategic leaders (or strategic independents) become partners, rather than subordinates, of the parent company being allowed a considerable degree of independence to develop lines of business for local, regional or global markets.

To date, there are few companies which could be described as truly transnational in organization, although there is some evidence of a trend towards greater geographical decentralization of headquarters functions. The British multinational BOC has relocated its international headquarters for health-care products to the US, while American MNEs such as Hewlett-Packard and Motorola have considerably broad-

Figure 3.10.   Generic roles of national organizations

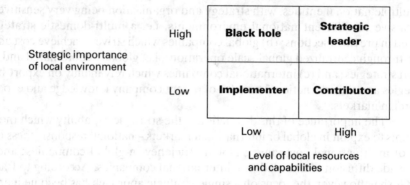

Strategic leader = National organizations with high international competence located in strategically important markets; develop and implement broad strategic thrusts jointly with HQs.

Contributors   = National organizations with strong internal competences but located in strategically unimportant markets; subsidiary competences used by parent company in worldwide opera-
tions.

Implementer   = National organizations with just enough competence to maintain their local operations in
non-strategic markets.

Black hole   = A weak subsidiary in a strategically important market.

Source: Derived from Bartlett and Goshal (1989).

ened the responsibilities of their subsidiaries in Europe. IBM has probably gone further than any other MNE in the direction of transnationality as discussed below. The
obvious employment effects of these trends is a significant enhancement of the quality
of employment at foreign subsidiaries and greater indigenous technological capability.

Since the late 1980s, IBM has introduced a number of organizational
changes designed to improve the company's competitiveness in the face of declining
growth in sales and profits. Major initiatives taken include a reduction in total
employment (but without compulsory redundancies); eliminating bureaucracy;
worldwide decentralization; external collaboration with "systems houses"; and a
more customer-orientated, rather than technology-orientated, strategy.

Two major changes, in particular, have shifted IBM towards a more transnational firm. First, responsibility for pan-European operations, long exercised by
IBM's Paris-based European headquarters, has been decentralized to country-based
strategic leaders. IBM UK has been given responsibility for European-wide strategy
for personal computers and for banking and financial services; IBM Germany has
been granted responsibility for mainframe computers and manufacturing industry;
France is responsible for telecommunications, maintenance, software and IBM's
internal computing system and Italy for mid-range machines, scientific computers
and the government and public sectors.

The drive towards transnationality was given a further major boost by the
decision made at the end of 1990 to transfer worldwide responsibility for one of the

company's main lines of business (the Communications Systems Division) from the US to Europe. This new headquarters in London will have global responsibility for communications system product planning and for coordinating geographically dispersed manufacturing plants and development laboratories. As part of the transfer, 120 senior US executives will move from the US to the UK. The decision to relocate was motivated by the rapidly growing European market for telecommunications as a consequence of deregulation, "1992" and the prospects created by political developments in Eastern Europe.

5.2 *MNE network strategies*

A second scenario for MNE strategy during the 1990s is that of multinational networks. Dunning (1988), for example, identifies three main stages in the evolution of MNEs: (a) as a confederation of loosely knit foreign affiliates designed to provide the parent company with natural resources or to supply local markets with manufactured products and services; (b) as a controller of a group of integrated value adding activities in several countries; (c) as an orchestrator of production and transactions within a cluster or network of cross-border internal and external relationships, which may or may not involve equity investment, but which are intended to serve its global interests. Thus, MNEs in the late 1980s and early 1990s are seen as a "central nervous system of a much larger group of interdependent but less formally governed activities, whose function is primarily to advance the global competitive strategy and position of the core organization". This third stage has been brought about by the rapid growth in the number of strategic alliances between firms (see Chapter 4).

Casson (1990) has extended Dunning's third stage by developing a "systems view" of international production in the 1990s which emphasizes inter-firm linkages in the production system. Rather than the production system being viewed as being organized as a series of competing single-product plants, it is characterized by complementary multi-product plants, linked to each other by intermediate product flows.

At least two important employment effects of MNE network systems are noteworthy. First, the growth of network relationships will increase further the already well-developed international division of labour through the increasing use of out-sourcing for intermediary products. Second, significant job losses may be expected as many MNEs streamline operations by concentrating on core activities and avoiding duplication of effort in alliance relationships.

6. Conclusions

Changing MNE strategies during the 1980s and 1990s have had both negative and positive employment effects. The main negative effects include:

- major plant closures and job losses in long-established MNEs, with the shift from multi-domestic to global strategies involving greater plant specialization and integration;

- in Europe, major job losses may be expected in the short-to-medium term as a consequence of MNE restructuring and the concentration of production into fewer, larger plants located in close proximity to major European markets. This will exacerbate the already wide regional imbalances in employment opportunities between core and periphery locations. The "new wave" of FDI into Europe in the run-up to "1992" may also have major adverse employment impacts through the displacement effect;

- in the 1990s, the growing importance of MNE network strategies will result in the increasing use of a core and periphery workforce and a greater international division of labour.

More optimistically, the (albeit) gradual shift towards transnational strategies will result in a greater geographical dispersion of key HQ functional responsibilities in MNEs, thereby enhancing employment quality in overseas subsidiaries. There is also some evidence of an evolution over time in MNE plant roles and responsibilities, which is particularly relevant to the debate on Japanese "screwdriver operations".

Bibliography

Baker, M.J. (ed.) 1991. *Perspectives on marketing management*, Vol. 2 (New York, John Wiley).

Bartlett, C.A.; Goshal, S. 1989. *Managing across borders: The transnational solution* (Boston, Massachusetts, Harvard Business School Press).

—; —. 1990. "Matrix management: Not a structure, a frame of mind", in *Harvard Business Review* (Boston), July/Aug.

Casson, M. 1990. *Enterprise and competitiveness: A systems view of international business* (Oxford, Clarendon Press).

Cecchini, P., et al. 1988. *The European challenge 1992 – The benefits of a Single Market* (Aldershot, Hampshire, Wildwood House).

Doz, Y. 1986. *Strategic management in multinational companies* (New York, Pergamon Press).

Dunning, J.H. 1988. "The new style multinationals – Circa the late 1980s and early 1990s", Chapter 13: "Explaining international production" (London, Unwin Hyman).

James, B.G. 1989. *Trojan horse: The ultimate Japanese challenge to Western industry* (London, Mercury Books).

Jatusripitak, S.; Fahey, L.; Kotler, P. 1985. "Strategic global marketing: Lessons from the Japanese", in *Columbia Journal of World Business*, 20, No. 1, Spring.

Paníc, M. 1991. "The impact of multinationals on national economic policies", in Bürgenmeier, B. and Mucchielli, J.L. *Multinationals and Europe 1992: Strategies for the future* (London, Routledge).

Porter, M.E. (ed.) 1986. *Competition in global industries* (Boston, Massachusetts, Harvard Business School Press).

Porter, M.E. 1986. "Changing patterns of international competition", in *California Management Review*, Vol. 28, No. 2 (Berkeley), Winter.

Savary, J. 1991. "European integration, globalization process and the future of industrial locations in Europe", in Proceedings of the UK Academy of International Business Annual Conference (London), April.

Servan-Schreiber, J.J. 1968. *The American challenge* (Atheneum, New York).

White, R.E.; Poynter, T.A. 1984. "Strategies for foreign-owned subsidiaries in Canada", in *Business Quarterly* (London, Ontario), Summer.

Young, S.; Hood, N.; Hamill, J. 1988. *Foreign multinationals and the British economy* (Beckenham, Kent, Croom Helm).

4

Cross-border mergers, acquisitions and strategic alliances

James Hamill

1. Introduction

Since the mid-1980s, multinational enterprises have favoured the use of mergers and acquisitions to expand their activities abroad. At the height of this wave of international take-overs in 1989, there was a total of 2,764 cross-border mergers and acquisitions valued in excess of $130 billion.[1] Accompanying this has been rapid growth in cooperation agreements and alliances between MNEs – a new form of international business collaboration – which in contrast to traditional forms of joint ventures involves enterprises that are in direct competition with each other.[2]

Strategic alliances and international acquisitions have been used by MNEs to respond to a number of new competitive challenges which emerged in the 1980s, the most salient of which were: major technological changes (the impact on production processes and on products of the new technologies – microelectronics, robotics, new materials and biotechnology); the globalization of markets, where the competition is among corporations worldwide; and the growing importance of various geographical regions (such as Asia/Pacific, North America and Europe).

This wave of cross-border mergers, acquisitions and alliances (MAAs) in the late 1980s and early 1990s raises important questions about the effects on employment of these new strategies. Generally speaking, when MNEs established new plants in a foreign country – so-called greenfield investments – there was a positive effect on host country employment. The effects, however, of these MAAs are much less clear-cut. The purpose of this chapter is to examine the likely employment effects of the boom in MAAs in the late 1980s and early 1990s. Section 2 describes the main trends in strategic alliances, mergers and acquisitions; section 3 examines the reasons for these MAAs in general and in a number of specific industries where MAAs are particularly common; and section 4 describes the employment effects of MAAs and sets out a conceptual framework in which the positive and negative employment effects can be identified.

---

[1] Data derived from *Acquisitions Monthly*, Washington, various editions.

[2] There is a large and growing volume of literature on strategic alliances. The main titles are reported in the bibliography to this chapter.

---

2. Cross-border trends in mergers, acquisitions and strategic alliances

2.1 Mergers and acquisitions

The initial focus of most cross-border mergers and acquisitions was the US between 1984 and 1988. Since then, there has been a shift in such activity towards Europe.

Foreign acquisitions in the United States

During the peak years from 1984 to 1988 (table 4.1), foreign companies acquired a total of 2,055 US companies for approximately $126 billion. This accounts for well over three-quarters of the total value of all foreign direct investment in this period.

Foreign acquisitions in the US have been highly diversified by sector, nationality of acquiring company and by size. They have been spread across a wide range of industries, including a large number in the service and manufacturing sector. British companies have been the most active, acquiring a total of 1,121 US firms between 1984 and 1988 for $86 billion.[3] Canadian, Japanese, French, German and Dutch companies have also been significant acquirers. Many acquisitions have been particularly large – between 1986 and 1988 foreign firms acquired 18 US companies for more than $1 billion each (table 4.2). Foreign acquisitions were, however, not confined to these mega-deals. A large number of small-to-medium sized companies have also been very active in acquiring enterprises in the US.

Foreign companies made their biggest acquisitions in 1988 with a total of 476 deals valued at approximately $47 billion. Since then there has been a significant downturn in both the number and value of deals, although several very large acquisitions have occurred recently, including Sony's acquisition of Columbia Pictures; Bass's takeover of Holiday Inns; ASEA-Brown Boveri's of Combustion Engineering; and Michelin's of Uniroyal Goodrich.

Cross-border acquisitions in Europe

Since 1988, the geographical focus of cross-border acquisitions has tended to shift from the US towards Europe. In 1989 and 1990, there was a total of 3,410 cross-border mergers and acquisitions in Europe, with a total value in excess of £63 billion (table 4.3). These have included both cross-border take-overs within the EC and a large number of European acquisitions by non-EC firms. US companies have been

---

[3] The wave of British acquisitions in the US have been examined in Hamill (1989). A series of case studies on British acquisitions in the US were published in *Acquisitions Monthly*, 1989, including: "Buying in the US building sector", Apr.; "Acquiring in the US food and drink industry", May; "What Dixons has gained from Cyclops", June; "Ferranti's merger with ISC", July; "Salvesen's US strategy", Aug.; "Low and Bonnar: US acquisitions produce mixed results", Sep.; "US acquisitions by the Dowty Group", Oct.; "US acquisitions by Smith & Nephew", Nov.

Table 4.1.   Foreign acquisitions in the United States, 1984-88

Year	Number of acquisitions	Acquisition value ($m)
1984	245	9 911
1985	367	12 997
1986	420	22 597
1987	547	33 765
1988	476	46 667
Total	2 055	125 937

Source: US Department of Commerce, *Foreign direct investment in the US*, various years.

Table 4.2.   Largest foreign acquisitions in the United States, 1987 and 1988

Acquiring company	Nationality	Acquired company	Sector	Acquisition value ($m)
Rob Campeau	Canada	Federated Dept. Stores	Retailing	8 800
BP	UK	Standard Oil	Oil & Gas	7 992
Unilever	UK/Neth	Chesebrough-Ponds	Cosmetics	3 100
Hoechst	F.R. Germany	Celanese Corp.	Chemicals	2 850
Bridgestone Corp.	Japan	Firestone Tire	Tyres	2 600
Maxwell Communications	UK	Macmillan (US)	Publishing	2 510
Sony	Japan	CBS Records	Music	2 000
Hanson Trust	UK	Kidde	Diversified manufacturing	1 800
Oppenheimer	S. Africa	Newmont Mining	Mining	1 551
Tate & Lyle	UK	Staley Continental	Food (sugar)	1 500
Ferruzzi	Italy	Himont	Chemicals	1 490
Blue Arrow	UK	Manpower Inc.	Management consultancy	1 350
Government of Saudi Arabia	Saudi Arabia	Star Enterprises	Oil	1 292
Government of France (Péchiney)	France	Triangle Industries	Metal products	1 260
Bonfman Family	Canada	Tropicana Products	Food	1 200
Alan Bond	Australia	G. Heileman Brewing	Brewing	1 200
Grand Metropolitan	UK	Heublein	Wines and spirits	1 200
Nippon Mining	Japan	Gould Inc.	Machinery	1 100

Source: US Department of Commerce, *Foreign direct investment in the US*, various years.

the largest acquirers in Europe in value terms. In 1989, they paid almost 41 billion ECU for European companies – over 40 per cent more than the top European cross-border acquirer, France, followed by companies from Sweden and the UK. Together these four nations accounted for 60 per cent of the total value of all cross-border deals in 1989. The largest cross-border take-overs in Europe in 1989 and 1990 are listed in table 4.4.

Table 4.3.   Cross-border acquisitions in the EC, 1989 and 1990

	Number of acquisitions	Acquisition value (£m)	% of acquisition value
Nationality of acquirer:			
United States	397	12 193	19
France	549	11 287	18
Sweden	238	7 359	12
United Kingdom	636	6 864	11
Germany	225	3 883	6
Switzerland	249	2 295	4
Japan	98	2 244	4
Belgium	94	1 804	3
Finland	121	986	2
Norway	40	346	1
Denmark	95	474	1
Canada	30	2 075	3
Others	638	11 482	18
Total	3 410	63 292	100
Nationality of target:			
United Kingdom	540	31 103	49
Germany	929	6 841	11
France	549	6 560	10
Spain	349	5 822	9
Italy	309	4 674	7
Netherlands	293	4 358	7
Belgium	184	1 749	3
Denmark	133	1 258	2
Ireland	34	511	1
Portugal	63	399	1
Greece	14	8	1
Luxembourg	13	9	1
Total	3 410	63 292	100

Source: Derived from *Acquisitions Monthly*, Feb. 1991.

Although there were considerable intra-EC cross-border mergers, according to a study by McKinsey & Co., EC-based companies were still spending three times more on acquisitions in the US than on cross-border purchases in the Community. In the first half of 1990, the same study estimated that EC companies spent 6.8 billion ECU on mergers and acquisitions within the EC itself compared to 13.6 billion ECU in North America and only 2.2 billion ECU in the rest of the world.[4]

[4] "The pattern of recent mergers and acquisitions", in *Panorama of EC Industries, 1991-1992*, Brussels, Commission of the European Communities, 1992.

Table 4.4.   Largest cross-border acquisitions in the EC, 1989 and 1990

Acquiring company	Nationality	Acquired company	Sector	Acquisition value (£m)
SmithKline	US	Beechams (UK)	Pharma-ceuticals	4 509
Philip Morris	US	Jacobs Suchard	Food	2 196
GEC-Siemens	UK/Germany	Plessey (UK)	Defence equipment; electronics	2 030
Northern Telecom	Canada	STC (UK)	Telecom-munications	1 836
BSN	France	Nabisco (5 Euro businesses) (US)	Food	1 581
Ford	US	Jaguar (UK)	Motor cars	1 560
Stora	Sweden	Feldmühle Nobel (Germany)	Insurance	1 453
Groupe AG	Belgium	Amev (Neth)	Insurance	1 354
AMP	Australia	Pearl Group (UK)	Insurance	1 243
CGE	France	Telettra (Italy)	Telecom-munications	1 100
Svenska Cellulosa	Sweden	Reedpack (UK)	Paper, packaging	1 050
IFIL/BSN	Italy/France	Galbani (Italy)	Food	1 005
National Australia Bank	Australia	Yorkshire Bank (UK)	Banking	977
Deutsche Bank	Germany	Morgan Grenfell (UK)	Banking	950
Pepsico	US	Smiths/Walkers (UK)	Food	856
MLVH	France	Guinness (12 per cent) (UK)	Drink	821
Fujitsu	Japan	ICL (80 per cent) (UK)	Electronics, computers	743
Brierley Investments	New Zealand	Mount Charlotte Investments (UK)	Property	644
Guinness	UK	Cruz del Campo (Spain)	Brewing	533
Wiggins Teape Appleton	UK	Arjomari-Prioux (France)	Paper	498
Grand Metropolitan	UK	Rémy Martin (49 per cent) (France)	Drink	200

Source: *Acquisitions Monthly*, Feb. 1990, 1991.

In terms of the nationality of the acquired company, nearly half the cross-border deals in Europe (in value terms) have involved the take-over of British companies, reflecting the more liberal acquisition environment in the UK compared to the Continent. Thus, the UK is in a unique position of being both the most important acquiring and acquired nation in Europe; although in terms of the former, British acquisitions abroad at least in value terms have been focused mainly in the US rather than the EC.

2.2 Strategic alliances

Accompanying the growth of cross-border mergers and acquisitions, since the mid-1980s there has been a rapid increase in international strategic alliances. Unlike acquisitions, there are no comprehensive statistics on the incidence of strategic alliances, and the estimates which have been made in different studies vary considerably. Morris and Hergert (1987), for example, identified 839 alliances in the period 1975-86, while a recent study by the consultants KPMG Peat Marwick McLintock identified no fewer than 669 corporate partnerships in the last three months of 1989 alone.[5]

Although it is difficult to give exact statistics, there is no doubt that alliances between competitors are becoming commonplace, with reports of new partnerships in the business press almost daily. As with mergers and acquisitions, strategic alliances involve large sums of money. In July 1992, Toshiba of Japan and Siemens of Germany announced their plans to develop advanced memory chips in a deal valued at $1 billion while on the same day Japan's Fujitsu and the US chip maker Advanced Micro Devices unveiled their plan to develop jointly advanced memory chips for the computer industry worth $700 million. Furthermore, although alliances are being established across a wide spectrum of manufacturing and non-manufacturing industries, they are particularly common in high technology industries such as semiconductors, telecommunications, aerospace and defence equipment and pharmaceuticals (Gugler, 1991).

3. The main motivations behind the spread of mergers, acquisitions and strategic alliances

Before discussing the employment and related effects of the recent boom in cross-border MAAs, the motivations underlying such activity need to be examined, since these will have important implications for post-MAA change and, hence, for employment. Unfortunately, there have been no previous attempts made to provide a comprehensive theory of international MAAs. In this section, we present an explanation which relates the boom in cross-border MAAs to the attempts made by MNEs to create a sustainable competitive advantage in global industries. Two main types of competitive advantage can be sought through cross-border MAAs: those which seek to strengthen product and geographical market portfolios, e.g. brand acquisition and international expansion; and those which seek to achieve lower costs and greater efficiency through sharing resources and achieving scale economies.

The two main strands of the literature relevant to an explanation of international MAAs are the economic theory of FDI and the literature on the causes and motivations of domestic acquisitions. International mergers and acquisitions are a form of FDI and it may be expected, therefore, that FDI theory could contribute to an understanding of the recent cross-border MAA boom. FDI theory, however, has focused mainly on greenfield investments and there has been little attempt to incor-

---

[5] Reported in *Financial Times*, 3 May, 1990.

Figure 4.1.   MAA motivations

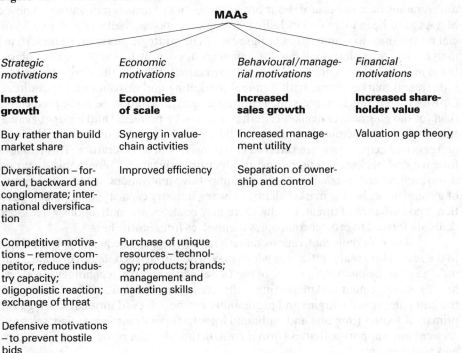

Strategic motivations	Economic motivations	Behavioural/managerial motivations	Financial motivations
Instant growth	**Economies of scale**	**Increased sales growth**	**Increased shareholder value**
Buy rather than build market share	Synergy in value-chain activities	Increased management utility	Valuation gap theory
Diversification – forward, backward and conglomerate; international diversification	Improved efficiency	Separation of ownership and control	
Competitive motivations – remove competitor, reduce industry capacity; oligopolistic reaction; exchange of threat	Purchase of unique resources – technology; products; brands; management and marketing skills		
Defensive motivations – to prevent hostile bids			

Sources: Derived from Cooke, 1986 and 1988; Buckley, 1975; Steiner, 1975; Morgan, 1988; Love and Scouller, 1990; Business International, 1982 and 1987, and Hamill, 1991(a) and (b).

porate MAAs into mainstream theory. The few attempts that have been made largely pre-date the international MAA boom of the late 1980s and early 1990s.[6] Recent work by Dunning and Casson, however, places greater recognition on the role of MAAs. Dunning[7] explains the growth of international MAAs as an attempt by MNEs to create and sustain ownership advantages which reflect both the individual hierarchical capacity of the firm and its sucess in combining these with other hierarchies (through MAAs) in such a way that their overall long-term competitive position is strengthened. Similarly, Casson[8] focuses on the internalization advantages which can be derived from MAAs. For MNEs to enter into MAAs, there must be some reason for integrating the operations of partners. In other words, there must be internationalization economies to be derived from MAAs otherwise partners would deal on an arm's-length basis.

While mainstream economic theories of FDI have only belatedly given attention to MAAs, there is an extensive literature on domestic MAAs which can be

[6] See, for example, Aliber (1971), Calvet (1982), Contractor and Lorange (1988), Dubin (1975), Hamill (1991a), Hisey and Caves (1985), Kogut and Singh (1985), Wilson (1980).

[7] Dunning (1988).

[8] Casson (1989 and 1990).

extended internationally.[9] An important feature of this literature is that MAAs are multi- rather than uni-causal. Four broad categories of factors motivating domestic MAAs have been identified including strategic; economic; behavioural; and financial motivations as summarized in figure 4.1. The strategic motivations underlying mergers and acquisitions fall into four main groups – growth, diversification, competition and defensive objectives. MAAs may be motivated by the desire for instant growth and market share, with minimal marketing and distribution expenditure. Growth rates through mergers and acquisitions may, in addition, be more predictable than for the alternatives available, in that they can be predicted at the target evaluation stage of the acquisition process. The diversification motivations underlying mergers and acquisitions are referred to extensively in the literature. This includes forward and backward integration; product diversification; geographical market diversification and internationalization. Competitive motivations include the removal of a competitor; buying market share; reducing industry capacity; oligopolistic reaction; and exchange of threat. Finally, there may be defensive motivations where such deals are formed to protect companies themselves from hostile bids.

The economic motivations underlying mergers and acquisitions are related to the search for greater efficiency which may arise through economies of scale; gaining access to the unique resources of the target company (e.g. technology, products, brands, management and marketing skills, etc.) and synergistic effects. As regards the latter, improved margins and profitability can be achieved through sharing both primary activities (inbound and outbound logistics; operations; marketing, sales and service) and support activities (firm infrastructure; human resources; technology; and procurement).

Behavioural or managerial explanations for mergers and acquisitions derive from the literature on the managerial theory of the firm and the separation of ownership from control in large organizations.[10] In this respect, MAAs take place to maximize management utility through sales growth rather than profit maximization. Financial explanations of MAAs, on the other hand, emphasize the impact of MAAs on shareholder value rather than on management utility and there is extensive literature on the shareholder impact and financial performance[11] of mergers and acquisitions.

The literature on domestic MAAs reviewed above can be extended to form the basis of an explanation for the boom in international MAAs since the mid-1980s. Clearly, the explosion in cross-border MAAs could have been, at least in part, due to managerial or short-term financial motivations. However, as the cases examined later show, the two main categories of factors contributing to an explanation of the recent boom in international MAAs are the strategic and economic motivations.

In conclusion, a wide array of different reasons can be adduced to explain the international MAA boom of the late 1980s. Generally, however, long-term strategic and economic influences rather than short-term financial or managerial motivations have predominated. Of these at least five factors (figure 4.2) can be identified:

[9] See Buckley (1975), Business International (1982, 1987 and 1988), Cooke (1986 and 1988), Goldberg (1983), Jemison and Sitkin (1986), Keenan and White (1982), Love and Scouller (1990), Morgan (1988), Payne (1987), Salter and Weinhold (1979), Steiner (1975).

[10] See Cyert and March (1963).

[11] See note 9.

Figure 4.2. Factors influencing the growth of strategic alliances

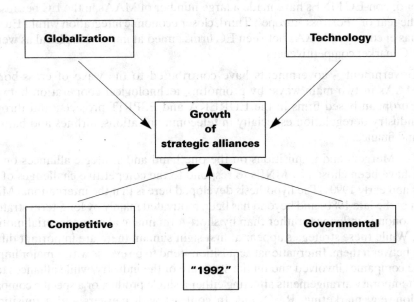

Source: The author.

■ Globalization – as a consequence of the globalization of markets (see Chapter 6), competitiveness in many industries is becoming increasingly dependent on firms achieving a "critical mass" in terms of market share, strong product portfolios and extended geographical market coverage. These motivations have been behind those MAAs which have been used to increase size and market share; build a strong portfolio of global products (brands); and to achieve rapid internationalization and geographical market diversification.

■ Global competition – closely related to the above, the emergence of global competition has encouraged cross-border MAAs for a number of reasons including economic motivations – to achieve scale economies and synergy in value-chain activities aimed at improving efficiency; and competitive motivations such as removing a competitor through acquisition or collaboration. The emergence of new global competitors, especially from the Far East, has resulted in considerable overcapacity in many industries e.g. automobiles, thus stimulating MAAs to reduce surplus capacity.

■ Technology – the accelerated pace of technology change and the increasing costs and risks associated with R&D have contributed to the wave of international MAAs, and these have been used to gain access to new technology or to share the risks and costs associated with technology development.

■ "1992" – proposals for a Single European Market have contributed to the boom in international MAA activity in at least three main ways. First, cross-border MAAs in Europe have been used to strengthen products (brands) and extend

European market coverage prior to the removal of internal trade barriers. Second, non-EC MNEs have made a large number of MAAs in the EC because of the fear of "Fortress Europe". Third, closer economic integration within Europe has encouraged MAAs between EC firms aimed at improving global as well as EC market competitiveness.

■ Government – governments have contributed to the wave of cross-border MAAs in two main ways: by promoting technological cooperation between European-based firms in the EUREKA and ESPRIT projects; and through industry deregulation especially in telecommunications, airlines and banking and finance.

Mergers and acquisitions on the one hand and strategic alliances on the other have been chosen by MNEs to respond to the competitive challenges of the 1980s and early 1990s. The hypothesis developed here is that the international MAA boom of the late 1980s and beyond has been motivated mainly by long-term strategic and economic influences rather than by short-term financial or managerial motivations. While these strategies appear at first sight similar, there are important differences between them. International acquisitions tend to be events with a major impact on the companies involved and on the structure of the industry, while alliances tend to be temporary arrangements affecting either a single product or a specific company function, e.g. marketing, R&D, etc. In contrast with mergers and acquisitions, alliances do not usually lead to the disappearance of one of the companies, or a restructuring of the companies involved or of the industry to which they belong.

Acquisitions and alliances also are not evenly spread across industries. On the one hand, MNEs in low and medium technology industries, characterized by weak demand, slow growth and overcapacity, have tended to favour international acquisitions as a means of enlarging their operations. Similarly, MNEs in the service sector have favoured mergers and acquisitions as a means of quickly acquiring the necessary scale to enable them to follow their MNE clients abroad, taking advantage of new opportunities arising from the deregulation of their industries. On the other hand, in the faster growing, high technology industries, MNEs have entered into cooperation agreements or strategic alliances to share escalating R&D costs and to obtain the widest market coverage in order to recoup these costs. Alliances have in many industries become a means by which an enterprise in spite of enormous challenges can remain an effective competitor in the business.[12]

These are of course only general trends: alliances often occur in technologically mature industries while acquisitions take place in high technology industries. Nevertheless, the distinction is a useful one in explaining the general factors behind the recent wave of MAAs, as can be seen when examining the use of these strategies in specific industries.

---

[12] See ECE/UNCTC (1986).

Figure 4.3.   Acquisitions and alliances in the European defence industry

Domestic

- GEC's acquisition of Plessey's avionics and underwater systems business and of Ferranti's radar division (United Kingdom).
- The merger of the flight electronics businesses of Thomson-CSF and Aérospatiale of France in a joint venture – Sextant Avionique – the fourth largest navigation, guidance and display devices company in the world.
- Daimler-Benz's take-over of Messerschmitt-Bölkow-Blohm, which grouped their aerospace, engines, weapons and military electronic businesses in a single company, Deutsche Aerospace.
- The merger of the electronic command and control systems activities of the Swedish-owned Bofors and Ericsson groups.

Cross-border

- The acquisition of Plessey's radar and military communications businesses by Siemens.
- Thomson's acquisition of the bulk of Philips' defence interests in the Netherlands, France and Belgium.
- The take-over of Short Brothers (United Kingdom) by Bombardier of Canada.
- The purchase of a 20 per cent stake in Bodenseewerk Gerätetechnik, a German missile system company by Matra of France.
- GEC's purchase of a 5 per cent stake in Matra and collaboration on space systems.
- The merger of British Aerospace's guided weapons businesses with Thomson of France in a joint venture company, Eurodynamics.
- Preliminary discussions between GEC-Marconi and Daimler-Benz regarding long-term collaboration.
- Long-term collaboration announced between Daimler-Benz and Mitsubishi of Japan.

Source: Derived from company accounts, press reports and *Acquisitions Monthly* (various editions).

3.2 Industry cases

Defence equipment: This is a high technology industry manufacturing weapons systems using advanced electronics and communications technology. The market for its products is in decline, especially since the end of the Cold War. Intense competition between contractors has developed for a dwindling number of contracts. The costs of developing new weapons systems are growing particularly as a result of the present demand for more sophisticated products and more integrated defence systems. The erosion of the principle of national procurement in defence spending has also meant that many firms have lost their guaranteed home market virtually overnight. In addition, the industry, particularly in Europe, is highly fragmented among a large number of small and medium-sized firms. Consequently, the profitability of firms has fallen sharply and contractors are actively seeking to diversify into other industry branches.

Both international acquisitions and alliances have become key strategies for those firms in the industry seeking to survive in such unfavourable market conditions (see figure 4.3).[13] It has become clear for several that only by reducing the number of

[13] See Hamill (1990).

rivals, nationally and internationally, can they restore profitability to the industry as a whole. A good example of a company using international acquisitions to achieve this objective is Thomson-CSF of France. In 1990, the company acquired the defence business of Philips of the Netherlands, as well as MEI, a military communications firm and affiliate of Thorn-Emi of the UK. Furthermore, in April 1992 the French company made a $450 million bid for the missile and aircraft division of the Dallas-based LTV Corporation. Like other leading defence contractors, Thomson-CSF had already acquired a number of smaller national rivals to ensure its share of a declining national market.

In addition companies have also made international alliances. The principal reason for these alliances is to share the costs and risks associated with the increasing use of electronics in weapons systems. A good example of this type of alliance is the consortium of European firms cooperating in the European Fighter Aircraft Project, whose design stage alone costs an estimated $5 billion. There is a strong commercial incentive for enterprises to provide customers with integrated weapons systems as well as to be the prime contracting company in specific projects. To fulfil this role, companies must have capabilities across a wide spectrum of technologies and products. Alliances have thus proved a convenient and less costly way for companies to acquire such a capability. Among the numerous examples of this type of alliance include: cooperation between Ferranti of the UK and Thomson to develop radar technology; and between Pilkington of the UK and Thomson in optoelectronics.

Survival for MNEs in this industry thus increasingly depends on their success in forging appropriate alliances and in acquiring firms to gain the critical mass to capture a sufficiently large share of a declining market. In Europe it is widely forecast that in five years' time, based on current market trends, there will be room for only two or at most three defence equipment companies – a prediction which, if accurate, presages a further round of international acquisitions.

Airline industry: This a good example of a service industry currently undergoing a period of structural change as a result of deregulation. Traditionally, competition between carriers has been limited by bilateral agreements under which capacity, pricing and market access were controlled. Gradually the scope of these bilateral agreements and the protection they afford national flag carriers is being eroded. Under EC policies to progressively establish a competitive Single Market in airline transport, domestic EC markets will cease to be the preserve of national carriers.

With this in mind, major airlines are expanding their activities internationally either by acquiring equity stakes in other major airlines or by buying smaller, regional airlines to serve as a feeder for their major routes.[14] Table 4.5 gives an overview of airline acquisitions in the late 1980s. In one of the largest deals to date, British Airways (BA) paid $750 million for convertible preference shares in USAIR, the US's sixth biggest carrier, that if converted in five years could give it up to 44 per cent of the equity capital of the airline. Through this deal BA gains access to a 39-state network, with routes to 210 cities and five major hubs including Pittsburgh, Washington and Baltimore. The US air travel market accounts for some 40 per cent of global air traffic and is thus a potentially lucrative market for European carriers.

[14] See Farmbrough (1990).

Table 4.5.   Airline industry acquisitions, 1985-89

Acquiring company	Acquired company	Value (£m)	Year
Wings Holdings (US)	NWA (US)	2 120	1989
USAir (US)	Piedmont (US)	850	1987
United Airlines (US)	Pan American (Pacific Division) (US)	603	1985
Delta Air Lines (US)	Western Air Lines (US)	584	1986
Federal Express (US)	Tiger International (US)	466	1988
Air France (France)	UTA (54.58 per cent) (France)	396	1990
USAir (US)	Pacific Southwest Airlines (US)	278	1986
Ueberroth (Peter) & Others (US)	Eastern Airlines (US)	273	1989
British Airways (UK)	British Caledonian (UK)	250	1987
America West Airlines (US)	Eastern Airlines (Bid No. 2) (US)	233	1989
Trump (Mr. Donald) (US)	Eastern Airlines (East Coast Shuttle) (US)	213	1988
Dictum (Mexico)	Aerovias de Mexico (Mexico)	188	1988
Trans World Airlines (US)	Ozark Holdings (US)	170	1986
Icahn (Mr. Carl) (US)	Trans World Airlines (23 per cent) (US)	159	1988
American Airlines (US)	ACI Holdings (US)	157	1986
Pacific Western Airlines (Canada)	Canadian Pacific Airlines (Canada)	151	1986
Texas Air (US)	Eastern Airlines (Air Shuttle Div.) (US)	126	1988
PWA Corporation (Canada)	Wardair (Canada)	117	1989
Swissair (5 per cent) (Switzerland)	Delta Air Lines (5 per cent) (US)	117	1989
Texas Air (US)	People Express (US)	81	1986

Source: *Acquisitions Monthly*, AMDATA.

Alliances have also emerged in the industry (see figure 4.4). New computer-based reservation systems – Sabre in the US, Amadeus and Galileo in Europe – have been established by consortia of leading airline companies. This cooperation between the main carriers has enabled travel agents to provide an improved global reservation system and increased protection for the passenger.

Although deregulation will encourage further collaboration, international authorities are monitoring these inter-firm initiatives for any anti-competitive effects. In 1990, for example, the Commission of the European Communities in Brussels forbade the proposed establishment of Sabena World Airlines – a joint venture between Sabena (60 per cent), KLM (20 per cent) and BA (20 per cent) on competition grounds.

Heavy electrical engineering industry: This industry consists of a variety of firms engaged in the manufacture of components and equipment for power plant construction. It covers a wide range of products, but the main elements in terms of cost are the boiler and turbine generator which are at the heart of thermal power stations. The manufacturing capability in these areas is complex and skill-intensive, requiring a considerable commitment in terms of R&D and production facilities. Many of the companies involved – e.g. Siemens, General Electric, Hitachi – have a wide range of other industrial activities including telecommunications, computers, electronics and defence, while for others, heavy electrical equipment represents all or a significant proportion of sales, e.g. ABB.

Figure 4.4. Selected strategic alliances by European airlines

British Airways
- Aborted attempt to establish Sabena World Airways (SWA); an alliance between BA, Sabena (Belgium) and KLM (Netherlands).
- Possible 40 per cent stake in Sabena following breakdown of SWA.
- Marketing alliance with United Airlines in the US.
- Link with Aeroflot (USSR).

Scandinavian Airlines System
- Partnership with Swissair.
- 24.9 per cent stake in British Midland.
- Acquisition of Norskair (Norway) in 1989 (£1 m).
- Equity holding in Continental US.
- Marketing alliance with Thai and All Nippon Airways.
- Establishment of Equal Quality Alliance, involving SAS, Finnair, Swissair and Austrian Airlines.

Others
- Mutual 5 per cent equity stake Swissair and Singapore Airlines.
- Swissair's 5 per cent shareholding in Delta of the US.
- Alliance between Lufthansa and Air France.
- Austrian Airlines and All Nippon alliance.
- Marketing link between KLM and Garuda (Indonesia).
- Air France alliance and acquisition of Air Inter and UTA.
- Virgin Atlantic marketing alliance with British Midland and Dan-Air.

Sources: Derived from *Acquisitions Monthly and Interavia*, various editions.

During the latter half of the 1980s and early 1990s, the industry was restructured on a world-wide basis as a result of a series of international mergers and acquisitions. In August 1987, ASEA of Sweden and Brown Boveri of Switzerland merged their two companies into one – ABB – which with combined sales of $16 billion and a total workforce of over 180,000, became the world's largest power plant manufacturer. In 1988, GEC of the UK and the French CGE company merged their power plant businesses into a single unit called GEC-Alsthom with total sales of $11 billion. Subsequent large-scale take-overs included ABB's acquisition of the transmission business of Westinghouse and Combustion Engineering, both of the United States and Rolls Royce's acquisition of Northern Engineering Industries of the UK. In addition, there were numerous smaller-scale acquisitions by leading companies in the industry within southern Europe (e.g. Spain, Portugal, etc.) and Eastern Europe (Poland and the former Czechoslovakia).

There were two main factors encouraging MNEs to adopt this strategy. First, in the 1980s the market for power plants in the US and Europe virtually collapsed. The electrical supply industry, the power generating industry's main customer stopped placing new orders for all types of power plant – fossil fired and nuclear. Existing power generating supply was more than adequate to meet the demand for energy at this time. Several firms were thus forced to either abandon or scale down their activities in the power generating field. Despite this steady withdrawal from the industry, a study commissioned by the EC Commission in 1988 estimated that world capacity for boiler manufacture was still running at ten times demand, while capacity utilization in the EC was running at only 30 per cent. The same report concluded that even if demand grew substantially, the industry was still too fragmented among too many small-scale competitors for existing enterprises to enjoy a sufficient level of return on investments. Many enterprises therefore took the matter into their own hands, and engaged in a series of international mergers and acquisitions which reduced industry capacity and brought supply more into line with demand.

Secondly, there was a decline in the principle of national procurement for power plant suppliers. Traditionally the power plant industry had been perceived by governments as a strategic element of the national economy. Foreign firms were not considered when awarding contracts for new power plants and governments, fairly openly, maintained lists of qualifying – i.e. national – suppliers. Gradually, however, the relationship between the electricity supply industry and the government has become more distant. In the United Kingdom, this came about as a result of the industry's privatization. In other EC countries and in countries applying for EC membership there has been a steady pressure for public procurement markets in general and the utility industries in particular.

Thus falling demand and overcapacity combined with the waning of government-supplier relationships have been the main factors encouraging firms to engage in international acquisitions and as a result to bring about the restructuring necessary to achieve a higher level of profitability.

This process has reduced the world market in power generating to just five major players, the three European-based suppliers (ABB, Siemens and GEC-Alsthom) and two US-Japanese groupings (GE-Hitachi-Toshiba and Westinghouse-Mitsubishi), and has gone some way towards reducing manufacturing overcapacity.

A new round of deals is now under way. These are of two types: the first is aimed at achieving market access via technology transfer or local manufacturing; the second is designed to share the costs of producing and developing the latest power turbines. An example of the first type was GE's association agreement with Elin Energieversorgung of Austria to win a contract for the two 40MW turbines to power a combined-cycle plant in Linz. Only by entering into agreements with local firms can GE win contracts in these markets. An example of the second was GE and GEC-Alsthom's cooperation to develop the world's most powerful gas turbine, the 50-hertz Frame 9F. Under this arrangement the European parties to the deal can sell the product in Europe while GE can market it in the US.

Packaging: This is a mature, low-growth and low-technology industry which has traditionally been highly fragmented among numerous firms supplying mainly national and local markets. In Europe in particular a number of new factors have emerged recently which offered firms in the packaging industry new opportunities for growth:

■ the increasing concentration of the industry's main customers – the region's food and drink and retail industries – as a result of international mergers and acquisitions;

- the growing inclination of these firms to adopt pan-European selling and distribution strategies;

- the removal of restrictions relating to packaging and labelling which had been justified on the grounds of protecting the consumer;

- the emergence of tighter regulations in the packaging field arising from concern over the environment.

All these factors in one way or another encouraged the leading packaging firms to expand abroad in search of a growing share of these new markets through international mergers and acquisitions. One of the most active acquirers in the European packaging industry in recent years has been the French company Carnaud SA. Between 1985 and 1989 a total of 28 packaging companies joined the Carnaud "Federation of Enterprises", covering France, Germany, Italy, Spain, Turkey and also the US. The most significant event, however, was the 1989 merger with Metal Box Packaging of the UK to form CMB Packaging – the largest packaging group in Europe and the third largest in the world.[15] In this move the two firms achieved the size and scale necessary to respond to the new challenges. This merger triggered other acquisitions by leading competitors in the industry. For example, Péchiney International, the packaging subsidiary of the French state-owned aluminium company, acquired American National Can (ANC) in 1989, followed by the purchase in 1990 of a 39 per cent stake in Technipack International (TPI), a leading producer of packaging for up-market cosmetics.

Pharmaceuticals: Mergers, acquisitions and alliances (MAAs) have been less common here than in many other industries. Over the last few years, however, a number of important agreements have been concluded which will have a major impact on industry structure. The factors motivating MAAs in other industries are beginning to become evident too in pharmaceuticals. These include the increasing costs of R&D, partly as a consequence of stricter safety and control standards, and the continued need for new product development; pressures by several governments to control drug prices for national health services; trade liberalization in the run-up to "1992" which may put downward pressures on prices due to the emergence of lower-cost countries such as Greece, Italy and Portugal; the increasing strength of the generic drug makers, which is threatening the profit margins of the large research-based medicine companies; and the growing importance of biotechnology in new drug development.

Acquisitions in the pharmaceutical industry fall within two distinct groups. First, there has been a number of acquisitions by large, multinational enterprises of small, start-up or developing biotechnology companies. Recent examples include: Schering's purchase of Triton and Codon; Rhône-Poulenc's acquisition of France's leading biotechnology company Transgene; Hoffmann-La Roche's merger with Genentech; and the acquisition of Genprobe by Japan's Chugai. Through this type of acquisition, the multinational gains access to a new technology which in all probability will create some of the industry's leading drugs of the future while the small biotechnology company gains access to the larger financial resources of the multinational to fund R&D, and to its greater management and marketing skills.

[15] See Hamill (1991b).

The second group includes acquisitions by multinational pharmaceutical companies of other MNEs and is motivated by the pursuit of global market leadership. For example, in early 1990 Rhône-Poulenc significantly increased its presence in North America – the world's largest pharmaceutical market – through its acquisition of the Canadian vaccine company Connaught Biosciences and of a 68 per cent stake in Rorer of the US valued at approximately $ 3 billion. In 1989 Beecham of the UK and SmithKline of the US merged to form SmithKline Beecham – one of the top three pharmaceutical companies in the world (the others are Merck and Bristol-Myers-Squibb both of the US). According to the companies, the merger would allow greater resources to be devoted to R&D and thereby bring new drugs onto the market more quickly; and increase selling power to promote the new group's leading pharmaceutical products. In 1991, the 35th and 37th largest pharmaceutical companies Sanofi of France and Sterling Drug of the US merged their companies into Sanofi Winthrop – which with annual sales of $ 2.3 billion has become one of the top 20 drug companies in the world.

As in the other industries considered above, the early 1990s will see a further consolidation of competition in world pharmaceuticals through MAAs.

4. Employment effects of cross-border mergers and acquisitions

The wave of cross-border MAAs since the mid-1980s raises important issues regarding the economic impact of such activity and in related policy concerns in the area of merger control. The EC, for example, has recently introduced new regulations governing mergers and acquisitions which require that all deals with a "Community dimension" be notified to the European Commission for approval. Included in the definition of "Community dimension" are mergers and acquisitions where the companies involved have worldwide sales of ECU5,000 million (about US$ 6,000 million) or more; at least two of the groups to which the companies involved belong have sales in the EC of ECU250 million (about US$ 300 million) or more; and the companies involved do significant business in more than one EC Member State.

The debate on MAA impact has focused mainly on the potential trade-off between the competition and competitiveness effects of such activity. Thus, the concerns which have been expressed about the anti-competition effects of MAAs through increasing industry concentration have been balanced by the recognition that some industry consolidation through MAAs may be necessary to improve international competitiveness. In this section, and given the focus of this book, we are concerned with the employment and related effects of cross-border MAAs, rather than with impact on competitive structure *per se*, although the two are closely related.

A number of problems arise in attempting to evaluate the employment effects of the recent boom in international MAAs. First, the full effects of many MAAs take between three and five years to work through. Thus, while the late 1980s and early 1990s were the years of the cross-border MAA boom, it will be the mid-1990s before the full impact of these deals on employment can be assessed. Second, there has been very little prior research on the employment effects of MAAs. The research which has been done on the impact of previous MAA booms has focused either on the financial performance of MAAs or their impact on industry concentration levels. Third, the employment effects of MAAs will vary considerably depending on the a priori assumptions made (e.g. the competitive position of partners in the absence of a deal) and by the type of MAA (e.g. vertical, horizontal, conglomerate MAAs, etc.). Finally, there are methodological problems in attempting to evaluate the employment effects of MAAs, especially concerning the level of aggregation – firms, industries, national economies, regions or the world. As the emphasis of the chapter is MNE strategy, the level of analysis chosen here is the level of the firm. It should be made clear, however, that different conclusions may emerge depending on the level of aggregation. Thus, at a micro-level, MAAs may enhance employment opportunities through improving the international competitiveness of partners. To the extent that such employment gains are at the expense of other firms, the overall macro-effects on the industry/national economy may be significantly different.

Bearing in mind these limitations, the best that can be attempted at present is to provide a framework within which the employment impact of cross-border MAAs can be assessed. It will take several years for the relevant aggregate empirical evidence to be gathered and this will require a much larger-scale research project than is possible within the scope of this chapter. The framework presented below will at least provide a starting-point for future empirical work on the employment effects of MAAs.

4.1 Employment impact

The employment and related effects of cross-border MAAs will depend to a very large extent on the motivations underlying such deals. It was argued earlier that the recent boom in cross-border MAAs can be explained as a strategic and economic response by MNEs to the rapidly changing international business environment of the late 1980s and early 1990s (see figure 4.1). The driving force behind many deals has been the attempt to improve long-term international competitiveness.

From the point of view of the employment effects of cross-border MAAs, it is important to identify the potential sources of competitive advantage arising from such activity. These are essentially twofold: first, cross-border MAAs aimed at improving international competitiveness through strengthening product and geographical market portfolios, i.e. MAAs which result in the acquisition of global brands, higher value-added products, and international market expansion; and second, cross-border MAAs which aim to improve international competitiveness through lower costs, increased efficiency and scale economies by achieving synergy in the value chain activities of partners. Thus, attempts to improve international competitiveness through cross-border MAAs may be driven by either international product/market expansion or cost/efficiency or some combination of the two (there are however difficulties in distinguishing between these two motivations as illustrated in the case of ABB: see box 4.1).

Box 4.1.   ABB: Employment effects of acquisitions in the ASEA-Brown Boveri Company, 1988-92

What are the effects on employees when their companies are taken over by multinational enterprises?

ASEA-Brown Boveri (ABB) illustrates some of these changes affecting employment, following its international acquisitions. Although ABB is only one company it is a useful case study because its background – a large firm facing increasing international competition in an industry undergoing technological change and difficult trading conditions – is shared by many MNEs at present.

ABB is one of the biggest manufacturers of power generators in the world. Worldwide sales for 1991 were over $29 billion. Its total staff of 215,000 are employed in 1,200 companies in over 25 countries. Following the merger in 1987 of Asea of Sweden and Brown Boveri of Switzerland, the newly created ABB acquired around 60 companies in over 20 countries with a total value of about $3.6 billion – including two major acquisitions in North America. Recently the company has made a number of acquisitions in Eastern Europe and as a result is now the region's largest Western employer.

Reasons behind ABB's merger and its acquisitions

The ABB merger took place as a result of the collapse of the market for power plants in the 1970s and 1980s (see section 3 above on the power generating industry). ABB's more recent acquisitions in the United States and Eastern Europe have occurred for the following reasons. First, these are two of the three markets in the world (the other is Asia) where most new orders for power-generating equipment are or will be placed in the next few years, and ABB's acquisitions are designed to capture this new business. Second, these newly acquired companies, particularly in Eastern Europe, are, in relation to ABB's existing plants, low-cost producers. The company intends to build and design its power plant equipment more cheaply there and to export to other markets.

Rationalization, restructuring and the transfer of production

In order to weld the companies it has acquired together, ABB has undertaken a huge process of company restructuring. Businesses are closed; exchanged with other companies; or transferred to other companies abroad. In all cases the overriding objective is to derive benefits from international economies of scale. Particular problems have arisen where operations that duplicated work being done elsewhere have been closed. This fusion and integration proved especially difficult in Germany, where there was a considerable overlap between the Asea and Brown Boveri. Consequently in 1988, 4,000 jobs (10 per cent of ABB's German workforce) were lost.

Reorganization also involves the shifting of businesses from one company to another — often to other countries — so that production of a particular product can be consolidated and done more economically in a single plant. For example, the Stromberg company of Finland, which ABB acquired in 1988, was responsible for producing the whole gamut of power equipment products — generators, transformers, drives, etc. However, the small size of its market meant that production was both uneconomical and of poor quality, and the company was only able to survive because of its protected market. ABB transferred the company's activities in the manufacture of AC motors to an ABB plant in Vasteras in Sweden while Stromberg became responsible for the production of one product — electric drives. ABB doubled the volume of production in Stromberg by making substantial investments in production technology (e.g. a new robot production line was installed) and in training and retraining staff. Through new investments ABB companies are thus transformed into dedicated plants manufacturing their products for both their home market and ABB's international network. ABB Stromberg, for example, was able to increase its exports to Germany and France tenfold because of its new access to ABB's distribution network, and this helped to strengthen the company's general position.

ABB tried to implement the reorganization following acquisition quickly so that conflict with its new staff is defused as far as possible and that the link with the company's traditional customers is not broken. Aware that transferring production out of a country can attract negative publicity, ABB has tried to show itself not to be favouring one country over another. It is no coincidence that the company is headquartered in "neutral" Switzerland and adopts English as its lingua franca. It is, however, important to the company that national interests do not sidetrack it from its task: hence its policy of always ensuring full control of acquisitions. Indeed, ABB has spent nearly $15 billion buying minority positions left over from joint ventures formed by ASEA and Brown Boveri when they were separate companies.

Losing headquarters

ABB breaks up the headquarters of companies it acquires. As a rule it cuts the staff by at least 90 per cent as follows: a third go to companies which are at the production line; another third leave the payroll but continue to provide the company with the same service on a contract basis; and a third are made redundant. In this way, the German HQ at Mannheim which had a staff of 1,600 was reduced to just 100; the Stromberg company in Helsinki, Finland which when acquired had a headquarters staff of 800 has now only 58 employees; and Combustion Engineering which had a staff at headquarters of 600, was reduced to just 90.

The company reports that such action is usually supported by production employees who they claim often resent the waste and opulence of activities at headquarters — Combustion Engineering before it was acquired operated a fleet of executive jets even though at the time it was continuously cutting back its production staff. ABB runs a small staff of 100 at its global headquarters in Zurich.

Decentralization and results-based management

To make sure that the performance of companies it acquires are completely transparent, ABB operates a radical policy of decentralization and results-based management. Authority over production, accounts, cashflow and dividends is given to the management of each company.

ABB thus breaks up large structures and creates more small companies in their place. Their single company in Germany for example was broken up in 1988 into 20 separate legal companies. In all ABB has created 1,200 legal companies, all with responsibility for their own profit and loss.

In this effort to encourage accountability, ABB has in the process created by industry standards very small production units. On average each of these 1,200 plants employs only around 200 employees; factories employing more than 1,000 are rare. Each of these companies are further subdivided into 4,500 profit centres with on average just 50 employees.

In-house competition

All senior managers are responsible for monitoring the performance of each company in their product area according to a set of critical parameters, such as failure rates, through-put times, inventories as a percentage of revenues and so on. Successful companies are held up to the other companies operating in the business area as examples of best practice. Comparing performance across borders puts ABB companies in competition with each other and generates strong pressure on them to succeed. According to senior managers, the pressure this puts management under – not to mention their staff – is more intense than from ABB's own competitors in the market-place.

New working methods

One of the most decisive challenges facing the workforce is the rate of improvement and the current focus on reducing total cycle time. This is not the brain-child of ABB but is borrowed from Motorola and its Time-Based Management System. In essence, this system is designed to cut working capital by shortening through-put time – the time taken from order to delivery – and is being applied to all areas of activity. The goal of the company is to reduce total cycle time by 50 per cent by 1993; that is from order to delivery the time taken in 1993 will be half of that of 1990.

ABB has contracted out to supplier firms more of the business it used to do in-house. As the largest producer in the industry, ABB can negotiate the best deals with suppliers on price, quality and delivery. ABB's supplier network therefore enables the company to cut product cycle times. ABB has also extended its supplier network internationally, most recently to Eastern Europe.

Redundancies

The first and most visible consequence of ABB's restructuring and rationalization is redundancies. In 1991, excluding turnover of staff through divestments and acquisitions, there were 13,000 redundancies within ABB and, in 1992, redundancies were running at 1,000 per month.

Acquisitions and in-group competition

One very important consequence of this enlarged group structure is the presence of many similar production plants and units. Turbines, for example, are manufactured in at least five different locations in Switzerland, Germany, the US, Sweden and Poland. Management is comparing the performance of these different units carefully. They are competing with each other in what appears to be a vast in-house race in terms of delivery, quality, "just-in-time" methods and cost.

Already the company has begun production in Poland of gas turbines for Western markets; German workers of ABB at Mannheim have criticized ABB for transferring production to Poland to exploit cheaper labour.

Time-based management and equalizing the differences between manual and non-manual employees

One result of the introduction of new working methods is that office work is done by operators at the shop-floor level – a well-known means of reducing production time; another is more teamwork among former white-collar workers, for instance between design and production technology. Recently ABB has started advocating a new kind of standardized associate agreement doing away with most differences between white- and blue-collar workers.

Size of plant and access to the real decision-takers

The radical reduction in the average size of ABB companies across the world – an indirect effect of ABB's policy of decentralization – presents trade unions with a practical, but none the less considerable, difficulty in organizing and representing the ABB workforce. In the same way, the company's matrix organization – under which a factory is under the authority of both the national company at the local level and the product manager who coordinates production at the international level – has increased confusion over which level of management has responsibility for dealing with workers' representatives. Workers at a local plant might very well have to choose between: the manager of the local company; his boss at the national headquarters; or the coordinator of the product group.

ABB's matrix organization, as well as the competition generated as a result of decentralizing authority within the company, tends to fragment rather than unite the workforce.

Conclusion

ABB's restructuring, following the acquisition of many new companies, has tended to affect the workforce in diametrically opposed ways: on the one hand, many employees will benefit from the training, new participatory forms of team production, greater responsibility, etc. They will also benefit from ABB's increased investment in new technology and, in so far as ABB's international network provides more business opportunities, they will also enjoy more incentives and job security (e.g. ABB Stromberg, Finland). For companies on the verge of collapse when acquired by ABB these are not inconsiderable advantages.

On the other hand, ABB employees who are marginalized by these developments, who do not fit into ABB's core products, who become suppliers to ABB, who are not trained in the new techniques, who are not the winners in ABB's in-house race to create the best factories or whose production is not cost-effective in relation to newly acqired plants will have a very different perspective towards ABB's restructuring.

Figure 4.5 presents four different scenarios concerning the micro-employment effects of cross-border MAAs distinguishing between the two main strategic motivations outlined above.

In **scenario 1**, a foreign company acquires a firm to gain access to the latter's product portfolio and/or to expand geographically. Since the acquisition is mainly growth oriented, there may be a significant transfer of capital, technology, marketing and management skills from the acquiring to the newly acquired subsidiary in the post-acquisition period. The latter may play an important strategic role in the international expansion of the acquiring company, and may emerge as a product specialist or strategic independent subsidiary (see box 4.1). As a consequence of the improved international competitiveness of the newly acquired subsidiary (through the resource transfer effect) and its wider product/market role, there may well be a significant increase in both output and exports. In such circumstances, positive employment effects may be predicted in terms of employment levels, job security, etc.

The importance of **scenario 1** is that it contradicts the often-held belief that acquisitions will always be job destroying; and there are many examples of such deals which could be quoted. For example, most foreign acquisitions in the US fall within this group, the acquisition being made to gain access to the acquired company's products or to establish significant US market share. Many of the cross-border acquisitions which have taken place in Europe are also in this category, the acquisition being made to strengthen products or extend geographical market coverage prior to the establishment of the Single Market.

Scenario 2. Acquisitions which fall under scenario 2 take place to reduce costs or to reduce industry overcapacity by removing a competitor. Significant post-acquisition rationalization and consolidation may take place to reduce costs and achieve synergy. For the acquired company, this may be highly negative, as it may result in a loss of responsibility in key functional areas of activity (e.g. R&D; marketing; product development, etc.) through the transfer of these functions to the new parent company. As a result, the newly acquired company may become essentially a "branch" subsidiary with limited product/geographical market responsibilities and with little decision-making autonomy from the parent. Significant job losses may be expected as a consequence. Many of the cross-border MAAs discussed in section 3 of this chapter fall within this group.

Scenarios 3 and **4** both cover mergers and alliances between companies, rather than outright acquisition. The essential difference between the two are that in scenario 3, any job losses as a consequence of rationalization and consolidation are more than compensated for by the improved international competitiveness of the partners. In scenario 4, on the other hand, the merger or alliance is mainly cost driven, resulting in significant job losses.

As shown in the next two sections, it is possible to present examples of the differential employment effects of MAAs aimed at product/geographical market expansion compared to cost/efficiency driven MAAs.

Figure 4.5. Employment effects of cross-border MAAs: Four scenarios

Scenario	Strategic motivations	Post-MAA impact	Employment effects
1. Foreign acquisition of host country firm	International expansion through product strengthening/geographical market diversification.	Resource transfers from acquiring to acquired company (capital technology, management, marketing, etc.); acquired company becomes product specialist or strategic independent; improved international competitiveness; increased output and exports.	Increase in employment levels through enhanced international competitiveness and access to global markets; improved quality of employment through technology transfers, etc.; transfer of innovative personnel practices.
2. Foreign acquisition of host country firm	To reduce industry over-capacity; cost driven.	Large-scale post-acquisition rationalization and consolidation; loss of subsidiary autonomy in R&D, marketing, etc.; restricted product/market role for the acquired company.	Significant job losses as consequence of post-acquisition rationalization and possible plant closures; reduced job security through restricted product/market role; reduced employment quality through centralization of R&D, etc.
3. Merger or alliance between host and foreign partner	International expansion through joint product strengthening/geographical market diversification.	Significant post-merger/alliance rationalization and integration of value-chain activities required to gain synergy.	Increase in employment because of improved international competitiveness compensates for jobs lost as a result of integration; reduction of job security in the short run, but increasing in the long run.
4. Merger or alliance between host and foreign partner	Improved international competitiveness through lower costs and greater efficiency.	Significant post-merger/alliance rationalization and integration of value-chain activities required to gain synergy and lower costs.	Major job losses as result of rationalization and integration, reduced job security and uncertainty about future.

Source: The author.

Figure 4.6.   Strategic gap analysis: British manufacturing industry in the early 1980s

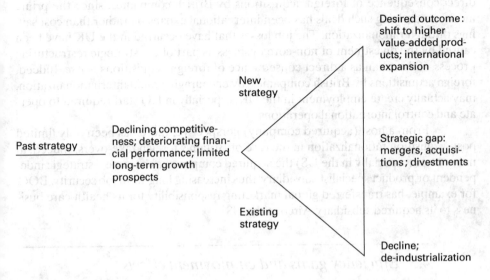

Source: Adapted from Jauch and Glueck (1988), p. 24.

4.2 Britain's foreign acquisitions

The wave of British acquisitions abroad since the mid-1980s fall within scenario 1[16] and can be explained by using Strategic Gap Analysis – where the term refers to the difference (gap) between the expected outcomes of existing strategies and the desired outcomes of a change in strategy (see figure 4.6).

In the early 1980s, British manufacturing firms undertook a drastic restructuring and downsizing of their domestic operations in response to highly unfavourable market conditions. By the mid-1980s, these companies' financial position had considerably improved, allowing them to consider new strategic options for attaining long-term competitive advantages. Two main actions were chosen:

- refocusing on higher value-added product sectors or sectors with greater growth potential;
- a shift away from the traditional foreign markets of British companies in developing countries to new foreign markets in industrialized countries with high growth prospects.

Mergers and acquisitions (and divestments) in the UK, but especially abroad, played a crucial role in achieving such strategic objectives. Given the strategic motivations described above, the employment effects of British acquisitions abroad have, at worst, been neutral and probably positive in the long-run, from both

---

[16] See Hamill (1991c).

a home and host country perspective. There have been few jobs lost in the UK as a direct consequence of foreign acquisitions by British companies, since the prime motive underlying such deals has been international expansion rather than cost savings through rationalization. The job losses that have occurred in the UK have been caused by the divestment of non-core business as part of the strategic restructuring process, rather than as a direct consequence of foreign acquisitions *per se*. Indeed, foreign acquisitions by British companies, by encouraging rapid internationalization, may actually create employment in the UK, especially in HQ staff required to operate and control international operations.

From a host (acquired company) perspective, there has been only limited post-acquisition rationalization in the case of Britain's foreign take-overs. Indeed, in many cases (especially in the US) the acquired company has become a strategic independent or product specialist subsidiary, thus increasing long-term job security. BOC, for example, has transferred global marketing responsibility for its health-care business to its acquired subsidiary Airco in the US.

4.3 *Efficiency gains and employment effects*

While cross-border acquisitions aimed at improving international competitiveness through product strengthening and geographical market diversification raise few concerns regarding employment impact, the same cannot be said of scenario 2 acquisitions. Cross-border acquisitions to reduce industry overcapacity, or to achieve cost savings through synergy, raise serious concerns regarding the potential adverse employment effects of post-acquisition rationalization.

There are many examples of cost/efficiency-driven cross-border acquisitions. In particular, many of the examples quoted earlier in the defence, airline, power generating and packaging industries have been driven by the search for cost-efficiency through post-acquisition rationalization. The potential for significant job losses as a consequence of post-acquisition rationalization will be especially high in the following areas:

■ consolidating HQ staff;

■ closing down unnecessary facilities;

■ eliminating redundant executive positions and unproductive personnel;

■ centralizing volume leverage functions (e.g. purchasing, insurance, data processing);

■ integrating operations (e.g. raw materials, manufacturing, distribution, marketing);

■ integrating R&D and technology development.

Large-scale job losses during the 1990s are expected in the industries referred to earlier as a result of post-acquisition consolidation and integration. For example, since the merger between SmithKline and Beecham to form SKB, the company has announced a 10 per cent reduction (5,000 employees) in its worldwide workforce involving the closure of 60 manufacturing, administrative and distribution sites.

5.   Conclusions

This chapter has presented a broad overview of the boom in cross-border MAAs in the late 1980s and associated employment effects. It is argued that the employment impact of cross-border MAAs will vary considerably depending on the motivations underlying the deal, a distinction being drawn between MAAs aimed at improving international competitiveness through product strengthening and geographic market expansion, on the one hand, and cost/efficiency driven MAAs, on the other. It is in the latter that the potential adverse employment effects are greatest as a result of post-MAA rationalization and integration of activity.

As both positive and negative effects can be adduced depending on the motivations underlying MAAs, it is clearly difficult to reach general conclusions on which effect will predominate. What can be said with greater certainty is that as a consequence of the cross-border MAA boom of the late 1980s, the next few years may see major job losses in many sectors as a result of post-MAA rationalization and consolidation. Indeed, a new era of MNE labour conflict may be approaching, reminiscent of the plant closure battles of the 1970s.

Bibliography

Borys, B.; Jemison, D.B. 1988. "Hybrid organizations as strategic alliances: Theoretical issues in organizational combinations", in *Graduate School of Business*, Stanford University, Mar.

Buckley, A. 1975. "Growth by acquisition", in *Long Range Planning*, Aug.

Business International, 1982. "Acquisitions in Europe", in *Business International Research Report*.

—. 1987. "Acquisition strategy in Europe", in *Business International Research Report.*

—. 1988. "Making acquisitions work: Lessons from companies successes and mistakes", in *Business International Research Report.*

Calvet, A.L. 1982. "Mergers and the theory of foreign direct investment", in A.M. Rugman: *New theories of the multinational enterprise*, Beckenham, Kent, Croom Helm.

Casson, M. 1989. "Theory of cooperation in international business", Chapter 3 in P.J. Buckley: *The multinational enterprise: Theory and applications*, London, Macmillan.

—. 1990. *Enterprise and competitiveness: A systems view of international business*, Oxford, Clarendon Press.

Commission of the European Communities (CEC). 1992. *Panorama of EC industries 1991-1992*, Brussels.

Contractor, F.J.; Lorange, P. 1988. "Competition vs cooperation: A benefit/cost framework for choosing between fully-owned investments and cooperative relationships", in *Management International Review*, Wiesbaden, 28, Special Issue.

Cooke, T.E. 1986. *Mergers and acquisitions*, Oxford, Basil Blackwell.

—. 1988. *International mergers and acquisitions*, Oxford, Basil Blackwell.

Creedy, K.B. 1991. "The cost of restrictive bilaterals", in *Interavia*, Mar.

Cyert, R.M.; March, J.G. 1963. *A behavioral theory of the firm*, New York, Wiley.

Devlin, G.; Bleackley, M. 1988. "Strategic alliances – Guidelines for success", in *Long Range Planning* (Elmsford, New York), Vol. 22, No. 5.

Dubin, M. 1975. "Foreign acquisitions and the growth of the multinational firm", Doctoral Thesis, Harvard Business School.

Dunning, J.H. (ed.). 1971. *The multinational enterprise*, George Allen and Unwin, London.

Dunning, J.H. 1988. *Explaining international production*, London, Unwin Hyman, Chapter 13.

ECE/UNCTC. 1986. *Recent developments in operations and behaviour of transnational corporations: Towards new structures and strategies of TNCs*, Publication Series No. 7, Geneva.

Farmbrough, H. 1990. "International aviation and the airline industry", in *Acquisitions Monthly*, Washington, Mar.

Fusfeld, H.J.; Haklisch, C.S. 1985. "Cooperative R&D for competitors", *Harvard Business Review*, Boston, Nov./Dec.

Goldberg, W.H. 1983. *Mergers – Motives, modes, methods*, Aldershot, Gower.

Gugler, P. 1991. *Les alliances stratégiques transnationales*, Editions Universitaires, Fribourg, Switzerland.

Hamel, G.; Doz, Y.L.; Prahalad, C.K. 1989. "Collaborate with your competitors – and win", in *Harvard Business Review*, Boston, Jan.-Feb.

Hamill, J. 1989. "British acquisitions in the US", in *National Westminster Bank Quarterly Review*, London, Aug.

—. 1990. "Defending competitiveness: Acquisitions and alliances in the European defence industry", in *Acquisitions Monthly,* Washington, DC, May.

—. 1991a. "Changing patterns of international business: Cross-border mergers, acquisitions and strategic alliances", Paper presented at the Academy of International Business, UK Region Annual Conference, 12-13 April, London.

—. 1991b. "CMB Packaging: A case study of the 1989 merger between MB Packaging (UK) and Carnaud (France)", Case Clearing House, Cranfield.

—. 1991c. "Strategic restructuring of British industry through international acquisitions and divestments", in *Journal of General Management*, Winter.

Harrigan, K.R. 1984. "Joint ventures and global strategies", in *Columbia Journal of World Business*, Summer.

Harrison, J.S. 1987. "Alternatives to merger – Joint ventures and other strategies", in *Long Range Planning*, Vol. 20, No. 6.

Jain, S.C. 1987. "Perspectives on international strategic alliances", in *Advances in International Marketing*, JAI Press Inc.

Jemison, D.B.; Sitkin, S.M. 1986. "Acquisitions: The process can be a problem", in *Harvard Business Review*, Boston, Vol. 64, No. 2, Mar.

Keenan, M.; White, L.J. 1982. *Mergers and acquisitions*, Lexington, Massachusetts, Lexington Books.

Kogut, B.; Singh, H. 1985. *Entering the US by acquisition or joint venture: Country patterns and cultural characteristics*, Wharton School, University of Pennsylvania, Pittsburgh, Discussion Paper.

Love, J.H.; Scouller, J. 1990. "Growth by acquisition: The lessons of experience", in *Journal of General Management*, Vol. 15, No. 3, Spring.

Mayer, C. 1991. "A flight plan for Europe?", in *International Management*, May.

Morgan, N.A. 1988. "Successful growth by acquisition", in *Journal of General Management*, Vol.14, No. 2, Winter.

Morris, D.; Hergert, M. 1987. "Trends in international collaborative agreements", in *Columbia Journal of World Business*, Summer.

Mytelka, L.K.; Delapierce, M. 1987. "The alliance strategy of European firms in the information technology industry and the role of ESPRIT", in *Journal of Common Market Studies*, Oxford, No. 26.

Norburn, D.; Schoenberg, R. 1990. "Acquisitions and joint ventures – Similar arrows in the strategic quiver", in *Business Strategy Review*, Autumn.

Ohmae, K. 1989. "The global logic of strategic alliances", in *Harvard Business Review*, Boston, Mar.-Apr.

Payne, A. 1987. "Approaching acquisitions strategically", in *Journal of General Management*, Vol. 13, No. 2, Winter.

Perlmutter, H.V.; Heenan, D.H. 1986. "Cooperate to compete globally", in *Harvard Business Review*, Mar.-Apr.

Pilling, M. 1991. "An industry turned upside down", in *Interavia*, Apr.

Porter, M.E. (ed.). 1986. *Competition in global industries*, Boston, Massachusetts, Harvard Business School Press.

Reich, R.B.; Mankin, E.D. 1986. "Joint ventures with Japan give away our future", in *Harvard Business Review*, Boston, Mar.-Apr.

Salter, M.S.; Weinhold, W.A. 1979. "Diversification through acquisition strategies for creating economic value", in *Free Press*, New York.

Steiner, P.O. 1975. *Mergers: Motives, effects, control,* Ann Arbor, University of Michigan Press.

Teece, D.; Pisano, G. 1987. "Collaborative arrangements and technology strategy", Berkeley Discussion Paper, Berkeley.

Wilson, B.D. 1980. "The propensity of multinational companies to expand through acquisitions", in *Journal of International Business Studies*, Spring/Summer.

5

Growth and structural changes of Japanese overseas direct investment: Implications for labour and management in host economies

Susumu Watanabe

1. Introduction

As a result of the unprecedented growth in its overseas direct investment[1] (ODI) during the 1980s, Japan had become one of the world's leading foreign investors by the end of the decade. The purpose of this chapter is to describe the implications for labour and management in host countries of this growth. Believing that the competitiveness of Japanese industries accrues largely from their organizational efficiency, host industrialized countries are particularly interested in Japanese managerial practices. Whether and how far Japanese practices will take root in host economies will depend on the scope for unpackaging the "Japanese system". It is particularly intriguing to see how other elements of the system will succeed where they are detached from the lifetime employment system.

Section 2 describes recent trends in Japanese ODI, section 3 examines its economic impact on recipient countries and section 4 assesses the attempts to transplant Japan's management and labour practices to foreign affiliates.

2. Growth and structural changes of Japanese ODI

2.1 Trends in Japanese ODI

Although Japan resumed its ODI activities in 1951, it was not really until the latter half of the 1980s (figure 5.1) that a real surge in Japanese outward investment occurred. Earlier increases in ODI – in the late 1960s and early 1970s and between 1978 and 1981 – were, in comparison, much less significant.

Between 1985 and 1989, Japanese ODI increased more than fivefold. Accounting for this rapid increase was Japan's chronic labour shortage which reduced

---

[1] Japanese investment is referred to as either "ODI" or "FDI" depending on whether it is considered from the perspective of the home or the host country.

Figure 5.1. The annual amount of Japanese ODI and the annual average dollar-yen exchange rate, FY 1965-90

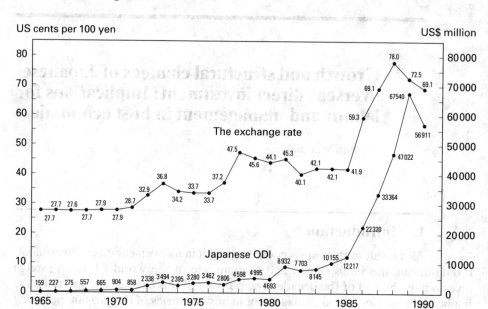

the price competitiveness of its exports, the prospect of a partially closed market emerging in Europe, and ever-worsening trade relations with the United States. At the same time, increased incentives and reduced restrictions by host governments stimulated investment in export-oriented offshore industries in the ASEAN-4 – Indonesia, Malaysia, the Philippines and Thailand. The strong yen, abundant capital supplies supported by high savings ratios, relatively low interest rates in Japan and the growing demand for services from Japanese firms abroad also boosted ODI in various branches of the tertiary sector.

After seven years of continuous rapid growth, Japanese ODI fell in 1990 as growth in the world economy began to slow down, the money supply in Japan became tighter, the yen weaker and major firms began to pay more attention to their domestic markets after years of rapid international expansion (Yuge, 1991).

2.2 The geographical and sectoral distribution

Until the early 1980s, Japanese ODI was more or less equally divided between industrialized and developing regions, the industrialized countries' share of investments in the primary and secondary sectors being no more than one-third of the total. Between 1986 and 1990, the situation changed with 75 per cent of the aggregate total and 77 per cent of the investment in the primary and manufacturing sectors going to industrialized countries. The shares of Africa and the Middle East, which had never been large, became negligible. Latin America managed to maintain its share in the aggregate total close to Asia's, but nearly 80 per cent of investment in that region was absorbed by financing and shipping tax havens. Thus, the impact of the phenomenal expansion of Japanese ODI during the 1980s was virtually confined to the industrialized regions and to Asia.

Within each region Japanese ODI is heavily concentrated in a few countries and areas. The United States received 96 per cent of the cumulative total in North America, and the United Kingdom, the Netherlands and Luxembourg 69 per cent in Europe. In Oceania, Australia has been virtually the only recipient, while the tax havens of Panama, Cayman Islands and the Bahamas accounted for 67 per cent of the cumulative total in Latin America and 76 per cent in 1981-90. In Africa, the tax haven of Liberia alone received 80 per cent of the cumulative total and 93 per cent of the total after 1980. In the Middle East, Kuwait and Iran absorbed 71 per cent of the cumulative total.

Finally, in Asia, the Japanese have invested almost exclusively (99 per cent over the entire period) in the newly industrialized economies (Hong Kong, Singapore, the Republic of Korea and Taiwan, China), the ASEAN-4 (Indonesia, Malaysia, the Philippines and Thailand) and China. The shares of the first two groups were 49 and 44 per cent respectively. Even among these groups the distribution of Japanese ODI is changing: the ASEAN-4 have received more of manufacturing investment than the NIEs since 1988. Investments aimed at global supplies of standardized products are now going to the former, while investments in the Republic of Korea and Taiwan, China, are primarily oriented towards local markets. It is not difficult to explain such shifts. As mentioned above, ASEAN governments recently added incentives for foreign direct investment (FDI) and reduced restrictions. In the Republic of Korea and Taiwan, China, on the other hand, labour costs and industrial disputes grew; so did trade frictions with Western countries, so much so that firms in these countries are now investing in ASEAN countries.

There were also important changes in the sectoral and subsectoral distribution of Japanese ODI (table 5.1). Investments in the tertiary sector rose from less than 50 per cent of the total to more than 70 per cent after 1980, while the primary sector declined from over 20 per cent to an almost negligible percentage. The proportion of manufacturing ODI in the aggregate total rose by 10 percentage points during the 1970s and then fell back to the previous level of 25 per cent. Against this overall picture are considerable interregional differences. For example, the proportion of investment in the tertiary sector varied, in the last subperiod, from about 50 per cent in the Middle East and Asia to over 90 per cent in Latin America and Africa with their tax havens. Manufacturing investment grew rapidly in all developed regions during the 1980s and in Asia after 1985, but it shrank in absolute terms in the other developing regions.

Within the manufacturing sector, the focus of Japanese ODI shifted from basic material processing (metal and paper) and labour-intensive light consumers' goods industries (notably textiles) before 1980 to metal engineering industries thereafter (i.e. electrical and electronic machinery, transport equipment and general machinery). Metal processing (e.g. iron and steel) remains an important area of investment, but the motivation of investment has changed: during the earlier periods it was aimed at securing supplies for industries at home, but more recently invest-

Table 5.1. Growth and structural changes of Japanese overseas direct investment, FY 1951-90 (US$ million)

Sector/industry	All regions				North America				Europe				Oceania			
	51-70	71-80	81-85	86-90	51-70	71-80	81-85	86-90	51-70	71-80	81-85	86-90	51-70	71-80	81-85	86-90
1. Primary sector	886 (24.8)	7094 (21.5)	4995 (10.6)	5659 (2.5)	184 (20.2)	648 (7.3)	675 (3.9)	1217 (1.1)	6 (0.9)	854 (22.3)	4 (0.0)	730 (1.5)	208 (74.0)	815 (36.3)	483 (28.1)	1855 (13.4)
Agriculture and fishery	82	827	312	876	8	246	114	268	0	2	–	34	9	99	46	259
Mining	804	6267	4683	4783	176	402	561	949	6	852	4	696	199	716	437	1596
2. Manufacturing sector	928 (25.9)	11645 (35.4)	11826 (25.1)	57213 (25.2)	217 (23.8)	2211 (24.9)	5278 (30.8)	32617 (29.0)	36 (5.8)	808 (21.1)	1244 (19.1)	10452 (21.7)	51 (18.2)	738 (32.9)	266 (15.4)	1248 (9.0)
Food	51	535	505	2994	3	207	298	1323	6	37	31	444	8	36	15	234
Textiles	180	1448	445	1915	6	175	63	516	1	137	55	672	1	4	1	6
Timber, paper pulp	212	546	362	1847	192	142	272	1455	–	0	–	21	5	89	33	30
Chemicals	50	2576	1356	6958	–	240	426	4154	16	88	111	1200	2	97	6	27
Metals	138	2481	2571	5119	1	371	667	3146	3	153	105	338	31	223	109	92
General machinery	68	826	1077	5961	7	213	555	3198	4	116	95	1580	0	22	15	43
Electrical and electronic machinery	73	1506	2166	16613	2	659	1493	8944	1	126	272	3922	3	18	13	72
Transport equipment	87	892	2395	7507	–	89	1126	3814	3	56	361	1477	1	220	26	700
Other	61	833	947	8297	3	115	377	6067	2	95	215	795	0	30	49	42
3. Tertiary sector	1763 (49.3)	14181 (43.1)	30331 (64.3)	164284 (72.3)	511 (56.0)	6027 (67.8)	11215 (65.3)	75387 (69.0)	597 (93.3)	2170 (56.6)	5282 (80.9)	37077 (76.8)	22 (7.8)	691 (30.8)	971 (56.5)	10757 (77.6)
Construction	36	360	401	1592	5	124	125	922	0	12	33	73	–	12	17	43
Commerce	381	5028	7269	18638	306	3187	3928	9563	29	788	1669	4214	12	236	339	1015
Financing and insurance	318	2108	8433	54459	110	841	3244	15199	61	761	2873	21434	9	53	277	1416
Services	49	1344	3293	29980	38	432	617	19654	6	91	154	3011	0	65	158	2520
Transport	–	–	5900	11538	–	–	70	439	–	–	28	199	–	–	15	153
Real assets trade	–	–	2533	43316	–	–	2076	28474	–	–	57	6540	–	–	79	5354
Other	978	5342	2500	4764	52	1443	1155	1136	501	518	468	1606	1	325	86	256
Total	3577	32920	47152	227157	912 [25.5]	8886 [27.0]	17167 [36.4]	109218 [48.1]	639 [17.9]	3832 [11.6]	6531 [13.9]	48262 [21.2]	281 [7.9]	2244 [6.8]	1718 [3.6]	13857 [6.1]
Average total per year	179	3292	9430	45431	46	889	3433	21844	32	383	1306	9652	14	224	344	2771
Growth index relative to the previous period	–	18.39	2.86	4.82	–	19.33	3.86	6.36	–	11.97	3.41	7.39	–	16.00	1.41	8.06

Sector/industry	Asia				Latin America				Africa				Middle East			
	51-70	71-80	81-85	86-90	51-70	71-80	81-85	86-90	51-70	71-80	81-85	86-90	51-70	71-80	81-85	86-90
1. Primary sector	315 (41.9)	2993 (32.9)	3239 (33.6)	1335 (4.8)	110 (19.4)	1275 (22.8)	307 (3.2)	287 (1.2)	59 (63.4)	469 (34.7)	135 (7.0)	27 (1.1)	— (—)	42 (2.2)	152 (21.3)	208 (45.4)
Agriculture and fishery	47	239	61	178	16	181	64	114	1	57	28	23	—	3	—	—
Mining	268	2754	3178	1157	94	1094	243	173	58	412	107	3	—	39	152	208
2. Manufacturing sector	320 (42.6)	4258 (46.9)	2946 (30.6)	11141 (39.7)	275 (48.5)	2505 (44.7)	1779 (18.8)	1723 (6.9)	25 (26.9)	71 (5.2)	119 (6.2)	17 (0.7)	4 (1.2)	1060 (55.1)	195 (27.4)	18 (3.9)
Food	23	125	108	912	9	125	55	78	3	5	—	—	—	4	0	0
Textiles	107	813	261	685	57	293	66	36	17	21	—	—	—	—	—	—
Timber, paper pulp	15	127	49	335	8	188	7	8	—	0	—	—	—	—	—	—
Chemicals	19	702	570	1350	8	493	56	218	1	0	5	5	—	944	180	6
Metals	34	997	666	1108	66	669	917	421	3	17	101	7	—	52	6	8
General machinery	15	258	307	1069	42	206	106	71	—	—	—	—	—	10	1	—
Electrical and electronic machinery	45	498	289	3342	19	193	94	331	—	—	—	—	—	—	—	—
Transport equipment	14	252	426	1006	69	264	447	505	1	3	3	1	2	9	2	2
Other	48	476	272	1335	5	74	28	55	1	6	8	2	1	3	—	—
3. Tertiary sector	116 (15.5)	1837 (20.2)	3449 (35.8)	15579 (55.5)	182 (32.1)	1822 (32.5)	7380 (78.0)	22838 (91.9)	8 (8.6)	812 (60.1)	1668 (86.8)	2413 (98.2)	330 (98.8)	823 (42.6)	365 (51.2)	230 (50.4)
Construction	4	72	149	516	27	109	51	37	—	19	1	4	—	12	28	—
Commerce	17	384	658	2734	17	420	664	1078	1	2	4	7	1	10	8	26
Financing and insurance	65	201	515	3450	71	227	1458	12895	0	2	1	35	1	24	69	32
Services	5	624	1271	3802	1	108	474	901	0	20	614	89	—	4	—	—
Transport	—	—	249	847	—	—	4512	7690	—	—	—	2209	—	—	3	—
Real assets trade	—	—	307	2683	—	—	14	196	—	—	1023	69	—	—	—	—
Other	25	556	300	1547	66	958	205	41	6	769	25	—	328	774	260	173
Total	751 [21.0]	9078 [27.6]	9634 [20.4]	28056 [12.4]	567 [15.9]	5602 [17.0]	9468 [20.1]	24847 [10.9]	93 [2.6]	1352 [4.1]	1924 [4.1]	2457 [1.2]	334 [9.3]	1925 [5.8]	713 [1.5]	458 [0.2]
Average total per year	38	908	1927	5611	28	560	1894	4969	5	135	385	491	17	193	143	92
Growth index relative to the previous period	—	23.89	2.16	2.91	—	20.00	3.38	2.62	—	27.00	2.85	1.28	—	11.35	0.74	0.64

1. For the definition of "ODI" and for the coverage of the database, see the appendix to this chapter. 2. "—" stands for a negligible amount. Due to these entries and rounding-up, the sum does not always equal the total or subtotal. 3. The figures in parentheses under the sectoral subtotals stand for proportions in the regional totals, and those in brackets show proportions in the world totals. 4. "Commerce" includes manufacturers' sales offices. "Transport" is largely related to ship registry in tax havens. "Other" in the tertiary sector includes figures for "branch offices" in the original source, as well as "real assets" up to 1980, after which date purchase of real assets was excluded from the ODI data.

Sources: Compiled using data from the Ministry of Finance, the Government of Japan: *Kaigai Chokusetsu Tōshi (Todokeide Bēsu)* (Overseas Direct Investment statistics on the reporting basis) published in *Zaisei Kinyū Tōkei Geppō*, Dec. 1989, and the Export and Import Bank of Japan: *Kaigai Tōshi Kenkyūjo-hō*, Nov. 1990 and July 1991.

ments were often made for the purposes of catering for Japanese firms' affiliates abroad and/or for supporting ailing foreign firms.

In the tertiary sector the focus of Japanese ODI shifted from the establishment of branch offices and marketing offices and systems to financing and insurance, transport, services and real assets trade. Some investment in the financing and transport industries is related to tax havens, as noted earlier. The sudden surge in investment in "services" and "real assets" in North America in the last subperiod is attributable to the acquisition of movie companies, skyscrapers, etc. – an entirely new feature of Japanese ODI.

2.3 Changes in the investment mode and ownership structure

Traditionally, Japanese firms rarely used mergers and acquisitions to enter foreign markets. According to the 4th Basic Survey on Japanese firms' overseas business activities by the Ministry of International Trade and Industry (MITI) (see appendix), only 5.7 per cent of Japanese affiliates operating abroad in FY 1989 had been established in this way. This changed towards the end of the decade however, particularly in developed countries. For example in the United States in 1988, 88 per cent of total Japanese investment took this form compared with 23 per cent in 1986 (Takaoka, 1990). Major examples included Firestone, CBS Recording Company, Columbia Pictures Entertainment, Gould, MCA (Universal Studios), CIT and a US convenience store chain.

Another new trend is the increasing tendency of Japanese affiliates to raise investment funds outside Japan and to use locally accumulated profits for investment purposes. Honda, for example, built its manufacturing subsidiary in the United States with funds earned by its sales subsidiary. As noted in the appendix, such investments relying on funds raised abroad are not reported to the Government of Japan, and are therefore excluded from the data summarized in figure 5.1 and table 5.1.

In addition, Japanese firms now prefer to fully own their operations abroad. MITI's 4th Basic Survey discovered that 79 per cent of the affiliates (70 per cent of the manufacturing sector) in industrialized countries were wholly owned. Minority ownership accounted for 5.6 per cent (8.6 per cent) only. However, in the developing regions in contrast, minority ownership remains common. Here, 31 per cent of the total (41 per cent in the manufacturing sector) were wholly owned, while 34 per cent (31 per cent) were minority owned. This is due both to the desire of Japanese companies to minimize the risks of doing business in these countries and to the local governments themselves, who often set limits on the amount of equity foreign investors can own. ASEAN governments have recently reduced such restrictions, especially for export-oriented FDI. Consequently, the proportion of wholly or majority-owned affiliates seems to be rising rapidly (cf. Tokunaga, 1990). However, a relatively high proportion of minority-owned affiliates is likely to persist in Asia.[2] This region

---

[2] Information supplied by the Small and Medium Enterprise Agency (Chûshô Kigyô-chô), which is based on the database of the Ministry of Finance. "Small and medium-sized enterprises" in the manufacturing sector are defined to be enterprises with fewer than 300 workers or less than 100 million yen capital.

Table 5.2.   Motivation of Japanese manufacturing ODI by region, fiscal year (FY) 1989 (percentage in total replies)

Motivation	North America	Europe	Oceania	Asia	Latin America
1. Access to the local market	80.4	79.8	63.9	61.2	62.1
2. Export to Japan	10.0	3.7	14.8	18.2	6.2
3. Access to other markets	12.5	36.8	25.3	25.3	13.0
4. Collection of information	26.2	19.9	13.1	6.7	5.6
5. "Trade friction"	16.4	16.3	1.6	1.8	0.6
6. Official incentives	9.4	20.2	23.0	32.8	37.9
7. Dividends earning	9.2	4.3	14.8	9.8	11.9
8. Supply of labour	14.6	20.9	16.4	64.3	48.0
9. Supply of raw material	8.9	1.8	23.0	6.5	14.1

Note: The totals exceed 100 because some firms gave more than one reply.

Source: MITI's *4th Basic Survey Report*, pp. 128-139.

attracts about 60 per cent of new affiliates established by small and medium-sized enterprises, and these firms often go into a joint venture with an indigenous partner or a Japanese trading company because they do not have enough knowledge of local conditions or essential business connections.[3]

2.4 Changing motivation

The rapid increase in Japanese ODI in the latter half of the 1980s (see section 2.1) would suggest that the motivation for Japanese ODI has also changed, but table 5.2 demonstrates that ODI, at least at the time of MITI's 4th Basic Survey, followed the traditional pattern. In industrialized countries the most common motive was to "gain access to the local market". This, allied to the related "trade friction", suggests that marketing motives were predominant. In developing countries, the most common motives are host government incentives (also of some significance in the case of developed countries) and "labour supply" (important due to Japan's own chronic labour shortage). More recent surveys, however, are beginning to point to a new set of motives for Japanese ODI.

In the Japan Exterior Trade Research Organization's survey of 270 manufacturing affiliates in Western Europe (JETRO, 1990c), "globalization of the parent firm's operations" was by far the most common motive, mentioned by two-thirds of

---

[3] With their well-developed information network, organizational and marketing know-how, general trading companies bring together companies with different capabilities (e.g. know-how in different business lines) to organize joint venture projects. They will participate, but usually remain a minority owner. See Kojima and Ozawa (1984) for a detailed analysis of Japanese general trading companies. According to Toyo Keizai (1990b), Mitsui had 552 overseas affiliates with 158,451 workers as of 1 July 1989. In terms of the number of overseas affiliates, Mitsui was No. 1 in Japan, immediately followed by six other trading companies.

respondents. The next most common replies were "expansion of local demand" and "to improve response to users' needs" (one-third each). "Protectionist restrictions on imports from Japan" and "EC 92" were mentioned by less than 20 per cent each. The "globalization" motive was no doubt related to these two considerations to some extent. Whatever its explanation, the high frequency of this reply suggests a shift in Japanese firms' strategies from defensive to offensive ones (cf. Ozawa, 1991).

Further evidence that Japanese ODI is increasingly motivated by "global" competition comes from numerous changes in the way Japanese companies operate internationally. In a recent survey by the Export and Import Bank of Japan, 77 per cent of the 247 major manufacturing companies cooperating for the study had been operating in an internationally consolidated accounting system.[4] Some of them introduced technological innovations at their overseas plant even earlier than at home (Kume, 1990). Particularly significant is the tendency to undertake R&D abroad. In 1990 some 42 per cent of companies interviewed by JETRO had some kind of R&D programme abroad while 41 per cent in Europe had been involved in a global R&D programme of their parent company (JETRO, 1990c and 1990d).

3. The impact on host economies

In attracting Japanese FDI, host governments, whether in industrialized or developing countries, are attempting to achieve a number of objectives, including most notably: the generation of employment; the boosting of value added and exports; and the raising of both the productivity and quality of local supplying firms. The following discusses how far Japanese FDI is achieving these objectives. It should be noted, however, that three-quarters of total accumulated Japanese ODI date from 1986 or after (table 5.1) and that the bulk of the new investments were not yet fully operational at the time of writing this chapter.

3.1 Direct employment

According to MITI's *19th Survey Report*, Japanese affiliates abroad employed 1,326,101 workers in March 1989: 79 per cent (1,053,477) in the manufacturing sector, 13 per cent (177,129) in commerce, 5 per cent (61,098) in the rest of the tertiary sector, and 3 per cent (34,397) in the primary sector. Of this total, 33,554 (2.5 per cent) were Japanese. The proportion of Japanese was 1.6 per cent in the manufacturing sector and 5.1 to 8.5 per cent in different branches of the tertiary sector. The metal engineering industries employed 650,603 workers, or 49 per cent of total employment and 61.8 per cent of manufacturing employment. The electrical and electronic machinery industry alone employed 368,425 workers and the transport equipment industry 181,233 workers. The share of the textile industry was only 7.7 per cent of the total and 9.7 per cent of manufacturing employment (102,101 workers).

---

[4] This practice, of course, enlarges the scope for "FDI dumping" whereby affiliates are set up in order to avoid "trade frictions" and to circumvent import restrictions, where product export from Japan is more profitable and preferable to their parent firms (Kojima, 1985). See Wong (1989) on related subjects.

Table 5.3. Employment at Japanese affiliates by region/country/area (No. of workers)

Region/country/area	MITI's 19th Survey, March 1989				Toyo Keizai Survey, July 1989	
	All sectors		Manufacturing		All sectors	
	Total	Japanese	Total	Japanese	Total	Japanese
North America	316 278	14 445	214 602	6 377	423 365	15 690
United States	293 047	13 590	202 313	6 040	389 706	14 823
Canada	23 174	n.a.	12 279	n.a.	33 659	867
Europe	137 322	5 946	93 505	2 052	n.a.	n.a.
EC	132 425	5 737	91 513	1 999	n.a.	n.a.
United Kingdom	37 015	n.a.	24 654	n.a.	50 476	2 721
Germany,Fed.Rep.of	28 556	n.a.	14 503	n.a.	30 635	1 774
Spain	20 595	n.a.	19 328	n.a.	20 286	223
France	20 067	n.a.	15 132	n.a.	20 038	533
Belgium	9 315	n.a.	5 851	n.a.	12 645	417
Oceania	53 129	1 228	32 956	315	n.a.	n.a.
Australia	42 195	n.a.	27 368	n.a.	88 711	1 112
Asia	656 845	9 511	583 282	6 466	n.a.	n.a.
NIEs	337 905	5 535	302 967	3 605	504 305	6 572
Korea, Rep. of	118 593	n.a.	112 320	n.a.	202 792	507
Taiwan, China	117 377	n.a.	113 547	n.a.	182 256	1 832
Singapore	65 655	n.a.	54 350	n.a.	72 143	1 976
Hong Kong	36 280	n.a.	22 750	n.a.	47 114	2 212
ASEAN	267 234	3 522	234 391	2 591	n.a.	n.a.
Thailand	99 016	n.a.	86 891	n.a.	153 174	1 860
Malaysia	71 923	n.a.	67 188	n.a.	82 376	836
Indonesia	63 604	n.a.	56 657	n.a.	66 727	912
Philippines	32 254	n.a.	23 610	n.a.	43 165	283
China	24 203	n.a.	20 778	n.a.	37 757	450
India	n.a.	n.a.	n.a.	n.a.	32 313	68
Latin America	142 891	1 874	118 033	1 015	n.a.	n.a.
Brazil	101 184	n.a.	82 138	n.a.	222 509	1 122
Mexico	18 840	n.a.	18 189	n.a.	33 313	364
Africa	11 834	297	7 309	74	n.a.	n.a.
Nigeria	n.a.	n.a.	n.a.	n.a.	13 778	84
Middle East	7 802	253	3 790	115	n.a.	n.a.
World total	1 326 101	33 554	1 053 477	16 414	1 941 236	38 120

Notes: (1) A marginal number of respondents to the MITI survey failed to indicate the country where they operated.   (2) Toyo Keizai's information includes planned affiliates and affiliates which are out of operation but not
yet withdrawn.   (3) Only the countries with employment exceeding 10,000 workers are listed.

Sources: Compiled from MITI's *19th Survey Report*, pp. 111-114, and Toyo Keizai, 1990b, p. 15.

Table 5.4.   Japanese affiliates' share in the manufacturing employment in selected economies, 1988

Economy	Total manufacturing employment	Employment at Japanese affiliates	
		No. of workers	% in total
Singapore	352 600	54 350	15.4
Malaysia	928 900	67 188	7.2
Taiwan, China	2 810 000	113 547	4.0
Thailand	2 300 000	86 891	3.8
Hong Kong	875 900	22 750	2.6
Korea, Republic of	4 667 000	112 320	2.4
Australia	1 203 600	27 368	2.3
Philippines	2 238 000	23 610	1.1

Note: Employment in 1988 except Malaysia (1987), Taiwan, China (1987) and Thailand (1986).

Sources: The second column is based on ILO: *Year Book of Labour Statistics, 1989-90*. The data for Taiwan, China, are from *Industry of Free China*. The third column is based on MITI's *19th Survey Report*, pp. 111-114.

One-half of the total employment and 55 per cent of the manufacturing employment were created in Asia, mostly the newly industrialized economies (NIEs) and the ASEAN-4, and just over 20 per cent in North America. The EC and Latin America accounted for 10 per cent each. Country-wise, the United States was by far the largest beneficiary, accounting for 22 per cent of the total and 19 per cent of manufacturing employment. The Republic of Korea, Taiwan (China), Brazil, Thailand and the other ASEAN countries (excluding Brunei) were the next largest beneficiaries, followed by Australia, Hong Kong, China and EC countries (table 5.3).

The impact of FDI is of course relative. Both the total employment and the employment in manufacturing generated by Japanese affiliates in the United States were substantial in absolute terms, but they were equivalent to no more than 0.3 per cent of the total and 1 per cent of manufacturing employment. There is no scientific benchmark as to how large a share is significant but even so the relative importance of Japanese investment to overall employment creation is small. Only in four economies – Singapore, Taiwan (China), Hong Kong and Malaysia – did employment at Japanese affiliates exceed 1 per cent (MITI, 19th Survey) while it was only more than 1.5 per cent in Singapore. In the manufacturing sector, the share rises to over 1 per cent in seven economies: all the Asian NIEs, ASEAN-4 minus Indonesia (table 5.4), but it was just below 1 per cent in Brazil and Indonesia, two of the world's largest economies.

In considering the direct employment effect of Japanese investment, other factors have to be taken into account as well. First, the response ratio in the survey was 78.8 per cent (see appendix). If we apply this percentage to the survey figures, total employment will rise to 1,682,869 including 42,581 Japanese, and manufacturing employment to 133,689 including 20,829 Japanese. As the non-respondents were mostly affiliates of small and medium-sized firms, the actual numbers at all the affiliates on the MITI list must have been somewhat smaller. On the other hand, the MITI list did not include all the existing Japanese firms abroad. Again, the missing firms were mostly small. To be conservative, we may put the global total employment at

1.6 million workers and the global manufacturing employment at 1.3 million workers, 2.5 per cent of the former and 1.6 per cent of the latter being Japanese.[5]

Second, the statistical data do not take into account the quality of employment. Considerable portions of official employment figures in the Third World consist of underemployed workers in agriculture and in urban "informal sectors". In the absence of reliable statistics, the number of "unpaid family workers" and "employers and own-account workers" are often used as a proxy. Although this is hardly acceptable in the context of an industrialized economy, it may be reasonable in the context of a developing economy. Around 1988, these categories accounted for 72 per cent of the economically active population in Indonesia, and between 50 and 30 per cent in the Philippines, Mexico, Malaysia and Brazil, as compared with over 20 per cent in Italy and Japan and below 10 per cent in the United States and the United Kingdom.[6] The Japanese affiliates' contribution ought to be assessed in terms of their share in the "formal sector" employment only. Dearth of data, however, forbids this.

Third, even where the Japanese affiliates' share in a country's employment is modest, their impact on certain local economies can be significant. This argument seems particularly valid in the case of Japanese manufacturers, whose investment tends to be clustered in depressed peripheral areas (see section 5 below). To a questionnaire sent to the United States by Nihon Keizai Shimbun (Japan Economic Journal) Co., 27 States responded, invariably expressing their desire to attract Japanese investment which would "contribute to the state economy and provide job opportunities".[7] Host governments' enthusiasm is understandable in the light of enormous numbers of job applications Japanese investors attract. In 1986-87, Nissan (UK) received about 11,500 applications when they had 500 posts to offer, and Komatsu (UK) 3,000 for the first 70 production line jobs.[8] The first company received some 20,000 applications for 1,000 posts in late 1990, when two other Japanese firms were also recruiting more than 4,000 workers in the depressed British automobile industry.[9] Similar was the case at Mitsubishi Motor Co. and Mazda in the United States.[10]

---

[5] ILO: *Year Book of Labour Statistics, 1989-90*. The difference between the two pairs of industrialized countries is partly explained by the prevalence of subcontracting in Japanese and Italian industries.

[6] Our estimates are considerably lower than the figures published by Toyo Keizai Inc. (the last two columns in table 5.3), although the latter appear to overestimate reality somewhat, e.g. because of inclusion of affiliates still at the planning stage and those out of operation (but not yet withdrawn). The 1989 survey by the Electronics Industries Association of Japan (EIAJ, 1989) found that, out of a total of 481 member companies, 178 had at least one affiliate abroad as of the end of June 1989, 765 affiliates in 39 economies in total. They employed a total of more than (because some did not give information) 406,431 workers, including 4,753 Japanese. This is 10 per cent more than MITI's figure for the same industry (368,425 workers), although the EIAJ figures understated reality partly because of non-reporting by some member companies and partly because there were outsiders who did not belong to the Association. In the light of the above, our estimation of total employment at 1.6 million seems to be conservative, but it may not be too far from the truth. In fact, the results of the 1987 Benchmark Survey of foreign firms' affiliates by the Bureau of Economic Analysis (BEA), US Department of Commerce, are consistent with this conclusion. According to this survey, Japanese affiliates in the United States employed 284,600 workers, or 9.0 per cent of the total employment at the foreign-owned firms in 1987 (Howenstine, 1989).

[7] *Nihon Keizai Shimbun*, 15 Mar. 1990, morning. For incentives offered by host governments, see, for example, Dunning (1986), Oliver and Wilkinson (1988) and Reed (1989).

[8] Oliver and Wilkinson, 1988, pp. 62 and 67.

[9] *Nihon Keizai Shimbun*, 1 Nov. 1991, morning.

[10] Lawrence, 1990, p. 19, citing Shimada and MacDuffie, 1987.

These figures eloquently indicate the values of the jobs created by these affiliates to the local communities.

For the sake of balance it should be recorded that not all the affiliates surveyed are wholly owned by the Japanese. Thus, employment at these firms is not entirely attributable to Japanese ODI. Nor can one simply apply their equity shares to assess their contribution, because at least some of the firms partially owned by Japanese investors could not have come into existence or survived competition without their participation.

Finally, in order to assess the total impact of Japanese ODI, the indirect employment effects – as measured by using the Keynesian multiplier effects and measuring backward and forward linkages – should also be taken into account. Using input-output analysis, Yamashita (1989, p. 19) argues that the total employment effect of Japanese investment in the ASEAN economies may be about three times as large as its direct effect. This is broadly consistent with Yokota (1987),[11] who estimates the ratio of total indirect to direct employment generated by foreign manufacturing firms in Thailand at 2.23:1, using the 1980 input-output table of the country. The ratio however is bound to vary from one country to another, depending on the structures of Japanese ODI and of the host economy.

3.2 Value added and exports

In fiscal year (FY) 1988 the total value added at the 7,544 affiliates cooperating for MITI's 19th Survey amounted to US$78,378 million. The manufacturing sector accounted for 49 per cent and commerce for 45 per cent. Geographically, nearly half the total was generated in North America, followed by Europe (22 per cent) and Asia (19 per cent). In the industrialized regions, commerce contributed more to the value added than the manufacturing sector, while the opposite was the case in the developing regions.

The same report provides country data only for the United States, which were equivalent to 0.7 per cent of the GNP and 1.8 per cent of the manufacturing GDP in 1988. The figures for the ASEAN-4 corresponded to 2.2 per cent of the combined GNP and about 9 per cent of the combined manufacturing value added of the group. Those for the NIEs were 2.8 per cent and 5.7 per cent, respectively.[12] In the case of the EC, a subregional analysis makes no sense, because the number of constituents is large and Japanese investment is concentrated in a few countries.

MITI's *4th Basic Survey Report* contains data on the market composition of the annual turnover and on the supply-source composition of the procurements in each region, which confirm well-known features of Japanese ODI in the manufacturing sector: it is almost entirely oriented towards local market in the developed regions and much more export-oriented in developing regions, especially in Asia,

---

[11] Quoted in Sibunruang and Brimble, 1988, p. 18.

[12] Calculated using data from *World Bank Atlas, 1989, World Development Report, 1991*, supplemented with data on Taiwan, China, from the Taiwan Liaison Office in Tokyo: *Chûka Minkoku 1989-nen no Kokujô Tôkei*, Aug. 1990 and Malaysian data from the Asian Development Bank: *Key indicators*.

while the situation varies more widely in commerce. However, such breakdowns were reported for less than 60 per cent of the global turnover and procurements. In Europe, some respondents reported transactions within the EC as "local" while others regarded them as "export" and "import". The data also seem to exaggerate the local market orientation of manufacturing affiliates and their degree of dependence on imported materials, particularly in North America and Europe, for the reasons explained below.

In the regions where the market is large, Japanese multinationals usually have separate subsidiaries specialized in manufacturing, sales or R&D. In the case of Honda, for example, these three areas are covered, respectively, by Honda of America Mfg. and Honda Power Equipment Mfg.; American Honda Motor Co.; and Honda R&D North America and Honda Engineering North America. The products of two manufacturing subsidiaries are sold to American Honda Motor Co. in order to be distributed either locally or abroad. Under this arrangement, the former subsidiaries appear to be entirely local-market oriented, although certain portions of their output are actually manufactured for export markets. Moreoever, as materials and components are imported directly and not through American Honda Motor Co., the import-export ratios become artificially high.[13]

According to the above-mentioned MITI Report's figures, the overall balance of trade was, in 1989, negative in North America, Europe and the ASEAN-4. In manufacturing it was also negative in Oceania and Africa.

The negative direct foreign exchange effect of FDI is not unique to the Japanese case. This has been a favourite subject of study among development economists. In the United States, the BEA's 1987 Benchmark Survey found that only affiliates from France and from the Middle East were, as a whole, net exporters. This survey, however, also revealed that the average import-export ratio of Japanese affiliates was higher than that of affiliates from the other countries: "affiliates' exports to Japan were over five times as large as those to any other country and accounted for 41 per cent of all affiliate exports. Affiliates' imports from Japan were over four times as large as those from any other country and accounted for almost one-half of all affiliate imports. A large portion of this trade was accounted for by Japanese-owned wholesale trade affiliates" (Howenstine, 1989, p. 126).

Confining the scope of their study to the US manufacturing sector, Graham and Krugman (1989) argue that "the only major difference between Japanese and other foreign manufacturing firms is a higher Japanese import propensity", and they speculate as follows:

> ...Japanese may be pressured to continue relying on domestic suppliers, or may simply not trust US suppliers, to a greater extent than other foreign investors. However, we speculate that the main reason is related to the mismeasurement of marketing firms as manufacturers and the selection bias that leads foreign firms to enter the US disproportionately in activities that make use of imported inputs; these factors may be at work in Japanese FDI, which is newer and less mature, to a greater degree than among foreign investors as a whole. Numerous studies of the behaviour of multinational firms indicate that as these firms become more experienced in the conduct of

---

[13] Based on the author's interview at Honda in April 1992.

international operations they tend to increase the local content of the output of their overseas subsidiaries (see, e.g., Vernon, 1966). Because Japanese firms are typically quite inexperienced in the role of foreign direct investors, it is reasonable to expect them to increase the domestic content of their US subsidiaries' output as they gain experience (pp. 60-61).

Large trade deficits by Japanese manufacturing affiliates in North America and Europe accrued partly from the import of capital goods which were to be installed at the new plants. This naturally grew when the rate of ODI accelerated. The above-discussed relationships between manufacturing and sales subsidiaries is another explanation.

As regards export promotion, suffice it to note that the "globalization" of Japanese multinationals is increasing trade among their subsidiaries worldwide because of product specific horizontal division of labour, so much so that in 1991 one out of every three cars exported from North America was produced by Japanese-owned firms.[14]

3.3 Local procurement of materials and components and technical cooperation for suppliers

The local procurement ratio in commerce basically depends on whether the affiliates in this business branch were established mainly as exporting or importing agents. Trading companies can help develop local industries, e.g. through provision of markets and technical advice and information. It is, however, primarily from manufacturing FDI that one expects significant contributions to this end.

Figures by MITI show that in FY 1989 the average local procurement ratio in Japanese manufacturing affiliates was 45.6 per cent (MITI, 1991, pp. 200-223). MITI (1989a, p. 15) also estimated that appreciation of the yen reduced the local procurement ratio by 7.3 percentage points between 1983 and 1986, by raising prices of imports from Japan relative to those of local goods. The value of the yen in terms of the US dollar rose by 40 per cent during that period. As it increased by another 30 per cent in the next two years (figure 5.1), the ratio must have been reduced further by this factor.

Such external conditions remaining constant, the local procurement ratio in the manufacturing sector will depend on factors such as the industrial composition of ODI, its age and the host government's policy. In the *4th Basic Survey Report* this ratio was over 80 per cent in timber, paper and pulp, food processing and chemicals; between 50 and 65 per cent in transport equipment, textiles, petroleum and coal products, steel and non-ferrous metals; and between 44 and 20 per cent in general machinery, electrical and electronic machinery, and precision machinery. By and large, it appears that the import ratio tended to rise with the degree of sophistication of the product.

---

[14] *Nihon Keizai Shimbun*, 26 Feb. 1992 (evening), based on a report published by the Motor Vehicle Manufacturers' Association of the United States Inc. (MVMA).

The length of time the affiliate has been established is a particularly salient factor in the level of local procurement. MITI (1989b, p. 192) reports that the local procurement ratio was 63 per cent among manufacturing affiliates established before 1970, 55 per cent among those established during the 1970s and 45 per cent among those established during the first half of the 1980s. Thereafter, the ratio rose to about 50 per cent, no doubt due to the increasing pressure from industrialized host countries. All the age groups anticipated that it would rise to 65-75 per cent in the next five years. JETRO (1990c) found that the average local procurement ratio at the responding affiliates in Europe had increased from 51.2 per cent at the beginning of their operations to 67.2 per cent by the end of 1989.

In the same way as Ford, GM and Volkswagen, the major Japanese automobile firms such as Toyota and Nissan are followed abroad by their suppliers. At home, Japanese firms rely on their "cooperative companies" (i.e. core suppliers) and subcontractors much more (about 70 per cent of their material costs) than their US and European counterparts. This means the potential scale of such foreign investments by Japanese supplier firms is much larger. However, such smaller suppliers often find it difficult to meet the demands of their larger Japanese customers abroad because of resource constraints. It would also be politically unwise to rely excessively on home suppliers. Japanese affiliates, therefore, are keen to use local suppliers. For example, in the EIBJ survey (1990), between 56 and 42 per cent of respondents in the United States, the EC and Asia stated their intention to increase purchases from local suppliers.

However, despite these intentions, JETRO (1990c) reports that 70 per cent of the affiliates in Europe were unhappy with their local suppliers. Out of a total of 117 respondents, 59 complained of unreliable delivery, 55 of poor quality and 46 of high costs. The automobile assemblers had the largest numbers of local subcontractors, but only one in nine was satisfied with them. According to Oda (1990), Japanese firms felt that the just-in-time (JIT) system was virtually impossible in the EC because of unreliable delivery, while Ishii (1990) reports that for political reasons Japanese automobile manufacturers in the United States would opt for locally owned suppliers, if they were as efficient as Japanese suppliers' affiliates. In reality, however, the latter were chosen more often because they were more reliable. Reportedly, the quality of parts and materials supplied by American firms was so uneven that Toyota had to check them upon delivery – a practice abolished in Japan for some time.

In response to indifferent service, Japanese companies, by encouragement and the use of incentives, try to improve the cost or quality of the product themselves. For example, they often show local suppliers how to reduce the costs of their components and, depending on their success, sometimes award suppliers with long-term contracts. In order to encourage such efforts, companies like Nissan and Toyota recently introduced a commendation system for local suppliers. From the United Kingdom, Dunning (1986) reports:

> Japanese firms are more prepared to give advice on product design, equipment and production methods and work organization than their earlier (or indeed their current) United States counterparts [...] In particular, there was widespread agreement – even among the very large United Kingdom suppliers – that their Japanese customers had helped upgrade their quality control, inspection and testing procedures

and, in some cases, had forced them to reappraise their production philosophy. Certainly, as compared with their dealings with their United Kingdom customers, domestic suppliers found the relationship with their Japanese counterparts less distant and more cooperative and stable. (p. 14.)

Oliver and Wilkinson (1988) argue similarly with reference to Komatsu (UK) and cite a local supplier saying that "The Japanese tend to camp out on your doorstep. We've got English firms that we see once or twice a year [...] it's nothing for the Japanese to turn up two, three or four times a day" (p. 131). Different authors report similarly from different parts of the world, either developed or developing, and some argue that buyer-supplier relationships among local firms are changing under the influence of Japanese firms.[15]

Thus, it can be seen that Japanese firms are attempting to repeat in foreign markets the success they had at home in building an effective supply network (Watanabe, 1983, Chapter 2). However, for reasons to be discussed below, progress to date has been slow.

In the Third World the problems of local suppliers are well known (cf. Watanabe, 1983, Chapters 5 and 7). One basic problem is the small size of the local market. To overcome this constraint, Japanese firms have started "networking" their affiliates, especially within Asia. The ASEAN governments encourage such arrangements under their Industrial Complementation Programme, whereby reduced import tariffs are applied to parts and components produced within the region. Export of automobiles built under such arrangements started from Thailand and Malaysia. A limited number of indigenous component manufacturers have emerged, such as Thai Engineering Products Co. (TEP) which, equipped with numerous CNC (computer-numerically controlled) machine tools, cater to most multinational automobile, motorcycle and agricultural machinery companies operating in the country (Watanabe, 1992, Chapter VII).

---

4. Managerial practices and industrial relations

The success of Japanese industry – at first attributed to the use of advanced production technologies – is increasingly being seen as due to their organizational prowess and in particular their "lean (or low waste) production system".[16] As a result, the Japanese system has become the focus of intense scrutiny, not to mention direct imitation.

The broad principles of this system have become well known. Japanese firms try to achieve "no defect production" or "total quality control (TQC)" and attempt to eliminate waste in all their business activity by means of the just-in-time

---

[15] See, for example, Lawrence, 1990, p. 35 and Ishii, 1990, pp. 18-19 for the United States; Conseil economique et social, the Government of France (1984) for France; Sibunruang and Brimble, 1988, for Thailand; and Watanabe, 1983, Chapter 5 for the Philippines.

[16] There is a long list of western literature on this subject, particularly in the United States. See, above all, Altshuler et al. (1984), Abegglen and Stalk, Jr. (1985), Dertouzos et al. (1989) and Womack et al. (1990). The main elements are discussed concisely in Chapter 1, Oliver and Wilkinson (1988), where the term "low-waste production system" is used. Womack et al. use "lean production system".

system and teamwork based on flexible task-sharing. Product design and production processes are simplified to enlarge the scope for low-cost automation. Industrial relations are maintained in a peaceful and cooperative spirit through a single enterprise union system and through close communication and consultation. Efficient and reliable suppliers are secured through close collaboration and through stable business relationships in a competitive climate. Japanese firms also continuously improve existing products and production facilities and procedures through constant efforts, notably in "QC (quality control) circles". These efforts to achieve small but continuous improvements have proved in practice to have a greater impact on productivity than some major technological reorganization, such as the installation of a robot production line. The system calls for highly motivated workers with diverse skills and knowledge ("Tanôkô"), developed through frequent retraining and job rotation. Although Western observers tend to ascribe Japanese workers' motivation in such teamwork to their culture, it is more related to economic incentives provided by the lifetime employment system, the pay and promotion system, largely but not entirely based on seniority, and the egalitarian remuneration system (cf. Watanabe, 1991).

There are a number of questions raised about the Japanese system and its transferability to other settings. How far has the Japanese system been effectively transplanted? Are there any specific conditions that make this transplantation easier or more difficult? How far have these principles been diffused to local firms? Finally, what has been the response of local people, workers and observers?

4.1 Transferring Japanese management practices abroad

As is clear from the above sketch, the Japanese production system relies on human factors for its smooth operation far more than its Western counterparts: "While the American firms try to develop a 'structure' which functions sufficiently well irrespective of the personalities and attitudes of the workforce, the Japanese approach is to create the right people, who can work effectively irrespective of structure" (Takamiya, 1985, p. 193). Japanese firms therefore endeavour to transplant their labour-management practices (e.g. highly selective recruitment, extensive in-house training, consultation and direct communication, and long-term employment for core workers) before manufacturing practices such as the JIT system and teamwork (Oliver and Wilkinson, 1988, p. 132). The former are prerequisites of the latter.

Labour-management practices at Japanese affiliates in the United Kingdom have been described as follows:

> Japanese affiliates in the 1980s are more inclined to adapt their labour practices to local needs. In particular, they are particularly sensitive to local criticism of their recruitment policies. They appear to make every effort not to poach from other firms; they have broadly conformed to nationally agreed wage levels; they offer few bonuses or monetary incentives; and, almost without exception, they are fully unionized. Their distinctive impact is shown in the area of hiring policy where they seek to recruit employees able and willing to work as part of a team; the adoption of a more open and consultative style of industrial relations; the creation of quality control cir-

cles; the provision of first-class working and social conditions; and the fact that they prefer to deal with only one trade union. The fact that most of their workforce is ... normally recruited in areas of high unemployment, has no doubt made it easier for them to adopt a more paternalistic stance towards, and be more demanding of, their workers ... (Dunning, 1986, p. 11.)

Kujawa (1986) and Lawrence (1990) report similarly from the United States.

In order to recruit workers who can adjust to their corporate culture and teamwork, Japanese firms spend enormous sums on training and retraining.[17] The goal of training workers to embrace the corporate culture leads to greater use of on-the-job training or in-house facilities. External training courses are however used for preparing employees for promotion (ML Expert Committee, 1990). The training method also varies, depending on local conditions. For example, in Malaysia and Singapore where Western influence is stronger, Japanese firms rely more on manuals than elsewhere. In training personnel for higher posts, more formal course methods are used. In contrast, in Thailand and Indonesia training is given mainly on the job (Yamashita et al., 1989). In developing countries, especially in the ASEAN region, some Japanese firms have established technical training schools not only for their own employees but also for those belonging to other firms.[18]

It is difficult to say if these practices can be transferred or learned through training. In Yamashita et al. (1989), 70 to 90 per cent of the Japanese respondents felt that the Japanese style on-the-job training and internal human resources development systems were applicable outside Japan, while 50 (Malaysia and Thailand) to 70 (Indonesia and Singapore) per cent felt similarly with the QC circle. The job rotation system was considered to be applicable by 40 per cent of the respondents in all countries, while 80 per cent thought the lifetime employment and seniority pay systems inapplicable.

Regarding manufacturing practices, Oliver and Wilkinson (1988, pp. 120-121) report that total quality control, flexible work, teamwork, statistical process control quality circles and the just-in-time system were practised in descending order by 100 to 64 per cent of the Japanese firms surveyed. The degree of success was in the same order, except that the positions of the first two reversed. Most difficult to transplant was the just-in-time system – a fact supported by other studies, e.g. Oda (1990).

Successful absorption of Japanese practices appears to have much to do with location. Aoyama (1988) attributes the success of job flexibility and rotation systems in affiliates in South Wales and South Scotland to the socio-cultural homogeneity of the labour force and extremely high unemployment rates in those regions. The latter factor permits a severe screening of workers at the time of recruitment, as Oliver and Wilkinson (1988) note. Both Dunning (1986) and Reed (1988) suggest that to Japanese companies which attach a great importance to workers' attitude, the absence of a

[17] See, for example, Kujawa, 1986, Chapter 8, Lawrence, 1990, and the studies cited therein for the United States; Oliver and Wilkinson, 1988, and the reports cited therein for the United Kingdom; Sibunruang and Brimble, 1988, p. 16 for Thailand; and Kiyota, 1988, for Mexico. Yamashita et al., 1989, and ML Expert Committee, 1990, provide empirical information on related subjects in the ASEAN region, plus Taiwan, China, in the case of the latter.

[18] See, for example, Panglaykim, 1983, p. 77. In Singapore, such schools have often been set up upon request from the host Government.

history of industrial conflict must be an important consideration in the choice of location. They also note that in depressed peripheral areas workers tend to be more open to solidarity appeals and "personalistic" style of business.

Timing of investment and the nature of the product may also be relevant. In the United States, Japanese automobile manufacturers are considered to have been more successful than electrical appliance manufacturers in simplifying job classification, increasing job flexibility and rotating workers through different jobs. In the manufacturing of colour television sets, for example, workers' duties are less varied and simpler than those in the automobile industry, so that the companies probably had less incentive to experiment on Japanese managerial practices which might cause frictions with their employees. Second, electrical appliance manufacturers were among the earliest Japanese investors in the United States, and they had to be more cautious in applying Japanese systems. Once they started with non-Japanese systems, however, it was not easy to switch to Japanese practices. Third, the workforce in electrical companies was socio-culturally mixed, while the automobile manufacturers are located in areas with more homogeneous inhabitants (ISS, 1990). Evidence of strong support from the workforce of Japanese management practices is limited, so far.

Table 5.5 reveals a very low rate of unionization of workers at Japanese affiliates, although the rate was slightly higher in the manufacturing sector. These rates however should be kept in perspective: the national rate of unionization of American workers was only 16.8 per cent in 1988, as compared with 46.9 per cent in the United Kingdom (1987), 40.9 per cent in Germany and 26.8 per cent in Japan.[19] Where workers are unionized, agreements are usually secured to enlarge the management's degree of freedom in modifying the production method and standards, job rotation, QC circle activity, etc. (Aoyama, 1988). For the purpose of labour-management "harmonization", a Japanese-style consultation system is set up. Where workers are not organized, close communications are maintained by various means (e.g. hot lines with workers' representatives, regular opinion surveys and meetings, bulletin boards, newsletters, and provision of production information for the team leaders) so that issues can be taken up by the management instead of a union (Ishii, 1990).

According to the US General Accounting Office, whether unionized or not, wages and benefits at Japanese-affiliated automobile firms are similar to those at other unionized auto plants (Lawrence, 1990, p. 17). This is consistent with Dunning's report from the United Kingdom. In that country, company-based representative bodies are set up for consultation, either to substitute for unions or to supplement each other: of a total of 20 companies examined by different authors, eight companies had both, four had a union but no representative body, and three companies had just a representative body (Oliver and Wilkinson, p. 129).

A no-lay-off commitment is sometimes made in writing, e.g., that the firm will not lay off workers unless compelled to do so by economic conditions and financial circumstances so severe that its long-term financial viability is threatened (Lawrence, 1990, pp. 17-19). During the business recession in the early 1990s, however, a number of wholly or partially Japanese-owned producers and distributors had

[19] Rôdôshô (Ministry of Labour): *Rôdô Tôkei Yôran* (Summary of Labour Statistics) for 1990, p. 228.

Table 5.5.   Unionization of workers at Japanese affiliates by region, FY 1989

Region/sector		No. of respondents	% of total respondents			
			Unionized		Sign of unionization	No sign of unionization
			No dispute	Disputes		
North America	(A)	1397	7.6	0.6	1.3	90.6
	(M)	492	16.5	1.0	2.0	80.5
Europe	(A)	809	14.1	1.0	1.9	83.1
	(M)	236	31.4	2.5	1.7	64.4
	(M)	49	36.7	12.2	0	51.0
Asia	(A)	1673	18.2	2.5	2.5	76.9
	(M)	1002	26.3	3.9	3.4	66.4
	(M)	128	38.3	15.6	2.3	43.8
Africa	(A)	40	7.5	20.0	2.5	70.0
	(M)	9	0	33.3	0	66.7
Middle East	(A)	32	6.3	3.1	0	90.6
	(M)	9	22.2	11.1	0	66.7

Note: "A" and "M" stand for "all sectors" and "manufacturing", respectively.

Source: MITI's *4th Basic Survey Report*, pp. 456-461.

to lay off some of their workers. Some cases of plant closure resulting in dismissal have also been reported. We will come back to this subject in section 5 below.

Japanese firms may stick to their no-lay-off rule more firmly in developing countries. Even at the expense of profitability, they sometimes try to maintain their workforce. An extreme case is a bearing manufacturer in Thailand who avoided lay-off during the recession of 1985-86 by diverting redundant workers to QC education, weeding of the factory site, goodwill visits to Thai army and police stations in the border areas, etc. (ML Expert Committee, 1990). Such behaviour may be motivated by different considerations. In most Third World countries lay-off and dismissals are restricted or forbidden by law. Where qualified workers are scarce, firms naturally tend to retain them during a recession. They may also try to contribute to economic welfare of the host developing nation.

4.2 Diffusion among local firms

The literature tends to give the impression that Japanese ODI is having a fairly noticeable impact on industrial relations and managerial practices in host economies. Oliver and Wilkinson (1988, pp. 142-249) report that after Toshiba and the EETPU agreed on the "strike-free" package in 1981, other newly investing firms followed the example. By the end of 1987, 28 companies were known to have similar agreements: nine Japanese, three American and 12 British companies. These agreements typically provide for most or all of the following: an emphasis on cooperation and common purpose, denying a conflict of interest between employer and employee; binding arbitration; extensive labour flexibility; the harmonization of terms and conditions; the establishment of company representative boards independent of the trade union; and sole recognition of the signing union. As regards manufacturing systems of Japanese firms, the same authors argue that their presence has made their practices "more highly visible, and existing companies in the UK are frequently pointing to these companies as models to be emulated" and that "there is strong evidence of the Japanization process at the level of individual companies" (pp. 134 and 159). They cite Rolls-Royce (aero-engines), Wedgwood Potteries and Jaguar Cars as particularly successful emulators, while Ford is considered to be the most successful among the US companies (Womack et al., 1990).

American authors are sometimes quite positive about the impact of Japanese FDIs. After a survey of literature, Lawrence (1990) argues:

> The new approaches to production technology, buyer-supplier relations and labor-management practices introduced by the foreign-affiliated automakers into their own operations are being diffused to their Big Three competitors. By engaging in joint ventures, US producers have not only learned valuable lessons about building small cars, but also important lessons about labor-management relations [...] the Japanese emphasis on training has given US workers valuable new skills and experience. Their emphasis on collaborative relationships with suppliers has diffused Japanese know-how to US autoparts makers.

In a survey conducted towards the end of 1989, more than 90 per cent of the responding chief executive officers (CEOs) in the United States replied that the following Japanese managerial methods were being practised in US firms: (1) continuous training aimed at the development of *Tanôkô*, (2) management with a longer time horizon, and (3) a worker's rotation to different duty posts. Between 80 and 85 per cent felt similarly about (4) workers' participation in workshop level decision-making, and (5) close labour-management relationships. About 70 per cent felt positively about (6) teamwork and (7) managers' engagement in workshop-level duties, while (8) the company union was supported by about 55 per cent. In contrast, 92 per cent of the respondents were sceptical of the seniority pay/promotion systems. The lifetime employment system was unacceptable to 45 per cent, while 23 per cent considered it positive.[20]

Japanese authors tend to be rather cautious in their assessment of the impact of Japanese practices on local industries. They often argue that despite the popularity of literature such as Imai's *Kaizen*, the concept of total quality control (TQC) or companywide effort at quality and productivity improvements does little more than fostering the sense of participation in corporate management. For example, a Japanese who had been directly involved in the GM-Toyota joint venture NUMMI (New United Motors Manufacturing Inc.) reportedly conceded that the diffusion of lessons learned at the plant to other GM plants was minimal. Managerial staff who were sent from GM to NUMMI for learning did not like to put these ideas into practice (e.g. working *with* blue collars), while those who wanted to do so were

---

[20] *Nihon Keizai Shimbun*, 12 Feb. 1990, morning. The survey was conducted by Conference Board Co. in November and December 1989 on behalf of the Japanese newspaper company.

not given sufficient authority and workers did not follow. Workers appeared to be apprehensive and did not accept the concept readily, partly because GM continued to close plants and lay off workers.[21]

A major obstacle lies with the foremen and middle managers who owe their positions of power to the old system and are less important in the new system, which is more oriented towards the production workers: they feel threatened by Japanese systems such as the QC circle, teamwork and direct worker-management communication.[22]

The shop floor is not without its problems, either. It has been suggested that in the United Kingdom the concept of total quality control did not work, partly because of the lack of motivation and identification with the company, but also because of the low education level, e.g. lack of knowledge of simple maths (Aoyama, 1988). In the United States too, at a conference at Stanford University in March 1990, where the applicability of Japanese managerial practices was discussed, a few US participants argued that the fundamental problem facing American industries was often workers who were drug addicts and who lacked minimum educational standards.

4.3 Socio-cultural conflicts

An influx of massive foreign investment causes almost instinctive fear and discomfort in the host nation. In this respect, there appears to be little difference between Western nations' reaction to Japanese FDI today and the European reaction to American investment in the late 1960s (cf. Tugendhat, 1973, Chapter 1). This time, however, the situation tends to be aggravated by the incomparably larger cultural gap.

As we have seen, British and American authors found no basic difference in the behaviour of Japanese firms compared with that of firms from other countries. Differences observed are largely attributed to the age factor, or the length of experience in overseas operations. Indeed, criticisms against them sometimes go like this: "Very much like their British and American predecessors, Japanese multinationals always use their own suppliers and have their own nationals for top management" (Reed, 1989, p. 222). Dunning (1986) also notes the relevance of the choice of products and target market to the managerial style, such as the degree of centralization of management, although he does not entirely deny the influence of culture.

These scholars' views appear to be broadly shared by business people. In the already cited survey of 407 CEOs in the United States, 57 per cent of respondents felt there was little difference between Japanese investors' behaviour and US firms' investment behaviour abroad during the "strong dollar" period, while 30 per cent found some difference between the two. Significantly, however, as many as 77 per

---

[21] *Nihon Keizai Shimbun*, 6 May 1990, based on an interview with Mr. Azuma, former president of NUMMI.

[22] Shimada and MacDuffie, 1987, cited by Lawrence, 1990, p. 29; Aoyama, 1988, p. 55; Onglatco, 1988, pp. 108-109; and Dertouzos et al., 1989, p. 76.

cent conceded that there were criticisms of Japanese investors rooted in cultural difference, and just below 70 per cent feared that a further expansion of Japanese FDI might aggravate frictions between the two countries. Forty-six per cent feared that it might result in the outflow of US technologies crucial to national security, 42 per cent agreed that it might enlarge Japanese economic power in the United States excessively, and 41 per cent felt that the Japanese style management was disagreeable to Americans.

Reed (1989, p. 211) argues that "at the state level, relationships with the Japanese are overwhelmingly positive", while "at the national level, the alarmists dominate and the overall tone of the dialogue has been negative". The problem seems to arise partly from "expectation gaps" between those local policy-makers, industrialists and workers who are directly involved on the one hand and more remote observers on the other.

One example of this expectation gap concerns the transfer of technology and R&D programmes to developing countries. Multinationals usually take it that R&D can be organized only where more immediate business capabilities of operation and maintenance of the production facilities, manpower development, general management, etc., have already been prepared. In contrast, intellectuals and bureaucrats in host countries tend to insist that R&D can be treated separately and transferred immediately. Significantly, local industrialists do not necessarily share this view, presumably because they know the business better. In fact, the very concept of "technology transfer" is open to question: people in developing countries tend to interpret it as synonymous with the "localization of technical posts" (Panglaykim, 1983).

It may be also true, however, that such mixed reactions "suggest an interesting dichotomy between the relatively successful experience of technology transfer to production workers at the workshop and the somewhat problematical managerial, social, political and cultural interactions. While problematical reactions stem partly from specific characteristics of the American economy and society, the peculiar patterns of Japanese corporate behaviour are also responsible for misunderstandings and conflicts" (Shimada, 1989, p. 205). Much the same assessment has been made of Japanese investment in Indonesia (Panglaykim, 1983).

The pros and cons of Japanese managerial practices are neatly summarized in the following:

> The criticisms of Japanese practices centre on claims that they entail work intensification and heightened control by companies over their constituent agencies – their workers, their suppliers and so on. On the other hand the advocates of the Japanization of British industry point to its benefits in terms of business efficiency, and hence the competitiveness of British companies in world markets, arguing that British industry either becomes more competitive internationally or ceases to exist in a significant form. Both critics and advocates would probably agree on the question of work intensification [...] The advocates would probably argue that the benefits of Japanese-style personnel practices (where they exist) compensate for this intensification; the critics may be unconvinced of this. Where the two sides appear to have an unbridgeable gap is in their perspective on control [...] The critics view Japanese-style practices as insidious control devices, the most immoral of which are represented by strategies to elicit loyalty and commitment to the company. The advocates

see loyalty and commitment as desirable and morally acceptable on the grounds that everyone benefits in the long run. (Oliver and Wilkinson, 1988, p. 174).

There seems to be little doubt that the discomfort of US CEOs with Japanese management style is linked to the concept of "management-by-stress" with which Womack et al. (1990) associate the "lean production system" (p. 101). In addition, as we have seen, flexible manufacturing also threatens their authority.

Finally, there is a risk that social and cultural hostility towards the Japanese will result from the way the new management techniques are being presented. It is worth recalling that the management of many Western manufacturing companies were fully aware of the advantages of these new techniques for some time but could not introduce them because of resistance from their workforces. Now there appears to be a new resolve to reintroduce these new techniques by associating them with the competitiveness of Japanese industry and in this way legitimate them as the *sine qua non* for industrial success. As Graham (1988) explains:

> The myth of JIT allows organizational changes to be implemented as an imperative, claiming that they must be introduced to defeat foreign competition [...]
> The strength of this myth is demonstrated by trade unions' acceptance of the changes in work organization and industrial relations practices which underpin JIT manufacture, for example, binding arbitration in disputes [...] the continual linking in the mass media of "Japan" with "industrial competitiveness" leads each individual's understanding of "Japanese production management techniques" to converge on "efficient production management techniques, which must be applied in Western companies if they are to remain competitive". The adjective "Japanese" creates an imperative for introducing changes in working practices (p. 74).

To the extent the workforce in particular dislikes the changes thus imposed (for example, work intensification), socio-cultural conflicts with the Japanese – not just with affiliates – are likely to increase. This danger is all the more real because Western companies are not offering those elements of Japanese systems which should be more attractive to workers, that is, job security and egalitarian remuneration.

5. Conclusions

By virtue of the large scale of Japanese FDI in recent years and its somewhat exaggerated unique cultural features, psychological frictions and a certain degree of discomfort are likely to persist, particularly among Western hosts. On a less emotional level, the criticisms levelled at Japanese FDI in different parts of the world can be summarized as follows: (1) Japanese firms do not use local suppliers, relying on their suppliers from home; (2) they do not appoint locals to top management posts, filling them with Japanese; (3) Japanese plants are "screwdriver" operations, and high-tech and high value-added operations are kept at home; (4) Japanese firms will, sooner or later, take home the profits generated in the host country; and (5) Japanese FDI will lead to economic dominance and political influence.

The first two issues are particularly salient and are discussed below, as well as another which has received less attention – namely, the problem of motivating workforces abroad without the capacity to use typical Japanese incentives.

5.1 Development of local suppliers

In section 3 we discussed Japanese affiliates' problems in securing reliable local suppliers and suggested that, despite their more than average effort, their progress in increasing local procurements was slow. Their effort in this domain has become imperative, largely because of the pressure from host governments and societies. In the case of the automobile manufacturers operating in the United States, a target of 75 per cent has been set.[23] Ironically, the pressure on Japanese automobile companies is occurring at the same time as US automobile manufacturers, like Ford, are increasing their dependence on foreign manufactured parts (Lawrence, 1990).

One basic cause of the problem in the United States is that not many local firms are interested in changing their practices and facilities to accommodate Japanese users' needs. Frequently, United States suppliers are unwilling to do joint R&D to develop new or better components (Ishii, 1990). Indeed, the United States Government Accounting Office (US GAO), in referring to complaints made by US suppliers that drawings received from Japanese firms were "fundamentally different from United States auto-makers and difficult to read or interpret", criticizes United States car makers for not modifying their drawings or specifications for foreign suppliers.[24]

In Europe a similar reluctance to modify products to a potential Japanese clientele prevails. In Germany, for example, a local mouldmaker preferred to continue to produce moulds to its very high quality standards despite the fact that this meant that delivery was far slower and the products twice as expensive as in Japan and despite the fact that these high standards – targeted to produce 100,000 metal pieces – were not necessary for their Japanese users, who would have changed their product design much sooner (Suzuki, 1988).

Western companies' reluctance to accommodate Japanese users' needs may be explained by the lack of competition in Western industries. For example, there were 872,000 establishments in the manufacturing sector in Japan against 348,000 in the United States in the early 1980s,[25] when the overall scale of the United States economy was twice that of the Japanese economy. A seller's market climate permits suppliers to expect their clients to adjust their needs to supplies offered. As we noted earlier, some Japanese firms' R&D programmes abroad have been set up exactly to do this. In order to enable Japanese affiliates to increase their procurements from local suppliers substantially without sacrificing economic efficiency and consumers' welfare too much, the latter firms will need a sort of "attitudinal revolution" or "consciousness revolution", similar to what the Japanese underwent during the 1950s and 1960s prior to their technological modernization and organizational rationalization (Watanabe, 1983, Chapter 2).

[23] The concept of "local content" varies from one country to another, and even within a country. The United States Government has left it undefined, and its judgement in the early 1990s on Honda's cars has triggered off a dispute with the Governments of Canada and Japan.

[24] US GAO, 1988, cited in Wassman and Yamamura, 1989, pp. 135-140.

[25] Based on the *1981 Establishment Census of Japan* and the *1982 Census of Manufacturing* of the United States.

The attitude of Western firms may partly be explained by the recent origin of Japanese affiliates and by uncertainties about their growth. In the initial years of operation, Nissan Manufacturing of United Kingdom (NMUK) found out that local suppliers were reluctant to comply with its requests to extend their capacity, largely because they had doubts about the feasibility of NMUK's expansion plans. In the light of actual achievements, local suppliers began to cooperate more readily and following NMUK's suggestions some started to install experimental facilities and hire design personnel.[26] Other Japanese affiliates in the world are probably experiencing a similar situation. This being true, the problems associated with local procurement may decrease with time.

Nevertheless, several economic and institutional factors will continue to account for a different evolution in the patterns of subcontracting outside Japan, e.g. differences between Japan and the other countries as concerns wage differentials among different firm size groups, cost of land and buildings, small entrepreneurship and the general attitude towards community interests. In Western countries, in particular, the subcontracting systems are likely to remain characterized by a few hierarchical layers of "cooperative firms" (i.e. main manufacturers of components), subcontractors and subsubcontractors, instead of half a dozen as is usually the case in Japan. Intra-firm relationships are also likely to remain less close, which implies higher constraints on technological cooperation among firms (Watanabe, 1983, Chapter 2).

5.2 Using local staff

In earlier periods, British and American multinationals commonly used their own expatriate managers to fill top posts in their subsidiaries. In contrast, Japanese firms have been reducing the expatriate-local ratio at their overseas affiliates to the same level as in firms of other nationalities (cf. Sibunruang and Brimble, 1988). The sensitivity to this issue seems to be due to Japan's weaker political position which makes them less sure of themselves, and partly because they know that their globalization plans will be seriously constrained from the manpower side unless they do something to change the situation. Results from MITI's 3rd and 4th Basic Surveys show that the proportion of Japanese in the total managerial staff continued to decline in all regions since 1980. A number of factors encouraged this trend: (1) at relatively old affiliates, local workers have acquired experience sufficient for middle management posts; (2) the increasing relative cost of Japanese compared to local staff; (3) the lack of Japanese managers to support rapidly growing overseas operations; and (4) pressure to promote locals.

In the 4th Basic Survey, the global average rate of nationals filling directors' posts was 45 per cent in all sectors and 54 per cent in the manufacturing sectors. It was highest in the personnel and purchasing units (56 per cent each), followed by the sales and R&D units (52 per cent), the planning units (49 per cent) and the accounting units (45 per cent). In general, Japanese firms tend to entrust to compatriots those units where close and accurate communication and understanding are required with

---

[26] The present author's interview with NMUK purchasing officer in July 1992.

head office, whereas British nationals usually head those units where a full under-standing of the local language, culture, business customs and psychology, and commercial law is needed (Dunning, 1986).

In the same survey, the proportion of Japanese nationals occupying the post of CEO varied from 82 per cent in North America to 63 per cent in Asia, broadly corresponding to the proportion of wholly owned subsidiaries. Generally, it can be argued that recruitment of local staff to top posts in Japanese subsidiaries would have been higher without the existence of the peculiar Japanese "human network" management style and the barrier of the language – factors which encourage foreign firms in Japan to appoint locals to top management posts. In addition, Japanese companies are reluctant to sacrifice their high quality control standards by recruiting local managers with insufficient knowledge of and training in these practices. Experience of other Japanese companies in the US, for example Nissan's plant in Tennessee, which relied heavily on local managers, and other foreign companies – Volkswagen's poor performance in the US market and its reliance on locally recruited managers – have taught Japanese companies about the dangers of "the premature localization of top management".[27] Finally, Japanese companies' severe screening of potential managerial recruits and its long-term programme of in-house manpower development tend to reduce the supply of local candidates that can readily fill top management positions in Japanese affiliates. The "humanware strategy", the "company-wide quality control" and business procedures based on informal rules and mutual understanding demand, as necessary qualifications of a manager, a more thorough knowledge of the corporate system and a more extensive network of human connections than elsewhere.

In a survey by the EIBJ (1990), in which 247 Japanese firms with a total of 1,677 manufacturing affiliates participated, securing and training of local managerial and technical staff was felt to be a problem by 96 per cent of firms with affiliates in the ASEAN-4, 87 per cent in Europe and about 80 per cent in the Asian NIEs and in the United States.

As is clear from the above, experience does not necessarily support Western authors' argument that prompt localization of management and decentralization of R&D are necessary conditions of survival in international competition.[28] For the reasons mentioned above, however, Japanese multinationals are now endeavouring to accelerate managerial localization. While promoting communication between Japanese and non-Japanese staff inside and outside the home country by more frequent use of English, they are institutionalizing special career development schemes and personnel evaluation systems for non-Japanese employees. Staff members are exchanged between the head office and affiliates in order to familiarize themselves with the corporate culture and local conditions and to build up a "human network".

---

[27] ASEAN researchers have also found some empirical evidence to justify Japanese firms' cautious approach. In Malaysia, local managers were less interested in marketing, training and development of an information system than the Japanese (Kawabe, 1989, p. 18, citing a local study). In Jakarta, affiliates with a Japanese manager usually had fewer Japanese technicians, and labour productivity and annual turnover were usually higher than elsewhere (Waloeyo, 1989).

[28] See Reich (1991), for example. Regarding the danger of excessive decentralization of R&D programmes, the Japanese often refer to Philips, which used to be their model in international operations but suffered from a setback in the semiconductor market, in their view, for this reason.

Training courses are offered for overseas affiliates' managerial staff at different levels of corporate hierarchy.

In order to recruit and keep those professional workers who are not interested in long-term job security but in immediate remuneration for capabilities they possess already, an increasing number of companies are introducing a contract work system as an alternative to the conventional (implicit) lifetime employment, combined with the seniority pay and promotion system.[29]

Since the problem is rooted partly in cultural differences, such efforts by individual firms will need support from various sources, especially from educational institutions. It is encouraging that the number of foreign students in Japan is growing rapidly (partly because of disguised job hunters) and that Japanese language and culture courses have been introduced in the school curricula in a growing number of countries. It will certainly be in their own long-term interests if Japanese multinationals devote slightly larger portions of their annual revenue to support foreign students in Japan and to promote grass-roots level language and culture courses in host countries.

5.3 "Japanese practices" without the lifetime employment system?

Any production system will collapse without a built-in mechanism to motivate the "constituent agencies" properly, no matter how perfectly built up superficially. The "Japanese production system" without lifetime employment and egalitarian remuneration elements is a dead machine. It is a myth that Japanese workers are "devoted" to their company and work because of their cultural tradition. In a recent survey, 20 per cent of Japanese workers in their QC circle programme made the effort "because it is good for the company". The others were all motivated by longer-term economic benefits, notably "development of work capabilities", which would be essential for their promotion and pay increases. Of course, what was "good for the company" was also good for the worker, because his or her welfare was dependent on the company's prosperity. Such longer-term economic calculation is warranted by the lifetime employment, seniority pay and promotion, and egalitarian remuneration systems.[30]

Given its importance, it is unfortunate that "lifetime" employment is so difficult to transplant. The lifetime employment system (no lay-off rule, more correctly)

---

[29] This is meant to accommodate diverse work attitudes of not only non-Japanese but also younger Japanese workers. It is also to meet high-tech industries' rapidly changing manpower requirements. One may interpret the change as a new evolutionary step of the Japanese employment and pay systems. Interestingly, however, no one has so far opted for the new type of employment contract at Sony, which was among the earliest companies to diversify career/employment routes for the employees. A statement of Mr. Morita, Chairman of Sony, in *Nihon Keizai Shimbun*, 31 May 1992, p. 24.

[30] See Watanabe, 1991, for a detailed discussion on this subject. The egalitarian remuneration system is extremely important to workers' morale. The average annual gross earnings of Japanese company presidents were 5.7 times higher than those of ordinary workers in 1985, whereas board members of American companies earned, on average, 33.5 times more. Companies reduce their losses by cutting the directors' remuneration before the ordinary workers.

works in Japan because everyone observes it. If it was not universally respected in Japan, and some companies could lay off their workers during a recession while others could not, those businesses which did not reduce staff would quickly collapse.

It must also be pointed out that "lifetime employment" does not mean "lifetime career with the same employer". In Japan, redundancy is often absorbed by means of transfer to other firms belonging to the same company group or to other "friendly" (e.g. user) firms. Where Japanese firms do not have such allies, they cannot resort to this tactic. Another common solution for redundancy is early retirement with premium bonuses. Because Japanese affiliates are usually very young, the scope of this solution is also limited. For these reasons, too, it would be extremely difficult for Japanese affiliates to guarantee their employees against lay-offs. The problem is compounded by a more limited geographical and inter-occupational mobility of Western workers.

Japanese firms abroad will no doubt try to abide by the no-lay-off principle to the extent possible because this is part of their very basic corporate philosophy, but with limited feasibility. The main question facing these firms is how to motivate their workers and at the same time maintain efficiency. Similarly, Western firms' experiments with "Japanese practices" may help improve their efficiency to some extent, but they should not expect too much out of it unless they are prepared to reform their employment and profit-distribution practices so as to motivate their workers properly.

Appendix

Japanese statistics on foreign direct investment

1. The Ministry of Finance data on overseas direct investment

Direct investment is defined to be long-term capital investment aimed at participation in business management. In the absence of an objective indicator of such intention of the investor, his share in equity capital is used as a proxy: 25 per cent before November 1980 and 10 per cent thereafter, according to the official definition in Japan. It includes equity investment, long-term loans and expenditure for the establishment and expansion of branch offices, the last element being included in "other" item of the tertiary sector in table 5.1.

After the Second World War Japan resumed its ODI in 1951. At first all the investment projects were subject to approval by the Ministry of Finance. From October 1969 onwards, however, its control was reduced in a number of steps. In December 1980, in principle, ODI became free except in some specified industries and countries, provided that every investment project exceeding a certain amount be reported to the Minister of Finance via the Bank of Japan within two months before the investment is made either in its totality or in part. If he finds any problem, the Minister can recommend or order a revision or cancellation of the project within 20 days of receipt of the report.

Apart from a number of specifically designated industries and trades, the cut-off point for reporting was 3 million yen between December 1980 and March 1984 and 10 million yen between April 1984 and June 1989. In July 1989 it was raised to 30 million yen, where it has remained since.

On the basis of this reporting system, the Ministry of Finance publishes statistics on Japanese ODI with respect to each fiscal year (FY), ending on 31 March. This database does not take account of possibilities of scaling down or non-implementation of a reported project, nor of withdrawals of invested capital. There is also some time lag, as reported investment may be carried out in a number of instalments. This implies possibilities of overstating the reality. On the other hand, the database tells nothing about the reinvestment of profits by already established affiliates and investments below the legally specified amounts mentioned above. Despite all these shortcomings, the database is commonly used for a quantitative analysis of Japanese ODI, as this is the most detailed official information.

2. MITI's annual and basic surveys on overseas business activities

In FY 1970, the Ministry of International Trade and Industry (MITI) launched an annual questionnaire survey on Japanese firms' overseas business activities. Since FY 1980 this survey has been replaced by a more comprehensive "Basic Survey" once every three years. In the text, these surveys are referred to as "MITI Survey" and "MITI's Basic Survey", respectively. *The 19th Survey Report* (for FY 1988) and *The 3rd and 4th Basic Survey Reports* (for FY 1986 and FY 1989) are particularly useful for our study, containing far wider and more detailed information than earlier reports. Unfortunately, however, considerable year-to-year fluctuations in the response ratio and changes in the sample forbid intertemporal comparison of their findings.

For these surveys MITI each year establishes a list of Japanese firms with overseas affiliates on the basis of the reporting system of the Ministry of Finance, eliminating non-respondents in previous years and adding those firms which had set up an overseas affiliate for the first time during the previous fiscal year. A questionnaire form is sent to each of the listed firms. The number of recipients of the questionnaire form increased from 1,100 to 1,600 in the early 1970s to over 3,000 by the mid-1970s and to over 3,500 by the late 1980s. Generally speaking, the response ratio is lower in a Basic Survey because the questionnaire is more comprehensive: 33.4 per cent in the 3rd Basic Survey and 50.2 per cent in the 19th Survey. It is also much lower among smaller firms than among major companies. As the number of affiliates tends to rise with the size of the investing firm, the coverage of affiliates is much higher than the response ratio: 64.4 per cent in the 3rd Basic Survey (4,579 out of 7,112 listed firms) and 78.8 per cent in the 19th Survey (7,544 out of 9,576). It was 72.3 per cent in the 4th Basic Survey (6,362 out of 8,804). In order to improve the response ratio, the sample was selected more carefully, which explains the reduction in the sample size and in the number of respondents. Partly because of the higher coverage and partly because of greater availability of related statistics in host countries, our analysis is sometimes based on the 19th Survey, rather than on the latest 4th Basic Survey.

Bibliography

Abegglen, James C. and Stalk, George Jr., in *Kaisha, the Japanese corporation* (New York, Basic Books), 1985.

Altshuler, Alan; Anderson, Martin; Jones, Daniel; Roos, Daniel; Womack, James: *The future of the automobile* (London, George Allen & Unwin), 1984.

Aoyama, Shigeki: "Nihon Kigyô no Takokuseki-ka to Koyô-Rôdô Mondai: 'Nihon-teki Keiei' no Tekiyô Mondai o chûshin ni (Japanese firms' multinationalization, employment and labour, with special reference to the applicability of 'Japanese-style management')", in Magazine *Keizai* (ed.): *Nihon Kigyô Kaigai Shinshutsu no Jittai* (Actual conditions of Japanese firms' overseas investment) (Tokyo, Shin Nihon Shuppan), 1988.

Conseil économique et social, the Government of France: "Le devenir de l'industrie française de l'automobile", Session de 1984, Séances des 12 et 13 juin 1984, in *Journal Officiel de la République Française*, 17 Aug. 1984.

Dertouzos, Michael L.; Lester, Richard K.; Solow, Robert M. and the MIT Commission on Industrial Productivity: *Made in America: Regaining the productive edge* (Cambridge, Massachusetts, MIT Press), 1989.

Dunning, John H.: "Decision-making structures in US and Japanese manufacturing affiliates in the UK: Some similarities and contrasts", Multinational Enterprises Programme Working Paper No. 41 (Geneva, ILO), 1986.

EIAJ (Nihon Denshi Kikai Kôgyôkai (Electronic Industries Association of Japan)), in *Kaigai Seisan Hôjin List* (A list of Japanese corporations manufacturing abroad) for 1989 (Tokyo), Oct. 1989.

EIBJ (Export and Import Bank of Japan), Research Institute of Overseas Investment (Nihon Yushutsunyû Ginkô, Kaigai Tôshi Kenkyûjo): "Kaigai Tôshi no Kyû-kakudai to Gurôbaru Keiei no Shinten (Rapid growth of overseas investment and the development of global management: A survey report)", in *Kaigai Tôshi Kenkyûjo-hô* (Bulletin of the Research Institute), Jan. 1990.

Graham, Edward M.; Krugman, Paul R.: *Foreign direct investment in the United States* (Washington, DC, Institute for International Economics), 1989.

Graham, Ian: "Japanization as mythology", in *Industrial Relations Journal*, Spring 1988.

Howenstine, Ned G.: "US affiliates of foreign companies: 1987 benchmark survey results", in *Survey of Current Business*, July 1989.

Imai, Masaaki, in *Kaizen: The key to Japan's competitive success* (New York, Random House Business Division), 1986.

Ishii, Shoji: "Hokubei ni okeru Nikkei Jidôsha Sangyô no Genchika Senryaku (Localization strategies of Japanese-owned automobile manufacturers in North America)", in *Kaigai Tôshi Kenkyûjo-hô* (Japan Export-Import Bank, Tokyo), Feb. 1990.

ISS (Institute of Social Science, University of Tokyo): *Local production of Japanese automobile and electronics firms in the United States: The "application" and "adaptation" of Japanese-style management*, ISS Reseach Report No. 3 (Tokyo), Mar. 1990.

JETRO, in *Kaigai Chokusetsu Tôshi* (Overseas Direct Investments) (Tokyo), 1990a.

—. *Hong Kong, ASEAN no Nikkei Kigyô Jittai Chôsa* (A survey of Japanese manufacturing firms in Hong Kong and ASEAN) (Tokyo), Mar. 1990b.

—. *Zai-ô-Nikkei Seizôgyô Keiei no Jittai* (A survey of Japanese manufacturing firms in Europe) for 1990, 1990c.

—. *Zai-bei Nikkei Seizôgyô Keiei no Jittai* (A survey of Japanese manufacturing firms in the United States) for 1990, 1990d.

Kawabe, Nobuo: "Japanese business in a plural society: The case of Malaysia", a paper presented at the Hiroshima Conference: *Beyond Japanese-style management in ASEAN countries: Assessments and adaptations*, Hiroshima, 12-13 October 1989.

Kiyota, Kenichi: "Technology transfer through recruitment and training: The case of US, Japanese and Mexican *maquiladoras*", a thesis presented to the Faculty of San Diego State University, Spring 1988.

Kojima, Kiyoshi: *Direct foreign investment: A Japanese model of multinational business operations* (London, Croom Helm), 1978.

—. *Nihon no Kaigai Chokusetsu Tôshi: Keizaigakuteki Sekkin* (Japanese overseas direct investment: An economic analysis) (Tokyo, Bunshindo), 1985.

Kojima, Kiyoshi; Ozawa, Terumoto: *Japan's general trading companies: Merchants of economic development* (Paris, OECD Development Centre), 1984.

Kujawa, Duane: *Japanese multinationals in the United States: Case studies* (New York, Praeger), 1986.

Kume, Gorôta: "Keiei no Gurôbaru-ka to Tôshisakikoku e no Kôken (The globalization of Japanese firms and their contributions to the host countries)", in *EIBJ Kaigai Tôshi Kenkyûjo, Chokusetsu Tôshi no Kyûzô to Keiei no Gurôbaruka* (Rapid growth of overseas direct investment and the globalization of Japanese firms) (Tokyo), 1990.

Lawrence, Robert Z.: "Foreign-affiliated automakers in the United States: An appraisal" (Washington, DC, The Brookings Institution), Mar. 1990.

Ministry of Finance: "Taigai Chokusetsu Tôshi (Overseas direct investment)", in *Zaisei Kinyû Tôkei Geppô* (Monthly bulletin of fiscal and financial statistics), Dec. 1989.

MITI (Ministry of International Trade and Industry), in *Daisankai Kaigai Jigyô Katsudô Kihon Chôsa: Kaigai Tôshi Tôkei Sôran* (The 3rd Basic Survey on Japanese firms' overseas business activities: Comprehensive statistics on overseas investment) (Tokyo, Keibun Shuppan), 1989.

—. *Dai-19-kai Waga Kuni Kigyô no Kaigai Jigyô Katsudô* (The 19th survey on overseas business activities by Japanese firms) (Tokyo, Ministry of Finance, Printing Office), 1990.

—. *Daiyonkai Kaigai Jigyô Katsudô Kihon Chôsa: Kaigai Tôshi Tôkei Sôran* (The 4th Basic Survey on Japanese firms' overseas business activities: Comprehensive statistics on overseas investment) (Tokyo, Keibun Shuppan), 1991.

ML Expert Committee (Ministry of Labour, Ajia Shinshutsu Kigyô Semmon Iinkai (Expert Committee on Japanese affiliates in Asia), in *Ajia Shinshutsu Kigyô Semmon Iinkai Hôkokusho* (A committee report), Mar. 1990.

Oda, Teruaki: "Chûshô Kigyô no EC Shinshutsu no Kanôsei o saguru (On the feasibility of small and medium-sized enterprises' investment in EC)", in *Geppô* (Monthly Bulletin) of Small Business Finance Corporation of Japan, June 1990.

Oliver, N.; Wilkinson, B: *The Japanization of British industry* (Oxford, Basil Blackwell), 1988.

Onglatco, Mary Lou Uy: *Japanese quality control circles: Features, effects and problems* (Tokyo, Asian Productivity Organization), 1988.

Ozawa, Terumoto: "Japan in a new phase of multinationalism and industrial upgrading: Functional integration of trade, growth and FDI", in *Journal of World Trade*, Feb. 1991.

Panglaykim, J.: *Japanese direct investment in ASEAN; The Indonesian experience* (Singapore, Maruzen Asia), 1983.

Phongpaichit, Pasuk: "Japan's investment and local capital in ASEAN: Post '85 era", a paper presented at the Hiroshima Conference cited under Kawabe, 1989.

Reed, Steven R.: "Japanese in the American South", in Yamamura, 1989.

Reich, Robert B.: "Who is them?", in *Harvard Business Review*, Mar.-Apr., 1991.

Shimada, Haruo: "Japanese management of auto production in the United States: An overview of humanware technology", in Yamamura, 1989.

Shimada, Haruo; McDuffie, John Paul: "Industrial relations and 'humanware'", briefing paper for the First Policy Forum MIT, mimeo., 1987.

Shook, Robert L.: *Honda: An American success story* (New York, Prentice Hall Press), 1988.

Sibunruang, Atchaka; Brimble, Peter: "The employment effects of manufacturing multinational enterprises in Thailand", Multinational Enterprises Programme Working Paper No. 54 (Geneva, ILO), 1988.

Suzuki, Akio: "Oshû ni okeru Nihon Kigyô no Genchi Seisan (Manufacturing activities by Japanese firms in Europe)", in Magazine *Keizai* cited under Aoyama, 1988.

Takamiya, Makoto: "Conclusions and policy implications", in Susumu Takamiya and Keith Thurley (eds.): *Japan's emerging multinationals* (Tokyo, University of Tokyo Press), 1985.

Takaoka, Hirofumi: "Nihon no Tai-bei Seizôgyô Tôshi no Genjô to sono Impakuto (Japanese investment in US manufacturing industries and its impact", in *Kaigai Tôshi Kenkyôjo-hô*, July, 1990.

Tokunaga, Shôjirô: "Nihon no Chokusetsu Tôshi to Tai Kôgyôka (Japanese ODI and the industrialization of the Thai economy)", Part 2, in *Keizaigaku Kenkyû* (Kyûshû Daigaku), Vol. 55, No. 3, 1990.

Toyo Keizai Inc.: *Kaigai Shinshutsu Kigyô Sôran 1990* (A compendium of firms with overseas direct investment for 1990), a special issue of *Shûkan* (weekly) Toyo Keizai (Tokyo), 1990a.

—. *Gyôshu-betsu Kaigai Shinshutsu Kigyô* (Firms with overseas direct investment by line of business) for 1990, a special issue of *Shûkan* (weekly), Toyo Keizai (Tokyo), 1990b.

Tugendhat, Christopher: *The multinationals* (London, Penguin Books), 1973.

US GAO (United States General Accounting Office): *Foreign investment: Growing Japanese presence in the US auto industry*, NSIAD-88-111. Mar. 1988.

Vernon, Raymond: "International investment and international trade in the product cycle", in *Quarterly Journal of Economics*, Feb. 1966.

Waloeyo, Doddy B.: "The role of Japanese private enterprises in ASEAN; Indonesia's case", a paper presented at the Hiroshima Conference cited under Kawabe, 1989.

Wassmann, Ulrike; Yamamura, Kozo: "Do Japanese firms behave differently? The effects of Keiretsu in the United States", in Yamamura, 1989.

Watanabe, Susumu (ed.): *Technology, marketing and industrialization: Linkages between large and small enterprises* (Delhi, Macmillan India), 1983.

—. "Labour-saving versus work-amplifying effects of micro-electronics", in *International Labour Review*, May-June 1986.

— (ed): *Microelectronics, automation and employment in the automobile industry* (Chichester, John Wiley), 1987.

—. "The Japanese quality control circle: Why it works", in *International Labour Review*, No. 1, 1991.

— (ed.): *Microelectronics and Third World industries: Employment, trade and "catching up"* (London, Macmillan), 1992.

Womack, James P.; Jones, Daniel T.; Roos, Daniel: *The machine that changed the world* (New York, Rawson Associates), 1990.

Wong, Kar-Yiu: "The Japanese challenge: Japanese direct investment in the United States", in Yamamura, 1989.

Yamamura, Kozo (ed.): *Japanese investment in the United States: Should we be concerned?* (Seattle, Society for Japanese Studies), 1989.

Yamashita, Shoichi: "Economic development of ASEAN and the role of Japanese direct investment", a paper presented at the Hiroshima Conference cited under Kawabe, 1989.

Yamashita, Shoichi; Takeuchi, Jôzen; Kawabe, Nobuo; Takehana, Seiji: "ASEAN Shokoku ni okeru Nihon-gata Keiei to Gijutsu Iten ni kansuru Keieisha no Ishiki Chôsa – Tai, Indonesia, Malaysia, Singapore no Yonka-koku Hikaku o Chûshin ni (A consciousness survey of managers on the Japanese-style management and technology transfer in ASEAN countries, with special reference to Thailand, Indonesia, Malaysia and Singapore), in *Nempô Keizaigaku* (Economic annals of the Faculty of Economics, Hiroshima University), Mar. 1989.

Yokota, K.: "Trade policies and employment in Thailand", unpublished term paper from MA programme, Thammasat University, 1987.

Yuge, Noriyasu: "1990-nendo no waga Kuni no Kaigai Chokusetsu Tôshi Dôkô Sokuhô (Preliminary report on trends of Japanese ODI in FY 1990)", in *Kaigai Tôshi Kenkyûjo-hô* (EIBJ), July 1991.

Part 2

Regional trends

6

Local sourcing and indirect employment: Multinational enterprises in northern Mexico

Noe Aron Fuentes F., Tito Alegria, Jeffery T. Brannon, Dilmus D. James and G. William Lucker

1. Introduction

In 1965 Mexico decided to take advantage of provisions in the United States Tariff Code and began encouraging the establishment of export-manufacturing processing and assembly activities along a 20 kilometre strip of her northern border adjacent to the United States. Known locally as *maquiladoras*,[1] the plants are permitted to import inputs into Mexico duty free, with only the value-added in Mexico subject to a customs tariff when the final product is exported to the United States. Most plants located in the border region are foreign owned. As we will see, the programme has enjoyed remarkable expansion. Today Mexico can claim to be the largest offshore production centre in the world, from which the nation earns more foreign exchange than any other industry except petroleum.

This chapter will highlight the indirect employment generated from purchases of locally made inputs by the *maquiladoras*. Our emphasis is on production facilities owned by foreign enterprises located in the northern border region, but those located in the interior will not be ignored entirely. Mexico was chosen as a case study for several reasons. First Mexico, like many other developing nations, has a dire need to create productive jobs. Second, economic policy is undergoing a sea change moving from an inward-looking, state-directed, import-substitution-industrializing strategy to a more liberalized, outward-oriented approach. New measures include the dismantling of a vast system of import licence requirements, tariff reductions, privatization of state-owned enterprises, and a relaxation of regulations governing the inflow of technology and direct foreign investment. Third, after 25 years of treating the *maquila* industry as an appendage or enclave, Mexico is making a concerted effort to integrate this important sector into the general economy.

Typically, any single economic activity creates employment indirectly in a variety of ways (see figure 6.1),[2] and in this respect *maquila* production is no excep-

---

[1] We will use *maquiladora(s)* when referring to a plant or plants involved in the programme and *maquila* when referring to the programme in general.

[2] Also see Jéquier (1989).

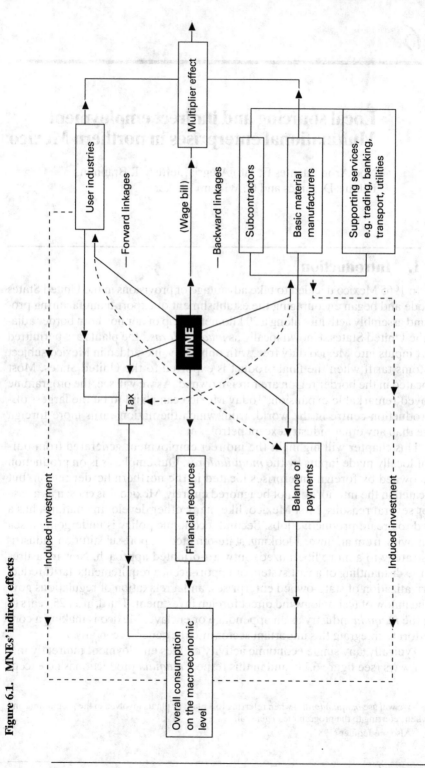

Figure 6.1. MNEs' indirect effects

tion. Some employment effects are rather weak. For example, internal forward linkages are negligible in Mexico because very little *maquila* output is sold inside the country.[3] Another instance of the impact of *maquila* production is the tax revenues paid by the *maquila* industry – which, aside from social security contributions and a 5 per cent levy on wages (earmarked for government construction of housing), are usually very low (Martinez, et al., 1988; Baker, 1989). Undoubtedly many other elements shown in figure 6.1 are significant. One would suspect that backward investment linkages, including expenditure on constructing industrial parks that often house *maquiladoras*, and investment in transport and warehousing infrastructure to support the industry, have a powerful employment effect.

Although we will present a global estimate of the indirect employment effects due to *maquila* workers spending their salaries and more detailed information on the impact of Mexican services supplied to *maquiladoras*, our study emphasizes a single avenue for promoting indirect employment. We focus on indirect employment from sales of Mexican material inputs to *maquiladoras* for three reasons: first, the proportion of Mexican content is extremely low compared with some other countries hosting significant amounts of offshore production; second, assuming policy measures can foster a higher Mexican-produced content, there is a latent opportunity for multiplying indirect employment associated with supplying *maquiladoras*; and third, increased employment is not the sole benefit that would attend an expanded network of subcontracting and other forms of local sourcing. Healthy backward linkages from *maquiladoras* to small and medium-sized Mexican suppliers would conserve foreign exchange, contribute to government revenues and, if competitive, increase efficiency. Furthermore, there is a less appreciated advantage of forging more robust linkages between local suppliers and producers of final products: small and medium-sized enterprises can serve as repositories for accumulating local technological capabilities and, not uncommonly, significant technical learning flows from the more sophisticated sourcing firm to the supplier.[4] In short, local-sourcing arrangements not only elevate levels of employment; there is an added dimension comprised of skill acquisition, heightened managerial know-how and upgraded technology, all of which lead to rising labour productivity.

The study relies heavily on three investigations conducted recently by various researchers at El Colegio de la Frontera Norte (COLEF) and the University of Texas at El Paso (UTEP): (1) the "Brannon/Lucker study", a survey of *maquila* workers in Cd. Juarez, (2) the "COLEF/UTEP study", a survey of *maquiladora* plant managers and chief purchasing officers of parent firms, and (3) the "Alegria study", an analysis estimating the amount of indirect employment in Mexico attributable to purchases made by *maquiladoras*.

---

[3] Currently, plants can market up to 50 per cent of their exports (which means up to one-third of their output) in Mexico, but there are a number of conditions that must be satisfied and most enterprises do not take advantage of the internal market.

[4] A typical observation is: "These backward linkages with local suppliers are known to be a potentially very important channel of technology transfer from foreign to domestic firms, as well as a major instrument for building up and developing the technological competence of domestic enterprises" (ILO/UNCTC, 1988).

Section 2 describes how Mexico's *maquila* industry has grown and evolved, while section 3 focuses on recent changes in the workforce employed by *maquiladoras*. Section 4 looks at the extent of Mexican-produced material inputs purchased by the plants; estimates of indirect employment generated by plant purchases made in Mexico are provided in section 5. Recent measures by the Mexican Government affecting *maquila* operations, including specific regulations targeting the *maquila* and macroeconomic policies that will have an indirect effect, are presented in section 6. Section 7 provides a summary and suggestions as to how Mexico might achieve a higher level of sales of Mexican-produced material inputs to *maquiladoras*.

2. Evolution of the Mexican *Maquila* Programme

The *maquila* industry began in 1965 as part of Mexico's Border Industrialization Programme (BIP). It operated under existing regulations through an exchange of ministerial memoranda until 1972 when provisions were entered. Basically the programme took advantage of Items 807.00 and 806.30 of the United States Tariff Code.[5] The former refers to a product, whose components originate in the United States, that is assembled abroad and is exported, in final form, to the United States. The latter applies to an American metal product having its form altered abroad and re-exported to the United States for further processing. Inputs for *maquila* production can enter Mexico duty free and United States content is not subject to American tariffs when the product is imported from Mexico.[6]

Mexico's motives included the need to increase employment after the end of the *Bracero* programme, which had permitted Mexican labourers into the United States to work, on a temporary basis, on American farms. Other objectives were to increase incomes in the border region, create a skilled labour force and incorporate Mexican inputs into the production process. As we shall see, some of these goals have been fulfilled more effectively than others.

As the international division of labour began to take shape, and a "global factory" became a reality, Mexico increasingly came to be regarded as an attractive location for offshore production. The country's political stability and proximity to the large United States market were factors. Also, from its beginnings when many customs disputes had to be decided on an ad hoc and time-consuming basis, there gradually arose rules of the game, both officially stated and informal, that were understood on both sides of the border. Repeated efforts reduced customs and other bureaucratic delays and impediments to doing business. Both the Mexican Government and private investors established industrial parks earmarked for *maquiladoras*. The parks simplified and shortened the gestation period for initiating production and, since the land and buildings could be rented, fixed costs of participating enterprises were

[5] The nomenclature has recently been changed to the Harmonized Tariff Schedule 9802.00.60 and 9802.00.80.

[6] Only a skeletal outline of the development of the *maquila* programme can be presented here. Readers will find useful Baerresen (1971) on its origin; Bustamante (1975) and Dillman (1975) for early development; and Grunwald (1985), Gonzalez-Arechiga and Barajas Escamilla (1989) and Sklair (1989) for more contemporary treatment.

Table 6.1. *Maquila* plants, employment, value added and exports, 1966-90

Year	No. of plants	Employment (thousands)	Value added (millions of US dollars)	Exports
1966	12	3.0		
1970	120	20.3		
1970	454	67.2		
1980	620	123.9		
1981	608	130.1		
1982	588	122.5		
1983	629	173.2		
1984	722	202.1		
1985	789	217.5	1 227.2	5 093.3
1986	987	268.4	1 294.5	5 645.9
1987	1 259	322.7	1 598.1	7 105.0
1988	1 490	389.2	2 337.4	10 145.7
1989	1 795	443.7		
1990	1 977			

Sources: INEGI, Estadística de la *Maquiladora de Exportación* (various issues); INEGI (1990); and USITC (1990).

reduced considerably. The programme received a valuable boost in recognition and prestige when, in 1968, RCA set up a plant in Cd. Juarez to manufacture yokes and high-voltage transformers for television sets (Barrio, 1988). In the early 1970s the first *maquiladoras* with Asian ownership appeared. In 1972 the Government allowed assembly firms to go beyond the stipulated strip along the northern border and locate in many parts of the Mexican interior.

As the data in table 6.1 indicate, Mexico's *maquila* industry has enjoyed vigorous growth in both employment and number of plants. Employment rose at an annual rate of 13.8 per cent annually from 1970 to 1985 (Gonzalez-Arechiga and Ramirez, 1989) and from 1986 to 1989 it grew by an additional 87.8 per cent. Looked at differently, *maquila* employment increased sixfold during the 1970s and well over threefold during the 1980s. The number of plants multiplied by 500 per cent during the 1970s and in excess of 300 per cent from 1980 to 1989.

This record may seem astonishing in view of the dismal performance of the Mexican economy in the 1980s, especially since 1982. Per capita gross domestic output fell from US$ 2,290 in 1981 to $ 1,954 in 1989 (measured in 1988 dollars) (IDB, 1990). *Maquila* sales, which were less than 3 per cent of Mexico's manufacturing output in 1980, had risen to almost 11 per cent by 1989 (Banco Nacional de Mexico, 1990).[7] The connection between a booming *maquila* and suffering economy seems less mysterious when it is considered that the Mexican real wage rate in 1980 began

[7] Parenthetically, Mexico does not treat her *maquila* industry as manufacturing in her balance of payments – rather they are treated as "transformation services". There may be plans under way to change the accounting taxonomy and move it to the manufacturing sector like the four "superexporters" of East Asia. Naturally, the current account balance would be unaffected, but the impact on the merchandise trade balance would not be trivial – instead of a US$ 645 million deficit in 1989, there would have been a $ 2.4 billion surplus (Banco Nacional de Mexico, 1990).

Table 6.2. **Value added by the** *maquila* **industry – product category, 1985 and 1988**
(millions of US dollars)

Product	1985	% of total	1988	% of total	% of change 1985-88
Food processing	10.3	0.8	23.3	1.0	126.2
Textiles, apparel	87.2	6.9	127.7	5.5	46.4
Shoes, leather goods	20.9	1.6	28.2	1.2	35.0
Furniture	49.9	3.9	126.5	5.4	153.5
Chemical products	1.8	—	18.3	0.8	916.6
Transport equipment	329.5	26.0	596.3	25.5	81.0
Equipment, tools, non-electric	20.3	1.6	37.3	1.6	83.7
Electrical, electronic machinery, equipment	240.5	19.0	382.1	16.3	58.9
Electrical, electronic materials, accessories	326.8	25.8	585.8	25.1	79.3
Toys, sports goods	39.6	3.1	66.4	2.8	—
Other manufacturing	88.1	7.0	282.9	12.1	67.7
Services	52.4	4.2	62.7	2.7	221.0
National total	1 267.2	100.0	2 337.4	100.0	19.7

Sources: Ministry of Programming and Budget; Bank of Mexico.

to fall sharply from 1980. Wages, including benefits, in the *maquila* industry in September 1989 were US$ 1.80 per hour. This undercut wages in offshore production in countries or territories like Taiwan, China ($ 3.71), the Republic of Korea ($ 2.94), Hong Kong ($ 2.48) and Singapore ($ 2.25) (ibid.).

Despite some episodic ups and downs, the expansion over the last 25 years has been impressive. However, mere quantification of the gains registered in employment, number of plants, value-added and export earnings fail to reveal some important evolutionary changes that have taken place within the programme. For example there has been a considerable flux in the product composition of *maquila* output. Grunwald captures the major shifts from 1969 to 1980 well:

> As the variety (of products) has increased, the composition of the product mix has changed. Textile products (including apparel), toys and dolls, and similar simple light industry constituted a fourth of all *maquila* output in 1969, but in 1981 they accounted for only a twelfth. Television receivers and parts, by far the most important single product group in Mexican assembly operations, now make up about a quarter of the total. Semiconductors and parts, which, with more than 16 per cent of the total, were almost as important as the television group in 1969, accounted for less than 6 per cent in 1980. Motor vehicle parts were not a significant assembly product in 1969, but in recent years they have occupied between the third and seventh place in order of importance of Mexico's *maquila* operations (Grunwald, 1985, p. 146).

During the early 1980s little change took place in the product mix because of the slow growth of the *maquila* programme, but the dynamism of recent years is well illustrated in table 6.2. Although from 1985 to 1988 there was little alteration in the rank order (not shown) of product group in value added, there were some significant shifts in proportions. Chemical products went from a negligible proportion to 8 per cent, and chemicals, other manufactures, furniture and food processing grew notably faster than the average, while services, shoes and leather goods, textiles and apparel, and electrical machinery shrank as a percentage of total value added.

There are good reasons to believe that *maquila* plants are becoming more capital-intensive. Several observers claim that there is a definite trend towards capital intensity for plants using more sophisticated technologies, and there is solid evidence that many *maquiladoras* are adopting modern technology.[8] Employment per plant has been rising. In the 1970-88 period, the average number of workers per plant increased from 170 to 260. In isolation this does not imply greater capital intensity, but it does when coupled with technological upgrading and a trend of industrial composition towards higher-technology products. Electronic products, for example, require larger-sized plants than, say, furniture manufacturing (Stoddard, 1987). The most convincing evidence is that, over the last decade, new capital requirements per additional job has been climbing by 4.4 per cent annually (Gonzalez-Arechiga and Ramirez, 1989). Therefore, we can say with some confidence that the capital/labour ratio is increasing, but only surmise that the capital/output ratio is moving in the same direction.

The pattern of national ownership and control is very difficult to pin down precisely. First, different gradations, from minority to total ownerships, are permissible. Second, there are "sheltered" *maquiladoras*, which are wholly owned by Mexican capital, but managed and operated by foreign, usually American, interests. Third, sometimes a *maquiladora* will be owned by an American firm which is, in turn, owned by an enterprise in another country – this is particularly common with Dutch and Japanese *maquiladoras*.

Some reports on ownership for the late 1970s are contradictory (Grunwald, 1985), but one with data that appear reasonable put foreign ownership of plants at 48 per cent, 95 per cent of which was American. The proportion of fixed investment by American interests at that time was probably much higher – one source said 90 per cent.[9] The situation in 1988 is shown in table 6.3. Perhaps the most notable trend in the 1980s is the decline in Mexican/United States participation and the appearance of Japan, and other Asian and European countries. Mexican participation in *maquiladoras* has always been much higher in the interior of the country.[10]

---

[8] See Palomares and Mertens (1987), Dominguez-Villalobos (1988) and Shaiken (1990).

[9] Grunwald (1985, pp. 149-150) cites Calderon (1981) and a table submitted by the Secretaria de Hacienda y Credito Publico to the Second Seminar on North-South Complementary Intra-Industry Trade sponsored by UNCTAD and the Brookings Institution, Mexico City, 18-22 August 1980.

[10] See Calderon (1981) for 1978 and Wilson (1990) for the current situation regarding Mexican *maquiladoras* in the interior.

Table 6.3.   Equity and investment in Mexico's *maquila* industry, 1988

Owner	No. of plants	%	Fixed investment[a] (in US$ million)	%
United States[a]	834	56.0	7 645	78.0
Mexico	566	38.0	1 450	15.0
Japan[a]	48	3.2	385	3.9
Joint ventures[b]	21	1.4	130	1.3
Others[c]	21	1.4	170	1.8
TOTAL	1 490	100.0	9 800	100.0

[a] Majority to 100 per cent ownership.   [b] Majority Mexican ownership.   [c] Includes companies from the Republic of Korea, the United Kingdom, France, the Netherlands, Spain, Sweden, the Federal Republic of Germany, Finland, Czechoslovakia, Brazil and Taiwan, China.

Source: Lee (1989).

3.   Changing characteristics of the *maquila* workforce

Over the past ten years or so the workforce in the *maquila* programme has undergone some important changes. We will concentrate on *obreros*, as opposed to technical and administrative personnel. Gender and geographic origin are featured, while worker turnover and skill profiles – the latter including a look at *técnicos* and engineers as well as *obreros* – are also examined.

Because individual firms and the industry had a highly elastic labour supply, conditions were quite favourable for *maquila* operations prior to 1983. Plants that cared to do so could be selective in hiring workers. *Maquiladora* managers showed a decided hiring preference for young, single females who were first-time entrants to the labour force. In view of the favourable labour supply conditions, employers could screen out, for the most part, men, older women, and recent arrivals to the border area. In 1982, females comprised almost 80 per cent of *obreros*.

After 1982, the most important benefit to the *maquila* industry was a sharp decline in dollar-denominated wage rates. The decline was brought about by the progressive depreciation of the Mexican peso in combination with a conservative Mexican Government wage policy. Government-determined increases in the benchmark minimum wage have lagged well behind the inflation rate. The real purchasing power of peso wages have fallen approximately 50 per cent since 1982. While this has proved a blessing to *maquila* operations in terms of wage costs, the labour markets along the border are considerably tighter due to the booming industry, which was, in large part, driven by these cost considerations.

Why, in the pre-1983 period, were young, single women preferred as workers? At the outset it should be noted that this practice has not been unique to the Mexican *maquila* industry. World-wide, a large percentage of workers employed by multinational corporations which produce for export in developing countries are unmarried females less than 25 years old (Grunwald and Flamm, 1985, p. 226; ILO/UNCTC, 1988, pp. 62-65). Women are often thought to be more dexterous than males and better suited for tasks requiring repetitive, discrete movements of the hands (ILO/UNCTC, 1988). In addition there are some who believe that they are more docile and submissive to authority, willing to work for lower wages, and less likely to be influenced by labour union organizers (Carrillo and Hernandez, 1982).

Evidently the pre-1983 minimum wages prevailing along the northern Mexico border were above the market clearing wages for females, thereby creating an excess supply of labour. Queues existed for available jobs and worker turnover rates were relatively low. Young females were attracted away from school and home production by manufacturing wages that probably far exceeded their opportunity costs. As long as the supply of labour with the preferred characteristics exceeded demand, the highly elastic labour supply for this segment of the labour market permitted *maquiladora* managers to be highly selective.

The *maquila* industry's reaction to tightening labour markets from 1983 to the present has been a multiple one. In order to prevent wages from spiralling far above the minimum, firms have been forced to alter their hiring criteria to include large numbers of previously excluded (or highly screened) segments of the labour force. They have also expanded non-wage benefits and tolerated higher turnover rates. Importantly, firms have sought interior locations where labour market conditions are more favourable. Finally, economic distress has quickened the flow of job-seekers to the border. The combination of these factors has allowed the labour supply to accommodate rapidly growing demands under conditions of first falling, and then stagnant, real wages.

Firms' decisions to relax their hiring criteria to adapt to tightening labour market conditions are most apparent in the relative growth of the male component of the labour force (see table 6.4). Despite managers' professed preference for female employees, the number of male workers grew almost two-and-a-half times faster than female workers after 1982. By December 1987, 34 per cent of *maquila obreros* in Mexico were men, compared to 22.7 per cent at the end of 1982. The rate of growth of male *obreros* in border *maquiladoras* was considerably higher than for interior locations (INEGI, 1988).

The labour turnover rate for a sample of about one-third of the assembly firms in Cd. Juarez for a 17-month period during 1987 and 1988 revealed that the monthly rate varied from a low of 5.28 per cent of the workforce to a high of 12.47 per cent. According to the Asociación de Maquiladora, A.C. (1988), this is roughly double the rate for border plants in 1982. Why should the already high incidence of labour turnover in 1982 go even higher? Increasing worker difficulties with transport, housing and child care are often cited. Also, the ease with which a worker can find another job in the industry encourages voluntary separation, often for minor reasons.

In our view, the conservative minimum wage policy coupled with monopsonistic behaviour of the *maquila* industry, whereby the minimum wage becomes a benchmark for a wage ceiling, has caused it to drift below worker compensation needed for market clearing. This accounts for the "shortage" of labour on the border. This condition does not prevail in interior locations where relatively large pools of available labour still exist because of lower female participation rates, fewer formal job opportunities and higher levels of unemployment and underemployment. Thus, a major attraction of interior locations is the opportunity to reduce hidden labour costs such as turnover, as well as to lower explicit costs.

Table 6.4. Mexico's *maquiladora obrero* workforce: Number of workers and gender composition, 1975-86

Year	Total obrero employees	Male obreros	% of total	Female obreros	% of total
1975	57 850	12 575	21.7	45 275	78.3
1976	64 670	13 686	21.2	50 984	78.8
1977	68 187	14 999	22.0	53 188	78.0
1978	78 570	18 205	23.2	60 365	76.8
1979	95 818	21 981	22.9	73 837	77.1
1980	102 020	23 140	22.7	78 880	77.3
1981	110 684	24 993	22.6	85 691	77.4
1982	105 383	23 990	22.8	81 393	77.2
1983	125 278	32 004	25.6	93 274	74.4
1984	165 505	48 215	29.1	117 290	70.9
1985	173 874	53 832	31.0	120 042	69.0
1986	203 894	64 812	31.8	139 082	68.2
1987[a]	262 000	90 800	34.7	171 200	65.3

[a] The 1987 data is for the month of December. It is unclear from the data source for the 1975-86 period whether the figures are year-end or a yearly average.

Sources: Instituto Nacional de Estadística, Geografía e Informática (INEGI), *Estadística de la industria maquiladora de exportación* 1975-86 (Mexico, 1988); idem: *Avance de información económica, industria maquiladora de exportación* (Mexico, June 1988).

Available evidence suggests that migrants to the border region have been another important source of labour supply to *maquiladoras* since 1982. Surveys of workers in Cd. Juarez by Fernandez-Kelly (1983) and Seligson and Williams (1981) conducted prior to 1982 revealed that 20 per cent or less of the respondents had lived in Juarez for five or fewer years. Carrillo and Hernandez (1982) interviewed 246 female workers who had migrated to Juarez and found that 21 per cent of those arriving from rural areas had been in the city for five years or less.

In 1987 the Brannon and Lucker study surveyed 200 *maquila* workers, evenly divided by gender; 36 per cent had lived in Juarez for five years or less. The 50-worker all-migrant study that Brannon and Lucker carried out in 1988 showed that 81 per cent had resided in Juarez for five years or less. George (1987) reported that 42 per cent of workers interviewed in his study had lived in that city for a similar period (see table 6.5).

According to Van Wass (1981, pp. 206-207), plants in Nuevo Laredo had "no set policy" on hiring migrants, but in Juarez few of the plants he visited recruited very recent arrivals. Further, he found that firms commonly "draw on the migrant pool only after a lag of one or two years after their arrival in the city". Until they had at least that much continuous residence in Juarez, their background and employment stability were open to question. In stark contrast, the 1988 Brannon and Lucker study found that male and female migrants to Juarez, on average, found work with a *maquiladora* in eight days and 11 days, respectively.

Table 6.5. Surveys of *maquila* workers

	Post-1983 surveys					Pre-1983 and 1983 surveys						
	Brannon and Lucker, 1988 N = 50		Brannon and Lucker, 1987 N = 200		George, 1986 N = 225	Fernandez-Kelly, 1983 N = 510		Seligson and Williams, 1981 N < 100		Carillo and Hernandez, 1982 N = 476		
	Male	Female	Male	Female	Male and female	Electric/electronic	Apparel	Male	Female	Electronics	Services	Apparel
Age	26.3	27.7	20.5	21.5	26.0	20[c]	26	25.2[c]	23.8	19	22	21
Marital status												
Married	40.9	36.0	22.0	22.0	42.0	39.0	46.0	31.0	35.1	33.0 (all industries)		
Single	54.5	40.0	73.0	72.0	53.0+			43.6	48.5			
Other[a] (percentage)	4.6	24.0	5.0	6.0								
Education (percentage with 6 years or less)	37	39	45.5[b]	52	29	41	67			46		
Birthplace (percentage)												
Cd. Juarez	95.5	0	44.0	44.0	55.0	41.0	27.0	30.1[d]		41		
Other cities in Chihuahua	4.5	20.0	23.0	17.0	25.0	29.5	27.7	36.8		59.0 (other cities in Chihuahua and other states)		
Other states	0	80.0	33.0	39.0	20.0	29.5	45.3	33.1				

[a] Includes those workers classified as divorced, widowed, separated and living in free union. [b] Percentage of total with eight years or less education. [c] Median age.

[d] Birthplace data for Seligson and Williams study include both males and females.

We know of no adequate study that sheds light on the change, if any, in the skill profiles of direct labour, or *obreros*. If, however, we examine the *maquila* workforce as a whole, there is little doubt that the skill level has been rising. The proportion of "technical workers", comprised of *técnicos* and engineers, represented 8 per cent of the *maquila* workforce in 1979 and 13 per cent in 1988. In the largest Mexican industrial park for assembly plants, which is operated in Cd. Juarez by Grupo Bermudez, the proportion of total employment of technical workers was 26 per cent in 1988 (Vargas and Williams, 1989). The park is comprised mainly of plants producing electric or electronic and automotive products.

This changing composition of *maquila* employment is driven by the adoption of new technologies associated with a greater degree of automation. In 1986, Mertens interviewed 35 *maquiladoras* that exported electronic products and found that 11 were using programmable equipment (Palomares and Mertens, 1987). Shaiken (1990) describes three electronics *maquiladoras* using modern technology and with productivities reputedly above similar plants in the United States. In 1987, Dominguez-Villalobos (1988) interviewed 20 large electronic, electrical and automotive plants in Cd. Juarez that accounted for about a quarter of *maquila* employment in that city. Twelve of the plants used a total of 286 micro-electronic machines, about half of which were robots (mainly for assembling electronic components). Computer numerical controlled machines were employed for a variety of activities, including moulding, welding, plastic forming and programming.

The trend towards more automation leads to increasing reliance on *técnicos* and engineers. Palomares and Mertens found that for 24 *maquiladoras* not employing programmable equipment, production, testing and maintenance *técnicos* constituted 8 per cent of employment (omitting administrative personnel) compared to 12.4 per cent for those using the modern equipment. The figures for engineers were 1.9 per cent and 4.6 per cent respectively. Dominguez-Villalobos (1988) reports that from 1984 to 1986, employment of engineers increased by 33.2 per cent for the eight firms using micro-electronic innovations, compared to 3.5 per cent for the 12 non-using firms. Once again, whether there is any systematic direction towards skill acquisition among *obreros*, we are unable to say.

---

4. Mexican material inputs

Very little Mexican content goes into *maquila* production. In fact, it has not amounted to 2 per cent of total purchases of material inputs during the 1980s and actually dipped below 1 per cent in 1985.[11] Roughly half of the Mexican-supplied material inputs come from the interior and the other half from the border region. Mexico's national content is considerably below that of other major centres of offshore production. In the late 1970s, the national content of the Republic of Korea was 33 per cent and that of Taiwan, China, stood at 27 per cent (Spinanger, 1984). Certainly differences in past economic and political experiences of Mexico vis-à-vis

---

[11] For data on Mexican-supplied inputs to the *maquila* industry from 1976 to 1983, see Grunwald (1985, p. 162); Banco Nacional de Comercio Exterior (1988, p. 873) provides data for 1980-87.

the Far East have something to do with the disparity (Wilson, 1990), as do differences in transport costs. Still, the gulf in terms of the proportion of national inputs seems inordinately wide. Since *maquila* production is dominated by multinational enterprises, one wonders why local sourcing is so low, because other studies report that subcontracting by multinational affiliates in developing countries is quite common (Halbach, 1989; Wright, 1990).

When inquiring about the paucity of Mexican-supplied inputs, three reasons will inevitably surface: high prices, inadequate quality and unpredictable delivery (Dobken, 1989; IMMM, 1989); yet this merely begs the question – why cannot these obstacles be overcome? If Mexico can increase her exports of manufactured goods, which do not include *maquila* exports, from US$ 2,234 million (15 per cent of total exports) in 1980 to $ 9,744 million (47 per cent of total exports) in 1987, why cannot Mexican entrepreneurs participate more fully in what is often referred to as "indirect exports", or sales to *maquiladoras*? Some argue that the Mexican business community has become accustomed to relying on the domestic market after years of following an inward-looking import-substitution-industrialization model of development. Another claim is that Mexican merchants shun high-volume, low-price marketing in favour of demanding a high price per unit on a low volume of sales. These arguments, however, run up against the same problem – they fit poorly with Mexico's ability to export manufactured goods.

There are numerous other explanations of which two are noteworthy – cost factors and purchasing decisions.[12] In purely economic terms, the Mexican supplier has faced three disadvantages in competing with American firms. First, until recently, Mexican inputs purchased by *maquiladoras* were subject to a 15 per cent value-added tax. Second, suppliers from both countries pay duties levied by their respective countries on most imported inputs. Typically, Mexican suppliers will acquire a higher proportion of their raw materials, semi-finished inputs, spare parts and equipment abroad and will, on average, pay higher duties than their American counterparts. Third, the cost of Mexican inputs count as part of the value added in that country and, as such, is subject to tariffs of the importing country. Santiago Ibarreche (1990) has estimated that the combined disadvantage of these three factors amount to about 40 per cent of the cost incurred in producing an item. Undoubtedly this gap would widen further if the higher interest rates borne by Mexican businesses were included in the equation. Some Mexican suppliers might enjoy an advantage in transport costs in selling to *maquiladoras*, but seldom can it predominate over the handicaps just enumerated.

There have been several studies of *maquiladora* purchasing practices,[13] but as far as we know, only the COLEF/UTEP study made an empirical investigation looking at differences in attitudes by purchasing authorities and relating them to sourcing practices in northern Mexico.

---

[12] For a more lengthy and inclusive exploration of why Mexican-supplied inputs are so skimpy, see Brannon, et al. (1990), a work which also has a more complete and detailed exposition of findings from the COLEF/UTEP study.

[13] See Patrick and Arriola (1987), Institute for Manufacturing and Materials Management (1989); McCray and Groff (1990), and South (1990).

The COLEF/UTEP investigation found that about 59 per cent of plant managers either had complete freedom to purchase, or could normally expect to have their requests approved by their home offices. The remaining 41 per cent were allowed to do no purchasing, or had difficulty getting approval for plant-level buying. This is important, because our findings indicate that corporate purchasing officers, compared to plant managers:

(a) *have a less favourable opinion about Mexican-made inputs*: one-fifth of head-office purchasing officers held negative views regarding Mexican suppliers or their products compared to only 1.7 per cent of plant managers;

(b) *are less likely to buy Mexican inputs*: 40 per cent of *maquiladoras* with no power to purchase or having difficulty in garnering home office approval were using Mexican inputs compared to 64 per cent of those with complete freedom or normal approval of purchase plans;

(c) *are less assiduous in soliciting Mexican suppliers*: about 64 per cent of enterprise headquarters frequently or occasionally sought out Mexican suppliers compared to 71.5 per cent of *maquiladora* managers.

In all likelihood, the barrier to local sourcing represented by purchasing practices of *maquiladoras* and their corporate headquarters has been considerably underestimated.[14] These patterns will be very difficult to alter. Like all institutional arrangements, the authority to purchase carries with it status and power along with a vested interest in maintaining these advantages. There are substantial transaction costs in actively seeking out suppliers in an unfamiliar environment, while abandoning comfortable ties with established vendors.[15] McCray and Groff report that *maquiladoras* whose parents maintain complete or tight control over purchasing often test and evaluate products of a potential supplier at corporate headquarters; one plant manager said that his corporation tested products for two years before making a decision (1990, pp. 35-36).

There is one more finding from the COLEF/UTEP investigation – a disturbing one – that should be added. Most products sourced by *maquiladoras* in Mexico are low value-added products and, as opposed to many of the *maquila* products themselves, require very little technological sophistication. The picture is bleaker still when we focus on the border region where products supplied were virtually devoid of any requirement for modern technology or design skills.[16] *Maquiladoras* are much less likely to source high or middle-tech items in Mexico (Diaz, 1990) and even less likely to do so in the northern border area.

---

[14] For example the Institute for Manufacturing and Materials Management (1989) study found no evidence that location of purchaser influenced the decision of what and where to buy.

[15] Octavio Diaz (1990), Procurement Manager in charge of Honeywell's Mexico International Procurement Office, provides useful insights into purchasing behaviour, as do McCray and Groff (1990).

[16] For the northern border carton boxes and packing materials were the most frequently cited purchases – others included shop supplies, pallets, solvents, gases, small tools, printing, office supplies, sponges, cleaning supplies, lubricants, wax, furniture, lumber, particle board, wooden mouldings, uniforms and thread.

Table 6.6. Survey results: Sourcing of Mexican inputs, 1989

	(1) Ciudad Juarez		(2) Chihuahua		(3) Tijuana		(4) Mexicali		(5) Total personal interview		(6) Total mailing		(7) Total (5 + 6)	
	#	%	#	%	#	%	#	%	#	%	#	%	#	%
Freedom to purchase locally:														
1. Complete freedom	6	30.0	3	30.0	12	41.4	3	50.0	24	36.9	18	50.0	42	41.0
2. Requests to purchase locally usually honoured by home office	9	45.0	1	10.0	2	6.9	2	33.3	14	21.5	13	36.1	27	26.0
3. Difficult to convince home office to purchase locally	0	0.0	1	10.0	2	6.9	0	0.0	3	4.6	n.a.	n.a.	3	3.0
4. Home office makes all purchasing decisions	5	25.0	5	50.0	13	44.8	1	16.7	24	36.9	5	13.9	29	28.0
TOTAL	20	100.0	10	100.0	29	100.0	6	100.0	65	99.9	36	100.0	101	100.0
Do you currently purchase material inputs in Mexico?														
1. Yes	12	57.1	5	45.5	15	51.7	4	66.7	36	53.7	26	70.3	62	59.0
2. No	9	42.9	6	54.5	14	48.3	2	33.3	31	46.3	11	29.7	42	40.0
TOTAL	21	100.0	11	100.0	29	100.0	6	100.0	67	100.0	37	100.0	104	100.0
How would you describe your actions in seeking local suppliers?														
1. Very actively seek	2	9.5	3	30.0	3	11.1	2	33.3	10	15.6	8	22.2	18	18.0
2. Occasionally seek	16	76.2	2	20.0	19	70.4	2	33.3	39	60.9	15	41.7	54	54.0
3. Virtually never seek	3	14.3	5	50.0	5	18.5	2	33.3	15	23.4	13	36.1	28	28.0
TOTAL	21	100.0	10	100.0	27	100.0	6	100.0	64	99.9	36	99.9	100	100.0

Source: COLEF/UTEP investigation.

5. Indirect employment

We can get a rough idea of the order of magnitude of indirect employment attributable to plant purchases of services and inputs from an investigation by Tito Alegria. Using a combination of official data published by government sources, unpublished government data and information collected by COLEF, Alegria was able to estimate the employment effect nationally and in each city hosting *maquiladoras*.[17]

Alegria used an input-output model comprised of the following sectors: (a) the *maquila*, (b) non-*maquila* manufacturing, (c) commercial activities, and (d) services. Spending by *maquiladoras* was divided into wages and salaries spent by employees, plant expenditures on services related to production and distribution, and plant purchases of material inputs. His results also incorporate the second "ripple" effects of spending of income by workers with jobs indirectly created by *maquila* operations. In 1989, of the *maquila* outlays totalling approximately US$ 2,500 million, the proportions were 61 per cent on wages and salaries, 33 per cent on services and 6 per cent on inputs.

These expenditures generated 514,516 jobs country-wide; 84 per cent by wage and salary expenditures, 15 per cent by purchases of services and only 1 per cent by purchases of inputs. Alegria has developed a separate model for estimating the impact of worker spending on indirect employment, but since these data are still being refined, nothing beyond this global estimate is presented here. We can, however, go into more detail regarding the other two categories. The direct employment of about 430,000 *maquila* employees in 1989 indirectly created 78,313 jobs in the service sector and 6,118 in the manufacturing sector.[18] Put differently, for every 200 jobs in the *maquila* industry, approximately 36 jobs are created in the service sector and three in the manufacturing sector.

Another model was applied to purchases of material inputs by *maquiladoras* the results of which are shown in table 6.7.

This direct-to-indirect employment multiplier changes according to the geographical zone being considered. The job multiplier for inputs is greater for the interior of Mexico than for the border region. This is probably due to the greater distance from the United States (the primary source for inputs) and the greater familiarity of *maquiladora* management with regional markets. In contrast, this differential multiplier effect does not apply to services because they are usually produced and consumed in the same location.

The employment multiplier for services and materials combined is one indirect job for every four *maquila* workers in the interior of Mexico, whereas the ratios are one-to-five for border cities and one-to-six for non-border cities in border states. The employment multiplier is most homogeneous among border cities, less similar

---

[17] The following sources were employed: Instituto Nacional de Estadística Geográfica e Informática (1980 and 1985), unpublished INEGI data on *maquiladoras* covering 1988 and 1989, Banco de Mexico (monthly) and COLEF (1987, 1988 and 1989).

[18] Since the 1985 census of services did not break down the data by municipalities, 1980 census data were used as a basis for calculating productivity in the service sector. To the extent that productivity has increased in this sector between 1980 and 1989, the figure for indirect employment creation due to purchases of services will be overstated.

Table 6.7. . Indirect employment generated by *maquila* purchases of Mexican services and inputs, 1989

Zones	Employment generated by zone (%)			Employment generated *maquila* employment (%)			Indirect employment as a proportion of					
							National			Within each zone		
	S	I	S+I	S	I	S+I	S	I	S+I	S	I	S+I
National	78 313	6 118	84 431	100	100	100	18.2	1.4	19.6	18.2	1.4	19.6
Border cities	63 760	3 288	67 048	81	54	80	14.8	0.8	15.6	19.0	1.0	20.0
Interior cities in border states	9 752	1 521	11 274	12	25	13	2.3	0.4	2.6	14.2	2.2	16.4
Interior cities	4 801	1 309	6 110	6	21	7	1.1	0.3	1.4	19.1	5.2	24.3

Note: S = services; I = inputs.

among cities away from the border, but within border states, and most heterogeneous among cities in the interior.

Among border cities, the ones with more *maquila* employment, which are the ones with the largest populations, generally have the highest job multipliers. Deviations from this tendency can emerge when: (a) the American "sister" metropolitan region, i.e., the one directly across the border, is larger than the Mexican counterpart, and (b) most production goes beyond simple assembly. In the former, competition from the American side dampens the multiplier, while in the latter the multiplier tends to be larger than average.

On balance, larger cities tend to have services with higher levels of efficiency, and in most of them, the manufacturing industry is more apt to supply inputs to the plants and/or have more adequate transport for moving inputs from other localities. Therefore the large urban size not only attracts more *maquiladoras*, but promotes the creation of more indirect jobs, thereby diversifying the local economy.

Clearly the most salient result from the analysis is the miniscule contribution to indirect employment creation due to *maquiladora*-sourcing of Mexican material inputs. This fact has not been lost on Mexican leaders. Moves are under way to integrate the *maquila* industry more fully into the economy-wide industrial sector.

6. Recent policy initiatives

The most concrete indication that Mexico is now determined to integrate *maquila* operations into her economy came in the form of a December 1989 decree, and official pronouncements made at a conference on *maquila* policy held on 9 March 1990 in Cd. Juarez.[19] The most important provisions of the decree (a) waived the value-added tax for inputs sold by Mexican enterprises to *maquiladoras,* (b) simplified rules governing transfer of equipment and supplies between *maquiladoras* or between a *maquiladora* and a supplier, and (c) increased the proportion of output that a plant can sell in Mexico, provided that several stipulations are met, to 50 per cent of a *maquiladora's* exports.[20]

Among the more important programmes announced at the 1990 conference were further simplification and streamlining of customs procedures; construction programmes geared towards improving transport, warehousing, communications and housing associated with *maquila* operations; and support for more industrial parks. Small and medium-sized enterprises that are potential *maquiladora* suppliers are to receive more credit on easier terms and are to be supported by various training programmes.

Furthermore, there have been notable shifts in macroeconomic policy. Regarding her trade regime, Mexico has systematically, and almost completely, dismantled her extensive system of import licence requirements, an accomplishment no doubt motivated by her entry into GATT in 1986. In 1983, import permits were

[19] "Respuesta del Sector Financiero al Desarrollo Integral de la Industria Maquiladora de Exportación y Proveedores". See Banco Nacional de Comercio Exterior (1990a) and Centro Bancario de Cd. Juarez (1990).

[20] See Banco Nacional de Mexico (1990b) and *Diario Oficial* (1989).

required for 8,459 tariff items; 8,117 of them had been eliminated by the end of 1987. By the end of 1988, licence requirements applied primarily to some agricultural products and products or inputs for the automobile, pharmaceutical, and computer industries (Pérez Núñez, 1990, p. 61). By early 1990 licences were required for only 230 items which applied to 7 per cent of American exports to Mexico (Sprinkle, 1990). Two other swipes at what little remained were taken when Mexico did away with import licences on computers and computer components (*Los Angeles Times*, 4 Apr. 1990) and import permits were eliminated on 46 of 80 inputs for the pharmaceutical industry. Licences on all pharmaceutical inputs are to be phased out by 1993 (*Financial Times*, 9 Feb. 1990).

Between 1983 and the end of 1987, Mexico had dropped her maximum tariff level from 100 to 20 per cent. Her average tariff, weighted by the value of imports, fell from 25.5 to 11 per cent from 1985 to 1988 (USITC, 1990).[21]

In addition to trade, Mexico has shown a liberalist tendency towards privatization and foreign investment. During the early part of the de la Madrid Presidency, the number of state-owned enterprises declined from 1,500 to 400. The programme was received with some scepticism because the vast majority of state entities that were abolished, merged or sold were small. Since then, however, large airline, steel, and chemical companies have been put up for sale, and a deal in excess of one billion dollars, involving foreign bidders, is under way for 20 per cent of Mexico's telephone system.

Indeed, privatization efforts have welcomed foreign capital. Foreigners probably already own around 25 per cent of Teléfonos de Mexico since it trades on the United States NASDAQ over-the-counter market in the form of American depository receipts.[22] Steps have been taken to denationalize Mexico's banking system, and again, foreign investors are being welcomed on board. In mid-1990, President Carlos Salinas de Gortari proposed legislation that would permit foreigners to own up to 30 per cent of banks and brokerage firms – for the latter this is the first time any foreign stake has been allowed.[23] In a move bound to shock those who remember the legal arguments surrounding the nationalization of Mexico's petroleum industry in 1938, Mexico has announced plans to privatize at least one-half of the country's state-owned mineral reserves during the next five years.[24] This cannot conceivably be accomplished without foreign participation.

In 1985, Mexico had an inflow of direct foreign investment that reached only about 5 per cent of her gross fixed investment, a share lower than any large country in the Western world (USITC, 1991). From 1986 onwards, however, Mexico's basic foreign investment law, passed in 1973, was interpreted more liberally and in the 1986-89 period direct foreign investment totalled US$ 11,930 million compared with $ 4,620 million during the previous four years. Further easing of investment practices took place in May 1989. The two most important changes were: (a) the opening of many

---

[21] Pérez Núñez (1990, p. 61) gives even lower figures. He claims that Mexico's average tariff, weighted by the value of imports, fell from 13.3 per cent in 1985 to 5.5 per cent in 1987 and that the weighted tariff dispersion around the mean went from 16.1 to 6.9 per cent during the same period.

[22] *Financial Times* (London), 18 June 1990.

[23] *Los Angeles Times*, 29 June 1990.

[24] *Financial Times* (London), 8 June 1990.

sectors of the economy, previously reserved for state and/or Mexican private capital (in the early 1990s, around 73 per cent of Mexico's economic production was open to 100 per cent foreign ownership) – one of the stipulations was that the investment be registered and approved by the National Commission on Foreign Investment, an autonomous arm of the Ministry of Trade and Industrial Development; and (b) a provision which could affect foreign subcontractors locating in Mexico and supplying *maquiladoras*: it is now possible for foreigners to have 100 per cent ownership in Mexico without the need to obtain approval. Authorization is automatic at the time of registration (1) if the initial fixed assets do not exceed US\$100 million, (2) if the funds come from abroad, (3) if, for industrial operations, they locate outside of Mexico City, Guadalajara and Monterrey, (4) if foreign exchange budgets are projected to be balanced within three years, (5) if the project involves the creation of permanent jobs and worker training and personnel development programmes are provided, and (6) technologies are compatible with environmental considerations (USITC, 1990).

In other areas of liberalization, in 1987, Mexico made important changes in its laws governing intellectual property rights by extending the lengths of patents; expanding the protection for new products, processes and trademarks; and giving trade secrets limited protection (USITC, 1990). Furthermore, in January 1990, Mexico softened its 1987 laws and announced that the nation will now abide by international standards in these matters. This removes a major impediment to both foreign investment and technology transfer. During the same month, Mexico eliminated ceiling rates for royalty payments for imported technology.[25] In addition, Mexico, the United States and Canada were taking serious steps to establish a North American Free Trade Agreement (NAFTA), under which *maquiladoras* will face "rules of the game" almost identical to regular direct foreign investment.[26] As to what this might mean for *maquiladora* operations along the northern Mexican border, there seem to be two views. Pessimists ask why prospective foreign investors would not look to interior locations where labour is more abundant and cheaper; technological capabilities are greater; domestic markets are larger and, although not without problems, infrastructure is more adequate. Others, however, point out that many firms prefer a border location because foreign (mainly American) executives can live in the United States, it is closer to the large United States market, communications with the parent enterprise is easier and it is nearer to activities such as plastic injection moulding, tool and die services and stamping operations on the United States side of the border.

We can say that two of the three economic disadvantages for Mexican suppliers vis-à-vis American competitors (mentioned in section 2 above) would be eliminated by the NAFTA. Mexican value added would not be subject to United States tariffs and a Mexican producer obliged to use more imported inputs would not suffer from import duties.[27] There is, however, no consensus on the broader, long-term repercussions of a Free Trade Agreement on *maquiladora* operations.

---

[25] *New York Times*, 11 Jan. 1990.

[26] " Indeed, the concept of the maquiladoras as distinct from other Mexican production facilities may cease to exist as the provisions of an FTA are implemented" (USITC, 1991, section 5, p. 5).

[27] As we have seen, the other disadvantage, a Mexican value-added tax, is now waived on sales to *maquiladoras*.

7. Summary and policy suggestions

The *maquila* industry is one of the most dynamic sectors of Mexico's economy and certainly is the spearhead of its northern region. Over the last 25 years secular growth has been striking. Product proliferation continues as does, for many establishments, the adoption of modern technology. Technical workers constitute a growing share of total *maquila* employment. Since the early 1980s, the proportion of male workers has been increasing, as has, in the northern region, the percentage of workers recently arriving from interior locations.

Indirect employment generated by wages spent by *maquiladora* personnel and by plant purchases of services has been significant. For a variety of reasons, however, the backward linkages from *maquiladoras* to Mexican-supplying enterprises have been anaemic. Furthermore, most Mexican inputs are not associated with sophisticated production techniques, and this is particularly true for the north. Only one job emerges indirectly for every 200 workers employed by *maquiladoras*. We have tried to make a convincing case that a more robust national content would entail beneficial externalities that go beyond the provision of productive job openings by fostering the accumulation of internal technological capabilities. Supplying enterprises constitute a locus for newly imparted (or generated) technical learning, and once a mutually satisfactory relationship is established, it is in the self-interest of the primary producer to assure the technological adequacy of its suppliers.

After an extended period of cavalier treatment, the Mexican authorities seem serious about incorporating the *maquila* sector into the nation's general drive towards industrialization. A series of recently instigated measures are targeted specifically at promoting *maquiladoras* and local suppliers. In addition, liberalization at the macroeconomic level appears to have improved the general economic climate for both domestic enterprise, returning Mexican flight capital and direct foreign investment. A NAFTA would give Mexican suppliers of inputs a more level playing field with foreign competition, but the ultimate effects on the *maquila* industry itself are in dispute.

Before suggesting how elevated levels of indirect employment can be forthcoming through expanded Mexican content, we might ask the question: What are reasonable expectations in this regard? The Banco Nacional de Mexico (1990), using an input-output matrix, estimated that Mexico's industrial growth between 1980 and 1989 would have been almost 27 per cent higher if the degree of integration of the *maquila* industry had equalled that achieved by non-*maquila* manufacturing. While constituting an interesting and informative simulation, the study does not, in our view, provide a realistic goal, except perhaps in the very long run. An often-repeated unofficial objective is to reach 5 to 10 per cent Mexican content over the next three years, a target which is more reasonable.

It is equally desirable to have realistic expectations as to benefits from greater integration of the *maquila* sector. In the border region, the vogue is to use an employment multiplier of two to two and a half. While the Alegria model may not have picked up all multiplier effects, certainly his more sophisticated approach leads us to believe that the employment multiplier for the *maquila* industry is somewhat below two. If we focus on the indirect employment associated with purchases of Mexican material inputs, if local sourcing rose to 5 to 10 per cent, as a conservative estimate, we can expect the generation of about 14,000 to 35,000 additional jobs. We reiterate, however, other gains aside from employment would accompany the strengthening of supplier linkages including saving of foreign exchange, higher tax revenues, and – as we have repeatedly stressed – the nurturing and strengthening of Mexican technological capacities. What can be done to attain greater integration?

Several strategies might have immediate impact: (1) promoting those items for which Mexico has a current comparative advantage (IMMM, 1989), (2) trying to attract plants that do their own purchasing (McCray and Groff, 1990), (3) recruiting vigorously those industries that use higher proportions of Mexican inputs, e.g., toys, (4) attracting Japanese firms that, anecdotally, are reputed to purchase more Mexican inputs (Darling, 1990), and (5) concentrating on the sale of Mexican services as well as material inputs (McCray and Groff, 1990). These are all meritorious and should be pursued, but we believe they will not get the complete job done – they are not sufficient to bring about sustained socio-economic development.

While current comparative advantage should not be ignored, the large potential gains lie in an evolutionary process whereby technology is upgraded and Mexican competitiveness encompasses a widening product mix. Policy-makers need to confront two decisions at the outset. First, is the objective to increase sales to *maquiladoras* nationally, or should a regional bias be included, aimed specifically at forging healthier supplier linkages in the border area? From the COLEF/UTEP and other surveys, it appears that *maquiladoras* in the north are technological enclaves. A priori it seems undesirable to have a broad geographic band with stunted endogenous technological abilities that is juxtaposed to a nation with enormous technical prowess. The second decision is the extent to which foreign suppliers located in Mexico are to be encouraged.[28] Will these suppliers merely extend the technological enclave one linkage backward, or can measures be taken to ensure that they contribute to national capacities?

Having made these observations we offer three concrete suggestions concerning (1) delivery dependability on the part of suppliers, (2) joint ventures for technology transfer and (3) the use of moral suasion.

As just-in-time supply and inventory practices become increasingly prevalent among *maquiladoras*, undependable delivery by Mexican suppliers becomes an overwhelming handicap. Yet, despite complaints about Mexican suppliers in this regard, we are aware of no studies that have attempted to determine the incidence of, and the reasons for, erratic delivery.[29] To what extent attitudes of Mexican subcontractors, financial difficulties, transport bottlenecks, or poor communication between sourcing and supplying enterprises play a part, no one knows. High priority should be placed on investigating the matter, as should corrective measures based on research results.

---

[28] Wilson (1990) observed that several Asian-owned suppliers have been established in the Tijuana area.

[29] Almost 14 per cent of both in-plant and home-office responses to the COLEF/UTEP survey gave "delivery takes too long" as one of the four main reasons for not purchasing supplies in Mexico.

Research by the United Nations Conference on Trade and Development (UNCTAD) in the early 1980s revealed that Third World enterprises interested in acquiring technology might find foreign small and medium-sized enterprises (SMEs) more attractive for entering into joint ventures vis-à-vis large multinationals. While SMEs can seldom organize and carry out large projects, UNCTAD's investigations found that SMEs, when compared to large multinationals, are more flexible both in decision-making and in production processes, have a greater propensity to procure material inputs locally, are more willing to sell specialized technical components or technologies rather than insisting on an investment package, are more amenable to engage in joint ventures, have less resistance to providing unpatented technology, are more willing to offer the latest technology and know-how, tend to have fewer restrictive clauses in agreements, are likely to offer more favourable terms regarding training of local employees, and have a greater propensity to offer better terms concerning improvements on the technology involved.[30]

As a second recommendation, we suggest that a series of workshops be conducted, each concentrating on specific "sister-city" regions, bringing together small and medium-sized manufacturing enterprises from both sides of the border. The purpose would be to encourage joint ventures for technology transfer. Aside from exchanging information on technologies needed and those available, workshops could provide practical guidelines for dealing with relevant legislation, regulations and administrative procedures involved in reaching an agreement and implementing its provisions.

It may be too naive to expect a wave of multinational enterprises (MNEs) with *maquila* operations to undertake voluntarily programmes assisting local suppliers, but some are likely to do so in an environment where it is clear that political "points" would accrue to such undertakings. Political persuasion could be complemented with studies that illustrate the economic gains that local sourcing can bring to firms within a reasonable time horizon. Examples of MNE assistance to Third World suppliers can be found all over the globe. Local affiliates of Philips have a wide range of assistance for approximately 1,600 local suppliers aimed at improving delivery times, bettering product quality, speeding product adaptation and decreasing inventory, among other goals. The parent firm assists suppliers with financial planning, negotiating new loans, accounting, R&D of new product lines, training, and purchase in large lots. Throughout much of Latin America, Sears and Roebuck has undertaken similar programmes. Exxon provided technical assistance to local spare parts suppliers in Argentina and helped solve product quality problems and, eventually, costs were reduced. These and many other examples can be found in a study by Wright (1990), the most comprehensive investigation on the topic to date.

These supplier-producer relationships are also found in Mexico. Shaiken reports on a non-*maquila* automobile assembly plant owned by a major American MNE that sources about 30 per cent of its parts in Mexico. The firm is, in general, very pleased with the relationships. "From the beginning, the company worked strenuously to impart to the suppliers its operating methods, particularly just-in-time

---

[30] For a review of UNCTAD's work and a complete bibliography of their related publications see Herbolzheimer and Ouane (1985).

inventory" (Shaiken, 1990, p. 41). Shaiken describes an MNE-owned computer man-ufacturer that has gone to some lengths to cultivate Mexican suppliers, initially because of local-content requirements placed on the computer industry, but now "this early impetus has been supplemented by a desire to lower costs and improve supply lines" (ibid., p. 114). In view of these cases, a healthy dose of governmental "jawboning", directed at *maquiladoras* and parent MNEs, might be warranted. We are not recommending compulsory local-content regulations for the *maquila* industry at this time, partly because it is very unlikely to be considered in the current climate of Mexican liberalization. However, we suggest that the possibility of initiating a moder-ate requirement be kept alive in order to render Mexican persuasion more effective.

One final set of observations: Mexico has initiated support measures for the *maquila* industry and/or Mexican suppliers featuring reduced bureaucratic impedi-ments, tax waivers, infrastructure, financing and training. We have three reservations regarding the newly emerging programmes: First, the obstacle of centralized pur-chasing by MNEs' headquarters should be weighed more heavily into the policy mix. This is a core, not a peripheral, issue. Second, the technological element in nurturing competitive Mexican suppliers is not proffered a central role, nor does there appear to be ample appreciation that backward linkages themselves can generate technical learning. When formulating and implementing measures for boosting local sourcing, the goal of elevating domestic technological capacities should be accorded equal weight with that of generating employment opportunities. Third, from the publicly available reports on the new drive to integrate the *maquila* sector more fully, it does not seem that there is sufficient recognition that the picture in the northern border region is especially disturbing, a situation that may justify, both politically and econ-omically, a regional dimension to integration policy.

To maximize socio-economic benefits, local sourcing must eventually look to an evolutionary process whereby the benefits of dynamic comparative advantage are captured and exploited. Reliance on low real wages as the primary competitive edge is not sufficient; increased productivity based on a steady progression of endogenous technological capacities is required. Increasing the number of jobs generated by the *maquila* sector goes hand in hand with a qualitative enhancement of worker skills, managerial know-how and entrepreneurial acumen in the Mexican supplying enter-prises. There is nothing intrinsically detrimental with selling *maquiladoras* wax, sol-vents or paper cups, so long as measures are pursued simultaneously that lead to a more fruitful constellation of products, processes and skills.

Bibliography

Asociación de Maquiladora, A.C. 1988. Mimeographed material supplied to one of the authors (Cd. Juarez).

Baerresen, Donald W. 1971. *The Border Industrialization Program of Mexico* (Lexington, D.C. Heath).

Baker, George. 1989. "Costos sociales e ingresos de la industria maquiladora", in *Comercio Exterior*, Vol. 39, No. 10, pp. 893-906.

Banco de México. Monthly-various issues. *Series mensuales de paridad cambiaria del peso frente al dolar*.

Banco Nacional de Comercio Exterior. 1988. "Maquiladoras: Más allá del empleo y las divisas", in *Comercio Exterior*, Vol. 38, No. 10, pp. 872-878.

—. 1990a. "Programa integral de Apoyo Financiero y Promocional para el Fomento del Comercio Exterior de Bienes y Servicios no Petróleos", in *Comercio Exterior*, Vol. 40, No. 3, pp. 199-211.

—. 1990b. "El sector financiero y las maquiladoras de exportación", in *Comercio Exterior*, Vol. 40, No. 4, pp. 318-319.

Banco Nacional de México. 1990. "In-bond industry", in *Review of the Economic Situation of Mexico*, Sep., pp. 454-461.

Barrio, Federico. 1988. "Historia y perspectivas de la industria maquiladora en México", in Thomas P. Lee (ed.): *In-bond industry/industria maquiladora*, pp. 7-9 (Mexico, D.F., ASI S.A., Banco Nacional de México and Asociación Mexicana de Parques Industriales Privados).

Brannon, Jeffery T.; Lucker, G. William. 1989. "The impact of Mexico's economic crisis on the demographic composition of the maquiladora labour force", in *Journal of Borderlands Studies*, 4:1 (Spring), pp. 39-70.

Brannon, Jeffery T.; James, Dilmus D.; Lucker, G. William. 1990. *"Purchase of Mexican-made material inputs by maquiladoras: Why is it so anemic and what can be done about it?"*, Paper, Association of Borderlands Scholars, Feb. (Tijuana, Baja California, Mexico).

Bustamante, Jorge A. 1975. "El programa fronterizo de maquiladoras: Observaciones para una evaluación", in *Foro Internacional*, Oct./Dec., pp. 149-174.

Calderon, Ernesto. 1981. "Las maquiladoras de los países centrales que operan en el Tercer Mundo", Lecturas de CEESTEM (Mexico, D.F., Centro de Estudios Economicós y Sociales del Tercer Mundo).

Carrillo Viveros, Jorge; Hernandez Hernandez, Alberto. 1982. *La mujer obrera en la industria maquiladora: El caso de Ciudad Juarez*, Tesis Profesional, Universidad Nacional Autónoma de México.

Centro Bancario de Cd. Juarez. 1990. *La Banca en Juarez* (No. 3, Mar.).

Colegio de la Frontera Norte (COLEF). 1987, 1988, and 1989. *Encuesta socioeconómica anual de la frontera* (Tijuana, COLEF).

Darling, Juanita. 1990. "Mexico is learning a new word for wealth", in *Latin American Times*, 1 May.

Diario Oficial. "Decreto para la Operación de la Maquiladora de Exportación", 22 Dec. 1989.

Dillman, Daniel C. 1976. "Maquiladoras in Mexico's Northern Border Communities and the Border Industrialization Program", in *Tijdschrift voor Economische en Sociale Geografie*, Vol. 3, No. 3, pp. 138-150.

Dobken, J. Chris. 1989. "Proveedores Mexicanos como exportadores indirectos de maquila", in Thomas P. Lee (ed.): *In-bond industry/industria maquiladora*, pp. 109-114 (Mexico, D.F., ASI S.A., Banco Nacional de México and Asociación Mexicana de Parques Industriales Privados).

Dominguez-Villalobos, Lilia. 1988. *Microelectronics-based innovations and employment in Mexico*. World Employment Programme Research Working Paper No. 208 (Geneva, ILO).

Fernandez-Kelly, Maria Patricia. 1983. *For we are sold, I and my people* (Albany, NY, State University of New York Press).

George, Edward Y. 1987. "Impact of the maquilas on manpower development and economic growth on the US-Mexico border", in *Issues in North American Trade and Finance*, No. 4 (Jan.), pp. 549-578.

Gonzalez-Arechiga, Bernardo; Escamilla, Rocio Barajas (ed.). 1989. *Las maquiladoras: Ajuste estructural y desarrollo regional* (Tijuana, El Colegio de la Frontera Norte and Fundación Friedrich Ebert).

Gonzalez-Arechiga, Bernardo; Ramirez, José Carlos. 1989. "Perspectivas estructurales de la industria maquiladora", in *Comercio Exterior*, Vol. 39, No. 10, pp. 874-886.

Gregory, Peter. 1986. *The myth of market failure: Employment and the labour market in Mexico* (Baltimore, Johns Hopkins University Press).

Gregory, Peter. 1987. "The Mexican labour market in the economic crisis and lessons of the past", in William E. Cole (ed.): *Mexico's economic policy: Past, present and future*, pp. 55-61 (Knoxville, Tennessee, Center for Business and Economic Research, University of Tennessee).

Grunwald, Joseph. 1985. "The assembly industry in Mexico", in Joseph Grunwald and Kenneth Flamm (eds.): *The global factory: Foreign assembly in international trade*, pp. 137-179 (Washington, DC, The Brookings Institution).

Grunwald, Joseph; Flamm, Kenneth. 1985. "Overview", in Joseph Grunwald and Kenneth Flamm (eds.): *The global factory: Foreign assembly in international trade*, pp. 217-236 (Washington, DC, The Brookings Institution).

Herbolzheimer, E.; Ouane, H. 1985. "The transfer of technology in developing countries", in *Trade and Development*, No. 6, pp. 131-148.

Ibarreche, Santiago. 1990. Personal communication to one of the authors.

Institute for Manufacturing and Materials Management (IMMM). 1989. *Maquiladora survey: Mexican content report* (El Paso, IMMM, University of Texas at El Paso).

Instituto Nacional de Estadística, Geográfia e Informática (INEGI). 1980. *VII Censo de Servicios* (Mexico, D.F., INEGI).

—. 1985. *XII Censo Industrial* (Mexico, D.F., INEGI).

—. 1988. *Avance de Información Económica: Industria Maquiladora de Exportación* (Mexico, D.F., INEGI).

Inter-American Development Bank (IDB). 1990. *Economic and Social Progress in Latin America, 1989 Report* (Washington, DC, IDB).

International Labour Office and United Nations Centre on Transnational Corporations (ILO/UNCTC). 1988. *Economic and social effects of multinational enterprises in export processing zones* (Geneva, ILO).

Jéquier, Nicolas. 1989. *Measuring the indirect employment effects of multinational enterprises: Some suggestions for a research framework*. Multinational Enterprises Programme Working Paper No. 56 (Geneva, ILO).

McCray, John P.; Groff, James E. 1990. "Maquila purchasing patterns: Opportunities and obstacles for US and Mexican border firms", in *Southwest Journal of Business and Economics*, Vol. 6, No. 2 (Fall), pp. 31-38.

Martinez, Raymundo; Monroy, Mauricio; Schell, Andrea. 1988. "Contabilidad e impuestos para las maquiladoras", in Thomas P. Lee (ed.): *In-bond industry/industria maquiladora*, pp. 35-41 (Mexico, D.F., ASI S.A., Banco Nacional de México and Asociación Mexicana de Parques Industriales Privados).

Palomares, Laura A.; Mertens, Leonard. 1987. "El surgimiento de un nuevo tipo de trabajador en la industria de alta tecnología: El caso de la electrónica", in *Analisis Económico*, Vol. 6, No. 10, pp. 31-53.

Patrick, M.L.; Arriola,R.S. 1987. "The economic impact of maquiladoras on border development: A Rio Grande Valley case study – Some preliminary findings", Paper, Western Social Science Association, 22-25 Apr., El Paso, Texas.

Pérez Núnez, Wilson. 1990. *Foreign direct investment and industrial development in Mexico* (Paris, Organization for Economic Co-operation and Development).

Programa Regional de Empleo en América Latina y el Caribe (PREALC). 1981. *Dinámica del subempleo en América Latina* (Santiago, PREALC).

Seligson, Mitchell; Williams, Edward J. 1981. *Maquiladoras and migration: Workers in the Mexico-United States border industrialization program* (Austin, Texas, Mexico-United States Border Research Program).

Shaiken, Harley. 1990. *Mexico in the global economy: High technology and work organization in export industries* (La Jolla, California, Center for US-Mexican Studies, University of California-San Diego).

Sklair, Leslie. 1989. *Assembling for development: The maquila industry in Mexico and United States* (Boston, Unwin).

South, Robert B. 1990. "Transnational 'maquiladora' location", in *Annals of the Association of American Geographers*, Vol. 80, No. 4, pp. 549-570.

Spinanger, Dean. 1984. "Objectives and impact of economic activity zones: Some evidence from Asia", in *Weltwirtschaftliches Archiv*, Vol. 120, No. 1, pp. 64-89.

Sprinkle, Richard L. 1990. "The US-Mexico Free Trade Area", in *El Paso Economic Review* 26:4 (July/Aug.).

Stoddard, Ellwyn R. 1987. *Maquila: Assembly plants in Northern Mexico* (El Paso, Texas, Texas Western Press).

United States International Trade Commission (USITC). 1990. *Review of trade and investment liberalization measures by Mexico and prospects for future United States-Mexico relations. Phase I: Recent trade and investment reforms undertaken by Mexico and implications for the United States* (Washington, DC, USITC), Apr.

—. 1991. *The likely impact on the United States of a Free Trade Agreement with Mexico* (Washington, DC, USITC), Feb.

Van Wass, Michael. 1981. *The multinationals' strategy for labour: Foreign assembly plants in Mexico's Border Assembly Program* (Ph.D. dissertation, Stanford University).

Vargas, Lucinda; Mitchell, William L., Jr. 1989. "Una historia de dos ciudades: El impacto de los maquiladores en Juarez y El Paso", in Thomas P. Lee (ed.): *In-bond industry/industria maquiladora*, pp. 120-126 (Mexico, D.F., ASI S.A., Banco Nacional de México and Asociación Mexicana de Parques Industriales Privados).

Watanabe, Susumu. 1981. "Multinational enterprises, employment and technology adaptations", in *International Labour Review*, Vol. 120, No. 6, pp. 693-710.

Wilson, Patricia A. 1990. *Maquiladoras and local linkages: Building transaction networks in Guadalajara*. Working Paper No. 32 (Washington, DC, Commission for the Study of International Migration and Cooperative Economic Development), Apr.

Wright, David L. 1990. *A study of the employment effects and other benefits of collaboration between multinational enterprises and small-scale enterprises*, Multinational Enterprise Programme Working Paper No. 60 (Geneva, ILO).

7

Employment and multinational enterprises in Indonesia

Hal Hill

1. Introduction

This chapter examines the impact of foreign direct investment (FDI) on the labour market in Indonesia, and in particular on employment creation, skills and human capital development. Special emphasis is accorded to the manufacturing sector, as the major recipient of FDI outside the oil and gas sector, and because the database and range of issues to be investigated are much richer than in the essentially "enclave" foreign investment in mining.

Indonesia constitutes a useful case-study of this topic for a number of reasons. First, as all major studies of FDI in Indonesia have stressed,[1] the policy regime has changed dramatically over the past 30 years, from outright hostility and nationalization (1958-65), a restrictive but still open stance (1974-84) to a more open posture (1967-72, 1986-present). Secondly, Indonesia has recovered strongly from a recession in the mid-1980s induced by a sharp fall in its terms of trade, to enjoy near-boom conditions in the late 1980s (as exemplified by the dramatic rise in non-oil exports); and foreign investment has played an important role in this process. Finally, Indonesia's data sources are reasonably good, both with regard to total inflows and approvals, and to the ownership data from several industrial censuses.

In general, FDI has numerous direct and indirect impacts on employment. First, there are the economy-wide effects of FDI. Foreign investors introduce a package of productive resources – capital, management, technology, marketing expertise – which provide the basis for their competitive advantage, and which overcome the intrinsic costs of "being foreign". The benefits which accrue to the host country depend on the extent to which the latter is able to capture these beneficial effects, whether in the form of new and better products, higher labour productivity, greater exports, and increased government taxation revenue. Second, there are the micro, enterprise-level impacts, such as the effects on industry structure (for example, new competitors, the demise of national, often smaller-scale, firms), on employment conditions and structures (for example, foreign firms generally recruit more skilled

---

[1] The chapter draws on the author's recent writings on foreign investment and industrialization in Indonesia (see in particular Hill, 1990a and 1990b), and on several earlier studies of foreign investment in Indonesia, including Dickie and Layman (1988), Hill (1988a), Kuntjoro-Jakti, et al. (1985), Sadli (1972), Thee (1984a and b), and Thee and Yoshihara (1987).

workers and pay higher wages), and on commercial relationships with upstream and downstream firms. The impacts are invariably extremely difficult to capture and quantify (to this writer's knowledge, there has not yet been a really detailed, enterprise-level assessment of the effects of FDI in Indonesia (Rice, 1974; Thee, 1990b; and Wells, 1973, come closest), but some of the general parameters may be identified and some broad assessments may be made.

This chapter is organized as follows. Section 2 analyses Indonesia's foreign investment regime since 1966. Section 3 provides a brief summary of the structure of and trends in the Indonesian labour market; section 4 takes a closer look at foreign investment in the manufacturing sector; section 5 assesses the wider impact of foreign investment, in particular on exports, skills, the development of linkages and subcontracting and how FDI itself has been affected by government policy; finally, section 6 presents the main conclusions.

2.   Foreign investment in Indonesia: An overview

Several major features of the Indonesian experience with foreign investment since 1966 need to be emphasized at the outset:

1.   From the end of the colonial era – effectively 1939 – until 1966 there was virtually no new foreign investment, as by the latter date almost all foreign capital had been either repatriated or expropriated.

2.   The "New Order" regime introduced a very liberal foreign investment code in 1967, and the door to FDI has remained open – sometimes wide open, sometimes just slightly ajar – ever since. These episodes in the country's foreign investment regime since 1966 need to be emphasized, because there has not been a consistent and coherent foreign investment "policy".

3.   It is convenient to think of FDI flows as comprising two roughly equal halves. The first constitutes investment in the oil and gas sector, and originates mainly in the United States. The second refers to all other sectors where Japanese investors have predominated. The two parts of the economy are administered under separate policy regimes and by different authorities.

4.   Related to this point, the data on FDI in Indonesia, while quite abundant, need to be used with great care. Official statistics refer only to the non-oil and gas sector; no official data are available on foreign investment in oil and gas. Moreover, for the non-oil sector, there are two sources of data: those published by the Capital Investment Coordinating Board (Badan Koordinasi Penanaman Modal – BKPM) which refer only to approved investments and which for several reasons greatly overstate the realized foreign capital contribution; and realized figures published by the central bank (Bank Indonesia – BI) which, with a delay, report estimated foreign equity investment (and loans). The accuracy of all sets of estimates is hampered by Indonesia's very open international capital market.

5.   Indonesia's ownership patterns are unusually complicated, for two reasons. First, it is often difficult to distinguish between the "state" and "private" sector. While

the State is a large direct investor, the Indonesian army also plays a direct role in business. (Is an army-run "yayasan" [foundation], existing mainly on government contracts, "state" or "private"?) Secondly, "foreign" and "domestic private" are often indistinguishable, owing in part to the presence of intense business contacts between Indonesian Chinese investors (the dominant domestic private group) and Chinese business interests in the broader East Asian regional economy. (Is a local firm's partner, a former Indonesian resident now living in Hong Kong, "foreign" or "domestic", for example?) This chapter adheres to convention below in identifying three groups: foreign, state, and (domestic) private, but it needs to be remembered that the distinctions between them are frequently blurred.

2.1 Government policy towards FDI

Indonesia's current Government, which took power in 1966, inherited a very weak economy characterized by triple-digit inflation, economic decline and sharp political divisions. Eager to obtain access to Western capital, technology and markets, the Government, in one of its first major decrees, introduced a new foreign investment code in 1967 (Law No. 1/1967). The new Law, together with a similar provision for domestic investment introduced in the following year, offered a wide range of fiscal incentives: tax holidays of two to six years, accelerated depreciation allowances, exemption from duty on the import of capital goods, loss carry-forward provisions, and a guarantee on profit and capital repatriation. Moreover, restrictions on the employment of foreign personnel were minimal, and foreigners were permitted 100 per cent ownership.

The initial open-door policy did not last long. In 1974, the Government introduced requirements that all new firms be joint ventures and that existing wholly foreign-owned firms invite a domestic equity partner within a decade. In addition, employment of foreign personnel was restricted and an increasing number of sectors were closed to foreign investors.

For the next decade, this fairly restrictive stance towards FDI was maintained. In the 1980s, however, declining international oil prices resulted in a sharp decline in government revenues (up to the early 1980s some two-thirds of the Government's revenue came from oil and gas taxes), and induced several policy changes. Regulations were relaxed in 1986, 1989 and 1992.

In 1986 foreign firms were placed on the same footing as domestic firms with regard to domestic distribution networks and state banks; exporting firms were given more liberal treatment; reinvestment of profits was facilitated; and the joint venture provisions became less harsh (see Hill, 1988a, p. 32). In May 1989, a Negative List (Daftar Negatif – DN) was announced which itemized only those sectors specifically closed to new investments. All other activities are now automatically deemed open, thereby allowing the BKPM to play a more effective role in promoting FDI. In 1992, foreign investors, provided their paid-up capital is in excess of US$ 50 million and if their project is situated in an industrial park in Java or Sumatra or is located outside these areas, now have the right to 100 per cent ownership of their business. Within five years of start-up, foreign investors must sell 5 per cent of their business to Indonesian interests, rising to at least 20 per cent within 20 years. This new law removes the initial difficulty faced by foreign investors of having to find a suitable Indonesian partner. Thus, by 1992 the regime had become more attractive to foreign investors.

2.2 Foreign direct investment since 1967

Foreign investors initially adopted a cautious attitude, and in 1968, the year after the introduction of the Foreign Investment Law, there was a net outflow (table 7.1).[2] By the early 1970s, however, the inflows were very sizeable, the real total for 1972 being the fourth largest of all years from 1968 to 1989. The picture becomes somewhat confusing in the mid-1970s, with the realized figure for 1974 being recorded as negative, in contrast to the very large positive approvals total. The explanation is that foreign investors became somewhat apprehensive at the prospect of political disturbances, yet this was also the year when the giant Asahan hydro-electric and alumina plant in North Sumatra was approved, which in turn contributed to the peak realized figure in the following year. Both approvals and realized flows then declined in response to the tighter investment regime. The realized figures in fact remained flat throughout the 1977-86 period owing to the restrictive BKPM policy, to occasional disputes in the petroleum sector over taxation and production sharing agreements, and to the sluggish domestic economy after 1982. Approvals data suggest strong investor interest from 1979 to 1984, peaking in 1983 as investors rushed to obtain approval before the introduction of a new, less favourable fiscal incentives regime. Part of the explanation for the high figure for the early 1980s relates to the Government's heavy industry programme. Although some of these projects commenced, many which had received approval were frozen during the government cutbacks of 1983-84, thus causing the very large discrepancy between the two columns over this period. More recently, both series rebounded strongly in the late 1980s in response to the more liberal investment climate and to the attractive investment opportunities for export.[3]

Within the BKPM sectors, manufacturing has been by far the largest recipient of foreign investments, absorbing nearly 60 per cent of the total over the period 1967-77, and 64 per cent from 1967 to 1989 (table 7.2). These figures exclude the very large investments in oil and gas.[4] The dominance of manufacturing is not surprising. Commercial opportunities in agriculture are not very great, apart from the heavily

[2] It is important to emphasize again that as no official data on FDI in the oil, gas and financial services sector are published, this part deals only with "BKPM sectors". For discussion of the data limitations, see Hill (1988a, pp. 157-164).

[3] The comparison in table 7.1 vastly understates the relative importance of domestic investment approvals because, unlike foreign firms, domestic firms are not required to obtain BKPM approval.

[4] The dominance of oil and gas in the total inflows is revealed by one set of estimates, which concluded that this sector accounted for 57 and 72 per cent of realized cumulative foreign investment up to 1977 and 1985 respectively (Hill, 1988a, p. 81). More recently, as petroleum investment has tapered off and manufacturing and service investments boomed, this share would have declined markedly. The omission of FDI in oil and gas also distorts the country shares of foreign investment in Indonesia. For the 1967-84 period, for example, Japan accounted for about 68 per cent of investment in BKPM sectors but only 3 per cent of oil and gas, giving it an overall share of 21 per cent. The respective shares for the United States were 5, 78 and 58 per cent (Hill, 1988a, p. 55).

Table 7.1. Foreign and domestic investment, 1968-89 ($ million)

Year	Nominal totals			Real totals		
	Realized	Approved		Realized	Approved	
	Foreign	Foreign	Domestic	Foreign	Foreign	Domestic
1989	735	4 150	7 190	665	3 757	6 507
1988	542	3 550	5 708	510	3 350	5 375
1987	446	843	3 407	430	814	3 283
1986	258	450	1 464	253	450	1 436
1985	310	859	2 833	310	859	2 833
1984	222	1 121	1 873	227	1 146	1 915
1983	292	2 882	7 707	306	3 018	8 070
1982	225	1 800	2 949	242	1 938	3 174
1981	133	1 092	2 676	151	1 242	3 044
1980	184	914	2 086	231	1 147	2 617
1979	226	1 320	1 242	314	1 833	1 725
1978	279	397	1 715	421	599	2 587
1977	235	328	1 386	383	534	2 257
1976	344	449	672	596	778	1 165
1975	476	1 757	593	880	3 248	1 096
1974	−49	1 417	554	−104	3 021	1 181
1973	15	655	1 465	36	1 594	3 564
1972	207	522	718	521	1 315	1 809
1971	139	426	939	358	1 098	2 420
1970	83	345	319	223	925	855
1969	32	682	101	90	1 916	284
1968	−2	230	13	−6	669	38

Notes: Foreign and domestic investment have been presented both in nominal terms (nominal totals), that is at current prices and in real terms or constant prices. Nominal totals have been converted to real totals using as a deflator the US producer price for finished goods, capital equipment; they are expressed in 1985 prices. Domestic approvals data have been converted at each year's exchange rate. BKPM data exclude the oil and gas and financial services sector; they refer to total planned and approved investments, include foreign and domestic equity and loan contributions.

Sources: IMF, *International Finance Statistics* for realized foreign investment; BKPM for approved foreign and domestic investment.

regulated plantations, fisheries and forestry sectors, and Indonesia's land regulations strongly discourage such activities. In services, too, the opportunities are limited for similar reasons, although the tourism sector has attracted a considerable volume of foreign investment in recent years; financial services are excluded from the BKPM's purview. Investments in mining have been substantial, in coal, gold, tin, nickel and copper. But these have been small in comparison with the huge inflows into oil and gas, and in any case state enterprises in mining have sometimes ruled out opportunities for foreign investors.

Within manufacturing, the drive towards industrial maturity has resulted in a pronounced change in the sectoral composition of foreign inflows. Whereas in the first decade textiles dominated, accounting (with food products) for almost half the total, for the period as a whole (1967-89) basic metals – mainly steel and related prod-

Table 7.2.   Realized foreign investment by sector (percentage of total)

Sector	1967 up to:	
	December 1977	June 1989
Agriculture	11.7	3.8
Mining	19.8	23.8
Manufacturing	58.7	64.4
Food products	3.5	2.7
Textiles	23.1	9.2
Wood products	0.7	0.8
Paper products	0.5	0.8
Chemicals	8.8	9.9
Non-metallic minerals	11.8	7.6
Basic metals	4.3	27.3
Metal products	5.8	6.0
Miscellaneous	0.2	0.1
Services	9.8	8.0
(Total: $ million)	(2 639)	(6 734)

Source: Bank Indonesia.

ucts – has been by far the most important. This sector, combined with the metal goods industries, has absorbed more than half the total from 1967 to 1989.

Outside the oil and gas sector, Asian – particularly North-east Asian – economies have been the major source of Indonesia's foreign investment (table 7.3; but see also note 4). Japan has played a dominant role, providing almost 41 per cent of the realized total through to 1989. Moreover if, as seems reasonable, the large "multi-country" group is allocated on a pro-rata basis according to single country shares, the Japanese figure approaches 60 per cent of the total – an impressive figure, which accounts for the fear in some Indonesian quarters of the Japanese "over-presence". The Japanese role is explained by a number of factors: the coincidence of liberalization in both investment regimes; the strong complementarity between a resource-poor and resource-rich economy; and strong political ties despite Japan's wartime occupation of Indonesia. Of course, Japan has been the dominant investor throughout Asia since 1970, and its sheer commercial size also explains the total.

The next major investor grouping has been the four Asian newly industrialized economies (NIEs), led by Hong Kong in the earlier years, but with large investments from the other three in recent years. These investments have been explained by a number of factors: proximity in all cases, buttressed by close commercial ties within East Asia's prominent Chinese business entities; the search for new low-cost investment sites, as in the case of textiles, especially since 1985 when all four economies have lost their comparative advantage in labour-intensive activities; obtaining access to Indonesia's rich natural resources has also been a factor, as in the case of Korean investments in timber and wood processing. As all four economies have been running current account surpluses in the late 1980s, their loss of comparative advantage has led to a rapid surge in investments in labour-intensive activities,

Table 7.3.   Major foreign investors (percentage of total)

	Realized		Approved
	to December 1977	to June 1989	to July 1990
Asia			
Japan	39.9	40.8	32.8
Hong Kong	10.2	8.8	7.7
Singapore	1.3	0.6	3.3
Korea (Rep. of)	0.1	1.2	1.9
Taiwan, China	n.a.	0.3	1.2
Europe			
Belgium	1.1	4.3	7.2
Netherlands	1.7	1.9	3.4
United Kingdom	1.0	1.2	2.1
France	0.5	0.4	1.6
Germany (Fed. Rep. of)	1.3	1.4	1.6
North America			
United States	6.7	3.5	11.8
Canada	0.1	0.1	7.7
Australia	2.7	2.0	4.0
Other countries	6.1	1.9	3.1
More than one country	27.3	31.6	10.6

Source: Bank Indonesia and BKPM.

the magnitude of which for Indonesia is understated in table 7.4 since these are cumulative totals. In recent years these four have been challenging Japan's position as the leading non-oil investor.[5]

European investors have generally played a far less significant role. Belgium is actually the largest investor, owing mainly to their country's involvement in Indonesia's now sizeable steel industry. The Netherlands is the second largest investor, reflecting the close economic and political ties between the two countries during the New Order period (and quite unlike the hostilities which were evident before 1966). North American investments in the non-oil economy have never been large, although the United States has been crucial as a market for Indonesia's newly emerging labour-intensive export industries.

Within manufacturing, and before the recent NIE investment surge became fully apparent, Japan and Hong Kong were the major foreign investors in most sectors. Japan's prominence in the large textiles and basic metals sectors is particularly apparent. Reflecting complementarities in relative natural resource endowments, and similarity in Asian diets, the NIEs have been important in wood and paper prod-

[5] For example, in 1989, approved investment from Japan totalled US$ 919.5 million (15.5 per cent of the total), compared to US$ 1,210.8 million (20.4 per cent) from the four NIEs, with investments from Hong Kong and the Republic of Korea being especially significant.

**Table 7.4.   Approximate estimates of ownership shares in Indonesia, late 1980s
(percentage of each sector's value added)**

	Domestic sector	Foreign	Government	GDP share (1988)[a]
Agriculture				
Food crops, smallholders, livestock	100	0	0	18
Fisheries, forestry, plantation	80	5	15	3
Mining				
Oil and gas	0	50	50	15
Other	30	30	40	1
Manufacturing				
Oil and gas	0	0	100	4
Other	59	17	24	14
Construction	90	5	5	5
Utilities	0	0	100	1
Transport and communications	50	0	50	5
Trade and tourism	90	5	5	16
Banking and finance	30	5	65	4
Government	0	0	100	8
Accommodation	90	0	10	3
Other services	100	0	0	4
Total	57	12	31	100
(excluding oil and gas)	70	5	25	

[a] Refers to share of GDP at current prices. These shares are used as weights to compute the ownership shares in the last two rows.

Source: Author's estimates, based on official statistics where possible.

ucts and food products. Only Belgium in basic metals and the United States in metal products have been exceptions to the rule of Asia's dominance in major branches of manufacturing.

Despite this international presence, it should be emphasized that overall foreign economic participation in the economy is small. Foreign firms probably generate a little over 10 per cent of Indonesia's GDP (and perhaps as much as 15 per cent of non-agricultural GDP), but only about half this figure if the oil and gas subsector is excluded.

In addition, by regional standards, the multinational presence in Indonesia is modest. Indonesia's aggregate inflows, in real terms, exceeded those of the Republic of Korea, the Philippines and Thailand, but were much less than those of the liberal regimes in Malaysia and Singapore, over the 1973-88 period (figure 7.1). Furthermore, the contribution of FDI to gross capital formation in Indonesia is one of the lowest. The ratio of FDI to GDP was relatively high in the mid-1970s, but has been low thereafter (figure 7.2). Similarly, on a per capita basis the total for Indonesia is very small.

Figure 7.1.   Total FDI, 1973-88 (in constant 1980 prices)

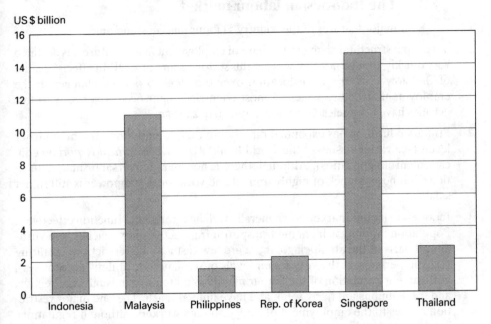

Source: National statistics.

Figure 7.2.   Ratio of FDI to GDP, 1973-88

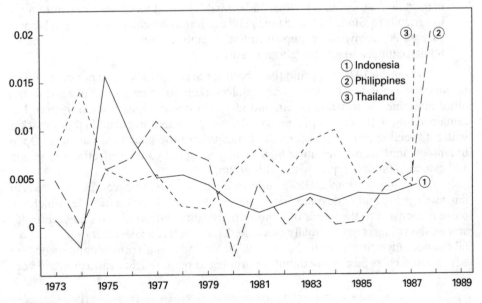

Source: National statistics.

3.   The Indonesian labour market

Four major features of the country's labour market stand out:

1.   Very rapid structural change: the share of employment in agriculture has declined very quickly, though not as steeply as this sector's share of GDP. In effect, because of the slow growth and dislocation over the 1939-66 period, changes in the employment structure which in most countries might occur over four to five decades have been telescoped into about 20 to 25 years.

2.   Primary education has expanded rapidly, but there is underinvestment at higher levels (see various issues of the World Bank, *World Development Report* on education enrolment ratios). Although there is now near-universal primary education, Indonesia's stock of highly trained and vocational manpower is still rather small.

3.   Indonesian labour markets are generally well integrated and function effectively. Population mobility is high, the transport infrastructure now reaches into virtually all parts of the archipelago, there are few caste/ethnic restrictions on hiring (except, perhaps, at the very senior levels of some non-"pribumi" enterprises), government regulation of the labour market is minimal and usually ineffective, and trade unions are fairly weak and have limited reach. The one major restriction relates to the employment of skilled foreign workers, although regulations have been eased in recent years.

4.   Wages and employment conditions in Indonesia have improved considerably over the past 25 years. Although accurate, finely specified longitudinal data are difficult to obtain, the evidence does suggest strongly that real wages have risen in most non-agricultural sectors, and probably also – though with less certainty – in agriculture. Since Indonesia may still accurately be characterized as a labour-surplus economy, these improvements mainly reflect an enhanced stock of human capital and greater labour intensity.

Over the 1971-85 period the labour force rose by about 60 per cent in size, became less rural, much better educated, less likely to be employed in agriculture, more feminine, more white collar, and less Java-based. Open unemployment has remained low, in the region of 2 per cent, although in an unregulated labour market without social security provisions the concept has little analytical meaning. Open unemployment is however quite high among educated youth, reflecting job search and extended family support within this group.[6]

The most serious challenge now facing the country's education planners is to improve quality and to develop vocational and higher education facilities which are more responsive to the needs of a modern, dynamic industrial economy. Illiteracy among the young is now virtually eradicated, a creditable achievement reflecting big oil-financed investments from the mid-1970s. Yet Indonesia's primary and secondary education sectors face many daunting problems: pupil-teacher ratios remain very

---

[6] The two major overviews of the Indonesian labour market are Hugo et al. (1987, Chapter 8), and Jones and Manning (1991).

high; physical facilities are inadequate, especially outside Java; school curricula are somewhat rigid and highly centralized; and the educational philosophy does not encourage creative and independent thought. In the higher and vocational sectors, the problems are more serious still, with generally poor facilities, inadequately trained and paid staff, and a lack of a tradition of critical scholarship (for more discussion, see Keyfitz et al., 1989). The tertiary sector produces large numbers of humanities and social science graduates, but there are increasingly acute shortages of accountants, computer operators, financial analysts, engineers, architects, surveyors, and those possessing a middle range of technical skills. This skill gap is of particular relevance to the discussion of foreign investment and technology transfer in section 5 below.

As noted, wages and conditions of employment in the non-agricultural economy have improved steadily since 1965, reflecting the growing employment opportunities and the better skill base. Even within agriculture there appears to have been some real increase in the 1980s, after a decade of stagnation in the 1970s. The strong growth in rice output, continuing investments in agricultural infrastructure, and even some localized labour shortages (in part owing to the Government's transmigration programme, to move people off Java) appear to have been contributing factors (Jayasuriya and Manning, 1990; Naylor, 1990). Wages in the construction sector have generally increased, while an analysis of the two industrial censuses (1974/75 and 1985/86) suggests that real wages have been growing by an annual average rate of about 5 per cent (Hill, 1990b).

4. Foreign investment in the manufacturing sector

Three main ownership groups dominate Indonesian non-oil manufacturing: (domestic) private, private-foreign joint ventures, and those comprising all three groups (table 7.5). All three, but especially the former, are quite distinct. Private firms are by far the most numerous, and employ the largest workforce. Yet they are much smaller – output per firm is just 8 per cent that of the huge government joint ventures while employment per firm is just one-sixth. The other four ownership combinations are unimportant. The very small figure for wholly foreign-owned firms may appear puzzling, but it simply reflects the prohibition on new enterprises of this type after 1974 and the pressure on existing ones to divest.

Private firms have always been the major actors in Indonesian non-oil manufacturing. Even during the latter years of the "socialist" Guided Economy, they provided over two-thirds of the jobs and consumed 60 per cent of the power (a proxy for output, data on which are not available; table 7.5). In fact, their relative importance has changed surprisingly little, falling to 47 per cent of output in 1974, following the rush of foreign investment after 1966, but rising thereafter as private firms grew in sophistication and confidence. They have always been considerably smaller than their government or foreign counterparts, although the differentials do appear to be narrowing over time (see bottom of table 7.5).

The inclusion of oil and gas has a dramatic effect on ownership shares (table 7.6). Treating oil refining as wholly government (Pertamina) owned, and gas processing as a government-foreign joint venture (between Mobil in Aceh, and Huffco and

Table 7.5. Summary indicators of major ownership groups, 1963, 1974, 1985[a]

	G	P	F	G/P	G/F	P/F	G/P/F	All firms	(Total)
(1) Shares									
1985									
Firms	0.9	92.2	0.4	0.6	0.1	2.7	3.1	100	12 909
Employment	1.0	74.9	1.3	0.4	0.2	7.4	14.9	100	1 684 726
VA	0.4	55.8	1.3	0.4	0.5	17.1	24.7	100	Rp.7 153 837
1974									
Firms	6.8	87.9	1.4	1.2	0.2	25.0	–	100	7 091
Employment	19.3	68.9	2.6	1.3	0.7	7.3	–	100	655 821
VA	25.9	47.2	10.8	1.5	2.2	13.3	–	100	Rp.478 446
1963									
Firms	4.7	95.3						100	10 586
Employment	31.1	68.9						100	527 717
Power	39.7	60.3						100	715 520 HP
(2) Indices of relative size (average = 100)									
1985									
VA/firm	40	60	328	64	833	641	794		
VA/employee	40	75	97	105	244	230	165		
Employees/firm	101	81	339	61	342	279	480		
1974									
VA/firm	398	54	756	88	1091	534	–		
VA/employee	129	68	418	123	315	183	–		
Employees/firm	285	78	181	106	346	292	–		
1963									
Power/firm	851	63							
Power/employee	127	88							
Employees/firm	668	72							

[a] The data for 1974 and 1985 refer to firms employing at least 20 workers, and exclude oil and gas processing. In this and following tables, G, P and F refer to government, private (domestic) and foreign respectively. Joint ventures refer to firms with equity held by more than one of these groups. There is no separate identification of G/P/F firms in 1974; presumably they were included in the G group. The 1963 data refer to firms employing at least five workers and using power. No reliable value added data by ownership are provided, so installed power capacity is used.

Table 7.6. **Ownership shares in Indonesian manufacturing, 1988**
(percentage of each industry's value added)

Industry		Private	Government	Foreign
311)	Food products	53.9	36.7	9.4
312)		53.8	18.6	27.6
313	Beverages	39.2	34.2	26.6
314	Tobacco	95.9	0.8	3.3
321	Textiles	68.1	7.1	24.8
322	Garments	98.0	0.2	1.8
323	Leather products	99.1	0.9	0
324	Footwear	86.9	0.2	12.9
331	Wood products	83.3	3.7	13.0
332	Furniture	91.8	1.8	6.4
341	Paper products	50.2	10.1	39.7
342	Printing and publishing	64.4	24.3	11.3
351	Basic chemicals	14.6	72.6	12.8
352	Other chemicals	54.6	7.8	38.6
353/4	Oil and gas processing	0	100.0	0
355	Rubber products	47.5	34.9	17.6
356	Plastics	91.2	0.3	8.5
361	Pottery and china	76.3	0.5	23.2
362	Glass products	88.5	3.6	7.9
363	Cement	24.8	61.5	13.7
364	Structural clay products	91.4	1.5	7.1
369	Other non-metallic minerals	95.9	4.1	0
37	Basic metals	6.0	89.1	4.9
381	Metal products	50.8	22.4	26.8
382	Non-electric machinery	31.9	31.0	37.1
383	Electrical equipment	59.9	13.8	26.3
384	Transport equipment	59.0	13.8	27.2
385	Professional equipment	77.0	0	23.0
39	Miscellaneous	88.3	0.2	11.5
	Total			
	Excl. oil and gas	59.1	24.2	16.7
	Incl. oil and gas	43.8	43.8	12.4

Note: Data refer to firms with at least 20 employees. The "Government" category includes also firms in which the Government is a joint venture partner.

Source: Unpublished data from BPS.

others in East Kalimantan), the share of firms with government equity rises to over 50 per cent of total manufacturing output; that of private firms falls to less than 40 per cent, while foreign firms (excluding their government joint ventures) become unimportant. The share of private sector firms rose over the period 1985-88, reflecting the impact of the Government's liberalization measures.

The ownership data clearly illustrate the accuracy of the description by Thee and Yoshihara (1987, p. 343) of Indonesia's industrial structure as one of "upstream socialism, downstream capitalism". The Government's strategic objectives of "industrial deepening" and controlling the "commanding heights" of industry, aided by the oil boom of the 1970s, explain much of the pattern of ownership in Indonesian industry.

In addition to oil and gas, government or related firms are dominant in basic metals (the two big investments, in steel and alumina), fertilizer and the small machine goods industry; they are also significant in cement, food processing (sugar) and paper goods. For various reasons the significance of foreign firms is understated in these figures. In any case, multinationals in Indonesia have tended to congregate – when permitted by the Government's own investment decisions and regulations – in activities where their superior technology or product advantages confer a decisive benefit. These factors explain their above-average shares in industries such as glass products, plastics, electronics, other chemicals, beverages, and textiles. Private firms play something of a residual role, being especially important in industries where local consumer preferences are important, in simple agricultural processing industries (rubber and food products for example), in labour-intensive industries where brand names are unimportant (garments, furniture, leather products, some non-metallic minerals), or where foreign ownership is actively discouraged (such as printing and publishing).

Foreign firms play a significant role in a wide range of industries (at a five-digit ISIC level), where the interrelated factors of brand names and technology are crucial. The former is of relevance in industries such as cigarettes, beer, pharmaceuticals, pesticides, batteries and dairy products; while the latter is important in spinning (mostly in synthetic fibres), sheet glass, agricultural equipment and motor cycles.

The factor proportions of the ownership groups vary enormously, using value added per employee as a proxy in the absence of reliable capital stock estimates (table 7.7). The inclusion of oil and gas obviously results in far higher capital intensities in the two government groups, that for the wholly government-owned group being especially high because of the much smaller group of non-oil firms with which the oil operations are combined. Excluding oil and gas, the overall averages accord with a priori expectations, the government joint venture and foreign firms being far more capital-intensive than private or government firms. These differences may be decomposed into those due to location in more capital-intensive industries and those due to the adoption of more capital-intensive techniques within industries.

Using a similar database for 1975 and 1983, the author undertook such a decomposition analysis (see Hill, 1988a, Chapter 6; see also Hill, 1988b). The main conclusion was that the generally higher ratio for foreign firms was explained by both sets of factors, that is, that these firms tended to locate in more capital-intensive industries, and they were on average more capital-intensive within a given industry (finely specified at the five-digit ISIC level); the latter exerted a somewhat greater effect. In the case of a higher ratio for government firms, the location in more capital-intensive industries was generally the dominant factor. These differences were evident in both years, although an important feature of the results was the narrowing of some of the differentials, which is presumptive evidence of Indonesia's greater industrial maturity. Moreover, foreign firms were hardly the "devil" in the story, in that it was the government joint ventures, rather than the purely foreign or private-foreign joint ventures, which recorded the very high ratios.

Table 7.7.   Labour productivity by industry and ownership, 1985[a]

Industry		Private	Government	Foreign	Government (JV)
311)	Food products	109	113	263	78
312)		74	41	415	122
313	Beverages	43	16	198	414
314	Tobacco	98	10	373	13
321	Textiles	74	65	246	140
322	Garments	102	36	68	82
323	Leather products	67	23	2 574	196
324	Footwear	46	–	377	–
331	Wood products	84	85	108	595
332	Furniture	97	21	245	75
341	Paper products	73	–	142	187
342	Printing and publishing	102	158	79	69
351	Basic chemicals	37	21	93	148
352	Other chemicals	79	90	148	163
353/4	Oil and gas processing	–	87	–	113
355	Rubber products	136	70	59	33
356	Plastics	43	18	1 674	15
361	Pottery and china	109	27	39	–
362	Glass products	22	–	301	66
363	Cement	156	73	498	121
364	Structural clay products	87	131	606	357
369	Other non-metallic minerals	109	68	–	31
37	Basic metals	22	–	26	168
381	Metal products	83	17	168	145
382	Non-electric machinery	41	18	186	213
383	Electrical equipment	66	13	153	271
384	Transport equipment	124	12	147	44
385	Professional equipment	75	–	502	–
39	Miscellaneous	71	2	278	797
	All industries				
	Excl. oil and gas	74	58	210	166
	Incl. oil and gas	47	832	133	237

[a] The data refer to value added per employee in firms with at least 20 employees, expressed as an index with each industry's figure equal to 100.

Table 7.7 indicates that the small government group of firms is the least capital-intensive in most cases, reflecting the older stock of machinery and probable inefficiency. Private firms, too, are usually less capital-intensive than the joint venture or foreign groups. But there are exceptions, especially in the more labour-intensive industries, characterized by mature, standardized technology. Thus private firms exhibit comparable or higher ratios in industries such as food products (where sugar pulls down the joint venture figure), garments, printing and publishing, rubber products, and some non-metallic minerals. The figure is high also for transport equipment, reflecting the strong licensing ties with foreign companies which are excluded from equity participation in several subsectors. The government joint venture group is less capital-intensive than foreign firms.

It needs to be emphasized that these figures have no normative implications, nor do they tell us much about efficiency. Rather, the data indicate simply that foreign and government joint venture firms tend to be located disproportionately in more highly capital-intensive industries (as measured by value added and, probably, capital), and segments within industries. Lacking comparable access to skills, technology, finance and overseas markets, average labour productivity in private firms is a good deal lower. But this in no way implies inferior efficiency; indeed, to the extent that their survival depends less on "rent seeking" behaviour and political or bureaucratic connections, the social efficiency of private firms could well be higher.

Two additional features of this comparative assessment of the major ownership groups should be stressed. First, the direct employment effects of foreign investment in Indonesia's manufacturing sector are very small. Accurate estimates of the size of Indonesia's labour force are impossible, owing to the large numbers engaged in cottage industry employment on a casual and seasonal basis. However, combining the results of the 1985/86 Industrial Census and the 1985 Inter-Censal Population Survey, a figure for the mid-1980s of 6,110,300 is probably not too far off the mark. Of this total, some 3,400,800 (or 55.7 per cent) were working in cottage industry (defined as fewer than five employees) and 840,500 (13.8 per cent) were in small enterprises (defined as five-19 employees). The remaining 1.87 million workforce were in firms of at least 20 employees, the genuine "factory sector", which includes all the foreign firms and whose numbers can be estimated with much greater precision. This group comprises about 30.6 per cent of the manufacturing workforce, or about 3 per cent of the nation's entire workforce. These figures underline the obvious point that, even with rapid growth, the factory sector of manufacturing can at best make only a modest contribution to labour absorption for at least the remainder of this century.[7]

Consider now the foreign-owned firms within the factory sector. In 1985 these firms employed a little under 9 per cent of this workforce, far less than the figure for private firms, and lower also than the government sector. In other words, foreign firms provided jobs for just 3 per cent of the total manufacturing workforce, or a minuscule 0.3 per cent of the national workforce. When it is recalled that the only sector in which the multinational presence is large in Indonesia is the highly capital-intensive mining group (table 7.4), and including also the small foreign presence in construction, trade and tourism, financial services and plantation agriculture, it is most unlikely that the share of all foreign firms in the national workforce would exceed 1 per cent.

Within manufacturing, foreign firms in no case employ more than 30 per cent of an industry's workforce. They are most prominent in other chemicals, glass

---

[7] Consider, for example, a simplified numerical calculation. At the current share of manufacturing in the labour force, and assuming the annual growth rates of the total and factory manufacturing workforces are maintained – respectively 2.5 and 5.6 per cent per annum – the factory sector could absorb no more than about 10 per cent of the increment to the labour force in the early 1990s.

Table 7.8. Annual labour costs by ownership, 1985[a]

Industry	Firm size (employees)	Ownership							
		All	P	P-F	G-P-F	F	G	G-F	G-P
All industries	1000+	100	64	196	141	124	59	–	–
	200–999	100	82	178	130	199	64	391	107
	20+	100	76	219	154	168	69	288	89
31340 Soft drinks	200–999	100	99			103			
32111 Spinning	1000+	100	90	111	149	92			
	200–999	100	84	132	92	75			
32112 Weaving	1000+	100	72	193	111				
	200–999	100	98	160	98		68		
33113 Plywood	1000+	100	89	183					
	200–999	100	95	120					
34111 Paper products	1000+	100	60	107	205				
	200–999	100	66		144				
35510 Tyres and tubes	1000+	100	64	296	43				
	200–999	100	46	202	113				
35521 Rubber smoking	1000+	100	91		111	49	36		
	200–999	100	139		95		49		
356 Plastics	200–999	100	89	295					
36310 Cement	200–999	100	130	67	100				
38320 TVs, etc.	1000+	100	53	191					
38330 Electrical supplies	1000+	100	119		132	86			
	200–999	100	71	137	217				
38430 Motor vehicles	1000+	100	97	93	110				
	200–999	100	106	99	59				
38440 Motorcycles	1000+	100	137	55					
	200–999	100	76	144					

a Data refer to indices of labour costs per employee for each industry and ownership group, with the figure for all firms in each industry equal to 100. Ownership groups are as defined in table 7.5.

products and electrical equipment, but none of these branches is a significant employer of labour.

The above analysis should not be construed as a criticism of multinationals. These firms are concentrated in a relatively small portion of the economy which is itself a fairly minor employer of labour. Moreover, the indirect employment effects are a good deal more important, as we shall discuss in the next section. Multinationals could hardly be expected to be major employers, even within their broad spheres of operation. Their principal contribution lies in the area of technology transfer, improving national efficiency and economic welfare, and encouraging the development of a stronger export sector. It is the domestic private firms – smaller in scale, less able to operate modern technology effectively, and mainly located in labour-intensive activities – which would be expected to make the major employment contribution.

Secondly, is ownership an important determinant of wage differentials? A simple comparison of aggregates might suggest it is – average wages in large and medium government-foreign firms are about four times those in private or government-owned firms (table 7.8, row 3). Even standardizing for scale (rows 1 and 2), wage differentials remain very large; indeed, for firms with a workforce of 200-999 workers the range across ownership groups is larger still. These differentials at least partly arise from the fact that foreign and government joint venture enterprises tend to be located disproportionately in high-skill and capital-intensive industries.

To obtain a clearer picture, the comparison needs to be undertaken at a more disaggregated level, correcting also for firm size. Focusing on the comparatively few industry cases of more than one ownership group among larger firms, the dispersions are generally much smaller. For the most common pair-wise comparison, private and foreign firms (the latter including private-foreign joint ventures), in about half the cases (11 out of 21) foreign firms pay more by a significant margin (at least 20 per cent higher). However, in six cases the difference is not significant, while in the remaining four, private firms offer better conditions. The differences are much less decisive in the 15 private-government joint venture comparisons: the joint ventures pay more in six cases, the private more in four, while in the remaining five they are smaller. The clearest differences emerge in the private-government comparison where, contrary to conventional wisdom, conditions are actually inferior in the latter firms.

On the basis of the available data we can conclude that: (a) among various ownership groups there are few distinct differences – foreign firms offer marginally higher wages; but (b) the major differences among groups are explained by variations in industrial composition of these firms.

5. The impact of foreign investment: Wider issues

This section assesses the broader "development contribution" of multinational enterprises (MNEs) in Indonesia, with particular reference to the FDI impact on four main areas – the impact on exports, the contribution to skill formation, the development of linkages and subcontracting networks, and the effects of the policy regime on these and other issues.

5.1 Impact on exports

At the start of the 1980s there was widespread "export pessimism" in Indonesia, based on the belief that the country could never emulate the success story of its East Asian neighbours. During the 1980-89 period, however, Indonesia's manufactured exports grew at the spectacular average annual rate of 30 per cent. Plywood, clothing and woven fabrics accounted for over 60 per cent of the total, but export growth was strong, with a recent trend towards diversification.

This impressive export performance was primarily due to the Government's sound management of the economy, e.g. its exchange rate policy boosted the competitiveness of Indonesian exports, and by the introduction of incentives for exporters in 1986. However, foreign investors have also contributed to the success of the export drive, as evidenced by the number of "export-oriented" foreign investment approvals in recent years. In 1986, 93 projects were approved, of which 20 (22 per cent) were export-oriented, rising to 130 projects (38 export-oriented) in 1987, 145 (105) in 1988, 294 (231) in 1989 and 204 (155) in the first half of 1990.

On the other hand, comparing the major export items with the foreign ownership share the contribution of MNEs appears comparatively modest. For example, as illustrated in table 7.6, foreign firms produced just 13 per cent of value added in wood products (encompassing plywood), 25 per cent of textiles, 2 per cent of garments, 6 per cent of furniture, 13 per cent of footwear, 13 per cent of basic chemicals, 8 per cent of glass products, 5 per cent of basic metals (which includes steel), 26 per cent for electrical equipment and 12 per cent for miscellaneous manufactures.[8] These figures do, however, understate the MNEs' contribution in at least two respects.

First, they refer to industry, not firm, data. There are no data on the comparative export performance of foreign and domestic firms in Indonesia, but the evidence from other countries and the theory of the multinational enterprise strongly suggest that foreign firms are likely to be more export-oriented (and more import-intensive, too) than local firms. Langhammer (1988) and Hiemenz and Langhammer et al. (1987) do touch on some of these issues for Indonesia and other ASEAN countries.

Secondly, the ties between domestic exporters and MNEs are considerably stronger than the data suggest. Recent research by the author on textiles and garments (Hill, 1991) underscores the important role played by foreign buying groups and "arms-length" yet close business ties between Indonesian-Chinese exporters and firms from the Asian NIEs. Foreign ownership in the garment industry is minuscule, but these international commercial contacts have been crucial in providing market and design intelligence. In footwear, a recent surge in Korean involvement – not all of it in equity form – has resulted in several huge factories being established east of Jakarta. In rattan furniture, design and marketing specialists have been brought from the Philippines, a country more advanced in such skills but whose raw material supplies are nearly exhausted, to promote the local industry. More generally, Indonesia's

---

[8] Note, however, that there is not an exact correspondence owing to the complex concordance between the trade figures reported in SITC and the product data of table 7.6 which are based on ISIC.

export-oriented development phase has coincided with the loss of comparative advantage across a spectrum of labour-intensive activities in the NIEs, explaining the surge of FDI from these countries (see note 5; see also Thee, 1990a) and the development of many other forms of commercial interaction not captured in the official foreign ownership data.

5.2 Contribution to skill formation

A comprehensive assessment of the contribution of MNEs to human capital would ideally take the form of a comparison of the earnings stream of MNE (current and former) employees with those of a non-MNE control group. Assuming that labour markets are competitive and that real wage differentials may be attributed mainly to skill, any differences between the two groups could then be attributed to the impact of MNEs. Unfortunately, such detailed information is not available and so the major source of evidence on the subject has to take the form of firm surveys of training and other labour market policies. Certainly the mere fact of higher wages paid by foreign firms, as reported in table 7.8, cannot be taken as evidence of the contribution of MNEs to skill formation. The difference could equally be due to the recruitment policies of MNEs in hiring more skilled and better educated workers.

One of the most detailed studies of technology transfer and adaptation from MNEs in Indonesian manufacturing is that provided by Thee (1990b) on the basis of his in-depth survey of 12 firms. He concluded that:

> [...] most local managers and technical personnel obtained their necessary qualifications mainly through on-the-job training and additional training by working for a certain period [...] at the [MNE's] plant in its home country or in its overseas plants in other advanced countries [...] In addition, extensive training was also provided to local employees by expatriate managers and technical experts by a [MNE] to work in a joint venture [...] for a certain period of time (Thee, 1990b, p. 232).

The intensity of these training programmes varied, but a common feature was at least on-the-job training for production operatives, and advanced courses abroad for senior staff.

Earlier studies at the firm level confirm these conclusions. Manning (1979) undertook a detailed study of training facilities in foreign and domestic firms in the cigarette and textile industries. Half the foreign firms he surveyed provided special training courses for production workers, while the other half provided formal on-the-job training. Training provisions among comparable domestic firms were somewhat less – only 20 per cent of these firms offered these special training courses, while 60 per cent provided on-the-job training courses. These training facilities were in turn far more extensive than those of smaller domestic firms. In a survey of 74 Japanese firms in Indonesia, Tsurumi (1980) cited management reports that productivity levels among Indonesian workers were initially some 50-60 per cent those of Japanese or Korean workers. However, "after 12 to 18 months of work experience and closely supervised training" (p. 314) Indonesian workers achieved 80-90 per cent of this level. Rice (1974) and Siahaan, Thee et al. (1978) have also investigated training issues among foreign firms and have found evidence of a strong commitment to training.

Thus the field survey data point conclusively to the fact that foreign firms do make considerable investments in training, on a scale at least equal and probably exceeding that of the largest domestic firms. MNEs have thus made an important contribution to Indonesian economic development, but such a conclusion requires qualification in a number of respects.

1. Indonesia's shortage of skilled manpower – highly skilled and vocational – is increasingly serious, and this may have limited the benefits Indonesia has derived from the MNE presence. While there is a tendency in some quarters to view FDI as a substitute for domestic training, in fact the beneficial spill-over effects are limited because skilled Indonesian workers are unable to interact productively with their foreign counterparts, and Indonesian workers are less likely to rise in the international hierarchy of MNEs.

2. There is some circumstantial evidence which suggests that the senior appointment possibilities of local staff are restricted, especially among Japanese firms (see, for example, Panglaykim and Pangestu, 1983). Some writers attribute this phenomenon to cultural factors or head office restriction, but it is equally likely to be the result of the shortage of experienced Indonesian staff.

3. Although foreign firms hire better quality staff and train them more, these firms in many cases are able to appropriate the benefits of their investments in education owing to very low turnover levels among their staff, especially at senior levels. This aspect is emphasized by Rice (1974) and several other researchers.

4. The evidence does not point conclusively to FDI as being the only vehicle for the transmission of skills from foreign to domestic parties. Licensing arrangements, even without equity tie-ups, provide training facilities, although the international evidence and discussions with some Indonesian firms suggest that licensors may be less inclined to undertake such intensive technology transfers as is the case with foreign equity partners, in part because the former often focus more on sales-based (or even lump-sum) royalties payments rather than overall company development.

5.3 The development of linkages and subcontracting networks

Inter-firm linkages, including subcontracting networks, are another important means through which the externalities associated with the MNE presence may be appropriated by domestic economic agents. Foreign firms create powerful demonstration effects in their products, marketing procedures and managerial capacities. While these can and do result in firm closures among domestic competitors, on a level commercial playing field the MNE presence can equally act as a competitive spur. In the case of inter-firm linkages, also, such spin-offs are evident, such as in subcontracting relationships between MNE firms and local suppliers.

Thee (1990b) studied these networks intensively in his firm survey, finding mixed results:

[...] only the firms in the automotive industry, which is engaged in implementing an official "deletion programme", have been increasing the local content of the final goods through the mandatory increase of purchases of locally made parts and components. In contrast, in the case of pharmaceuticals, virtually all basic raw materials had to be purchased from the [MNEs] [...] In the case of food processing and chemical companies, various raw materials were procured locally, but in general these linkages did not involve an appreciable increase in the technical capabilities of local suppliers (Thee, 1990b, p. 231).

Thee's conclusions of weak subcontracting ties, except where the Government forces the pace (and even here, the Government has relaxed its deletion requirements in response to indifferent results) is supported by the research of Witoelar (1983) and the author's own interviews. They contrast sharply with the results of the Indian case study conducted by Lall (1980), although they are somewhat similar to the case of the Philippines (see Hill, 1985).

Three reasons can be given to explain these weak links between MNEs and local subcontractors. First, the capacity of local suppliers is generally weak, reflecting limited technological capability, unsophisticated commercial expertise, and poor quality control facilities. In interviews the author conducted with MNE assemblers in the automotive industry, for example, even well-disposed management with a strong preference for subcontracting reported numerous and costly delays in supply schedules and indifferent quality. A second reason is that, despite official support for subcontracting, the Government's protectionist policies have encouraged the opposite response. This is because of the "cascading" structure of protection, which offers very high effective protection to final stage assembly production, but low or even negative protection for intermediate inputs such as electrical and automotive components. In the absence of trade reform, it is difficult to see how this commercial obstacle can be overcome. Finally, it is sometimes alleged that ethnic fractures in the Indonesian business community – in particular between large Chinese concerns and small "pribumi" enterprise – may inhibit the development of such networks. While this may be a factor in certain circumstances, it is unlikely to be a key explanation: the large Chinese firms now employ increasing numbers of "pribumi" staff at senior levels, and in any case foreign firms would be less constrained in their commercial relationships.

In sum, this aspect of MNEs' contribution to Indonesian development is rather small. But it can be expected to develop over time as the quality of the potential pool of subcontractors improves and on the assumption that the Government continues with its programme of trade policy reform. MNEs have essentially responded to the market signals rather than being the primary cause of the problem.

5.4 The effects of the policy regime

The above discussion has alluded to the importance of the domestic policy regime in providing an environment conducive to maximizing the net domestic benefits of the MNE presence. However, in several respects the lack of an appropriate policy framework has limited the MNEs' contribution to economic development to economic development in Indonesia.

Firstly, Indonesia's trade regime has reduced the benefits which the country could have extracted from MNEs. In spite of the recent reforms, Indonesia's system of protection features high – and highly dispersed – effective protection for many manufactures, drawing resources into uneconomic activities and discriminating against low protection activities (see Fane and Phillips, 1991). Many of the high protection items, such as steel and automotive products, are capital-intensive; conversely, some of the labour-intensive activities, such as garments, "receive" very low, or even negative, protection. In both cases the effect of the protection regime is to draw resources out of the labour-intensive activities and thus retard badly needed employment growth.

Protection hampers the emergence of an efficient industrial sector in other respects. Some MNE-intensive industries exhibit negative value added at international prices, as a result of the inefficiency induced by extremely high levels of protection, thereby resulting in very little domestic benefit from the foreign investment. High protection and high concentration often go hand in hand (see Hill, 1987), resulting in very weak competitive pressures. This has important implications for choice of technology and employment creation, as Wells' (1973) case study revealed: firms in competitive industries often adopted excessively capital-intensive technologies when managers were able to express their preference for a "quiet life" or for sophisticated engineering equipment. More generally, protection has encouraged the development of a rent-seeking, politicized atmosphere in which entrepreneurs – foreign and domestic alike – are encouraged to lobby governments rather than pursue commercial objectives.

A major concern in Indonesia until the early 1980s was that government-induced distortions encouraged firms to adopt excessively capital-intensive technologies. This distortion occurred primarily in the capital market, where government banks offered subsidized credit, often at negative real rates of interest. Less important were tax incentives which cheapened the cost of capital, labour regulations which drove up the price of labour, and other regulations such as the ban on the import of second-hand equipment. However, following the capital market reforms of the 1980s and the removal of most of the subsidized credit programmes, these anti-employment biases became much less important. In any case, their primary impact – at least in the case of the credit programmes – was on domestic firms, since foreign firms were in principle denied access to loans from state banks.

Throughout the period since 1967, the benefits Indonesia has been able to extract from FDI have been mitigated somewhat by a widespread ambivalence towards foreign ownership and by structural deficiencies in the political system sometimes labelled the "soft state syndrome". The contrast in these respects with neighbouring Singapore is stark. The latter has established clearly defined entry rules for MNEs, it adopts a positive, welcoming posture towards them, and it operates a fiscal regime which ensures that foreign firms are properly taxed. In contrast, at least until recently, Indonesia's BKPM "… had not yet resolved whether its mission was exclusively to regulate foreign investment or simultaneously to promote that investment" (Encarnation and Wells, 1986, p. 71). Until the negative list, investment priority areas were ill-defined, procedures were cumbersome and time-consuming, and fiscal supervision was lax. In effect, MNEs built a large risk premium into their calculations, but often redeemed it through lower tax obligations or high protection. In such circumstances the domestic benefits were smaller.

Other aspects of the domestic policy regime have been discussed above. Indonesian governments have under-invested in education and training programmes, and in research and development (R&D) facilities. The recruitment of skilled foreign personnel has sometimes been curbed excessively. And sudden changes in the policy environment unsettle foreign firms and encourage them to focus on short-term, fast-yielding projects.

6. Conclusions

Our principal conclusions are threefold. First, foreign firms have entered Indonesia in increasing numbers since the liberalization of 1967, and the annual trends can be explained by the interplay of domestic and international economic circumstances and the domestic policy regime. Foreign investors have – where the policy regime permits – entered sectors which are consistent with the theory of FDI: large-scale mining activities, some of the more technology-intensive manufacturing industries, and a few niches of the service sector. Despite their growing presence, however, the inflows and ownership reach are comparatively modest in international perspective, and generally less than most of the country's neighbours. Foreign firms play a far smaller role than (domestic) private and state firms.

The second conclusion is that foreign firms have made a significant contribution to Indonesian economic development since 1966. There is hardly a firm in Indonesia's modern sector that has not had some commercial or technological tie-up with overseas interests, whether taking the form of close equity links of the type discussed above; or of strong licensing arrangements which, even without the equity interest, bind the foreign and domestic partners together; or of occasional commercial encounters through the supply of machinery and marketing information. MNEs have been especially important in providing training facilities; they have also contributed to the export drive, though in other respects the spin-offs are a good deal weaker.

A third key theme of this chapter is that the Indonesian policy regime has meant that the economic benefits associated with the MNE presence have not always been as great as they could have been. MNEs have been permitted to operate in highly concentrated industries behind import protection. This regime has virtually guaranteed them high profitability, even though some of the industries concerned have generated negative value added at international prices. The country's fiscal regime has also been unnecessarily lax. And the "stop-go" ambivalent policy environment may have created much uncertainty in the minds of foreign investors, encouraging them to select quick-yielding high-return projects. Appropriate changes in the domestic policy regime should be able to play a role in strengthening MNEs' contribution to economic growth in the country.

Note   An earlier version of this chapter appeared as *Working Paper* No. 67 in the ILO's Multinational Enterprises Programme. Some of the data and discussion in the original version have been omitted.

Bibliography

Dickie, R.B.; Layman, T.A. 1988. *Foreign investment and government policy in the Third World: Forging common interests in Indonesia and beyond*, London, Macmillan Press.

Encarnation, D.J.; Wells, L.T. 1986. "Competitive strategies in global industries: A view from host governments", in M.E. Porter (ed.): *Competition in global industries*, Boston, Harvard Business School Press.

Fane, G.; Phillips, C. 1991. "Effective protection in Indonesia", in *Bulletin of Indonesian Economic Studies*, Canberra, 27(1).

Hiemenz, U.; Langhammer, R.J., et al. 1987. *The competitive strength of European, Japanese and US suppliers on ASEAN markets*, Kieler Studien 211, Tubingen, J.C.B. Mohr (Paul Siebeck).

Hill, H. 1985. "Subcontracting, technological diffusion and the development of small enterprise in Philippine manufacturing", in *Journal of Developing Areas*, 19(2), pp. 245-261.

—. 1987. "Concentration in Indonesian manufacturing", in *Bulletin of Indonesian Economic Studies*, Canberra, 23(2), pp. 71-100.

—. 1988a. *Foreign investment and industrialization in Indonesia*, Singapore, Oxford University Press.

—. 1988b. "Some neglected issues in factor proportions and ownership: An Indonesian case study", in *Weltwirtschaftliches Archiv*, Kiel, 124(2), pp. 341-355.

—. 1990a. "Foreign investment and East Asian economic development: A survey", in *Asia-Pacific Economic Literature*, Canberra, 4(2), pp. 21-58.

—. 1990b. "Indonesia's industrial transformation, Parts I and II", in *Bulletin of Indonesian Economic Studies*, Canberra, 26(2), pp. 79-120, and 26(3), pp. 75-109.

—. 1991. "The Emperor's clothes can now be made in Indonesia", in *Bulletin of Indonesian Economic Studies*, Canberra, 27(3).

Hugo, G.J., et al. 1987. *The demographic dimension in Indonesian development*, Singapore, Oxford University Press.

Jayasuriya, S.K.; Manning, C.G. 1990. "Agricultural wage growth and rural labour market adjustment: The case of Java 1970-88", in *Working Papers in Trade and Development*, Canberra, Research School of Pacific Studies, Australian National University, No. 90/2.

Jones, G.W.; Manning, C. 1991. "Labour force and employment during the 1980s", in A. Booth (ed.): *The oil boom and after: Indonesian economic policy and performance in the Suharto era*, Singapore, Oxford University Press.

Keyfitz, N., et al. 1989. *Indonesian universities at the crossroads*, Jakarta, Center for Policy and Implementation Studies.

Kuntjoro-Jakti, D. 1985. "Indonesia", in *Patterns and impact of foreign investment in the ESCAP region*, Bangkok, United Nations Economic and Social Commission for Asia and the Pacific, pp. 69-95.

Lall, S. 1980. "Vertical inter-firm linkages in LDCs: An empirical study", in *Oxford Bulletin of Economics and Statistics*, 42(3), pp. 203-226.

Langhammer, R.J. 1988. "Investment and trade flows: The case of Indonesia", in *Bulletin of Indonesian Economic Studies*, Canberra, 24(1), pp. 97-114.

Manning, C.G. 1979. *Wage differentials and labour market segmentation in Indonesian manufacturing*, unpublished doctoral dissertation, Australian National University, Canberra.

Naylor, R. 1990. "Wage trends in rice production in Java 1976-1988", in *Bulletin of Indonesian Economic Studies*, 26(2).

Panglaykim, J.; Pangestu, M. (collab.) 1983. *Japanese direct investment in ASEAN: The Indonesian experience*, Singapore, Maruzen Asia.

Rice, R.C. 1974. "The interfirm externalities of foreign investment in manufacturing in Indonesia", in *Ekonomi dan Keuangan Indonesia*, 22(2), pp. 127-153.

Sadli, M. 1972. "Foreign investment in developing countries: Indonesia", in P. Drysdale (ed.): *Direct foreign investment in Asia and the Pacific*, Canberra, Australian National University Press, pp. 201-225.

Siahaan, L.; Thee, K.W., et al. 1978. *Japanese direct investment in Indonesia: Findings of an experimental survey*, Tokyo, Joint Research Program Series No. 9, Institute of Developing Economies.

Thee, K.W. 1984a. "Japanese direct investment in Indonesian manufacturing", in *Bulletin of Indonesian Economic Studies*, Canberra, 20(2), pp. 90-106.

—. 1984b. "Japanese and American direct investment in Indonesian manufacturing compared", in *Ekonomi dan Keuangan Indonesia*, 32(1), pp. 89-105.

—. 1990b. "Indonesia: Technology transfer in the manufacturing industry", in H. Soesastro and M. Pangestu (eds.): *Technological challenge in the Pacific*, Sydney, Allen & Unwin, pp. 200-232.

—. 1990a. "The investment surge from the East Asian newly industrialising countries into Indonesia", seminar paper, Department of Economics, Research School of Pacific Studies, Australian National University, Canberra.

—; Yoshihara, K. 1987. "Foreign and domestic capital in Indonesian industrialization", in *Southeast Asian Studies*, 24(4), pp. 327-349.

Tsurumi, Y. 1980. "Japanese investments in Indonesia: Ownership, technology transfer, and political conflict", in G. Papanek (ed.): *The Indonesian Economy*, New York, Praeger, pp. 295-323.

Wells, L.T. Jr. 1973. "Economic man and engineering man: Choice of technology in a low-wage country", in *Public Policy*, 21(3), pp. 319-342.

Witoelar, W. 1983. "Ancillary firm development in the motor vehicle industry in Indonesia", in K. Odaka (ed.): *The motor vehicle industry in Asia*, Singapore, Singapore University Press, pp. 17-84.

8

Effects of foreign direct investment on employment in the former "centrally planned economies" of Central and Eastern Europe

Martin K. Welge and Dirk Holtbrügge

Of all the areas discussed in this book where FDI is taking place, virtually none have attracted more interest than the countries of Central and Eastern Europe. Yet as any reader of the morning's newspaper knows, the previous evening's television broadcast has usually rendered it obsolete before it has even been printed. Thus when this chapter was commissioned, Gorbachev was in power, the Soviet Union still existed, the Baltic States had not yet declared their independence, Czechoslovakia was written in one word and Yugoslavia was not yet in a state of civil war.

Although subsequent attempts were made to catch up with post-coup and post-Soviet Union results, the basic problem remains that events are moving too quickly to permit conclusive statements and meaningful analysis. In addition, none of the countries of Central and Eastern Europe shared much in common with each other, except for all having had "centrally planned economies".

The UN/ECE database provides the most accurate statistics on joint venture registrations up to about the third quarter of 1991, after which time the breakup of the former USSR and the increasing ability of enterprises to enter Eastern Europe without central registration has considerably complicated the task of having comparable data available for statistical purposes.

Thus while this chapter was intended to focus on the former USSR, Hungary and Poland, it is obvious that few generalizations are possible and that most FDI in the Commonwealth of Independent States is concentrated in Russia and the Ukraine. Section 1 describes briefly the move to market economies in these countries; section 2 examines the role of foreign investment; section 3 outlines general labour market conditions and section 4 the local labour laws as they affect foreign investors; section 5 looks at the employment effects to date of foreign direct investment, while the conclusion outlines some of the main issues emerging in these countries with respect to the employment effects of foreign investment.

Editor's Note.

1. Central and Eastern European economies in transition

The move to a market economy in all former centrally planned economies (CPEs) is a new and unique experience for these countries. This change, however, is taking place without any model for the selection and timing of appropriate action. Most programmes focus by default more on intentions and objectives rather than on ways and means. In addition, all former CPEs are not only confronted with the problem of transforming their societies into market economies, but are also simultaneously faced with the necessity of achieving economic stabilization and providing basic food and consumer goods.

Another serious problem facing the former CPEs, where for more than half a century the right to work had been a basic right guaranteed by the Constitution, is unemployment. This problem did not emerge all at once. The relatively low levels of open unemployment recorded in the early stages of the transition, despite the large and widespread falls in output, testified to the fact that the "soft budget" constraint was still operating in these economies. However, in 1991 the picture changed considerably: the number of persons registered as unemployed in Eastern Europe more than doubled in the year to December 1991 and reached 4.1 million in March 1992 (excluding the former GDR and USSR). Unemployment rates in Poland could be estimated to range around 10 per cent in December 1991 and some 7-8 per cent in Czechoslovakia and Hungary (UN/ECE 1992, p. 6). In the Republics of the Commonwealth of Independent States, official registration of unemployment has only recently begun and to date the numbers of registered unemployed are low. However they are increasing: in Russia, in January 1992, 692,000 registered as unemployed in comparison to 151,000 in April of the same year (Ecotass, 1992).

As in Western economies, the burden of this unemployment has tended to fall more heavily on women rather than on men, on the young, and on manual workers rather than on the skilled and more educated. Since restructuring is in its early stages and there is still a large number of unprofitable state enterprises facing inevitable bankruptcy, the level of unemployment will rise considerably and even beyond the time at which output begins to recover. Social pressure to resist unemployment is going to be a decisive factor in influencing political developments in the region.

Finally, the liberalization of public life has fuelled previously suppressed nationalist and ethnic tensions which, now released, are becoming obstacles to reform. In the Commonwealth of Independent States conflict may still lead to the breakup of economic relations between the former Union Republics and to a further fragmentation into several autonomous States with different political, economic and legal regimes.

As early as the late 1970s several leading Eastern European economists (e.g. Kornai, 1980) were already pointing out that supply shortages, low productivity and long innovation cycles were a result of soft budget constraints and thus system-immanent to a centrally planned economy. Since the early 1980s, it was well known that the economic situation in Eastern European was deteriorating with increasing rapidity. The chronic and familiar problems associated with central planning and the

Table 8.1.   Recent economic developments in Central and Eastern Europe

Country	Population 1990 (million)	GDP 1990 (US$ bn)	GDP decline in 1991 (%)	Employment decline in 1991 (%)	Registered unemployment March 1992 ('000s)
Ex-USSR	289	512	n.a.	n.a.	n.a.
Poland	38	62	9	5.5	2238
Romania	23	36	14	11.6	461
CSFR	15.6	47	16	7.4	503
Hungary	10.6	32	10	6.0	478
Bulgaria	9.0	22	17	14.5	453

Source: World Bank, OECD, 1992.

command economy such as stagnant growth, low productivity, poor quality goods and zero innovation were becoming more and more acute. This permanent crisis manifested itself in the form of severe shortages, inflation, mounting budget deficits, and increasing social and environmental problems.

Up to the mid-1980s, gradual economic reforms had been adopted to cope with mounting pressures. But by the late 1980s, it became evident that the severe crisis could not be met with piecemeal reform but only by a radical overhaul of the entire system including the introduction of a multi-party, democratic system of government and a market economy. Thus with the collapse of the communist system in Central and Eastern Europe, all these countries quickly embarked upon the setting up of new political regimes and the moving from an overly centralized command economy to a more decentralized market system. Of immediate import in the economic sphere was the issue of the speed with which the market mechanism should be introduced.

In **Poland**, "shock-therapy" was adopted in 1989 aimed at stabilizing the economy, drastically reducing inflation, and simultaneously transforming the existing system into a market economy. This programme consisted of: (a) reducing the budget deficit and tightening credit and monetary policy; (b) limiting wage increases in state enterprises; (c) abolishing most administrative price controls and introducing market-oriented pricing; (d) removing bureaucratic restrictions on the private sector; and (e) sharply devaluing the zloty followed by the introduction of internal convertibility[1] to increase competitive pressures on Polish enterprises and to prevent undesirable capital flows.

The initial euphoria over "shock-therapy", however, quickly turned sour. Although the International Monetary Fund forecast a growth in private consumption and GDP as well as a boom in capital investment, GDP in the first half of 1991 actually declined by 5-10 per cent and investment by 20 per cent. In 1991, output contin-

---

[1] Internal convertibility only includes convertibility for transactions on current accounts by residents (and not transactions on capital accounts). Foreign-owned enterprises operating in Poland count as residents.

ued to fall and the rate of inflation remained high. The results of privatization and enterprise restructuring in particular have been even more disappointing. The Government has been especially criticized for overemphasizing the economic benefits accruing from privatization while neglecting to mention the psychological and social problems. With the benefit of hindsight it now seems that the prediction expressed at the time that economic growth would occur simply through privatization and the free play of market forces was over-optimistic. It is also true that many reformers and policy advisers greatly underestimated the amount of time required to pass the necessary economic legislation and actually implement agreed decisions. This is true not just for Poland but for all the economies in transition.

Hungary, in contrast, has followed a more gradual strategy of economic transformation both because it had already introduced elements of market mechanism over the last two decades and because the country's own more precarious financial state meant that a "big bang" approach carried with it more risks. A key element of the Act on Economic Associations (Company Act) of 1988 was to generate an entrepreneurial spirit through the privatization of state companies and the development of small- and medium-sized enterprises. Like in Poland and the former Czechoslovakia, a State Property Agency (SPA) was set up in March 1990 to regulate the process of selling state-owned enterprises and their assets. The SPA was empowered to put a halt to so-called "spontaneous privatization" – in practice a sophisticated form of theft from the State – whereby the former managers turned their enterprises into joint-stock companies and sold the shares to foreigners in return for such favours as a guaranteed job, or signed over property rights to private ventures which they subsequently owned. The majority of Hungarians perceived this practice to be unfair since it permitted the former unsuccessful managers to take over enterprises without paying a fair price as well as preserving the power base of the former "nomenclatura".

Although privatization has been most successful in Hungary there have been considerable problems due to delays, the lack of financial resources and of buyers, valuation problems and arguments about compensation to past owners. Thus by the end of 1991, of the 20 enterprises earmarked for privatization under the **First Privatization Programme,** only four had been approved for privatization by the Board of Directors of the SPA. Although other programmes have been started, according to the Government only around 10 per cent of former state property had passed into private hands by the end of 1991 with total revenues of some HUF 31.38 billion.

In the **former USSR**, following the drastic political and economic reforms introduced by Gorbachev, four alternative plans for a thorough transition to a market economy were presented to the Supreme Soviet in 1990 – from the conservative approaches of Abalkin and Aganbegyan and the radical Shatalin-Yavlinsky "500 days programme" to Gorbachev's "Guidelines". None of them, however was implemented, in the light of the dramatic political events of August 1991.

After the replacement of the former USSR by a Commonwealth of Independent States in December 1991, most of the new independent Republics announced rapid economic and political reforms. In Russia, for example, after many postponements most administrative price controls were abolished, trade was freed and a programme of privatization announced. It is planned to end shortages by allowing prices, wages and the exchange rate to fluctuate according to the market. By allowing the rouble to float freely, at least at the start of the programme, it is hoped to achieve currency convertibility instantly. Until recently, however, the members of the new Commonwealth have failed to create a new workable system of economic and monetary coordination. Furthermore, many think that the Commonwealth may be too weak to withstand the forces of nationalism which are still gathering strength. Overall, the political and economic situation in many of the former Union Republics seems to remain unstable and unpredictable at least in the short term.

The transformation to a market economy made rapid progress in the **Czech and Slovak Federal Republic**, despite political moves which led to the dissolution of the federation at the end of 1992. Before that, a highly ambitious privatization pro- gramme was under way (more than 8.5 million citizens were planned to take part in the mass distribution programme which aimed to turn over US$ 9.9 billion worth of state-owned equity to private shareholders), most subsidies and restrictions on prices and foreign trade had been removed, and the legal basis for the development of the private sector had been completed with the passing of a new Commercial Code in December 1991. In **Bulgaria**, **Romania** and **Albania**, the transition process is also under way but it remains still in its early stages.

2. The role of foreign direct investment as a potential catalyst for change

Within the new economic policies of all former CPEs, foreign direct invest- ment (FDI) is expected to play an important role. Although the aims vary from country to country, the following common objectives may be identified:

■ the improvement of the foreign exchange position through expanding export- oriented industries and import substitution;

■ the achievement of spin-off effects through the modernization and restructuring of the host economy by importing capital and technology and introducing market-oriented management techniques in domestic companies;

■ the improvement of the quality and quantity of raw materials, manufactured products, consumer goods and services for the domestic market; and

■ the creation of new jobs, improved productivity, training for host country techni- cal and managerial personnel and the transformation of the country's employ- ment structure.

From the foreign investors' point of view, former CPEs are attractive at least in the long term for several main reasons: a large, untapped potential market consisting of almost 400 million people; a reasonably skilled, low-cost labour force; an existing industrial structure which, no matter how obsolete, was able to manufac- ture a vast range of useful products and in some cases to export to industrialized economies; and (especially in the former Soviet Union) a strong capacity for pure and applied scientific research, as well as a rich untapped reservoir of raw materials and mineral resources.

2.1 Recent changes in investment legislation

By now new, more liberal legislation has been adopted in almost all former CPEs in an attempt to establish conditions to attract foreign investment. Now only in Albania is a foreign investor legally required to form a joint venture with a local partner; all the other countries of the region allow foreign companies to fully own corporate assets in their territories.

Taking all the changes in the legislation together it can be argued that while other barriers to foreign investment may exist, there are now no longer any major legal impediments to the establishment and operation of companies with foreign participation in these countries. Nevertheless, constant changes to laws are unhelpful in creating the sort of stable and predictable climate necessary to inspire confidence amongst foreign investors. While this is no longer a problem in Central Europe – Hungary, Poland, the Czech Republic and Slovakia have by now established a fairly settled legislative framework for foreign investment – in some of the Republics of the CIS, the laws are far from being clear and stable. Here, following the collapse of the Soviet Union and the failure to create in its place any central legislating body, the Parliaments of each Republic have assumed the task of enacting all the new business legislation. Thus, until each Republic has its own company law, labour code, taxation system, etc., foreign investors, particularly those who were established under the old but no longer valid Soviet laws, will have to endure considerable uncertainty.

In 1971, **Romania** was the first CPE country to actually pass a law allowing domestic enterprises to run JVs with foreign partners. However, the nine JVs established during the 1970s were subsequently liquidated. After the 1989 revolution, the Provisional Council for National Unity issued a new decree subsequently amended and made more attractive to FDI. Now only one Agency, the Romanian Development Agency, is responsible for issuing consent to new investment proposals; while applications are by law required to be processed within 30 days.

In **Hungary**, JVs have been authorized by a decree of the Minister of Finance since 1972, but the Company Act and the Foreign Investment Act of 1988 signified a considerable change in the Hungarian attitude towards FDI. As of January 1989, foreigners could acquire a 100 per cent share of domestic companies, and in the following year foreign companies, even those wishing to establish fully owned enterprises in Hungary, no longer required authorization from the Government. All industries from production and commerce to services (including banking and insurance) and trade, with the exception of activities excluded or restricted by law, are open to foreign participation. They can engage in foreign trade without restriction and enjoy special tax incentives. On the whole, Hungary's FDI regime is the most liberal of all former CPEs and is as open – if not more so – than most Western market economies.

In **Poland**, foreign legal and physical entities have been authorized to run certain strictly limited types of economic activities since 1976. An attempt to attract FDI was made in 1982 through the law on foreign small manufacturing enterprises. However, exporting and importing were restricted and the maximum number of employees was limited to 200. In 1986 another law was passed, enabling foreign investors to do business in the public sector and enter into JVs with public sector companies. Since January 1989, the economic activity of foreign investors has been based on the same general principles binding all Polish economic entities. Finally, in July 1991, a revised Foreign Investment Act came into effect. The new law abolished the minimum capital requirement and the rule that foreign equity participation above 10 per cent required approval. It also permitted the repatriation of 100 per cent of after-tax profits and invested capital.

In the **former USSR**, legislative changes proceeded more gradually and in ad hoc manner. No unified foreign investment law was actually passed until just before the events of August 1991. Substantive liberalization prior to this generally took the form of Presidential Decrees: in October 1990 two such decrees authorized foreign investors to set up wholly owned subsidiaries on Soviet territory and to repatriate in full the profits earned in local currency. Furthermore the Soviet law of July 1991 gave to the Republics the full right to legislate for foreign investment in their own territories although several had already passed their own foreign investment laws, e.g. Lithuania in December 1990 and Kazakhstan in January 1991.

Russia was one of the first States to pass a privatization law, the "Law on Privatizing State- and Municipal-Owned Enterprises" (November 1991), which envisaged the possibility of foreign companies buying a 100 per cent stake in the state enterprises that were to be privatized. The Russian privatization programme, however, has been criticized for only providing incentives to the employees of privatized enterprises and not to the foreign investors themselves. So far, the attempt to attract large Western companies to major industries in the Russian market has not been very successful.

In **Czechoslovakia**, a Law on Companies with Foreign Participation took effect in January 1989. However, since FDI flows following the promulgation of this law proved disappointing, the Czech and Slovak Federal Republic's Federal Assembly approved new amendments on 19 April 1990. In particular, the possibility of full foreign ownership was established, approval procedures simplified, JVs with private Czech and Slovak citizens legalized and full repatriation of profits allowed. Tax incentives were also offered, but fewer than in Poland or Hungary. In **Bulgaria**, FDI has been permitted since 1980. In February 1992 the country passed its third foreign investment law in 18 months. Reflecting political changes, this new law substantially liberalizes the investment regime for foreign companies. Finally, in July 1990, **Albania** overcame its ideological reservation against foreign economic assistance and made a first step in the creation of legal conditions for encouraging FDI (UNECE, October 1990).

It is important to point out that foreign investment laws are only one gauge of a country's degree of openness to foreign investors. Of particular importance are the privatization laws in these countries. Generally and not surprisingly given the relative values of state-owned enterprises under prevailing prices, these laws place various restrictions on foreign participation in the sale of state-owned enterprises and their assets. Negotiations with foreign investors over the sale of state firms often become protracted.

Figure 8.1.   Number of FDI registrations in Eastern Europe

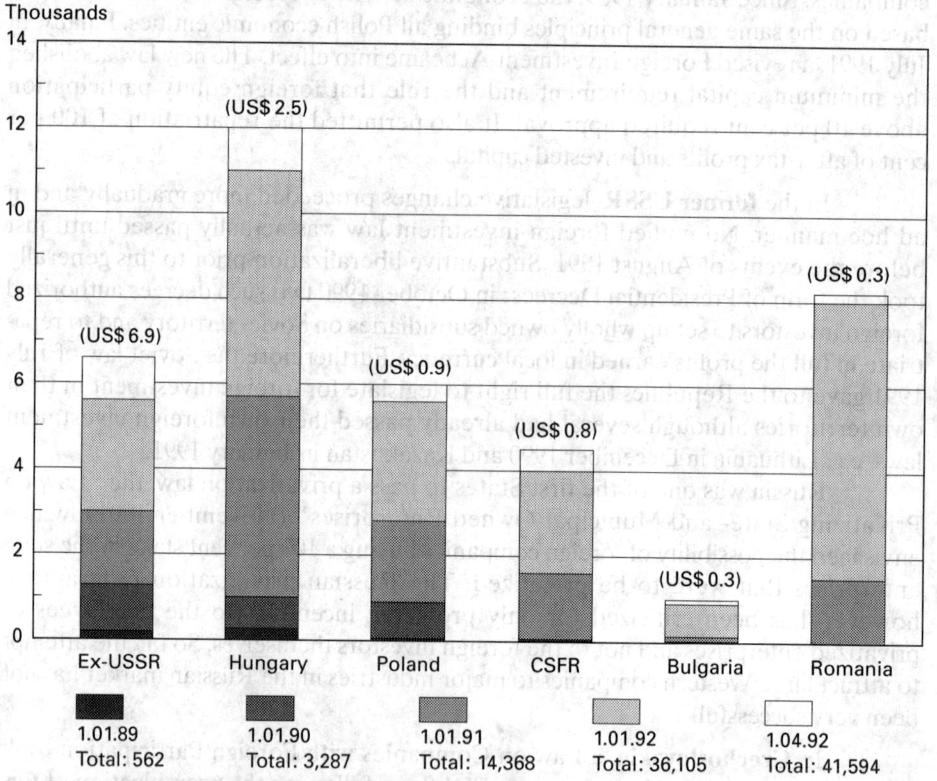

Thousands

Note: Estimated value of foreign capital in brackets (US$ billion).

2.2 The recent evolution of FDI

The liberalization of legal and economic conditions for FDI in most Eastern European economies has attracted the interest of foreign investors and caused a rapid increase in the number of JVs and in the amount of capital invested from abroad in recent years (see figure 8.1). Still, the rapid growth may not be entirely accounted for in the existing statistics of the host countries. It is not unreasonable to assume that the central authorities do not have the full picture, since foreign participation in local enterprises can also be registered in regional and local offices, in addition to the principal ministries. Available information is also often incomplete and potentially misleading in the way in which key indicators are presented and classified according to economic activities which do not correspond to recognized standards. Finally, no information is collected on items such as the origin of production inputs, the value of the technology contributed by the Western partner, the amount of credit provided and the related interest payments.

Table 8.2.   Foreign investment registrations in Eastern Europe, 1992 (number and estimates of foreign capital in US$ million)

Country	1.1.1992		1.4.1992	
	Number of registrations	Foreign capital	Number of registrations	Foreign capital
Former USSR of which:	5 600	5 900	6 600	6 900
Russia	2 500	3 400	2 900	4 200
Ukraine	500	900	600	960
Estonia	1 100	105	1 496	150
Latvia	250	45	300	50
Lithuania	220	33	292	35
Hungary	11 000	2 250	12 000	2 500
Poland	5583	832	6000	900
CSFR	4 000	760	4 500	850
Slovenia	1 000	650	1 100	700
Romania	8 022	269	10 394	323
Bulgaria	900	250	1 000	270
TOTAL	36 105	10 911	41 594	12 443

Note: Values in national currencies converted in US$ at current official rates.

Source: ECE Secretariat.

A detailed look at the available information, however, can spread some light on the nature of the investment process. In spite of the exponential increase in the number of FDI transactions, the overall picture is rather disappointing.

■   First, not all JVs registered in the statistics are operational. In the USSR, only 40 per cent of approximately 3,000 JVs registered at the Ministry of Finance by the end of 1990 were actually functioning.

■   JVs are more numerous in Hungary and Poland than in the much larger former USSR. And half of the operational JVs are reported to be in Hungary alone.

■   On the whole, JV capitalization is very low and has even declined most recently. In the former USSR, for example, the average size of a JV's statutory capital decreased from 7 to 2 million roubles between 1987 and 1990. Taking all registrations together, the average size was only 2.4 million roubles. In Hungary, the average capitalization of all JVs operational at the beginning of 1990 was HUF 90 million. Cumulatively, the average foreign contribution to statutory capital was HUF 40 million, or US$ 653,000 (at the official exchange rate in January 1990). In Poland, 80 per cent of all JVs in operation by March 1990 had a foreign capital share of less than US$ 100,000. In the CSFR finally, 80 per cent of the 1,200 JVs or FDI transactions approved between May and December 1990 had capital of Kcs1 million or less.

■   An analysis by country of origin shows that a high percentage of invested capital comes from neighbouring countries: i.e., from Finland in the former USSR; from

Austria in Hungary; from Germany in Poland; and from Austria and Germany in the case of the CSFR (see table 8.2). The investors from these countries are, therefore, exploiting their locational advantage, knowledge of the market and possession of products and technologies needed by the host countries. Conspicuous by their absence are Japanese and British companies – two of the world's leading foreign investors.

■ In the former USSR, the size of foreign manufacturing start-ups (actually in operation) was limited (42 per cent) relative to investment in business and distributive services, and in computer-related activities (table 8.3, see also IMF, et al., 1991, Vol. 2, p. 77). The percentage of JVs in the manufacturing sector in Poland and Hungary is higher, yet most investment occurred in component manufacturing. Therefore, the degree of value added and the contribution of FDI to the economic growth of the host economies is restricted. In ex-Czechoslovakia, FDI in the manufacturing sector has been limited relative to the perceived potential, even if more recently there appears to have been signs of stronger interest by big Western firms, particularly from Germany.

■ The regional distribution of FDI within countries is also interesting. In the former USSR, more than 60 per cent of all JVs were located in Russia and 10 per cent in the Ukraine. More than 50 per cent of all JVs are located in Moscow and the surrounding region, and 25 per cent in other large cities like St. Petersburg, Tallin or Kiev. In Hungary, the concentration is even higher – 72 per cent of the operational JVs and 75 per cent of JVs formed in 1990 are located in Budapest. Only in Poland, can one find an approximately even distribution. Therefore, the FDI contribution to regional policies and development until now has been minimal.

In a new development in many former CPEs, local authorities are trying to attract foreign firms by setting up free economic zones (FEZs). These FEZs are intended to offer more liberal conditions for investment as concerns duties, taxes, labour legislation and currency exchange. Unlike export processing zones (EPZs) in developing countries, these Eastern FEZs are more like *import processing zones* and intended to try out market structures and provide orientations for restructuring the entire economy. Moreover, it is expected that the concentration of FDI will accelerate economic transformation in an area. FEZs have already been established in Hungary and Bulgaria. In the former USSR, FEZs are planned in Vyborg, Novgorod, Kaliningrad, St. Petersburg, on the Black Sea coast as well as in the Far East. The independent Baltic Republics likewise plan to set up FEZs. Up to now, these attempts have sometimes been blocked by central authorities who feared that economic regionalization could further undermine central political power. Those that have gone ahead have not been notably successful. It is worth recalling that in the former USSR the rationale for establishing FEZs was to create special conditions inside a zone and thereby obviate the necessity to open up the territory to investors elsewhere. Thus the opening up of all of Russia to FDI negates the original rationale for these special zones.

It is premature, at this stage, to draw any strong inference from the scarce data available and the limited experience with FDI in Eastern Europe. However, it

Table 8.3. **Number of JV registrations in the former USSR, Poland, Hungary and the CSFR, by origin of foreign partner**

Country/Region	Former USSR		Poland		Hungary		CSFR	
	Number	Foreign capital (US$ m)	Number	Foreign capital (US$ m)	Number	Foreign capital (US$ m)	Number	Foreign capital (US$ m)
Western Europe	1228	1870.9	2296	301.0	797	530.6	195	71.8
EEC	700	1074.4	1661	201.5	412	257.1	90	53.2
France	70	181.2	130	14.3	9	8.8	7	13.0
Germany	281	346.1	981	109.1	252	78.6	56	12.7
Italy	130	289.8	131	19.4	46	42.9	9	0.3
Luxembourg	7	1.4	5	0.3	5	54.5	–	–
Netherlands	24	34.4	108	26.6	24	17.2	7	8.3
Spain	29	39.7	14	1.0	7	0.7	1	0.0
United Kingdom	112	115.4	145	13.9	48	44.5	7	6.6
EFTA	468	685.4	613	96.7	374	269.8	102	18.6
Austria	115	143.0	200	22.0	257	200.9	80	11.9
Finland	183	356.9	20	1.5	9	9.5	2	0.0
Liechtenstein	18	14.6	24	6.6	21	14.7	–	–
Sweden	66	95.7	256	32.4	24	14.3	4	0.3
Switzerland	78	78.1	90	14.5	61	30.2	16	6.3
Other Europe	60	111.1	22	2.8	11	3.7	3	0.0
Yugoslavia	32	91.0	5	0.5	3	0.0	3	0.0
United States	247	360.2	214	29.4	65	91.6	4	0.0
Canada	53	86.7	48	3.9	17	1.5	–	–
Japan	33	46.4	5	1.0	2	1.0	–	–
Developing countries	130	148.9	42	5.6	15	58.0	2	0.2
Former CPEs	145	273.4	54	3.8	16	11.1	12	17.0
Bulgaria	45	151.3	2	0.1	1	0.2	1	0.3
USSR	–	–	48	3.5	14	10.7	7	11.5
Hungary	27	48.9	3	0.2	–	–	3	5.3
Poland	75	65.3	–	–	1	0.1	1	0.0
China	25	26.8	–	–	–	–	1	5.0
Korea, DPR of	11	27.0	–	–	–	–	–	–
Other	54	48.2	39	8.8	4	0.6	–	–
Multi-Party	121	262.5	101	20.4	74	153.0	13	37.3
Unknown	3	0.6	3	1.0	16	0.5	1	0.0
Total	2050	3151.6	2799	373.8	1006	847.8	228	131.4

Note: For the former USSR, Poland and Hungary as of 1 January 1991; for CSFR as of 25 March 1991. Figures may not add to totals because of rounding.

Source: UNECE Data Bank on Joint Ventures.

appears that foreign investors are, on the whole, risk averse, e.g. investing a small amount but by no means disinterested. Investors from neighbouring countries have been generally more active (e.g. in the case of Finland, Germany, Austria), but actual investment – concentrated in either small ventures or those with some form of foreign capital participation – has been modest. The activities of expatriates who use their previous knowledge of local markets (e.g. in Poland, Hungary and the former CSFR) to exploit opportunities for profits which derive from existing distortions may partly explain the pattern of investment. Initially, investment was also skewed to hard currency markets, e.g. foreign enterprises, Western tourists, etc. Especially in the USSR, it also seems that many JVs were established merely to gain experience and in order to become an insider with an advantageous position for the future penetration of the domestic market ("wait-and-see-JV"). The immediate positive economic effect of this "illusory" form of FDI is likely to be marginal (IMF, et al., 1991, Vol. 2, p. 79). Actual JV performance has not yet conformed to the expectations of host governments and nationalistic feelings against foreign speculation and dominance are emerging.

With privatization, however, a new stage in foreign company involvement in the economies in the region has begun which has far greater significance for employment both inside Eastern Europe and in the Western economies. In many industries, notably low-priced consumer products, automobiles and heavy electrical engineering, Western MNEs are competing fiercely with each other to acquire companies in the East and gain market share. In some cases these newly acquired companies are being integrated into the multinational production network of these firms, so that goods and components will be made in the East and exported to Western markets. For example, ABB has shifted the production of its gas turbines for world markets to its plant in Poland. Already, ABB trade unions in the West have voiced alarm at the creation of new production capacity in this region, declaring that it is designed to exploit cheap Eastern European labour.[2]

The leading MNEs from the major industrialized countries, particularly Japan, are nevertheless conspicuously absent from the picture. East European markets are less attractive for their higher valued products, while cheap labour is of less strategic importance for these companies which rely on more sophisticated process technology and production methods. In addition, political problems still restrict Japanese investors particularly with regard to investments in Russia. Nevertheless, expectations about business opportunities in the Eastern European economies are still generally high and there are probably few major Western MNEs which have not at least considered these opportunities at length. As a matter of fact, as reported in the press, many European and American MNEs are planning to undertake large investments in these countries in the next years. For example, General Motors has decided to invest US$ 150 million in a car-producing JV in Hungary, where 850 people will be employed. A similar contract has been signed by the Japanese Suzuki company. Volkswagen AG plans to employ approximately 16,000 in its JV with Skoda in former Czechoslovakia, and the JV plans to buy components from more than 200 local subcontractors. Adding people employed at these component suppliers, the project may

---

[2] "4,000 employees protest against planned job cuts at ABB", in *Frankfurter Allgemeine Zeitung*, 4 Sep. 1991, p. 24.

account for some 85,000 jobs in former Czechoslovakia. In the former USSR, there are some large-scale projects planned, too. As mentioned above, the large-scale privatization of state-owned assets currently under way in Eastern Europe constitutes an opportunity for investment by the largest Western companies. Some of the first companies to arrive, e.g. Siemens, GE and ABB, have already acquired companies in Eastern Europe whose employees total more than 10,000. Indeed by 1995, ABB plans to employ over 20,000 in the region as a whole (see box 4.1 on ABB).

It would, however, be a mistake to suggest from this increased activity that investments in these countries do not contain numerous risks for foreign investors. These are caused by various factors:

- with reference particularly to the CIS – the inadequacy of the regulatory framework, political and legal uncertainty as well as administrative and bureaucratic delays;

- the lack of inputs caused by the breakdown of central planning and distribution;

- the absence of an efficient information system to identify potential partners, suppliers, customers and even products, etc.;

- the lack of basic infrastructure in areas such as banking and related financial services, telecommunications, hotel and office facilities;

- the shortage of local managerial experience and the low motivation of the workforce; and

- for the former USSR, Bulgaria and Albania only – restrictions on access to hard currency and on the repatriation of profits caused by the non-convertibility of domestic currencies.

3. Labour market conditions

The structure of employment in the former CPEs is significantly different from that in Western industrialized countries and presents an added problem for foreign investors. Since the allocation of the labour force was directed and controlled by central planning authorities, the sectoral structure of employment reflected the industrialization policy aimed at developing heavy industries. At the opposite end, the tertiary sector was largely underdeveloped. Beyond that, the private sector was of some importance only in Poland and in Hungary.

The labour market is also largely unbalanced by region, occupation, qualification and demography. Labour mobility is limited and in the same country there may exist regions with an excess and with a chronic shortage of labour. Beyond this, there is an acute shortage of qualified specialists. Overall, workers' general education is not worse than in Western countries; what is lacking, however, is particular skills. The large majority of managers and technicians are accustomed to orthodox management techniques and working methods. Only a few managers in foreign trade organizations, firms with foreign trade rights or science-based cooperatives have sufficient knowledge of Western management techniques. In general, workers are not familiar with modern equipment such as CNC-machine tools, lasers or with production logistics. In some branches of industry in the former USSR, for instance, the supply of personnel that is able to serve computer-aided automated production falls short of the requirements by more than 40 per cent. Demand is growing fast for engineers and technicians in electronics, bio-engineering, systems analysis and other high technology sectors, too.

Another major difference from Western market economies is that wages and salaries have been traditionally fixed by state authorities. Collective bargaining or other machinery to fix wages is absent. In general, labour costs are very low, both in absolute terms and relative to other European or even South-East Asian countries. In the former USSR average monthly earnings in 1990 were around 270 roubles (equivalent to US$ 165 at the official exchange rate of 1 rouble = US$0.61). Corresponding figures for Poland in the beginning of 1990 were about 617,000 zloty, or US$ 65. In both countries, earnings in industry and transport were above average, while those in agriculture, housing, health, education, culture and art were below average throughout the 1980s.

Poor work motivation and performance also seem to be a major characteristic of centralized economies. A primary reason for the economic decline of the former CPEs was the low productivity of labour in state enterprises caused by poor work discipline and motivation, high labour turnover and absenteeism, low loyalty and commitment. Since state enterprises did not operate under budget constraints, human resources were hoarded irrespective of their actual profitability. Overall, three main sets of factors can explain work outcomes and job dissatisfaction: (a) macro-environmental factors, e.g. obsolete central planning, waste and misallocation of human resources, counterproductive wage system; (b) micro-environmental factors, e.g. technological backwardness of machines and tools, discontinuities of the production process because of missing supplies, faulty work organization, low workers' participation; and, finally, (c) intra-personal factors, e.g. lack of a work ethics, low state or the misconceived nature of training, or even passive attitudes toward work (Holtbrügge, 1990). The governments of the former CPEs repeatedly tried to improve labour productivity through various reforms since 1957, but all attempts failed to achieve the desired results because of the constraints mentioned above and the strong influence of central management and planning bodies which placed limitations on the individual enterprises' personnel policies. Foreign investors, however, have some important competitive advantages over domestic enterprises. They employ modern technology and Western management techniques and can adequately reward employees.

4. Labour legislation governing foreign direct investment

In most former CPEs the general reform of the labour legislation towards Western standards is a main item on the policy agenda for the 1990s. A comprehensive critical evaluation of the labour legislation currently affecting FDI is therefore highly tentative. However, on the whole, the way in which the existing regulatory system applies to JVs' employees seems to provide for vastly superior treatment as compared to domestic enterprises. Indeed, labour market regulation is not perceived by most foreign investors as an important constraint to FDI in comparison to other obstacles (Rosten, 1991, p. 95). Still, foreign investors may experience practical difficulties in adapting to local personnel practices and labour laws, and in dealing with trade unions.

In the former USSR, the work of the employees in JVs was regulated by the Fundamental Principles governing the Labour Legislation of the USSR and Union Republics of 15 July 1970, and the Code of Laws on Labour of the respective Union Republic (Barabasheva and Mogilevskii, 1990, pp. 180-190). This legislation also applies to foreign citizens employed in JVs, who normally were to be used only in highly qualified jobs, except for matters of payment, leave and pensions. The Decree of 2 December 1988, however, meant an important relaxation of Soviet labour legislation, in that it allowed for freer hiring and firing of staff, and fixing of wages, salaries and bonus payments simply by agreement between the partners and without intervention of trade unions or the State Committee for Labour and Social Issues (Goskomtrud). This flexibility not only enabled JVs to deal more freely with their staff, but also made them more attractive to Soviet workers, in comparison to state enterprises.

In the other former CPEs, labour legislation varies only in minor ways. In Poland, the work of the personnel of foreign-owned small-scale productive firms (FSME) and JVs is governed by the provisions of the Labour Code adopted in 1980. The concrete conditions of work, e.g. salaries and wages, are set out in the contract or other documents of the JV, or by decisions of its organs. In Hungary, wage-fixing for domestic and foreign employees is governed by the JV memorandum of association and the contracts of employment (Bischof, 1987, pp. 53-54). In Czechoslovakia, after the 1988 amendment, the Labour Code applied to employees in JVs, too. However, the Czeck and Slovak Governments may adopt differing provisions concerning the conclusion, modification or dissolution of labour contracts, the working hours and the form and amount of wages or salaries. As in the former USSR, Poland and Hungary, wages cannot be paid in foreign currencies.

5. Employment effects of foreign direct investment

5.1 Direct employment effects

Employees in joint ventures and foreign enterprises

The number employed in JVs has so far been negligible compared to the size of host economies. In the former USSR, around 110,800 people were employed in JVs as of 31 March 1991, the majority of them in Russia (97,700) and in the Ukraine (13,900) (Goskomstat SSSR, 1990). The largest JV is the Salamander-Proletarian Victory shoe-producing JV Lenwest in St. Petersburg, where around 2,700 people were employed at the beginning of 1991. Another prominent example is McDonald's fastfood restaurant in Moscow which has already hired 1,150 people (Morawetz, 1991, p. 57). However, the average JV employs only 117 people.

In Poland, a total of 168,200 people (including 390 foreigners) were employed in JVs by the beginning of 1991, less than 1 per cent of domestic employment. According to the Polish Ministry of Labour and Social Policy, this figure was likely to reach 330,000 by the end of 1991. Investment is concentrated in paper and allied products, food and tobacco, textiles, leather and clothing, chemicals and allied industries, and other manufacturing (mainly wood) (Foreign Trade Research Institute, 1990, p. 70).

Moreover, FDI has not normally been greenfield investment but a merger with local partners, in which local facilities partially, or even in total, become part of the new enterprise. Thus it does not create any additional employment, but is a more efficient and presumably more capital-intensive organization of production. Net employment creation (gross employment directly generated, minus total employment displaced) might have been only very minimal, if not negative. Since traditionally local partners were largely over-staffed, employment restructuring usually followed foreign entrance. For example, within one year of General Electric of the United States taking a 50 per cent share in Tungsram (Hungary), employment was reduced from 17,000 to 13,000. According to an empirical study in the USSR, on the average 30 to 40 per cent of the former workforce of the local partner – especially non-productive workers, e.g. drivers, porters, accountants, party and trade union officials, etc. – were dismissed (Holtbrügge, 1990).

Wage levels

In most JVs the basis of determining wage and salary rates is individual performance. Blue-collar workers are normally paid on a piece-rate basis with performance and standards corresponding to those in the foreign investors' headquarters. In order to increase productivity and the quality of labour, JVs pay their employees considerably more than local companies. In the USSR, the average wage level in JVs was 535 roubles at the end of June 1990 and around 625 roubles at the end of March 1991 (IMF, et al., 1991, Vol. 2, p. 102). Taking a median monthly income in state enterprises of 270 and 350 roubles respectively, during the same period, we see that wages and salaries in JVs lie approximately 80 to 100 per cent over the national average. In Poland, JVs paid on average 236,500 zloty in 1989 and 1.061 million zloty in 1990 (Foreign Trade Research Institute, 1990), while in Hungary, wages lie approximately 50 per cent over the domestic wage level (Eschenbach, Horak and Plasonig, 1989, p. 149).

However, employees of JVs may be sent abroad on business trips, particularly for training in the facilities of the foreign investors. Beyond this, a certain percentage of their salaries is paid in terms of foreign consumer goods like clothes, shoes, hi-fi equipment, television sets or even cars (cf. Hitch, 1990, p. 30).

Training

The problem of finding suitably qualified managers to operate their projects in Eastern Europe has been identified by Western companies as a main factor preventing the speedy and effective implementation of their business plans in Eastern Europe. Unlike investing in developing countries, Western investors face no shortage of managers in Eastern Europe. However, Eastern European managers brought up in a centrally planned economy have no experience or training of how to run a business in a competitive environment. Thus, foreign investors have initially preferred to use expatriate staff or biculturally qualified staff to run their operations in the East, that is, managers who left the country in their youth but who have acquired managerial business experience in the West.

In addition, Western investors – particularly those who are intending to produce goods in the East – are themselves having to develop the human resources they require. As application-oriented knowledge is especially needed, employees are gradually moved to the headquarters of the Western partners for training on the job. Beyond this, off-the-job training in international marketing, finance, business management, logistics, employee motivation, controlling, etc., is undertaken at Eastern or Western universities and institutes.[3]

As training and management development programmes are very expensive, Western investors are interested in keeping their cadre of personnel on a long-term basis. Opposed to this is the government's main objective of developing overall managerial capacities. For this reason, governments are interested in the systematic training of domestic specialists in JVs and in transferring them to state enterprises as soon as possible. In most JVs turnover of labour is low and does not exceed 3-5 per cent of the workforce so far. Mobility of skilled workers is above average, as many cooperatives and newly established small-sized enterprises try to attract specialists which previously trained at the Western partners' headquarters (Holtbrügge, 1990).

In comparison to domestic enterprises, JVs place higher demands on qualification and motivation of their employees. Moreover, they offer better working conditions, e.g. wages and salaries, physical working conditions, methods of production and status. Thus FDI activates a brain drain of trained and highly motivated specialists from state enterprises to JVs. Foreign investors are sometimes even alleged to create labour élites and thereby increase social friction. On the other hand, there are many young and highly qualified specialists who have not been able to find appropriate jobs in state enterprises for many years. By providing adequate conditions of work, JVs reduce the need for emigration and intellectual exodus. There are also indications that a large number of JV employees do not come from state enterprises, but from the secondary economy. The brain drain is thus compensated by a more efficient use of domestic intellectual potential.

---

[3] In the former USSR, for example, Moscow International Business School offers MBA programmes and extra courses for JV specialists. Some JVs, as for example the Russian-Italian JV MIRBIS or the Milan's Bocconi University-St. Petersburg University JV IMISP, as well as the Association of Joint Ventures, International Unions and Organizations, offer training to JV employees, too. Finally, special courses are organized by various foundations such as the Carl Duisberg Society and the Otto Benecke Foundation, or private management consultants such as Roland Berger. According to foreign managers interviewed in Russia, it is not very promising to train former directors or others who owe their previous leading positions at Soviet enterprises or ministries not to excellent skills but to their loyalty to the Communist Party. In some cases, they did not use their new knowledge and skills for improving productivity but only to protect their own power and privileges. Consequently, it is more successful to train college graduates or hitherto underprivileged young and well-trained specialists. Thus the reaction time is delayed but a greater amount of social energy is set free (Holtbrügge, 1990).

5.2 Macroeconomic and indirect employment effects

Beyond direct employment effects FDI may bring about beneficial macro-economic repercussions and generate employment *indirectly* throughout the local economy. Up to now, however, spending by JV workers or shareholders in the various former CPEs has been minimal in relation to national income. Even in a long-term perspective, macroeconomic effects due to additional spending may not be of any importance. Moreover, given the low quality of domestic consumer goods, higher wages and salaries paid by foreign investors will be spent mainly on imported rather than domestic products.

At the other end of the spectrum, a former centralized economy could quickly derive large benefits from foreign direct investment as long as FDI helps in easing bottlenecks in production which occur mainly as a result of the lack of effective market coordination, including the rationing of imports of intermediate inputs because of foreign exchange constraints. Foreign investors are more efficient than domestic enterprises (based on superior technology, knowledge and management) and much more responsive to price signals. For example, they can react more promptly and effectively to signals of supply shortages. In this way, they could help avoid disruption in production elsewhere in the host economy, and thereby protect and promote employment. The size of these effects is virtually impossible to measure, but their contribution to increasing in the productivity of the entire system is probably far from negligible.

Inward investment may have indirect employment-creating effects, too, via the purchase of inputs, services, demand for construction and public infrastructure, and subcontracting. Cooperation with local suppliers can create opportunities for local businesses, boost the emerging generation of entrepreneurs and support government policy of industrial restructuring. However, the supply of JVs with energy, raw materials and other goods faces several problems. In the former USSR, for example, in some cases 90 per cent of the capacity of state enterprises was taken by state orders. Since these orders have priority, only a very limited percentage remains for direct supplier orders. As a result, many JVs complain that very often production inputs ordered from local subcontractors do not arrive in time and with the quality required. Moreover, in many cases domestic partners of JVs were accustomed to obsolete technology and production inputs. Their relations with traditional suppliers very often could not be maintained and new subcontractors had to be found. In order to avoid a shutdown in production due to lack of inputs, critical items had to be imported in hard currency. Following the model of the most successful state enterprises, many JVs have integrated themselves backwards through the acquisition of domestic suppliers. For instance at Lenwest, the degree of company-produced assets reaches approximately 90 per cent (Chekinev, 1990, p. 47).

Finally, employment may be indirectly generated by JVs among their local customers (distributors, service agents, etc.). Such forward linkages, however, are minimal. Since an efficient distribution system does not exist yet and deficit goods very often disappear in the shadow economy, distribution is often handled by the JVs themselves. In addition, part of the production is exported in order to raise badly needed hard currency. In the former USSR, for example, JVs exported fish and seafood, wood and paper, chemicals and allied, and oil and derivatives mainly to Japan, Germany, Italy and Austria.

As a consequence of the structurally low integration of JVs in the host economies, former CPEs can benefit only to a limited extent from "spillovers" through JVs' local purchases or emulation by local firms. One might expect, however, that in some activities local cooperatives and private small-scale enterprises will gain importance as subcontractors. These units are traditionally independent from the central supply system; they are prone to market behaviour and can work more efficiently than large state enterprises. In some cases, work requiring high quality control standards is already carried out by them.

Another potential contribution of FDI concerns the "de-monopolization" of the domestic economy. State-owned companies in the former CPEs have not been exposed to national or international competition. The privatization process and the breakup of entrenched domestic monopolies are expected to be propelled by the activity of foreign investors. Foreign-directed firms are also expected to play a decisive catalytic role in fostering innovative and market-oriented behaviour and attitudes among local entrepreneurs. Until now, however, the market share of JVs in most industries has been too small to force domestic enterprises into more competitive behaviour. In the USSR, sales by JVs in 1989 were 2.750 million roubles, which is only 0.6 per cent of total domestic sales (Goskomstat, 1991). In Poland, this figure was less than 2 per cent (Foreign Trade Research Institute, 1990). Moreover, the activity of foreign investors might not affect the decisions of domestic enterprises since most JVs "create their own markets" by producing goods or services that were not produced before and therefore met demands otherwise unsatisfied (Hertzfeld, 1991, p. 81). Under the circumstances currently prevailing in most former CPEs, particularly in those economies where liberalization and the move to a market system are lagging behind, horizontal employment effects of FDI are not likely to loom large at least in the immediate future.

6. Concluding remarks

In spite of a tremendous interest by foreign investors, actual FDI in the former CPEs has been below its perceived potential, mainly because of political uncertainty, the negative economic environment left by the collapse of centralized command of the economy and the slowness of these countries' privatization programmes. Up to now, investment has been led mainly by the (individual) exploitation of limited opportunities for profits, perhaps due to existing distortions, the existence of hard currency local markets and "first mover" motivations. The direct and indirect FDI contribution to higher productivity and domestic production and employment has been quite limited so far.

Host country policies play an important role in encouraging foreign direct investment. In general the following measures have the most favourable results:

- the uniform, transparent, clear-cut and long-term definition of the scope of state intervention;

- the unambiguous determination of the status of private sector activity within the emerging legal framework, with a clear allocation of responsibilities to the different levels of government and, especially in the former USSR, between the new Commonwealth of Independent States, its member States and the local authorities;

- confidence-building measures including the enhancement of investment security by legal and economic guarantees;

- the rapid development of domestic wholesale markets and local financial markets;

- the improvement of the conditions for direct supplier relations by helping local suppliers to adapt to higher technological and qualitative requirements and by providing information about would-be subcontractors to foreign investors; and

- especially in the new Commonwealth of Independent States, the creation of at least internal convertibility of the domestic currencies and the reduction of the existing large distortions between domestic and world market prices.

It is difficult to predict, however, if the positive discrimination of FDI vis-à-vis domestic enterprises would partially offset the existing distortions and structural inadequacies of the host economies, or if it would further accentuate some of the current negative public opinion towards foreign investment and increase the obstacles to the entry of MNEs.

Beyond the incentives directly influencing the concrete conditions for foreign investors, the evolution of FDI and especially the investment decisions of large MNEs will mainly depend on the progress towards political and economic stabilization and liberalization of the host economy. The countries where this process is more advanced, namely Hungary and Poland, have been the most successful to date in attracting FDI. Hungary in particular appears the most "westernized" country among the former CPEs and proportionally has already received the bulk of existing investment. On the other hand, scepticism and disappointment among Hungarians is greater than in other countries, since the discussion about liberalization and privatization started already more than 20 years ago and has so far produced less tangible benefits than expected. Czechoslovakia was in a relatively favourable position, too, since it had at least partly usable assets to build on and – in contrast to Hungary – it was not faced with the legacy of an enormous foreign debt. The case of Poland shows that drastic stabilization and reforms and a rapid move to economic liberalization may have a negative social impact and bring about political instability which can ultimately hurt foreign investment. The cautious attitude of private foreign investors is perhaps a clear indication that confidence about the outcome of the transition in former CPEs is far from established. In addition to the potential opportunities for FDI and the incentives provided by the receiving countries, financial support, the opening of trade opportunities, and the provision of technical assistance by industrialized countries will probably be decisive in putting the transition process on the right track.

If Poland, Hungary, the Czech Republic and Slovakia succeed in economic and monetary reforms, the introduction of market mechanisms, and large-scale privatizations which do not exclude foreign participation, and if domestic political and social consensus are maintained, MNE investments may be expected in the medium and long term. In addition to jobs directly generated, FDI could also contribute to the establishment of a responsive and competitive economic environment which would lead to a higher integration of FDI in the local economy and therefore expand its horizontal and vertical effects.

In the Commonwealth of Independent States, the investment conditions seem more uncertain given the unstable political situation. In addition, there are less advantageous legal and economic conditions for FDI as compared to other parts of Central and Eastern Europe. Still, in the long term, Russia and the Ukraine offer attractive opportunities for large-scale FDI because of their vast internal markets, their critical need for an efficient expanding consumer goods industry and their enormous natural resources. The sheer size of these countries however is such that even in the medium term, any new employment generated by FDI will not alone be able to compensate per se for large-scale unemployment and labour market problems during the transition period. The importance of FDI for the transformation of these economies therefore lies mainly in the transfer of ideas and skills and as role models for the new private business sector.

Bibliography

Adirim, I.: "A note on the current level, pattern and trends of unemployment in the USSR", in *Soviet Studies*, Vol. 16, No. 3, 1989, pp. 449-461.

Barabasheva, N.; Mogilevskii, S.: "Organizatsiya i oplata trudarabotnikov sovmestnych predpriyatii", in V. Uckmar and A. Vengerova (eds.): *Italiya-SSSR: Sovmestnye predpriyatiya*, Moscow, Progress Publishers, 1990, pp. 175-190.

Bischof, H.: "Erfahrungen von Gemeinschaftsunternehmen (Joint Ventures) mit deutscher Beteiligung in Ungarn", in *Forschungsbericht der Friedrich Ebert Stiftung*, Bonn, 1987.

CCEET (Centre for Co-operation with European Economies in Transition): "Hungary", in *OECD Economic Surveys*, Paris, 1991.

Chekinev, I.: "Salamandra v SSSR, kak eto delaetsja", in *Joint Ventures*, Vol. 1, 2-3, 1990, pp. 44-47.

Ecotass, Moscow, No. 31, 6 July 1992.

Eschenbach, R.; Horak, C.; Plasonig, G. (eds.): *Ost-West Joint Ventures auf dem Prüfstand*, Manz, Vienna, 1989.

Foreign Trade Research Institute: *Foreign investments in Poland: Regulations, experience and prospects*, Warsaw, 1990.

Goskomstat (Gosudarstvennyi komitet SSSR po statistike): "Ekonomika SSSR v. 1990 godu", in *Ekonomika i zhizn'*, 5, 1991, pp. 9-13.

Hertzfeld, J.M.: "Joint ventures: Saving the Soviets from Perestroika", in *Harvard Business Review*, Vol. 69, Jan.-Feb. 1991, pp. 80-91.

Hitch, J.T.: "Critical overview of recent experiences of joint ventures in the USSR: Western perspective", in United Nations Centre on Transnational Corporations (ed.): *International Workshop on Negotiating Joint-Venture Agreements, 19-23 March 1990 in Moscow, USSR*, Geneva, 1990.

Holtbrügge, D.: "Joint Ventures in der UdSSR: Privatkapitalistische Inseln oder intersystemare Unternehmungskooperationen?", in *Aussenwirtschaft*, Vol. 44, No. 3/4, 1989, pp. 399-424.

—: *Human resource management in joint ventures in the Soviet Union*, paper presented at the Conference on Strategies for Business Ventures in Eastern Europe, Budapest, 12-15 Nov. 1990.

IMF, et al. (International Monetary Fund, World Bank, Organisation for Economic Co-operation and Development, and European Bank for Reconstruction and Development): *A study of the Soviet economy*, Paris, 1991.

Kornai, J.: *Economics of shortage*, Amsterdam, North-Holland Publishing Company and New York, Oxford University Press, 1980.

Korösi, I.: "Situation, problems and prospects of joint ventures in Hungary: An overview of past experience in the light of domestic research and literature", in Hungarian Scientific Council for World Economy: *Foreign Direct Investments and Joint Ventures in Hungary: Experience and Prospects*, Budapest, 1990, pp. 69-95.

Kühnl, K.: "Das neue tschechoslowakische Joint-Venture-Gesetz", in *Osteuropa-Wirtschaft*, Vol. 34, No. 3, 1989, pp. 243-249.

Laski, K.: "The stabilization plan for Poland", in *Wirtschaftspolitische Blätter*, Vol. 37, No. 5, 1990, pp. 444-457.

Malecki, M.: "Legal aspects of East-West investment (Joint Ventures)", in *Osteuropa-Wirtschaft*, Vol. 34, No. 3, 1989, pp. 224-236.

Morawetz, R.: *Recent foreign direct investment in Eastern Europe: Towards a possible role for the Tripartite Declaration of Principles concerning Multinational Enterprises and Social Policy*, Multinational Enterprise Programme, Working Paper No. 71, Geneva, ILO, 1991.

Pysz, P.; Quaisser, W.: "Nach dem 'Runden Tisch': Polens Wirtschaftsreform an der Wende?", in *Osteuropa-Wirtschaft*, Vol. 34, No. 3, 1989, pp. 175-187.

Rosati, D.K.: *Poland: New Opportunities for Western Companies*, Discussion Paper No. 9, Warsaw, Foreign Trade Research Institute, 1990.

Rosten, K.A.: "Soviet-US joint ventures: Pioneers on a new frontier", in *California Management Review*, Winter, 1991, pp. 88-108.

UNECE (United Nations Economic Commission for Europe): *East-West Joint Ventures News* (various issues).

—: *Economic Survey of Europe in 1991-1992*, New York, United Nations, 1992.

Part 3

Future issues

9

Multinational enterprises in the service sector: Conceptual and policy issues

Ana T. Romero

1.   Introduction

The growth of employment, trade and investment in services over the last two decades has sparked widespread interest in that heterogeneous group of activities comprising the service sector. According to recent estimates, services now account for at least one-fifth of the total value of world trade, between 50-60 per cent of world stock of foreign direct investment (FDI) and almost 60 per cent of annual FDI flows worldwide. All indications are that this is likely to continue.[1] Moreover, in an increasing number of countries, the sectoral share of services in GDP has been on the rise the 1970s. OECD member countries registered average annual growth rates of 2.2 per cent in industry between 1980 and 1989, and 3.1 per cent for services over that period (as opposed to 0.6 per cent per year for services between 1973 and 1980).[2] While the share of services in the GDP of developing countries is generally lower than that of industry, average annual growth rates for this sector during the 1980s were in many cases higher than in the previous decade. They were particularly significant in Asia, where between 1980 and 1989, the yearly rates were 6.3 per cent and 7.7 per cent in South and East Asia respectively.[3] In the area of employment, there has also been a noticeable shift from industry to the service sector, which includes activities in both public and private enterprises. In 1970, 50 per cent of the labour force in the industrialized market economy countries was said to be in services. By 1990, the figures had either approximated or in many cases exceeded 60 per cent.[4] Among the developing countries there are marked inter-country differences in the share of the workforce employed in services. None the less, employment in this

---

[1] UNCTC, 1990, p. 2; *The Economist*, 8-14 Dec. 1990; UNCTC, 1989, p. 2; UN: Transnational Corporations and Management Division, 1992, pp. 16-17.

[2] World Bank, 1991, table A.8, p. 187.

[3] ibid., p. 187.

[4] OECD: *Quarterly Labour Force Statistics*, No. 4, 1991, various pages, and *Labour Force Statistics 1969-1989*, Paris, OECD, 1991, p. 325. For example, in 1990, between 55 and 59 per cent of the civilian workforce in Spain, Germany, Italy and Japan was employed in services. In France, the Netherlands, Norway, Sweden, Australia, the United Kingdom and Finland, it was between 60 and 69 per cent. In the United States and Canada, the figures were 70.9 and 71.2 per cent, respectively.

sector is also estimated to be on the increase, especially in middle-income countries and in the newly industrialized economies.[5] In the case of Central and Eastern Europe, it is forecast that the privatization of state-run service enterprises and the modernization of infrastructure would help to stimulate both foreign investment and employment in this sector.

The changing role of services in the processes of economic growth and development has become a major subject of research and discussions among governments as well as employers' and workers' organizations, at both the national and international levels. Within the business community, coalitions of service suppliers and groups representing major users in the private sector were either formed or strengthened, in an endeavour to promote proposals for the liberalization of trade in services. Multinational enterprises (MNEs) were at the forefront of those initiatives, which were largely responsible for the debate on services being placed on the agenda of several international institutions. Multinational enterprises rank among the largest and most efficient suppliers of those services in which they have been allowed to compete. Moreover, by virtue of their competitive advantages, they are well-placed to expand in world markets once barriers to international trade in services are reduced. Consequently, their role in the internationalization of service transactions will continue to be critical.

The main purpose of this chapter is to identify the issues to which the participation and interest of MNEs in the service sector have given rise. First, it examines the differences between transactions in services as opposed to the production and trade in goods, as well as the reasons for which the presence of MNEs in this sector has provoked a number of conceptual and policy issues. Secondly, it focuses on the implications of incipient trade and investment liberalization measures for the activities of service MNEs and the efforts that have been made in the Uruguay Round of multilateral trade negotiations to address the conceptual and policy issues. Thirdly, it gives an overview of some major social policy and labour-related concerns that have either already emerged or are likely to surface in the future as cross-border trade and foreign direct investment by service MNEs expand. Some possible areas for future research will also be identified.

---

[5] By the late 1980s services provided jobs for more than 50 per cent of the workforce in several countries of Latin America and the Caribbean. Economic Commission for Latin America and the Caribbean, 1990, p. 43; and *ILO Yearbook of Labour Statistics*, 1991, tables 2A and 3B. For data on Asia where employment in services ranges from 24 per cent in Thailand to 63 per cent in Singapore, see Organisation for Economic Co-operation and Development: *OECD Economic Outlook*, July 1991, table 3.1, p. 66 and IMD International and World Economic Forum, 1990, p. 148.

2. The characteristics of services

The actual and potential impact of MNEs in the service sector, and particularly in those activities that have been generally protected from competition, cannot be divorced from the nature of services and the requirements for delivering them in international markets. Moreover, since these needs vary according to the activities, so too do the policy considerations to which they give rise.

The fundamental difference between goods and services is that the former are tangible, quantifiable items which can be traded without requiring a change in the location of the consumer and/or the factors of production. These are features that are inherent to all merchandise and they remain unchanged notwithstanding the growing service content of many goods. In the case of services the situation is not the same. Pure cross-border transactions are more the exception than the rule. To date, they are dependent on telematics infrastructure, the accessibility to which has provoked concerns that make cross-border trade in services no less complicated for MNEs than their delivery by other means. On the whole, consumers either have to move to the location of the supplier or vice versa. Since suppliers may be either natural persons (a national or permanent resident of a given country) or juridical persons (e.g. an enterprise) it means that the international movement of labour and capital is a prerequisite for carrying out these transactions.

Labour is central to the provision of services. The quality of a service is determined by the manner in which it is delivered. This in turn depends to a large extent on personal attributes such as knowledge and competence which determine the performance of the supplier. Some services (such as project design, planning, management, supervision and inspection related to construction; retailing and building cleaning) may be relatively more labour-intensive than others (e.g. freight transportation), in which the physical capital component predominates. Some services bring about qualitative changes without leaving any tangible indication that they have been rendered (e.g. entertainment and tourism-related services), while in other cases, there is material evidence that a transaction has taken place (e.g. construction and software implementation services). For most, consumption and production take place simultaneously, thereby necessitating the physical proximity of the provider and consumer (e.g. medical and dental services). Some services such as remote data entry and software development are highly transportable by means of telecommunications and information processing technologies (telematics). There are services that display two or more of the above characteristics as the following examples illustrate. In the case of remote data entry, there is a heavy reliance on relatively low-skilled labour as well as capital-intensive telematics facilities. The service is also highly transportable. In contrast, construction, which comprises various services, requires labour (human capital) that spans the gamut of skill requirements – from semi-skilled workers to engineering/professional personnel. It is also capital-intensive since equipment, machinery and finance are essential inputs. Although developments in the field of computer-aided engineering and design have made it possible for certain construction-related services to be provided at long distance, the temporary physical presence of natural persons at the construction site continues to be indispensable, and in the end, there is material evidence that the services have been supplied.

Goods are no less diverse than services. However, because they are tangible, there has not arisen the problem of conceptualizing that which the term "goods" denotes. In contrast, services, by virtue of their heterogeneity, their unique characteristics, and the different modes by which they are delivered have eluded efforts to arrive at a widely accepted definition that adequately embraces all activities in this sector.[6]

In the absence of a consensus with regard to the definition of services and the coverage of this sector, the practice so far has been either to include in bilateral trade agreements a list of the activities concerned, or to provide for the parties to specify those for which they will be prepared to negotiate commitments under the agreement. A similar approach has been adopted in the Uruguay Round of multilateral trade negotiations in which there is, for the first time in the history of such negotiations, a Group responsible for elaborating a regime for the progressive liberalization of trade in services. Up to the time of writing, the trade talks, which were launched in September 1986, were not concluded. However, the Group of Negotiations on Services (GNS) has succeeded in drawing up a draft General Agreement on Trade in Services (GATS) which embodies the definitions, principles and rules on which a consensus has been reached so far. This draft agreement, which will serve as the basis for the final discussions to be undertaken in the Uruguay Round, does not contain a definition of services. Rather, it states that the term "… 'services' includes *any* service in *any sector* except services supplied in the exercise of governmental functions …".[7] The Secretariat of the General Agreement on Tariffs and Trade (GATT) has drawn up a provisional classification list of some 156 activities which include construction but not factor services (i.e. investment, royalties and workers' remittances). While they comprise mainly intermediate or producer services which are critical for the operations of firms in all economic sectors, consumer or "final" services such as health care and education are also covered.[8] Proposals for the opening of the service sector to participation by MNEs and other private enterprises implies the need for a revision of public policy, since many of the activities in question are provided by state-run or parastatal enterprises that are not exposed to competition.

Another significant difference between goods and services is that in the case of the latter, their unique characteristics have implications for the manner in which they are produced and delivered to customers. Conceptually, international transactions in services do not fit into the conventional notion of "trade" as it applies to mer-

---

[6] The difficulty in defining a service is discussed in Nusbaumer, 1984.

[7] The terms of the exclusion of services supplied in the exercise of governmental functions will be subject to further review and discussions in the Group of Negotiations on Services. "Draft General Agreement on Trade in Services", GATT, 20 Dec. 1991, Part I, Article I, 3(b), p. 6.

[8] The major groups of activities are: business services; communication services; construction and related engineering services; distribution services; educational services; environmental services; financial services; health-related services; tourism, travel and leisure services; transport services; and other services not included elsewhere. GATT: "Services sectoral classification list", informal note by the Secretariat, 24 May 1991, 8 pp. The proposed classification list drew on the Common Product Classification (CPC) as developed by the UN Statistical Office in collaboration with member countries of the UN. It was also based on the reference list contained in GATT, op. cit.

chandise. After years of debate over the sensitive question of the cross-border movement of labour and capital for the purpose of providing services in foreign markets, a compromise has been reached as reflected in the definition of "trade in services" in the aforementioned draft General Agreement which identified four modes of supply. These are: cross-border transactions; the movement of the consumer to the territory where the service provider is located; the presence of "service providing entities" from one territory in another and the cross-border movement of "natural persons".[9]

A common perception of the acts that are to be considered as constituting a service transaction is also lacking, essentially because of the particularities of the activities. The agreement so far is that the supply of services encompasses their "production, distribution, marketing, sale and delivery".[10] This definition acknowledges that service suppliers, whether they are individuals or enterprises, may need to use a combination of means for gaining access to a given market. The demands of service MNEs have been a sensitive issue because the commitments which they require for facilitating trade in services imply the need for the revision of immigration rules, foreign investment policies and regulations as well as statutory provisions governing the operations of state-run service enterprises.

In the following section, the presence of MNEs in the service sector will be discussed drawing examples from producer services such as business, communication, and construction and related engineering activities and certain consumer services such as hotel and fast-food restaurant services.

2.1 MNEs in the service sector

The OECD estimates that in the early 1970s, 25 per cent of total foreign direct investment originating from the major industrialized countries went to the service sector. By the end of the following decade it had surpassed 40 per cent.[11] This trend has been confirmed by UN sources which state that the "rapid increase in investment flows in the 1980s was accompanied by a shift in the sectoral composition of both flows and stocks towards services".[12] Financial and business services, wholesale and retail trade, transport and communication accounted for most of this investment.

Whether revenues, market shares or the geographical coverage of company operations are used as the criteria for ranking the major providers of producer and consumer services, MNEs from the OECD countries stand out as the main actors in these international transactions.[13] In 1988, 75 of the world's top 100 corporate hotel chains (by number of rooms) and 91 of the top 100 construction firms (ranked by total contracts) originated from these countries.[14] In 1990, the leading 20 information

[9] GATT, 20 Dec. 1991, Article I, 2(a)-(d), p. 6.

[10] ibid., Article XXXIV(b), p. 29.

[11] *OECD Economic Outlook*, No. 50, Dec. 1991, p. 52. The sectoral distribution of foreign direct investment flows is discussed in other chapters of this book.

[12] *World Investment Report*, 1992, op. cit., p. 16.

[13] For more on the role of MNEs in the service sector see Dunning, Mar. 1989.

[14] Moody's Investors Service and UNCTC, 1990, calculated from data on pp. 260-263 and 192-193.

technology MNEs had their headquarters in the United States (9), Japan (6), France (1), Germany (1), Italy (1), the Netherlands (1) and the United Kingdom (1).[15] The supply of software and maintenance services has become a critical component of the business activities of manufacturers of information technology products, accounting for about one-third of their total revenues. In 1990, the leading 100 US firms in this industry derived 37 per cent of their earnings from software, hardware maintenance and related services.[16]

According to the *Directory of the World's Largest Service Companies*, MNEs stand out as the most efficient suppliers of a wide range of business and consumer services. The high profile of multinationals in this sector has inevitably stirred interest in identifying the factors that account for this. Research findings as well as arguments put forward by representatives of these enterprises in favour of liberalization have shown that technological developments in the fields of telecommunication, informatics and transport have given an impetus to the overseas expansion of service MNEs and provoked demands for improved access to foreign markets. The diversification of activities, the growing tendency to procure services from external suppliers, as well as the introduction of regulatory and policy reforms in this sector, are all factors that are helping to facilitate the internationalization of services.

2.2 The role of telematics

Advances in telecommunication and computer technologies have revolutionized the service sector. Telecommunication, which is the transmission and reception of signals by any electromagnetic means, is itself a service that is playing a critical role in changing the management and operations of enterprises. The convergence of modern telecommunication and informatics technologies (telematics) has opened up tremendous avenues for suppliers of information-intensive services to engage in cross-border trade, and in some cases, to relocate certain low-skilled labour-intensive operations to other countries. Some airlines, insurance companies, publishing companies and producers of on-line databases have moved their routine data entry and data processing work to a number of developing countries.[17] With telematics, banks, insurance companies and data processing firms can broaden their clientele by providing transportable services in markets where investment rules do not permit them to establish a commercial presence through a branch, representative office or other form of juridical person. Even in some cases where there is commercial presence, there are reports of plans by certain firms to install computerized systems which will enable them to enlarge the range of services that could be offered to customers.[18] These technological developments and their implications for cross-border trade in services were at the centre of the early debate on services. Through bodies such as

---

[15] *Datamation*, Vol. 37, No. 12, 15 June 1991, p. 11.

[16] ibid., Vol. 36, No. 12, 15 June 1990, pp. 184-197 (various tables).

[17] For more on the impact of information technology on services see, Rada, 1987, pp. 127-171.

[18] "A Belgian bank plots cross-border invasion using computer links", in *The Wall Street Journal*, 7 Feb. 1992, pp. 1 and 22.

the Business and Industry Advisory Committee (BIAC) and the International Telecommunication User Group (INTUG), service MNEs introduced – in various international forums – proposals for liberalizing telecommunication policies and rules to facilitate both intra-corporate and other commercial transactions.[19] Telematics has not only enhanced business opportunities for MNEs, it is also heightening their interest in expanding into new markets. As will be shown in the following paragraphs, several other developments account for the high profile of MNEs in the tertiary sector, and policy changes in the external environment seem likely to strengthen their position in world markets.

2.3 Factors accounting for the overseas expansion of service MNEs

The diversification of activities is a key factor that accounts for the growing presence of multinationals in the service sector. MNEs have utilized their technical and organizational capabilities, as well as their human and physical capital resources to venture into activities which may or may not be closely linked to the industry in which they have their main operations. Some, such as airlines and travel agencies have built on their ownership-specific advantages and taken advantage of the synergies between different travel-related industries to diversify into the hotel, car rental and other tourism-related services. Others, through selective acquisitions or the forging of strategic alliances with other service firms, have gone into new areas. One such example is that of a multinational in the public and residential property development business which has become involved in oil and gas exploration, related construction services, passenger and cargo shipping as well as hotels and resort facilities.[20]

Where the national legislation permits, MNEs have established a commercial presence through foreign direct investment. Some have followed manufacturers of their particular group of companies to which they provide business services. For instance, between the beginning of 1980 and October 1990, the number of businesses in the Mexican export processing zones (EPZs) that were classified as service enterprises grew from 31 to 84. This is significant when one considers the results of a 1990 survey which showed that manufacturing firms in those EPZs generally relied on subsidiaries belonging to the same group of companies, for the cleaning and maintenance of equipment, land transport, and customs and legal advisory services.[21] In cases where service firms are located outside of EPZs, they would be, depending on the laws governing the scope of their operations, even better placed to take advantage of their reputation for quality and efficiency, to attract clients other than affiliates of their group(s) of companies. Moreover, the future of specialized service firms

[19] The Business and Industry Advisory Committee continues to be actively involved in consultations within the Committee for Information, Computer and Communications Policy (ICCP) of the OECD, making known the difficulties faced by MNEs which not only supply data, communications and other transportable services but also rely on them for managing their operations.

[20] The reference is to Trafalgar House PLC (United Kingdom). Directory of the world's largest service companies, pp. 249-250.

[21] Quintanilla, 1991, table 1, p. 863. González-Aréchiga, et al., 1991, p. 245.

seems bright, with the growing externalization of services. Many of these establishments not only meet the needs of the parent company and the affiliates, they also operate as independent entities competing for contracts on the open market.

Market opportunities are being given a boost as more and more enterprises contract specialized firms to provide business services which would otherwise have been supplied by in-house units. Manufacturing plants using "just-in-time" systems are increasingly relying on specialist operators which have invested in sophisticated data communication, automated warehouses and transport/distribution facilities. The practice is becoming widespread as entrepreneurs streamline their operations. The European Service Industries Forum estimated in 1990, that by contracting out to service enterprises, a company could improve its operating efficiency by as much as 20 per cent. In the United Kingdom, the market for business support services was said to be worth £42.5 billion in 1990 (or 5 per cent of GDP) and likely to grow by more than 11 per cent per annum up to the year 2,000.[22] The diversity of enterprises to which, for example, one MNE in the consulting business provides services attests to the scope of this practice. The main activities of its clients range from retailing and investment banking to the manufacture of heavy equipment, consumer electronics and soap.[23] The practice of externalization is spreading even to public sector enterprises in many countries, where state-owned and parastatal companies are being restructured to promote efficiency, and contracts for the supply of certain services are now being given to private firms of both local and foreign origin.

Regulatory reforms that facilitate foreign equity participation and competition are external developments which are also contributing to the emergence of a favourable environment for the internationalization of services.

Franchising, the conclusion of management contracts, partnerships and joint ventures are other means by which service MNEs are internalizing their advantages while at the same time gaining access to foreign markets.[24] The use of franchising is widespread among restaurants and fast-food chains. In 1988, 1,093 of the 2,606 foreign-based McDonalds restaurants were operated by franchisees and 671 under joint venture agreements. The situation was similar in the case of the Kentucky Fried Chicken Corporation, for which 2,145 of its 2,862 overseas establishments were set up under franchise and 408 were joint ventures.[25] Large hotel chains are known to use mainly management contracts and franchising in developing countries, while

[22] "Contracted business services", Financial Times Survey, Section IV, *Financial Times*, 11 Mar. 1990, p. I. Estimates for the United Kingdom were reportedly made by the Oxford Forecasting Unit.

[23] Sears, Roebuck and Co., Salomon Brothers, Caterpillar Inc., N.V. Philips' GL and Dial Corporation were among the major clients that procured services from Andersen Consulting in 1989. See *Datamation*, 15 June 1990, p. 79.

[24] One of the ways in which firms may seek to maintain their competitiveness is by internalizing the market, that is by "internally controlling and coordinating ownership-specific and location-specific advantages with other assets owned ... rather that licensing the right to use these assets to indigenous firms located in the country of production". Dunning, 1989, p. 13.

[25] The McDonalds Corporation and Kentucky Fried Chicken Corporation ranked first and second among the world's 50 leading restaurant chains (by number of units and value of sales) in 1988. *The directory of the world's largest service companies*, op. cit., pp. 552 and 556. The Burger King Corporation, which is also of US origin, held fourth place. Of its 558 units operating outside of the US, 473 were franchised restaurants. See p. 540.

Table 9.1. Largest foreign-linked computer software and services firms in selected Asian countries, 1989

Country/Firm		Details of links with foreign MNEs	No. of employees
India	Tata Unisys Ltd. (Bombay)	Joint venture, minority interest Unisys (US)	460
	Citicorp Overseas Software Ltd. (Bombay)	Wholly owned subsidiary of Citicorp (US)	200
Singapore	Arthur Andersen Consulting	Member of Arthur Andersen Worldwide (US)	80
	EDS International (Singapore)	Wholly owned subsidiary of EDS/General Motors (US)	62
	Far East Computers	Subsidiary of Hindustan Ltd. (India)	59
	Coopers & Lybrand Management Consulting	Member of Coopers and Lybrand International (US)	60
	Peat Marwick Management Consultants	Member of KPMG (US)	50
	Chungco Technology	Wholly owned subsidiary of Computer Associates (US)	37
	SW International Systems	Joint venture, and ICL (UK), SW (Australia) and local entrepreneur	25
Philippines	SGV-Arthur Andersen	Member of Arthur Andersen Worldwide (US)	480
	The Pact Group	Subsidiary of SRI (France)	70
	Nixdorf Computer R&D Center	Subsidiary of Nixdorf (Germany)	45
	TSD Software Inc.	Subsidiary of TSD Corp. (Japan)	35
Korea, Rep. of	Systems Technology Management Corp.	Joint venture 50% EDS (US) and 50% Lucky Goldstar	1055
	Samsung Data System Co.	Joint venture Samsung 67% and IBM 33%	470
	Young Hwa Computer Center	Affiliate of Young Hwa/Arthur Young International	298
	Hyosung-Hitachi Data Systems	Joint venture, Hyosung Industries and Hitachi	188
	Samil Management Consultants Inc.	Affiliate of Samil Accounting/ Coopers and Lybrand	130

Source: Thierry Noyelle: "Computer software and computer services in five Asian countries", UNCTAD/UNDP: *Services in Asia and the Pacific*, Selected Papers, Vol. I, UNCTAD/ITP/51, New York, UN, 1990, compiled from data in tables 4, 7, 10, 14, pp. 129, 132, 135 and 139.

equity participation and the setting up of wholly-owned hotels are more common in industrialized countries.[26] Accounting and advertising MNEs have a tendency to enter into partnerships, while, as the selected examples in table 9.1 show, multinationals in the information technology business have made extensive use of joint ventures to establish a commercial presence in India, Singapore, the Philippines and the Republic of Korea. Such arrangements are also advantageous to local service enterprises which, by virtue of their association with a well-established foreign partner, stand to benefit from its technological capability, reputation and global experience.[27]

2.4 The changing external environment

The operating strategies and investment options of service MNEs play a critical role in determining the scope of their activities in international markets and the potential areas for expansion. Another critical factor is the external environment in which they have to operate. Deregulation and privatization policies are providing service MNEs with unprecedented opportunities for enhancing their position in some markets.

The demands of private enterprises for the liberalization of trade coupled with the need to reduce public spending, are motivating many governments to dismantle barriers to competition and to sell either all or part of the assets of some state-owned corporations including in the tertiary sector.[28] These policies are exposing banks, telecommunications, airlines and other services to the participation of private capital and *ipso facto* to investment by MNEs. In the case of telecommunications, the upgrading of existing systems in developing countries has also provided avenues for equity participation by MNEs wishing to gain access to markets for equipment and services. For example, the Jamaica Digiport International which was set up in the Montego Bay Free Zone to attract investors and promote the export of value-added information and communication services, is a joint venture involving American Telephone and Telegraph (35 per cent), Cable and Wireless (35 per cent) and Telecommunications of Jamaica (30 per cent). There are numerous other examples of MNEs that are either being invited to participate in or have already concluded joint venture agreements in developing countries, and in Central and Eastern Europe where extensive infrastructural development programmes are being undertaken.[29]

Privatization is only one avenue through which service MNEs are finding it possible to make inroads into foreign markets. Deregulation is another. In a number

---

[26] ibid., p. 259.

[27] For example, the director of one Indian service enterprise, Mafatlal Consultants, is reported to have said that, "it is absolutely necessary for Indian companies to have a good foreign partner, at least in the take-off stage". Lakha, 1990, pp. 54-55.

[28] "In Eastern Europe, Latin America, the new dictum is privatise", in *The Asian Wall Street Journal*, 22 May 1990; "Privatization takes hold in Eastern Europe", in *Transnationals*, Dec. 1990, pp. 3 and 7; "Peru to privatise 19 state companies", in *Financial Times*, 18 Feb. 1992.

[29] The activities of some of these MNEs are described in Postal Telegraph and Telephone International, 1991. "India switches line on foreign telecom investments", in *Financial Times*, 14 Oct. 1991; "Telmex in private hands by year-end", in *Latin American Weekly Report*, 16 Aug. 1990, p. 4.

of OECD member States, MNEs are being allowed to enter markets for value-added networks (VANs) and enhanced telecommunication services. These regulatory reforms are helping to advance the internationalization process by enabling MNEs to compete as service suppliers in an increasing number of countries. The majority of OECD countries now permit subsidiaries of foreign banks, insurance companies and brokerage houses to operate in the local market[30] and several developing countries are also moving in this direction, albeit at a relatively slower pace. Where the legal and institutional framework for promoting deregulation has been established, entrepreneurs have been showing keen interest in entering these markets. In the case of Mexico, the partial relaxation of regulations governing the purchase of producer services from foreign suppliers is said to have had the dual effect of stimulating foreign investment by MNEs involved in activities that have a high "service content" and opening the market to the importation of services.[31]

Where deregulation has made it possible for foreign enterprises to have private satellite links for their voice and data communication, this has also encouraged the offshore location of certain service activities. For service multinationals which handle large volumes of information, access to communication facilities at reasonable cost is vital to their operations. For example, the New York Life Insurance Company, which set up a data processing centre in south-west Ireland for the analysis and settlement of dental claims, has direct communication links with its headquarters in the United States. So too does Texas Instruments, which has a large facility in Bangalore, India, where software design and related operations are carried out.[32]

The discussions so far have shown that foreign investment and cross-border trade by means of telematics are two major modes of supply through which service MNEs have been penetrating foreign markets. Legislative and institutional changes at the national level, together with the use of business strategies such as collaborative and joint venture agreements, diversification and subcontracting, have been furthering this process. While initiatives to ease restrictions on trade in services are being undertaken at the bilateral and subregional levels, the pace at which service MNEs continue to expand in world markets will undoubtedly be determined by the international framework of principles and rules that is being negotiated in the Uruguay Round. Since the policies and practices of governments and the business community will be shaped by the resultant regime, it is worthwhile to examine both the proposals that have been put forward to deal with the conceptual and policy questions that have emerged, and the consensus that has been reached at the multilateral level so far.

---

[30] Marie-France Houde: "Foreign direct investment", in *The OECD Observer* (Paris), No. 176, June/July 1992, p. 12. "Canada starts race to deregulation [in financial services]", in *Financial Times*, 4 Dec. 1991, p. 21.

[31] González-Aréchiga, et al., p. 247.

[32] "White collar jobs go offshore", in *International Herald Tribune*, 7 Oct. 1991, p. 17; "Drudge work goes offshore", in *Datamation*, 1 Aug. 1986, pp. 26-27.

3. The activities of service MNEs: Conceptual and policy issues

One of the salient features of the draft General Agreement on Trade in Services is the recognition that the international movement of human and physical capital is a prerequisite for selling services in foreign markets. Under the proposed Agreement, parties that undertake market access commitments will be unable to maintain or adopt measures that would have the effect of limiting the number of natural persons that may be employed by service enterprises, foreign equity participation, and the type of business organization through which the supplier may choose to operate in a given country.[33] The concepts of market access and trade in services therefore embrace both cross-border transactions and international factor movements.

3.1 Foreign investment and commercial presence

The production and sale of services are processes that are not as distinguishable as they are in the case of goods. This is borne out by the fact that the definition of the "supply of a service" as agreed so far in the multilateral trade talks, refers to its production, distribution, marketing, sale and delivery. The notion of "commercial presence" became central to the discussions on trade in services, because market access for the provision of many services necessitates either the establishment of wholly foreign-owned enterprises or some form of equity participation in entities through which services could be delivered. According to the draft Agreement, commercial presence denotes "... any type of business or professional establishment ... within the territory of a party for the purpose of supplying a service". It includes the setting up, acquisition or maintenance of a juridical person (i.e. a corporation, partnership, joint venture, sole proprietorship or association) or the creation or maintenance of a branch or representative office.[34] Foreign investment and commercial presence are therefore synonymous.

The scope of activities in which service MNEs would like to have a "commercial presence" in order to supply services raises sensitive policy questions because they encroach on the operations of public utilities and other industries that have long been the preserve of private and public monopolies, and some of which may not survive in a competitive environment. Since the presence and conduct of monopolies and exclusive service providers are regarded as constituting barriers to trade, this has posed problems because governmental policies and institutional arrangements that protected public utilities and certain exclusive service suppliers are being called into question. By virtue of the scale of their operations and the fact that they have been traditionally identified as contributing to social and economic development, public utilities such as telecommunications, rail transport, postal services and broadcasting are generally considered to be "natural monopolies". Foreign

---

[33] GATT, 20 Dec. 1991, Article XVI, 2(d), (e) and (f), pp. 20-21.
[34] ibid., Article XXXIV, (d)(i) and (ii), p. 30.

competition has also been restricted from the supply of certain services for reasons of national security, consumer protection and regional development. Air transport, banking, insurance, educational and health-related services fall into this category. Governments are being urged to assess the economic costs of protecting them and to consider taking measures to expose them to competition.

Both the demands for competition and the arguments in favour of monopolies have been addressed in the draft Agreement which proposes that the scope of monopoly rights and the areas open to competition be clearly defined.[35] This would also apply to exclusive service providers. In this respect it is important to draw attention to the annexes of related provisions that have been elaborated to cover three services – telecommunications, financial services and air transport – which are still supplied by monopolies or select providers in many countries.[36] In the case of telecommunications, which is both a distinct sector and an intermediate service, "access to and use of public telecommunications transport networks and services" are included among the means for supplying these services. Under the proposed Agreement, intra-corporate communications of a non-commercial nature and the supply of services on a commercial basis are to be facilitated. The responsibilities of suppliers of public services are identified and so too are the measures that would have to be taken to remove barriers to competition.[37] Cross-subsidization by monopolies, that is, the use of revenues derived from profitable services to support those that are not profitable, is to be reduced and eventually eliminated. The draft provisions propose that rates for the use of public networks and services be "cost-oriented" and that a flexible approach be taken as regards the choice of operating standards, equipment and arrangements for utilizing these facilities.[38] The Agreement addresses the real need to be responsive to demands for competition and the responsibility of governments to assure the provision of "universal" telecommunication services to all areas, including those that are less profitable and would not be likely to attract private suppliers. However, if the measures recommended for obtaining market access are to be implemented, it means that government policies and rules would have to be revised to give foreign enterprises the option of using infrastructure and services, other than those provided by state or private monopolies. Competition in the market for equipment and value-added services coupled with the elimination of cross-subsidization would inevitably have an impact on employment, and in some cases, pose a threat to the very viability of some enterprises. Consequently, special provisions governing the pace of policy reforms particularly in developing countries and the implementation of measures for the development of indigenous service industries would therefore constitute a critical feature of new arrangements for progressively opening service markets to service MNEs.

[35] ibid., Article VIII(2) and (5), p. 14.

[36] ibid., "Annex on Telecommunications", pp. 39-44; "Annex on Air Transport Services", pp. 45-46; and "Annex on Financial Services", pp. 35-38.

[37] ibid., "Annex on Telecommunications", Articles 5.6 (5.6.1-5.6.3) and 5.7 (5.7.1-5.7.6), pp. 41-42. These include, inter alia, the safeguarding of the technical integrity of networks and services and the setting of criteria for obtaining access to and making use of public telecommunications infrastructure and services.

[38] ibid., Articles 5.1, 5.2, 5.3 (5.3.1-5.3.3), pp. 40-41.

3.2 National treatment and transparency

Closely related to the question of market access and competition is that of the conditions under which the supplier of a service is to operate in foreign markets. The delimitation of the areas in which foreign and local suppliers of services can compete would be meaningless without a commitment to afford all providers an opportunity to carry out their activities on an equal footing. While this issue is not at all peculiar to services, it does assume special importance, because the tertiary sector is characterized by the presence of monopolies and exclusive service providers as well as extensive certification and other statutory requirements for the exercise of professions. As a result, competition may be limited by governmental policies as well as the rules and practices of professional bodies. For example, multinational law firms have argued that the scope of their overseas activities is hampered by licensing requirements, limitations on the fields in which their lawyers can practise and restrictions on the professional association between local and foreign lawyers.[39] These problems have been addressed in the draft Agreement that prescribes standards of conduct based on the principle of national treatment which is fundamental to the GATT.[40] It is also recommended in the OECD Declaration on International Investment and Multinational Enterprises and there is an OECD instrument devoted to the subject. In these cases, it applies to foreign investment. However, by virtue of the characteristics of services, the application of national treatment would also extend to immigration-related policies which would have an impact on the supply of services.

The concept of transparency is important for the effective application of standards of non-discrimination in services open to competition. The action necessary for promoting transparency inevitably has a bearing on the administrative practices of governmental and non-governmental bodies that formulate policies and rules that are of relevance to service transactions and the scope and content of which might discriminate against non-local enterprises. This is taken into account in the draft multilateral agreement which provides for the publication of "... all relevant laws, regulations, administrative guidelines and all other decisions, rulings on measures of general application ...".[41] The reporting of amendments, and the introduction of sector-specific guidelines and regulations, will also be required.

Just as transparency is important to new entrants wishing to compete in this sector, so too it is vital for the employers and workers of enterprises which must face the challenges of operating in a changing environment. Consequently, it may be argued that commitments to improve market access should be matched by a corresponding commitment to promote, as recommended in paragraph 10 of the Tripartite Declaration of Principles concerning Multinational Enterprises and Social Policy, "consultations between MNEs, the government and, wherever appropriate, the national employers' and workers' organizations" on the social and labour effects of reforms and competition in the service sector.

---

[39] *Directory of the world's largest service companies*, op. cit., p. 319.

[40] GATT, 20 Dec. 1991, Article XVII, p. 21.

[41] ibid., Article III, p. 7.

The presence and interest of MNEs in the international market for services have not only posed challenges for governments with regard to trade and investment policies, they are also giving rise to situations that will have a bearing on regional development, employment, training and the social protection of workers.

4. Social and labour issues

The international debate on services has so far been driven mainly by commercial concerns. Although the skills of service providers, cross-border labour mobility and the exposure of public monopolies to competition have social and labour implications, they have been eclipsed by demands relating to the negotiation of rules for trade in services. This section is intended to give an overview of some of the issues that are of relevance to the service sector and to which governments and employers' and workers' organizations will have to respond.

4.1 Regional development

With the exception of certain highly transportable services such as software development and data processing, it is virtually impossible to separate labour-intensive segments of the production processes necessary for providing services and relocate them to countries where they could be produced using relatively low-cost labour. Consequently, the human and physical-capital intensity of subsidiaries of service MNEs are likely to be more similar to those of the parent company than would be the case for subsidiaries of manufacturing MNEs. It therefore means that for most services, even if the scale of operations differ, the material infrastructure and human resources in a potential location must be of the same or comparable quality as that required in another country. This accounts in part for the need for service MNEs either to bring in their own personnel or recruit from third countries, and to either establish or seek access to modern communication, storage and transportion systems.

The availability and cost of distribution, transportation and telecommunication systems play a major role not only for the supply of services but also in the making of choices about the location of manufacturing as well as service enterprises.[42] Whether firms enter a market to service the affiliates of foreign MNEs, local customers, or both, the choice of location will be influenced by the accessibility and quality of the infrastructure necessary for delivering services. Interregional disparities in the levels of industrial activity, in the quality and cost of infrastructure as well as in the availability of well-educated and skilled labour, will be decisive for the contribution that service multinationals can make to stimulating regional development in a given context.

While the final decision with regard to establishment in a given site is that of the investor, governments have a major part to play in promoting regional devel-

---

[42] "Look for a fast road near regular flights", in *Financial Times*, 5 June 1990.

opment as recommended in paragraph 35 of the Tripartite Declaration of Principles concerning Multinational Enterprises and Social Policy.[43] In some cases such initiatives are already being made, as evidenced by some of the replies to the fifth survey on the effect given to the Tripartite Declaration over the years 1989 to 1991. Various policies and programmes were reportedly implemented to encourage decentralization and industrial development in less developed parts of the countries concerned.[44] Also, with the aim of attracting investors, several governments have set up, sometimes with the participation of local or foreign private capital, industrial/technology parks and export processing zones (EPZs) equipped with sophisticated communication, transportation and warehousing facilities. For example, software development, remote data entry and other data services are being carried out in such facilities in India, China, the Philippines, Jamaica, Barbados, the Dominican Republic and Ireland.[45] In some cases measures are being introduced to strengthen the service sector in order that it would, with manufacturing, constitute the two main pillars of the economy.[46]

Access to infrastructure and skilled labour for delivering services, coupled with changes in foreign investment regulations to facilitate "commercial presence", would undoubtedly enhance the attractiveness of certain countries, particularly for small and medium-sized service companies seeking to enter new markets. Small US enterprises in the fields of finance, education, insurance, information and restaurant services are said to have a growing interest in establishing a commercial presence abroad and particularly in the emergent Single European Market. The prospect of gaining a foothold in Central and Eastern Europe has also made joint ventures and other collaborative arrangements become attractive options for small service firms,[47] and low-wage countries which have relatively large supplies of skilled and professional labour could also become potential destinations for foreign investment by service MNEs. However, market forces will almost certainly pull service suppliers, irrespective of their size, to establish in areas where there is infrastructure, and a level of industrial activity likely to generate a demand for services that are complementary to industrial production. Also of importance is the presence of sizeable communities, in which there is likely to be a significant demand for a wide range of consumer services such as restaurants, hotels, retailing and entertainment. In the light of these considerations, the contribution of service MNEs to the social and economic development of

---

[43] This voluntary ILO instrument was adopted by the Governing Body of the ILO at its 204th Session (Geneva, November 1977). Service MNEs are covered by the provisions of the Tripartite Declaration which state that "Multinational enterprises include enterprises, whether they are of public, mixed or private ownership, which own or control production, distribution, *services* or other facilities outside the country in which they are based". ILO: *Tripartite Declaration of Principles concerning Multinational Enterprises and Social Policy*, 2nd edition (1991), para. 6, p. 2 (emphasis added).

[44] ILO Committee on Multinational Enterprises, 1992, p. 32.

[45] "Drudge work goes offshore", in *Asian Business*, Vol. 27, No. 7, July 1991, pp. 41-42; Lakha, 1990, pp. 49-50; Joint Trade Unions Research Development Centre, 1992.

[46] Singapore, the Republic of Korea and Mauritius are examples of countries which are moving in this direction. "Asian manufacturing migrates to South-East in a shift in priorities", in *The Wall Street Journal*, 6 June 1991.

[47] "Small US service firms find big profits overseas", in *The Asian Wall Street Journal*, 2 Apr. 1991.

less developed regions would depend primarily on governmental policies with regard to the modernization of communication and transport facilities, foreign investment, industrialization and community development.

4.2 Privatization, deregulation and employment

Proposals and initiatives for the privatization of state monopolies as well as the exposure of local service firms to competition have met with much opposition from workers in a number of countries.[48] Public monopolies in the service sector are known to be large employers. Moreover, as providers of low-cost "universal" services, they are heavily subsidized and unused to competition. With the participation of private capital, there are fears that there would be a reordering of policy objectives and the reorganization of these debt-ridden establishments in a bid to make them efficient. The evidence so far is that the privatization of unprofitable enterprises in any sector tends to be accompanied by changes in operations with resultant lay-offs. This is borne out by a few of the replies to the fifth survey on the effect given to the Tripartite Declaration from 1989 to 1991,[49] and, given the size of the staff in public service enterprises, redundancies are likely to be considerable.

Another major concern is that new styles of management and decision-making structures may be introduced in privatized firms, with no guarantees that labour-management consultations would be held on sensitive matters such as manpower plans and changes in operations. Privatization and competition from service MNEs are also likely to have some impact on indirect employment, to the extent that long-standing arrangements between public enterprises and exclusive local suppliers of goods and services may not be continued, unless these entities are competitive. However, it may be argued that while former suppliers may lose their privileged position if they cannot fulfil the new requirements, other local firms, either independently or in collaboration with foreign partners, may be well-placed to seize the opportunities that may emerge in a competitive environment.

4.3 Employment and training

Even when non-market services (e.g. public administration) are excluded, the pace at which jobs are growing in the tertiary sector is outstripping that of employment in manufacturing in industrialized countries and in an increasing number of developing countries. This expansion, and promising forecasts of further growth, have drawn considerable attention to a number of employment-related questions that have become pronounced, by virtue of the nature of services.

---

[48] For example see: "Unions everywhere are resisting the region's privatisation policies", in *Latin American Weekly Report* (London), 29 Nov. 1990, p. 1; "Privatisation fears of Uruguay's very public workforce", in *Financial Times*, 10 Oct. 1990; "Thailand: Plans to privatise port triggers union protest", in *Social and Labour Bulletin*, 2/90, 1990, pp. 155-156; "Morocco-Privatization: Unions fear unemployment", in *Social and Labour Bulletin*, 3/90, pp. 231-232.

[49] ILO Committee on Multinational Enterprises, 1992, para. 70, p. 28.

First, non-standard forms of employment, and especially part-time work, are said to be more prevalent in services than in agriculture, manufacturing and the extractive industries. Information collected by the ILO in the late 1980s showed that one in seven workers in the OECD countries was employed on a part-time basis, and that, in this workforce, there was a predominance of women, ranging from 62 per cent in Italy to as much as 88 and 90 per cent in Austria and Germany respectively. Moreover, more than three-quarters of all part-time workers were in the tertiary sector, particularly in retailing.[50] The situation has not changed in the 1990s. For example, it was forecast in January 1993, that by the year 2000, more than half of the jobs that will be created in services in the United Kingdom will be filled by part-time workers.[51] Hotels and restaurants, retailing, and certain data and communication services make extensive use of such employment arrangements. In the case of retailing, the move towards longer opening hours and weekend trading is providing compelling arguments for the introduction or increased use of part-time work. For example, it was recently reported that this was one of the reasons for which the Burton Group, in which more than one-third of all staff in retailing work on a part-time basis, planned to cut 2,000 full-time jobs and create some 3,000 part-time positions.[52] Secondly, implicit in the very terms "non-standard", "atypical" or "precarious" which are used often interchangeably to describe part-time, short-term or temporary work, is the notion that the workers are in a disadvantaged position because the employment relationship is not governed by the standards concerning wages and working conditions and social security that apply to persons in full-time employment. Thirdly, the broad range of skill requirements and the concomitant differences in remuneration and working conditions in a given service, have also drawn considerable attention even though it can be argued that these are not peculiar to service enterprises. There is even the extreme point of view that employment in this sector is being polarized into low/semi-skilled, poorly paid, precarious jobs on the one hand and highly skilled, well-paid jobs which offer flexibility as well as relatively good benefits and working conditions on the other. The main argument is that non-unionized casual, temporary or part-time workers (e.g. data entry clerks) are in a weaker bargaining position as opposed to technical and professional employees (e.g. systems analysts) who may work under similar contractual arrangements. Fourthly, the application of telematics in the service sector is creating opportunities for telework, which could in the future increase the numbers involved in non-standard forms of employment. According to an ILO report, teleworkers include "female and often semi-skilled workers" who are considered to be relatively vulnerable to the negative aspects of such arrangements,[53] and this is the category of worker on which most attention has focused over the years. By way of example, one workers'

---

[50] ILO: *Conditions of Work Digest*, Vol. 8, No. 1, 1989, pp. 34-37.

[51] "Just the job for the future", in *Financial Times*, 8 Jan. 1993, p. 13

[52] "Burton Group cuts 2,000 jobs in big restructuring", in *Financial Times*, 8 Jan. 1993, p. 6.

[53] Occupations for which the use of telework is suited "... can be divided into two major groups: clerical and secretarial occupations on the one hand, and technical and managerial or professional on the other. This is a fundamental distinction because these two groups usually have quite different characteristics: a mainly female and often semi-skilled workforce in the first group; a skilled and largely male workforce in the second group. Their bargaining positions, working conditions and employment status may differ greatly". ILO: *Conditions of Work Digest*, Vol. 9, No. 1, 1990, p. 8.

organization, in its reply to the fifth survey on the effect given to the Tripartite Declaration, reported that in 1991 a multinational operating in the country in question laid off 280 telemarketers with one day's notice.[54] Irrespective of the frequency of such incidents, they do provide the basis for arguments that certain categories of service workers have less security of employment than others. Non-standard forms of employment have therefore contributed to mounting concerns about job security, which is a priority in all sectors. However, in recent years, it has become a key issue especially for workers in several consumer services that have been hard hit by recession, with a resultant decline in the demand. Retailing, hotels and restaurant services are examples that come readily to mind, and they are known to employ significant numbers of part-time and seasonal workers.

One of the unique characteristics of services lies in the inseparability of their quality from the attributes of their provider. As the vice-president of a major service corporation said, referring to the quality of services, "you can't use the traditional manufacturing tools to measure it or inspect it before you deliver it ... employees create it ...".[55] Whether it concerns consumer services such as retailing, hotels and restaurants and passenger transport, or producer services such as engineering design and building cleaning, there is a growing demand for efficient, well-educated and skilled workers on whose performance the success of service enterprises depends. The reputation for providing services of high quality constitutes an important source of competitive advantage for enterprises both in domestic and world markets.

In view of the wide range of skill requirements of service suppliers engaged in different activities, it is of interest to look at the implications for human resource development policies in the service sector. If one takes the example of data services, there is – at one end of the spectrum – repetitive data entry and data processing tasks, for which a basic knowledge of the language in which the individuals work, may not even be a requirement for recruitment. In some cases, this lack of knowledge is said to be preferred, since the worker would not be distracted by the content of the text.[56] Where such operations are moved to offshore locations, the enterprise may not have an interest in investing in the training of workers carrying out these routine and low-skilled activities, unless it has a long-term strategy of upgrading its offshore activities. Also, where there is a relatively high turnover of workers, the commitment to invest in training may be low. In contrast, where more value-added operations are carried out, training is likely to be considered worthwhile. For example, Digital has most of its software written in India, where in 1990, the average salaries of professionals in informatics were said to be between one-sixth of those of their British counterparts and one-eighth of their American peers. Within two years of its establishment, the enterprise is said to have trained 240 staff members.[57]

---

[54] "Reply of the Communications Workers of America (CWA)", Supplement to ILO: *Summary of the reports ...*, p. 32.

[55] The statement was made by J.A. McEleny, Vice-President for corporate quality improvement at Chicago and North Western Transportation Co. See Larry Armstrong and William C. Symonds: "Beyond 'may I help you'", in *Business Week* (New York), 2 Dec. 1991, p. 58.

[56] "Drudge work goes offshore", op. cit., p. 41, and "Life will be different when we're all on-line", in *Fortune*, 4 Feb. 1985, pp. 48-52.

[57] Lakha, 1990, p. 51.

One factor that is likely to motivate employers to invest in human resource planning and development at the enterprise level is the concern about "quality". The quality of service and the competitiveness of service firms are increasingly being determined by not only the skills of the individual providers but also the distinctiveness of their organizational methods and the technical know-how. The growing sophistication of the technologies used for delivering services would therefore be a compelling reason for putting an emphasis on in-house training for service personnel.

Since there may be a reluctance, on the part of some employers, to make considerable investments in the training of workers who may subsequently leave the enterprise, government-sponsored schemes would be critical. They can offer two advantages. The enhancement of human capital which, when coupled with other factor endowments, could induce service MNEs to upgrade their existing operations and encourage new investors to locate in regions where there is an available supply of skilled labour. For instance, the raising of educational standards and skills in the south of the United States has been identified as being vital for attracting service enterprises to invest in this region.[58]

In addition to training promoted by service enterprises and governments on an independent basis, there are joint approaches that could be adopted. In the case of Singapore, the National Productivity Board, which is a governmental agency and Singapore Airlines, which has an international reputation for quality, have set up a training institute for service workers. Between the end of 1990 and November 1991, the Service Quality Centre is reported to have trained more than 6,000 persons of all occupational categories from subsidiaries of MNEs including Citibank, Kentucky Fried Chicken and Shangri-La Hotels.[59]

The dearth of suitably qualified personnel for the service sector and the need for further training are problems that industrialized as well as developing countries now face. The Government of Australia in its reply to the fifth survey, noted that in a particular region there was a shortage of qualified and skilled workers for a number of service industries that had expanded between 1990 and 1991.[60] In other industrialized countries, there are increasing numbers of service enterprises investing vast sums in training and in the information technologies that have become indispensable for carrying out certain transactions efficiently. Moreover, according to one quality consulting firm, such action is likely to increase, particularly among enterprises involved in financial services, health care and retailing.[61]

Although there already exist arrangements in many countries for governments and industry to cooperate in the training of workers in all sectors, most pro-

---

[58] "American South puts emphasis in new skills", in *Financial Times*, 13 Jan. 1993, p. 4.

[59] In 1988 Singapore Airlines, which is renowned for the high quality of its service, ranked fifteenth among the world's 100 leading airlines, according to *The directory of the world's largest service companies*. See also, "Singapore camp tries to polish service sector", in *The Asian Wall Street Journal*, 8-9 Nov. 1991, pp. 1 and 5.

[60] "Reply of the Government of Australia", ILO: *Summary of reports submitted...*, p. 100. The reference was to New South Wales.

[61] For example, at the end of 1991, the Mariott Corp. was reported to be providing some 70,000 hotel workers with "empowerment training" in order to enable them to take initiatives to solve guests' problems. See *Business Week*, 2 Dec. 1991.

grammes are still designed to meet the needs of manufacturing and extractive industries. What is necessary, without duplicating enterprise-specific activities, is the introduction of training programmes that are targeted to meet the requirements of those services which have been identified as priorities for the development of competitive industries in this sector.

4.4 Cross-border labour mobility

One of the more politically sensitive questions that had to be handled during the multilateral discussions on trade in services was that concerning cross-border labour mobility. Of the six working groups set up to examine specific services in the Uruguay Round, labour mobility was the only group created on a means for supplying services rather than on a service. Among the activities singled out for special attention were construction and engineering – the very ones that had provoked a controversy when some developing countries called for rules to facilitate the international movement of relatively large numbers of natural persons for the purpose of delivering services.[62]

Once the trade talks got under way, governments as well as the representatives of industry made detailed inventories of the services for which market access was being sought, the barriers to trade that had been encountered and the requirements for gaining access to potential customers. It soon became evident that virtually all service transactions required some degree of mobility of human capital and that if the developing countries were to participate meaningfully in the negotiations, the competing proposals on the question of labour mobility would have to be accommodated.

As a result of the negotiations to date, the draft General Agreement on Trade in Services contains an Annex with provisions governing the "entry and temporary stay" of "... natural persons who are service providers of a party, and ... natural persons of a party who are employed by a service provider of a party, in respect of the supply of a service ...".[63] It therefore covers situations in which the service provider recruits workers/employees from a third country to supply services in another. The responsibility and right of governments to control immigration and ensure national security are duly recognized, and specific commitments applying "... to the movement of *all categories* of natural persons providing services under the Agreement" may be negotiated.[64]

Several low-wage countries have shown an interest in exporting not only services requiring unskilled, semi-skilled and skilled labour, but also certain profes-

---

[62] The other working groups dealt with Maritime Transport Services, Land Transport Services, Air Transport Services and Telecommunication Services. Brazil, Mexico and the Republic of Korea were home countries of construction firms that ranked among the top 100 in 1988. Brazil, Mexico and India were strong proponents of the facilitation of cross-border mobility for low-cost labour.

[63] GATT, 20 Dec. 1991, "Annex on movement of natural persons providing services under the Agreement", p. 34.

[64] ibid., paras. 2, 3 and 4, p. 34 (emphasis added).

sional services.[65] Among the ASEAN countries, the Philippines is considered to have a "good potential" for exporting skilled and unskilled labour for construction as well as skilled labour for professional services, in the 1990s. Malaysia is said to have "good potential" as regards unskilled labour for construction work, while in the case of Singapore, the potential is considered to be "good" for the export of skilled labour for construction, transport, financial and professional services.[66] Certain producer services may require the involvement of a relatively wide range of professional activities, virtually all of which are governed by specific regulations. Financial services constitute a good example of this. Since it was one of the first to be raised for discussions in GATT, it is not at all surprising that detailed provisions in this regard have been elaborated. The draft Agreement contains in one of its annexes provisions that specify the categories of managerial and professional personnel to be granted temporary entry, by parties undertaking commitments with respect to trade in financial services. They include: senior managerial personnel; specialists in the fields of finance, computer and telecommunications services; accountants; lawyers and actuaries.[67]

The temporary relocation of labour raises considerations that differ somewhat according to the occupational category of the workers involved and the arrangements under which they are being assigned to work abroad. When it concerns persons already employed by the service supplier, the conditions for temporary work in another country are likely to be negotiated between either the individual and management, or the representative workers'/employees' organization and the management of the enterprise. The arrangement will be subject to the guidelines of the companies concerning the terms and conditions for the transfer of personnel and there will be established procedures for determining the pay, benefits, conditions of work and protection of the workers concerned. In principle therefore, there should be fewer problems than those that are likely to arise in situations where the personnel concerned are not salaried employees and professional workers with considerable bargaining power, or in cases where there is no representation by workers' organizations.

As enterprises take steps to export services by means of the temporary migration of unskilled/semi-skilled and skilled labour, unions will inevitably press for the inclusion of such issues on the agendas for collective bargaining and labour-management consultation. It is worth mentioning that the International Federation of Commercial, Clerical, Professional and Technical Employees organized the First World Conference for Property Services Employees, in New York from 1 to 3 December 1992. Among the major items discussed were union cooperation in multinationals and collective bargaining for cleaning and building maintenance personnel. Should the temporary relocation of workers in these and other services become widespread practice in the future, the demands of unions for improved cross-border information and consultation procedures are likely to intensify. So too would the

---

[65] The interest of Mexican entrepreneurs in setting up enterprises abroad as well as in relocating teams of cleaning personnel on a temporary basis is discussed in Manuel Luna Calderón: "Servicios de limpieza de edificios en México", in González-Aréchiga, et al., 1991, pp. 226-229.

[66] Pang and Low, 1990, table 10, p. 175. For an assessment of the situation with respect to Indonesia and Thailand as well as the other services for which Singapore, the Philippines and Malaysia are said to have "some potential", see also table 10.

[67] See "Understanding of commitments in financial services", in GATT, 20 Dec. 1991, p. 53.

pressure on governments to draw up policies and regulations governing recruitment, working conditions and rights of those migrant service providers who are not covered by rules that apply to government-sponsored programmes.[68] Such frameworks are necessary to guarantee the protection of employees/workers in general and especially those who may not be organized.

As the following example shows, problems can arise, irrespective of the occupational category of workers, when governmental policies, union representation or enterprise-based procedures for labour-management consultation are either lacking or not effectively implemented. "Body shopping", or the assignment of professionals in the computer industry to work on contract abroad, is said to be a widespread practice in India. In 1990 it was reported that many of those employees who signed individual contracts of employment subsequently expressed dissatisfaction with the conditions of work and pay, the lack of opportunities for career advancement, and the inequality of treatment when compared with the prevailing standards in the host country. In the wake of a significant number of "departures" (many of the employees found jobs with other enterprises in the host country), it is reported that some Indian enterprises now oblige employees to sign a bond, the value of which must be paid if they were to discontinue their contract.[69]

In the absence of information about the general conditions of employment of such employees it is not possible to comment on the contractual arrangements. None the less, situations of this kind attest to the need for home and host country governments to accord as much weight to the social and labour dimensions of cross-border labour mobility as that which they would give to other aspects of market-access commitments regarding the supply of services. International trade in services in general and the cross-border movement of service workers in particular, raise social policy and employment-related questions that are covered by ILO instruments pertaining to migrant workers as well as occupations in a number of the services that are the focus of the trade talks.[70] The Tripartite Declaration, which is addressed to governments as well as employers' and workers' organizations, and MNEs, also provides useful guidelines for all of the parties concerned. In this regard, it is worth mentioning that, should the draft General Agreement come into force, there is, under Article XXVII, the possibility for consultations and cooperation with "UN specialized agencies concerned with services".[71] This will provide the framework within which the social and labour aspects of trade liberalization in services could be addressed within the ILO, which is the appropriate forum for discussing these questions.

---

[68] In several countries there are government-sponsored programmes under which seasonal migrant labour is recruited to work in the agricultural sector, construction and other industries as agreed in government-to-government arrangements.

[69] Lakha, 1990, pp. 53-54.

[70] Construction, maritime industries, hotels, catering and tourism and salaried employees and professional workers are among the many services covered by sectoral meetings of the ILO.

[71] GATT, 20 Dec. 1991, p. 27.

5. Conclusions

The information in this chapter has shown that the growth of the service sector is having profound consequences for trade, investment and social policy. The economic significance of the service sector, as well as the demands of certain governments and the international business community, have been responsible for the unprecedented attention that has been given to international transactions in the tertiary sector. It was shown that MNEs, by virtue of their competitive advantages, are already major suppliers of those services for which demands for trade liberalization were made. These enterprises are key players in the ongoing process of the internationalization of services through cross-border trade and various forms of foreign investment. They are therefore well-placed to seize the opportunities for market access which will be progressively facilitated with the establishment of a multilateral framework for trade in this sector.

The conceptual and policy issues that have emerged are inseparable from the unique characteristics of services, the need for the international movement of human and physical capital as well as the importance of service suppliers gaining access to foreign markets through the use of distribution, transport and telecommunications facilities traditionally provided by public or private monopolies. The concept of "trade in services" was shown to embrace cross-border delivery, labour mobility and foreign investment. The draft General Agreement on Trade in Services was frequently cited because its provisions, which are the result of the consensus reached so far by trade negotiators representing more than 100 countries, would constitute the normative framework of a future international regime for trade in services.

It was demonstrated that the concept of "market access" implied the need for statutory reforms with respect to the operations of public sector and private monopolies involved in activities including telecommunications, ports, transport and banking. The entry of "new" service suppliers implies that changes in the management and organization of activities may be required to suit the new environment in which there would be competition for the provision of certain services. It was found that the concept of "market access" as accepted by the participants in the Uruguay Round, spanned the lifting of barriers affecting the use of infrastructure to enable cross-border trade, equity participation of foreign capital, the entry and temporary sojourn of migrant workers of different occupational categories and the establishment of wholly owned service-providing entities. As regards the concept of "commercial presence", which was one of the thorniest issues that had to be dealt with at the start of the talks, the consensus so far is that it covers the establishment of wholly or partly foreign-owned service-providing entities by various means, including through acquisition.

The chapter also shed some light on the contribution of technological developments to the process of the internationalization of services. Examples were drawn from telematics – the combined use of telecommunication and computer technologies – which has made a number of services transportable, that is, tradeable at long distance. Moreover, when combined with other factor endowments such as low-cost labour, these technologies have encouraged the offshore location of certain labour-intensive data services, thereby making it possible for certain firms to gain market access through both cross-border trade and a commercial presence.

Finally, it was argued that the introduction of more liberal policies and regulations was likely to give an impetus to the overseas expansion of service MNEs and that this would have significant social implications for the host country. Deregulation and privatization policies were gradually enabling market penetration by MNEs in services traditionally protected from competition, and the participation of MNEs has already provoked misgivings in some quarters about the social and employment effects of the possible restructuring of privatized and deregulated enterprises. There are also concerns over possible changes in the pricing of services, the choice of location of service entities, procurement policies and labour-management relations.

As regards regional development, it was argued that this would be greatly influenced by the choice of location of service enterprises. These are likely to be drawn to areas where there are many industries, adequate communications and transport infrastructures as well as abundant potential consumers of final services. The policies of governments with regard to infrastructural, community and industrial development would therefore be critical in determining the gains to be derived from the liberalization of trade and foreign investment in services. It was noted that a number of governments were already taking measures in this regard, by setting up industrial and technology parks and EPZs, sometimes with the participation of the private sector, in order to create favourable conditions for investment by service enterprises.

Training was identified as being important for both the making of decisions about the choice of location of service industries and for competitiveness, since the quality of the service cannot be divorced from the attributes and performance of the providers. Human resource development is an area in which it is desirable that both governments and employers take joint initiatives if national development priorities and the needs of industry are to be fulfilled in a mutually beneficial manner. Moreover, workers' organizations have a contribution to make in the planning of programmes for the training of service personnel at all levels.

Since the debate on services has been motivated mainly by commercial considerations, attention was drawn to the social implications of cross-border mobility for the purpose of providing services. The need to guarantee the social protection of service workers temporarily relocated in other countries was also emphasized, as was the importance of consultations between labour and management on working conditions and other labour-related matters affecting these workers.

In conclusion, it was said that by virtue of its mandate and the focus of its sectoral activities, the ILO was the appropriate forum in which to discuss the social dimensions of changes taking place in the service sector. Its tripartite structure would also enable all the parties concerned to hold consultations with a view to balancing public policy objectives, commercial interests, and concerns about protecting the rights and welfare of workers in service industries. The participation of MNEs in this sector through privatization and deregulation has raised concerns about possible social and labour effects, which are worth researching. One common argument is that while MNEs may bring to privatized state-owned service corporations, capital, managerial and technical expertise and technologies that would make the entity competitive, their entry may also lead to the reorganization of operations with resultant job losses. Policies for the training and career advancement of professional and technical employees as well as the effects of privatization on direct employment in selected service enterprises could be subjects of comparative country studies. Another controversial issue that could be explored concerns the indirect employment effects of possible changes in policies for the procurement of goods and support services in privatized firms. Case studies of policies and arrangements for subcontracting, and their effects on local enterprises which either had those contracts before or have been given such contracts after the change in the structure of ownership of the establishment, would help to shed light in this area. While deregulation may create opportunities for new service providers, pressures for wage reductions might also be introduced with the arrival of competitors that may not be bound by collective agreements. Conditions of work and pay, together with industrial relations in selected services could also be an interesting topic for research. Finally, a study of pay, benefits and working conditions of part-time workers in those services where they constitute a relatively high percentage of the workforce, may be appropriate, in view of the increasing use of such working arrangements and the polemics that have arisen over the status of these workers vis-à-vis those in full-time employment.

Bibliography

Asian Business (Hong Kong), Vol. 27, No. 7, July 1991, pp. 41-42.

The Asian Wall Street Journal (New York), various issues.

Datamation (Newton, Mass.), various issues.

Dunning, John H.: *Transnational corporations and the growth of services: Some conceptual and theoretical issues*, UNCTC Current Studies, Series A, No. 9, ST/CTC/SER.A/9 (New York, UN), Mar. 1989.

Economic Commission for Africa: *African socio-economic indicators, 1988* (UN), 1991.

Economic Commission for Latin America and the Caribbean: *Statistical Yearbook for Latin America and the Caribbean* (Santiago), 1990.

The Economist (London), various issues.

Financial Times (London), various issues.

Fortune (New York), 4 Feb. 1985, pp. 48-52.

General Agreement on Tariffs and Trade (GATT): "Services sectoral classification list", Document MTN.GNS/W/50, Informal Note by the Secretariat, 24 May 1991 (Geneva), 8 pp.

—: "Draft General Agreement on Trade in Services", in *Draft final Act embodying the results of the Uruguay Round of multilateral trade negotiations*, MTN.TNC/W/FA, 20 Dec. 1991, Special distribution, pp. 1-55.

González-Aréchiga, Bernardo; Ramirez, José Carlos; Aguas Gómez, Fanny: "Maquiladoras e intercambio de servicios", in *México: Una economía de servicios*, reporte del proyecto, MEX/87/026; UNCTAD/ITP/58 (New York, UN), 1991, pp. 233-253.

Houde, Marie-France: "Foreign direct investment", in *The OECD Observer* (Paris), No. 176, June/July 1992, pp. 9-13.

International Herald Tribune (Neuilly, France), 7 Oct. 1991, p. 17.

International Labour Office (ILO): *Conditions of Work Digest* (Geneva), Vol. 8, No. 1, 1989 – Part-time work.

—: *Conditions of Work Digest*, Vol. 9, No. 1 (Geneva), 1990 – Telework.

—: *ILO Yearbook of Labour Statistics* (Geneva), 1991.

—: *Social and Labour Bulletin* (Geneva), various issues.

—: *Summary of reports submitted by governments and by employers' and workers' organizations for the fifth survey on the effect given to the Tripartite Declaration of Principles concerning Multinational Enterprises and Social Policy*, TDME/REP 5 (Geneva), 1992.

—: Supplement to the *Summary of the reports submitted by governments and by employers' and workers' organizations for the fifth survey on the effect given to the Tripartite Declaration of Principles concerning Multinational Enterprises and Social Policy* (Geneva), 1992.

—: *Tripartite Declaration of Principles concerning Multinational Enterprises and Social Policy* (Geneva), 2nd edition, 1991.

—: Committee on Multinational Enterprises: *Report of the Working Group entrusted with analysing the reports submitted by governments and by employers' and workers' organizations*, GB.254/MNE/1/4, 254th Session, November 1992.

International Institute for Management Development (IMD) and World Economic Forum: *The World Competitiveness Report 1990* (Lausanne), 1990.

Joint Trade Unions Research Development Centre: *Jamaica Digiport International* (JDI), Feb. 1992 (mimeo.), 7 pp.

Lakha, Salim: "Growth of computer software industry in India", in *Economic and Political Weekly* (Bombay), Vol. XXV, No. 1, 6 Jan. 1990, pp. 49-56.

Latin American Weekly Report (London), various issues.

Moody's Investors Service and United Nations Centre on Transnational Corporations (UNCTC): *Directory of the world's largest service companies*, Series 1 (New York, UN), Dec. 1990.

Nusbaumer, Jacques: *Les services: nouvelle donnée de l'économie* (Paris, Economica), 1984.

Organisation for Economic Co-operation and Development (OECD): *Quarterly labour force statistics*, No. 4 (Paris), 1991.

—: *Economic Outlook* (Paris), various issues.

—: *Employment Outlook* (Paris), various issues.

—: *Labour Force Statistics 1969-1989* (Paris), 1991.

Pang Eng Fong; Low, Linda: "Labour mobility, trade in services and the Uruguay Round: The perspective of ASEAN countries", United Nations Conference on Trade and Development: *Services in Asia and the Pacific: Selected papers*, Vol. 1, UNCTAD/ITP/51 (New York, UN), 1990, table 10, pp. 141-175.

Porat, Marc Uri: *The information economy: Definition and measurement*, US Office of Telecommunications, Department of Commerce, OT Special Publication 77-12(i) (Washington, DC), May 1977.

Postal, Telegraph and Telephone International: *Multinationals in telecommunications – Update* (Geneva), Summer, 1991.

Quintanilla, Ernesto R.: "Tendencias recientes de la localización en la industria maquiladora", in *Comercio Exterior* (Mexico), Vol. 41, No. 9, Sep. 1991, pp. 861-868.

Rada, Juan F.: "Information technology and services", Orio Giarini (ed.) for the Services World Forum (Geneva), in *The emerging service economy* (Oxford, United Kingdom, Pergamon Press), 1987, pp. 127-171.

United Nations: Transnational Corporations and Management Division, Department of Economic and Social Development: *World investment report 1992, Transnational corporations as engines of growth* (New York, UN), 1992.

United Nations Centre on Transnational Corporations: *Transnational corporations, services and the Uruguay Round* (New York, UN), 1990.

—: *Foreign direct investment and transnational corporations in services* (New York, UN), 1989.

Transnationals (New York), Dec. 1990.

The Wall Street Journal (Brussels), various issues.

The World Bank: *World Development Report 1991* (Washington, DC), 1991.

10

The globalizing firm and labour institutions

Duncan Campbell

1. Introduction

Globalization is a growing tendency which implies an increasing disparity between the way in which the world's economy works – how markets and production are organized, how companies are structured and restructured, how capital flows through the global system – and the way that societies – their political and educational systems and their cultural and labour institutions – are structured. While the nation-state remains the main point of reference for societies, it is becoming less relevant for economic matters. Global economic trends have "clearly proceeded at a more rapid pace than the capacity of the international community to develop supporting norms and institutions" (UNCTC, 1988, p. 1). Meanwhile, however, norms and institutions that have been firmly rooted at national and sub-national levels may be increasingly subject to economic influences external to those which they were traditionally designed to regulate.

Globalization can affect labour and labour institutions in two ways. The first is through the creation of what might be called a "regulatory deficit", where the national institutions which govern the labour market are rendered less effective by the internationalization of markets. For example, longstanding national policies on education and training may once have been up to the task of helping to ensure the smooth functioning of the labour market. Now, however, these same policies may be overwhelmed by demands placed upon them by the internationalization of markets.[1]

The second is the multinational enterprise (MNE), the "engine" of the tendency toward globalization. The process of globalization creates pressure on MNEs to become global actors, resulting in far-reaching organizational changes *within* and *between* these firms. Global coordination may characterize not only the intra-firm organization of production, but the very same pressures to go global (viz. market access, technological convergence, high costs and risks) have led to a variety of inno-

---

[1] Of course, this loss of policy autonomy is not at all the same as saying that policies and institutions have declined in significance – just in the relative independence they may once have enjoyed. Globalization may in fact open up policy options and present opportunities for institutional reform – for example, through local economic strategies to integrate into the international economy, new partnerships between local authorities, businesses and labour, etc. Innovations in local development may be becoming an increasingly important response to globalization.

vations in the inter-firm organization of production, such as "strategic alliances" among competitors or the spread of longer term, cooperative relations among contracting firms and suppliers. The globalization of the firm thus entails its own restructuring and also the restructuring of its relations with other firms, and it is from this process of organizational restructuring that the consequences for labour and labour institutions derive.

The purpose of this chapter is to examine the changing strategies and organizational structures of the MNE as a result of the process of globalization and its impact on labour and labour institutions. Section 2 defines the term "global" firm and identifies the main factors behind its tendency to become "global". Section 3 examines the implications of a new *intra-firm* organization of production on labour while section 4 describes the impact of new *inter-firm* organizations of production. Section 5 analyses the impact of "global" firms on local industrial relations and the prospects for its adjustment to the new reality. Section 6 summarizes the positive and negative effects of globalization on labour.

2.   The "global" firm and the motivations to go "global"

2.1 What is a "global" firm?

A global firm is one whose products are sold in all key markets of the world and whose worldwide activities are *integrated* across national markets (Porter, 1990). These two criteria, market presence and (relative) integration of activities, may not be the only defining characteristics of the global firm, but they are the most important. Of course, not all multinational enterprises have a global strategy and structure: "In multidomestic competition, multinationals have largely autonomous subsidiaries in each nation and manage them like a portfolio. In global competition, firms seek to gain much greater competitive advantage from their international presence, through locating activities with a global perspective and coordinating actively among them" (ibid., p. 55).

The essence of a global strategy is the cross-border coordination of steps in the value chain, but because there are many steps in this chain, the organizational implications of becoming a global firm are major. They are so significant, in fact, that the difference between a "multinational" and a "global" firm has been thought of by some as qualitative, rather than just one of degree. Consider, for example, Petrella's (1990) view of globalization as affecting: "all of the phases of innovation, development, production, distribution and consumption of goods and services...[Globalization] translates itself into the structural change of organizational types and forms and of the management of the firm" (p. 4).

This is not to say that there is any one model of a global firm. For example, a firm may limit production to one or a few locations in order to maximize economies of scale. The aerospace industry is a case in point (Porter, 1990). There are many reasons why the location of production and the relative integration across production units may vary. For example, some geographically dispersed industries, such as chem-

Figure 10.1. Integration-responsiveness grid

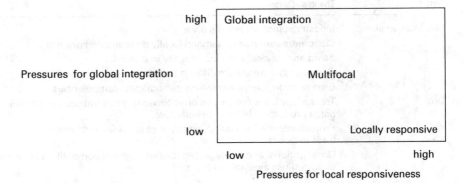

A summary of the characteristics of the three international groups

Cluster 1: Global integration	This international business group is characterized by intense competition domestically and internationally. The predominance of global competitors and competitors having a presence in all key markets contributes to this intensely competitive context. The group is distinguished by the view that customer needs are standardized worldwide and global awareness exists for their products, allowing businesses in the group to market a highly standardized product throughout the world. The degree of standardization and the considerable volume potentials associated with operating worldwide are consistent with the economies of scale that also characterize the group.
Cluster 2: Locally responsive	This international business group is certain that worldwide standardization of product technology, global distribution channels, global economies of scale, and standardized customer needs are not pressures that they confront. Generally, intense competition exists: however, this group's most distinguishing characteristics are the high level of customer service required in all markets and the existence of variable factor costs across locations.
Cluster 3: Multifocal	This final group is characterized by intense competition accompanied by the presence of global competitors similar in nature to Cluster 1. However, this group is clearly distinguished from Cluster 1 in that competitors do not market a globally standardized product and little standardization of product technology exists. Customer needs worldwide are not viewed as standardized nor are customers thought of as being aware of the product. The lack of market and product standardization is accented with the perception that government intervention and local customer service in each market are very characteristic of their industry.

Source: Roth and Morrison (1990), pp. 544-555.

icals, rely on locally available production inputs. Imports in that industry may consequently be relatively low and local content high. For others, such as automobiles, the international sourcing of parts and components may be high. For firms in some industries, remaining regulatory barriers or distinctive, "local" consumer tastes may dictate local presence and minimize the opportunities for cross-border integration of production units. The food industry, for example, is often cited as one where local product preferences are resistant to standardization across markets.

Table 10.1. Some impediments to globalization

Author	The impediments
Morrison, et al.	Industry standards remain diverse.
	Customers continue to demand locally differentiated products.
	Being an "insider" remains critically important.
	Global organizations are difficult to manage.
	Globalization often circumvents subsidiaries' competencies.
Doz	Technology does not always drive towards globalization, since small-batch production is now cost-effective.
	Protectionism is increasing, and applies to trade in knowledge as well as trade in goods.
	Organizational and strategic capabilities of global competitors lag behind opportunities available to them.

Source: Morrison, et al. (1991) and Doz (1987).

Diversity is thus clearly the critical watchword in any effort to classify the global firm, and, as the few examples above show, the industry is the context in which competition occurs and where firms' strategies are shaped. Not all "global" industries, however, are globally integrated. Figure 10.1 describes the range of strategies along industry lines from "global integration" to "multi-focal" to "locally responsive" (or "multi-domestic") as being determined by the different characteristics of the market faced by firms in different industries.

Strictly speaking, then, truly globally integrated industries may be rather few in number. Some of the major impediments to globalization are noted in table 10.1. Morrison (1990), for example, identifies only 11 global industries in which American firms are competitors. In fact, so rigorous are the measures of Morrison's criteria of product standardization and degrees of international competition that several of the technology-intensive industries – e.g. chemicals, pharmaceuticals, computers, telecommunications – do not figure in Morrison's classification as globally integrated. But there can be little doubt that the excluded industries are nevertheless dominated by firms whose strategies are highly coordinated across national and regional markets. For example, Petrella (1991, p. 394) observes that "car manufacturing is obviously very global", and, indeed, is often popularly associated with the globalization of the firm.

The extent of a firm's market presence is of course a necessary component of any definition of a global strategy. On the other hand, a global strategy cannot be defined uniquely in terms of the global standardization of the firm's product market: firms that operate "multi-focal" strategies (see figure 10.1) do not assume that their products and markets are standardized. Rather, they spread production over several local markets and tailor it to those markets. This does not mean, however, that such firms cannot have globally coordinated strategies in such areas as overall product planning, component sourcing, distribution and marketing, finance, etc. These firms may be less than fully globally integrated, but the coordination across functions that they engage in is the essence of a global strategy.

There may be good reason to assume that present global strategies focus on many other areas of cross-border integration than the standardization of a final product. For one thing, firms that based their strategies on an assumed standardization of tastes in the early 1980s were frequently disappointed (Kanter, 1991; Morrison, et al., 1991). For another, applications of advanced manufacturing technology facilitate a "multi-focal" approach in allowing firms to gain "economies of scope" through small-batch production while, at the same time, not impeding the realization of global economies of scale across various other functions. This ability is implied in the stated aims of some firms, e.g. Asea-Brown Boveri, to be "multi-local" rather than global in the markets in which it operates, or Sony's strategy of "global localization" (Ohmae, 1990). General Electric's chief executive summarized the company's objective as having simultaneously the reach and power of the global firm (i.e. coordination), and the flexibility to respond to changes in the market of the small firm (Robins, 1990).

2.2 The "logics" of globalization within the firm

The diversity of these examples suggests that there is no one "logic" of globalization applicable to all firms. Nevertheless, it can still be argued that there is a number of specific elements that, in different combinations, are the principal motivations for the globalization of the firm:

Cost elements: Coordinating units of activity worldwide may allow some firms to reap the cost advantages of economies of scale in production or in other functions. Particularly as products or their inputs (including their components, but also such services as marketing or distribution) approach a level of standardization, it is less cost-efficient for the firm to operate fragmented, duplicative operations. Coordinating worldwide activities induces the globalizing firm to "rethink" the specific competitive advantages of its various locations and to shift production to those where it can best exploit these advantages.

Market access: The global firm is not merely defined by its presence in all key markets worldwide, it *must* have such presence if it is not to be overtaken by competitors with deeper organizational and financial resources. One characteristic of global competition is the use of profits generated in one location to finance competitive battles in another. (To take one concrete example: now that Honda, Nissan and Toyota have established production facilities in Europe, for how long can Mitsubishi afford not to be present?) Many of the international mergers and acquisitions, particularly in the EC, have been motivated by the need to gain market access. Many new partnerships or alliances among competitors are also motivated by this objective.

Rising R&D costs: In many industries, the costs (and risks) of new product development have risen substantially. One reason for this is the shortening of product life cycles and, as figure 10.2 below illustrates, there is a strong inverse relationship between the length of product life and R&D costs. Two related pressures result: (i) the higher cost of new product development encourages product launching on a broader ("global") market for costs to be amortized; (ii) the shorter product life encourages firms to launch products simultaneously rather than sequentially on key markets.

Applications of information technology: Coordination across widespread geographical locations is facilitated by advances in information and communications technologies which overcome barriers of time and space at ever-reduced costs. Analogous impacts on the demand side of the market may also be at work here. New trends in *inter-organizational* relations are being driven in part by the convergence of new technologies, e.g. audiovisual electronics with computers, or telecommunications with computers, or the rising proportion of electronic components in mechanical engineering (the car).

3. A new intra-firm organization of production

The transition from a "multinational" to a "global" or more globally integrated firm poses a number of intra-firm, organizational challenges, all of which create closer linkages among farflung operating units. Four aspects of this change have a potentially significant impact on labour:

3.1 The decline of the "miniature replica" model of the subsidiary

The implications of the new intra-firm organization of production tend toward the eclipse of the old model of parent/subsidiary relations in which the subsidiary was conceived of as a "miniature replica" of the parent, and it was assumed that products were first developed by the firm for its home market and, once proven in that market, were exported and ultimately manufactured in the host country. But this "product life cycle" hypothesis assumes a model of expansion which is too slow for the present competitive environment. Indeed, the recent predominance of international mergers and acquisitions as market-entry strategies emphasizes the objective of immediate market access in a world of heightened cross-national competition and diminishing product life cycles.

The organizational geography of the earlier model of the multinational implied a relatively unintegrated or "replicable" pattern of production organization. However, the forces that compel firms to launch products more rapidly (and simultaneously) on as broad a market as possible are in some cases inducing major changes in the respective roles of subsidiary and parent. For example Philips, the Dutch electronics company: "a key element in restructuring was the establishment of international production centres. The revamped manufacturing facilities were assigned worldwide production of product lines. Microwave ovens for worldwide distribution, for example, are now produced in Sweden; office dictating equipment is made in Vienna", and this reflects a "shift from a previously geographically oriented structure to one that is more product-oriented, with its centralized product management team" (Van Houten, 1990, p. 104).

The respective roles of "parent" and "subsidiary" seem to be being redefined. In consequence, does the subsidiary become more autonomous or more dependent upon its parent? Is decision-making within the multinational character-

Figure 10.2. Product life and R&D costs

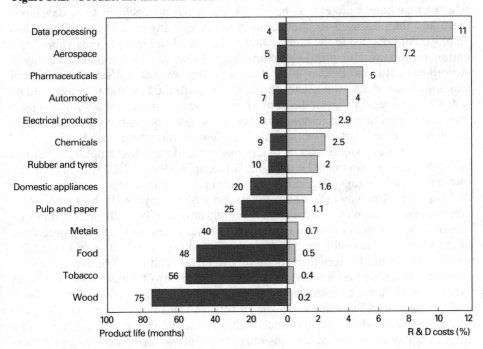

Source: Adapted from Canadian Council of Professional Engineers (1983), p. 8.

ized by greater centralization or decentralization? Most likely, the answer is "both" to each question. For example, responsibility for worldwide production of key products or components may be decentralized to subsidiary level to take advantages of economies of scale in production. On the other hand, the subsidiary's increasing role within a centrally coordinated production web may result in a decline in its relative autonomy, since scale economies can be obtained by the parent in centralizing the coordination of overall product strategy, purchasing and distribution networks, etc.

3.2 The "statelessness" of the global firm?

In the popular business strategy literature, the global firm is thought to aspire to true "statelessness". Consider, for example, Ohmae's (1990) view of the global firm:

> Before national identity, before local affiliation, before German ego or Italian ego or Japanese ego – before any of this comes the commitment to a single, unified global mission. You don't think any longer that the company you work for is a Japanese automaker trying to build and sell its products in the United States. You work for Honda or Nissan or Toyota. The customers you care about are the people who love your products everywhere in the world [...] Country of origin does not matter. Location of headquarters does not matter. The products for which you are responsible and the company that you serve have become denationalized (p. 94).

For some multinationals, the source of their competitive advantage is less reliant on the home market than before: products may be less likely to be developed there and then diffused to "host countries". A growing percentage of sales and employment are outside the home country. The disadvantages of being viewed as a national company with worldwide, subsidiary operations have arguably increased. According to Robins (1990, p. 23), "What is prefigurative about News International and Sony is not simply their scale and reach, but also the fact that they aspire to be stateless, 'headless', decentred corporations. These global cultural industries understand the importance of achieving a real equi-distance, or equi-presence, of perspective in relation to the whole world of their audiences and consumers."

This statelessness may be of less concern to these firms' employees, owners and shareholders than might be thought. For example, Reich (1991) has argued that ownership is of declining national importance in economic and employment terms.[2] A "domestic" firm may in fact have the majority of employees, the bulk of its sales, and even the location of its most technologically advanced or strategic activities outside of its home country, while the "foreign" firm may contribute an increasing share of employment, the skill base, tax receipts, etc., in the "host" country. Ownership would seem to matter less than the ability to attract and retain high value-added activities, an ability measured increasingly in the quality of a location's workforce. What is more, the deregulation and global integration of capital markets increasingly enable "foreigners" to own "domestic" assets, and vice versa. "Foreign" firms are increasingly quoted on national stock exchanges, and firms' ability to raise capital through equity or debt is increasingly unrelated either to the home country or to the host location for which capital is being sought.

3.3 A new economics of location

The cross-border coordination of steps in the value-added chain in order to take advantage of competitive advantages may shift the location of production. In the pharmaceutical industry, for example, the "logic" of globalization appears to be tending toward a decentralization of the core function of research and development (de Granrut, 1990).

Presence in the local market has of course long been the critical factor in locational decision-making, and the global firm's need to be present (and thereby to gain "insider" advantages) in the world's key markets is already widely recognized. What is new in locational decision-making, however, is not the objective of servicing

---

[2] As noted at the outset, we should remind ourselves that the global firm is at this stage more of a hypothetical construct than a reality. For the overwhelming number of multinationals, their workforces and operations continue to be concentrated in their respective home countries. They continue to be predominantly owned and governed by home-country citizens, and their most sensitive, core activities (R&D, for example), from which they derive their competitive advantage, remain concentrated in their home countries. For most, home-country taxation and other policies continue to matter most. "Global strategies" are the product of (home country) corporate-level decision-makers and, in any case, such strategies may be displaced by properly regional strategies tailored to the three wealthiest regions in the world – excluding the great majority of the "globe's" population. Armed with such arguments, Reich's thesis has been criticized as unduly futuristic. See, for example, Tyson (1991), and Thomsen (1992). On the continuing (indeed increasing) importance of the "home country", see Porter (1990).

a final market, but the lure of a site's various other factors now that declining costs (and greater speed) of communication and transport mitigate the disadvantages of distance. The location of an activity for inclusion in a global production web can be determined predominantly on grounds of relative factor costs – the attraction of relatively inexpensive, well-disciplined, unorganized labour in some Asian countries, for example, or the "cheap brains" sought by firms in the Indian software industry – or of such factors as the availability of highly skilled labour, the quality of local universities and local infrastructure, etc.

The globalization of the firm may be altering the locational economics of MNEs and may thus be contributing to change in the international division of labour. Although location decisions are still based on market presence and the availability of fixed factors of production, such as land and natural resources, factors that can be created, e.g. a skilled workforce, may be becoming more important criteria in the decision. Attracting and retaining high-quality global foreign firms has risen as a priority in the agendas of national policy-makers.[3]

3.4 The intra-firm organization of work

The globalization of the firm may be contributing to the decline in Taylorist or Fordist patterns of work organization. For some years now, both the academic and popular business literatures have described the intra-firm tendencies toward flattened hierarchies, broader job descriptions, the decentralization or devolution of authority, the organization of work into teams, incentive-based and firm-specific pay systems and policies to build worker motivation and commitment, and the closer integration of formerly discrete production and planning spheres.[4] The (unknown) diffusion of this new model has much to do with two main factors behind the globalization of the firm: the widespread effects of information technology, and the "demonstration effect" of Japanese firms.

First, the new technologies have brought a radical departure from the old work organization model associated with mass production which relied on narrow job definitions, unskilled and semi-skilled production workers, dedicated or inflexible

---

[3] Consider the case of the formerly British-owned computer manufacturer, ICL. When a majority of its shares was purchased by Fujitsu, ICL was excluded from the consortium of "European" firms receiving EC financing for research in the pre-competitive phase on next-generation semiconductor technology. Significantly, membership in the consortium is predicated not on the national origin of the parent – the European operations of the American-owned IBM participate in the consortium – but on the European location of the firm's most strategic function, research and development. The US firm appeared to have passed the test, but not so the newly Japanese one.

[4] The new work organization is consistent with the "organization-oriented" rather "market-oriented" firm (Dore, 1989), the theory of "flexible specialization" (Piore and Sabel, 1984), or that of "diversified quality production" (Streeck, 1991), and the observed trend toward "cooperative dependency" in workplace relations (Frenkel, 1991). The new work organization is also consistent with the "core-periphery" model of internal labour market segmentation of Atkinson (1984). In fact, as Dore (1989) has observed, what all the classifications above seem to share to varying degrees is the assumption of a more closed internal labour market for at least "core" employees and a growing periphery of employees whose working conditions may be characterized by less stability and security – and by outright job loss. At the core, moreover, is the strong assumption of cooperative labour-management relations as a necessary ingredient of lean production.

Table 10.2. Advanced manufacturing technologies, the direction of organizational change and industrial relations implications

Organizational characteristic	Comment	Industrial implications
Skill changes	Different skill requirement ("mental" or problem-solving, rather than physical). Usually higher average skill.	Do firms rely on external labour market for required skills? Is training negotiated? Do state policies support investment in training?
Work organization	Greater interdependence among work activities requiring flexible (multi-skilled) employees responsible for more planning and diagnosis, operating and maintenance duties.	Are there constraints on job boundaries posed by union structure or collective bargaining traditions? Does firmly established management hierarchy mitigate against decentralization?
Employment	Need for a high retention rate of well-trained workers because of: greater investment in training, higher capital investment per employee, more costly and immediate consequences of downtime.	Do industrial relations patterns emphasize employment (versus job) security? How are displaced employees accommodated/retrained?
Labour/management	Strong partnership between management and trade union/employees with greater and earlier information sharing, co-planning of selection and implementation of technology and organization changes, co-solving of problems.	Is the labour/management relationship characterized by "adversarialness" or cooperation? Are rights to information/consultation firmly established by custom or law? Does the structure of employee representation help or hinder cooperation?

Source: Adapted from *Human resource practices for implementing advanced manufacturing technology*, Washington, DC, National Academy Press, 1986, pp. 2-3.

machinery, and a high level of hierarchical supervision (Piore and Sabel, 1984). The independent significance of advanced manufacturing technology's influence on transforming work organization is briefly summarized in table 10.2. Although the description applies to the manufacturing setting, many similar conclusions on the impact of technology on work organization in the service industries could also be argued.

Secondly, the spread of the Japanese model of work organization is having a major impact on non-Japanese competitors, e.g. the concept of "lean production" used in the Japanese auto industry. The concept has three principal organizational implications: the organization of work takes on many of the attributes described above as employees are invested with a greater degree of employment security, training, responsibility and variety of tasks; the organization of production between firms is characterized by close, long-term relations among the firm and its suppliers, which are organized along the zero-buffer principle of "just-in-time" production and delivery; finally, the very basis upon which firms compete emphasizes high quality, continuous improvement, and closeness to the consumer (Womack, et al., 1990).

Womack et al. argue that the new model conveys both social advantages, in terms of improved job satisfaction and employment security, as well as economic advantages. As global firms face up to the competitive strength of the lean production model, the encounter may encourage a model of "global best practice" within major firms (Hoffman, 1991), one that would possibly lead to a cross-border convergence of work organization within the global firm (although it would be wrong to assume that this possibility would involve a wholesale imitation of Japan).[5] The prospect of a cross-border convergence occurring in work organization is plausible. First, the efficiency advantages of "lean production" have much less to do with technology than with social or organizational innovations. For example, with no differences in technology from an American firm, a Japanese car plant in the United States employs only half of the typical workforce of a domestic plant to produce the same output (Mendelowitz, 1988). Second, if a global firm is one in which production is more tightly coordinated across borders, each business unit is under pressure not to diverge from "global best practice".[6]

The assumption of convergence has a number of social or institutional implications. First, a sort of global, "firm-centric" social system is implied in the logic of convergence. How will this cross-border model change (or be changed by) distinctive, national settings with their particular institutions? Second, the new model of work organization is consistent with high labour standards for "core" employees: "globalizing" this trend through the vehicle of the multinational corporation would thus be a positive outcome. Third, however, the diffusion of high labour standards would simultaneously apply to fewer and fewer employees, as the quantitative impact on employment of the transition to "lean production" is, as the very expression implies, likely to be strongly negative.

This third implication is of profound importance. Here, it can be imagined that the principal risk is one of labour market exclusion. A greenfield or start-up

---

[5] The unqualified, enthusiastic endorsement of Japanese work and production organization by Womack, et al. (1990) has left some researchers unconvinced. See, for example, Berggren, et al. (1991) who, in their study of Japanese "transplants" in the United States, found work practices to be militaristic, stress-engendering, and resembling a "refined brand of Taylorism".

[6] Thirty years ago, an American school of industrial relations research hypothesized that industrial relations systems would tend toward convergence as a result of the widespread use of the same technologies (Kerr, et al., 1960). That the subsequent evolution of such systems revealed more divergence than convergence appeared to show the limits of a purely technological determinism on social systems (and the theory was indeed "revisited" by the original authors early in the 1970s). Greater cross-border integration at firm level valorizes a sort of "enterprise corporatism" or overarching "corporate culture" at the supranational level: if far-flung, organizational units are to derive their roles from within an integrated web of production, their cooperative fit within this production system must be assured. Arguably, cultural deviance or distinctiveness is less tolerable and, indeed, this multinational system of production becomes more vulnerable to disruption by any one of its links. For Hamill, the more pronounced dependencies within this new organization of production may greatly empower trade unions at any "local" link in the system, and therefore incline the multinational toward union avoidance. This is not a necessary conclusion to draw, however. The new vulnerability of decentralized production, however, underscores the extent to which *cooperation* across units of activity grows in significance. Union avoidance may well be one strategic option. Institutionalizing labour-management cooperation is another. The greater pressure for cooperation, moreover, may be arising not just across physically separate units of activity, but within the units themselves through new patterns of work organization.

facility is one matter, but what of the *conversion* of an existing facility? In addition to the significant employment loss projected in such a transition, which labour market groups will carry most of the burden of adjustment? If the new, high-commitment employee is uniformly young, more physically healthy, better trained and better capable of continuous training, then employment displacement will occur in a stratified way, disproportionately affecting the older worker, the less-skilled worker, etc. This process of exclusion will be all the more catalytic when new, start-up facilities enter into direct competition with established, conventionally organized ones.

4.   A new inter-firm organization of production

In addition to the creation of these new types of intra-firm organization, globalization is also forging new forms of cooperative relations *between* firms unrelated (or only partially related) by ownership. "Quasi-market" relations, situated somewhere between "markets" and "hierarchies", belonging to neither but having properties of both, are recent innovations in organization which, to varying degrees, may be replacing traditional, arm's-length relations between major firms in the market.

4.1 Managing markets through inter-firm networks

One way in which firms appear to be adjusting to the greater competitive challenge of an open global economy is by cooperation with other firms. Inter-firm cooperation as a competitive strategy has many motivations and many forms. Most, however, share the common feature of reducing the risks and costs that would otherwise be incurred from full-scale confrontation in the marketplace as a single firm: they mediate the full brunt of market forces by trying to shape these or by trying to impose order on volatile or competitive markets. They are in some sense the purely private, firm-level equivalent of industrial policies pursued by some States. The decline of arm's-length rivalries with at least a few of the firm's competitors arguably allows the firm to devote greater resources to those which remain.

The new cooperative arrangements among firms may at base be characterized by two types. The first kind are those relations bearing on cooperation between firms that are otherwise competitors – "strategic alliances": indeed the word "alliance" conveys their essence – they are primarily *horizontal* relations between or among firms that otherwise are competing with each other, allies in toto may diverge, but on a limited range of objectives they converge. In definitional terms, then, a strategic alliance is one established between actual or virtual competitors. The second type of innovative, inter-firm relations refers to changes in *vertical* linkages between firms.

An example of the first type, or horizontal relationship, is the recent agreement between the French computer group, Bull, and IBM. While competitors in their final markets, they agreed to an alliance through which Bull will gain access to needed technology (the RISC semiconductor technology), while IBM will gain access to Bull's market and distribution system over a selected range of products. IBM has taken an as yet undisclosed equity stake in the French company, the majority of whose shares are held by the French Government. NUMMI, the much discussed joint venture between Toyota and General Motors, is another example of a horizontal, inter-firm relationship. While Toyota gains additional access to the American market through General Motors' distribution network, GM's major objective is the transfer of Toyota's management, work, and production organization system.

4.2 Three axes of classification for horizontal relationships

Many of the strategic alliances that have been forged over the past 15 years can be located at some point along three, separate but not unrelated axes. First, alliances can occur at any one of several points along the value-added chain – from "pre-competitive" research consortia, to technology-sharing or co-production agreements, and finally to shared marketing and distribution channels. Second, there is great variety in the nature or form of an alliance, from various forms of licensing or cross-licensing arrangements, other forms of non-equity contracts or agreements, to equity arrangements up to and including international joint ventures. Whether an alliance takes an equity or non-equity form (the difference, for example, between NUMMI and the IBM/Bull alliance), an alliance is nevertheless qualitatively different in its strategic intent and market impact than a merger or acquisition. Table 10.3 isolates a few of these different forms of alliance, and also summarizes some of the costs and benefits attaching to each form.

A third classificatory approach centres on the strategic motivations of the partners themselves in constructing these alliances. Different strategies are apparent in specific industries. For example, "market access" appears as the most important strategic objective behind alliances in the automotive, consumer electronics, microelectronics, and food and beverage industries. In aviation and defence industries, however, the high cost of developing new products is a most important motivation for alliances among competing firms.

Three motivations behind strategic alliances are of greatest importance. These are: (i) the growing technological complementarity across formerly discrete industries; (ii) the increasingly rapid rate of technological change and innovation; and (iii) gaining access to the global market.[7] Strategic alliances can thus be viewed as a structural response to many of the same factors associated with the globalizing firm. The most basic of these relate to the competitive pressures to reduce product innovation cycles, which increase both the risks and the costs of research and development, and to amortize the higher cost of new product development by rapidly gaining access to markets. Unlike certain tendencies of the intra-firm organization of production, however, strategic alliances may be a vehicle for the coordination of production without any change in the location of production or of a strategic function. Therefore, a firm may benefit from cooperative alliances in R&D without decentralizing its own R&D function away from headquarters. Alliances in this sense may substitute for direct investment or locational shifts. They may therefore act as a curb, not so much on the globalization of the firm (since such alliances may still be regarded as

[7] These findings are from the Dutch MERIT/CATI data bank and are cited in OECD (1990).

Table 10.3. Global strategic alliances

Strategy	Organizational design	Benefits	Costs	Critical success factors	Strategic human resources management
Licensing-manufacturing industries	Technologies	• Early standardization of design • Access to new technologies • Ability to capitalize on innovations • Ability to control pace of industry's evolution	• New competitors created • Possible eventual exit from industry • Possible dependence on licence	• Selection of licensee that is unlikely to become competitor • Enforcement of patents and licensing agreements	• Technical knowledge • Training of local managers on site
Licensing-servicing and franchises	Geography	• Fast market entry • Low capital cost	• Quality control • Trademark protection	• Partners compatible in philosophies and values • Tight performance standards	• Socialization of franchises and licensees with core values
Joint ventures-specialization across partners	Function	• Learning a partner's skills • Economies of scale • Quasi-vertical integration • Faster learning	• Excessive dependence on partner for skills • Deterrent to internal investment	• Tight and specific performance criteria • Entering a venture as "student" rather than "teacher" to learn skills from partner • Recognizing that collaboration is another form of competition to learn new skills	• Management development and training • Negotiation skills • Managerial rotation
Joint ventures-shared value-adding	Product or line of business	• Strengths of both partners pooled • Faster learning along value chain • Fast upgrading of technological skills	• High switching costs • Inability to limit partner's access to information	• Decentralization and autonomy from corporate parents • Long "courtship" period • Harmonization of management styles	• Team-building • Acculturation • Flexible skills for implicit communication
Consortia, keiretsus and chaebols	Firm and industry	• Shared risks and costs • Building a critical mass in process technologies • Fast resource flows and skill transfers	• Skills and technologies that have no real market worth • Bureaucracy • Hierarchy	• Government encouragement • Shared values among managers • Personal relationships to ensure coordination and priorities • Close monitoring of member company performance	• "Clan" cultures • Fraternal relationships • Extensive mentoring to provide a common vision and mission across member companies

Source: Lei and Slocum (1991), p. 48.

part and parcel of a firm's "global strategy"), but on the firm's locational repositioning of its worldwide activities.

4.3 A new "vertical" inter-firm organization of production

The topic of inter-firm relations or even commercial links among networks of firms is not new. Indeed, there are entire industries (e.g. steel) whose output is destined solely to other firms and thus whose markets are exclusively inter-firm. An increasing percentage of all international trade is accounted for by inter-industry trade among firms in international supply networks. But inter-firm linkages can no longer be fully accounted for by the assumption that they are arm's-length, commercial transactions: the web of firms related in a vertical production organization may, as with strategic alliances, be increasingly characterized by their cooperative rather than arm's-length relations. Unlike strategic alliances, however, the firms involved in these vertical networks are not often direct competitors.

4.4 Redefining the boundaries of the firm: Externalization

In their bid to remain flexible and cost-efficient, firms have restructured in a variety of sometimes conflicting or opposite ways. Thus, for some firms, a return to "core businesses" may involve the hiving-off of non-central concerns. For example, there has been a marked trend toward the "externalization" of businesses or services formerly owned (or internalized) by the multinational. The principal advantage to the firm of the trend toward "vertical disintegration" is the flexibility that it gains in responding to volatile (or, at the very least, rapid) changes in demand in its product markets. On the other hand, there are a few noteworthy examples of vertical reintegration: Sony's purchase of Columbia Records, for example, enables the audio/visual hardware manufacturer to integrate "downstream" with a major "software" producer. Still, there can be little doubt that one of the ways in which firms are seeking to gain flexibility is to separate themselves from the ownership of non-central businesses.

The archetype of the "flexible multinational" is the Italian apparel company, Benetton, whose extended network of subcontractors allows the firm to respond rapidly to changes in tastes and styles without, in fact, manufacturing anything (Amin, 1991). The Benetton example may be extreme, but it is not unique. Even so, other multinationals have pared their activities to just those that define the corporation: "A firm's position in the market may be best protected by obtaining control over a few core functions and contracting the rest. In the auto industry, subcontracting of component production has gone so far that some foresee that the automobile company may soon become a kind of higher order design house and marketing agency. Its chief function would be to coordinate the work of other design houses (the systems suppliers), connect the subassemblies, and distribute the final product" (Lazerson, 1990, p. 15). At the logical extreme, a multinational's presence in key markets may rely more on the projection of a brand name than on any particular product or service that it itself provides.

4.5 *Just-in-time and the location of production*

Greater cooperation between multinational corporations and their suppliers based on greater long-term cooperation – rather than on "arm's-length", market-determined relations based on price – is an additional organizational innovation commonly attributed to the diffusion of the Japanese model of organizing production. Encouraging this trend are the dual motives of competition based on quality rather than price alone, and the productivity advantages and cost savings of reducing inventory holdings. "Just-in-time" (rather than "just-in-case") production methods affect the location of production, since this form of inter-firm relationship requires close geographical proximity. As the UNCTC (1988, p. 47) observed:

> The adoption of the new technologies and organizational methods in manufacturing is leading to significant changes in sourcing patterns and practices. In automobiles, supplier industries are increasingly located in physical proximity to assembly plants, as the latter shift to flexible manufacturing methods. This has clearly been the case of the automobile production facilities recently built by Japanese corporations in the United States and the United Kingdom, which are using just-in-time inventory systems. But a similar process is taking place in United States automobile production companies, which are restructuring their domestic-production facilities. In a related development, United States automobile manufacturers are increasingly using long-term, single-source contracts for key components. Ford, for example, has five-and ten-year single-source contracts for transmissions, axles, clutches, frame assemblies and engine parts.

Closer working and planning links in the new subcontracting relationships may be furthered by the technical ability for the instantaneous exchange of information, product specifications, etc., through computer networks. A recent international survey nevertheless casts some doubt on the diffusion of the new subcontracting relations. While many companies claim to have long-term relationships both with their customers and suppliers, in practice, customers are kept at "arm's length" and suppliers only a little closer. Only a small minority of companies claiming long-term supplier relationships train suppliers or work closely on product development with those suppliers (Kanter, 1991, p. 162).

In quantitative terms, the consequences on employment of changes in work organization are likely to be negative: (1) as the primary contracting firm relies more and more on the quality and efficiency gains associated with (employment-shedding) "leanness" in the supplier or subcontractor; and (2) as the primary contracting firm sharply reduces the number of subcontractors with which it enters into more cooperative relations.

In qualitative terms, the impact of these relations are on balance more likely to be positive. As the market link between firms in a supply relationship becomes one based less on price alone and more on quality, reliability, etc., the formerly integrated large firm would transfer its know-how in work and production organization to its subcontractors. On the negative side, however, is the greater dependence of the subcontractor on the contracting firm.

4.6 The blurring of firms' boundaries and inter-firm dependencies

As noted closer, more cooperative and longer-term relations among firms and their suppliers suggest a higher level of inter-firm dependency than in traditional, arm's-length inter-firm relations. Dependency may not be entirely a disadvantage, however: the dependent firm may be relieved from devoting its scarce management resources over the full range of functions required by an "independent" firm, e.g. marketing, strategic planning, etc., and therefore be in a position to devote fuller attention to improving productivity through implementing changes in work organization, improving product quality, etc. (UNCTC, 1988). It is not obvious, moreover, that it is always in the interest of the primary firm to have contracting firms solely dependent upon it. If firms are externalizing greater shares of their skill- or design-intensive work (Hoffman, 1990), the primary firm may wish to encourage its suppliers to gain learning and experience through diversifying their markets. As the dependent firm's independent reputation for quality and innovation grows, moreover, diversification becomes more possible.

Dependent, inter-firm relations may have direct consequences for the quality of employment and working conditions. Under the sort of "quasi-market" relationship implied by just-in-time production, for example, the individual firm may have difficulty in retaining control over its own organization of working time, its own "wage/effort" policy and its own pace of work. Such traditional elements of a firm's personnel practices can become subject to influence by the blurring of organizational boundaries implicit in this "quasi-market" form of inter-firm organization. It is questionable how these new patterns of relationships between firms will fit with established patterns of industrial relations and employee representation.

4.7 Inter-firm strategies, costs and benefits for labour

To some observers, such as Porter (1990), horizontal, inter-firm relations are inherently unstable and thus of only temporary strategic importance to the multinational enterprise. Amin and Dietrich (1991), on the contrary, observe a growing concentration of multinational market power as a result of these horizontal webs: "Corporate power ... is becoming increasingly centralized on two levels: first, the locus of strategic control is extending beyond the formal boundaries of the firm; second, a heightened degree of cooperation between oligopolists is occurring" (p. 22). The substitution of normal market relations with "loose-tight webs of partners, subcontractors, and collaborators" (Amin, 1991) may portend a "cartelization" of international markets (Petrella, 1990).

Questions of what may or may not be happening to industrial structures aside, the employment effects of horizontal relationships depend on the strategic focus of the partners and whether the alliance is successful. When it is, the employment consequences may not only be positive but long-term, since the temporary nature of an alliance will also depend on the strategic balance of the alliance that the parties forge. For example, the joint venture between the US firm General Electric and the French company SNECMA, has been a long-term, successful endeavour to develop propulsion systems too costly and risky for either to have undertaken alone.

It is self-evident that the parties to a strategic alliance hope to gain mutually from their cooperation. Such positive synergies, however, are not the only possible outcome. It can be said of another example involving General Electric that:

> some venture partners deliberately enter into such arrangements to learn about or to gain access to another firm's research or proprietary technology. The single biggest cost may be one partner's loss of skills and other sources of competitive advantage to a partner that then becomes a more direct and more potent competitor. This occurred when GE entered into a specialized joint venture with Samsung to produce microwave ovens. Now Samsung competes with GE in its full line of household appliances (Lei and Slocum, 1991, p. 54).

Reich and Mankin (1986) similarly observed strategic differences along national lines in their study of Japanese-US joint ventures in the US electronics industry. The American partner was typically interested in a quick infusion of capital, whereas the Japanese partner was interested in access to proprietary technology. The authors predicted an ultimate erosion of the skill base of the US electronics industry as the outcome of these strategic alliances.

5. Global firms, local industrial relations

5.1 Labour market regulation and globalization

At the same time as changes have taken place in the cross-border, intra- and inter-firm organization of production, national systems of labour market regulation have begun to show signs of strain. Many trade union movements in advanced market economies have declined in strength, in some instances dramatically in recent years, while the State has in many countries withdrawn to varying degrees from an active role in labour markets. New patterns in the organization of production would have in any case exposed a gap in the regulation of the labour market: the gap or "regulatory deficit" seems all the greater in the weakened institutional environment of the early 1990s.

The sources of this regulatory deficit are twofold. First, national regulatory frameworks whose coverage may once have been more or less co-extensive with a nation's economic activity are no longer so, as markets and competition erode the significance of national boundaries. Industrial relations systems and, indeed, national social policies generally, are being called upon to adjust to market conditions that are increasingly not of their own making and outside of their ambit of control. One thinks in this regard of John R. Commons' observation in early twentieth century that trade union organization must cover the extent of the product market if "wages" – and, by extension, all standards governing labour – were to be "taken out of competition". In fact, the concept of an internationally "level playing field" governing the conditions under which labour would be employed was at the very origin of the International Labour Organization. Second, a higher degree of integration across geo-

Table 10.4. Five channels of labour's strategic influence in a global economy

At the national level	
Private agreements	Labour-management agreements that implicitly or explicitly address the greater international openness of competition are commonplace. The most "proactive" contractual responses would focus, for example, on methods of improving productivity (e.g. eliminating narrow job boundaries in return for greater employment security, guarantees of retraining, etc.) rather than concessions in the area of wages or working conditions alone.
National legislation	Ideally, fully tripartite, active labour market adjustment policies would probably best ensure the equitable balance of costs and benefits among all parties in competition in an open economy. The aim would be to continually adjust and redirect human resources in a manner least costly to people. The objective, however, is a difficult one. Which national labour and trade policies benefit a nation's workforce and the stability of its labour institutions without doing so at the expense of another nation's workforce? That is, can protection occur and protectionism be avoided? For example, do "social clauses" accompanying trade legislation (Van Liemt, 1989) work if not subscribed to by all nations in a trading system? Or do they invite evasion through changes in trading partners/patterns?
At the international level	
International legislation	The European Community remains the only region in which labour laws are concluded at the supra-national level. The aim of EC labour law is not to "take wages out of competition" for the region, but to take other working conditions out of competition in an integrated market, e.g. differences in the treatment of temporary and part-time workers, or in the organization of working time, or in the differential degrees of the institutionalization of worker participation. The slow pace of the construction of the EC's social dimension shows that the desire for a firmly institutionalized basis for international social policy is far from being fully accepted. The ILO's labour standards are forged internationally, but acquire active significance only when ratified by member States. This disparity between the level at which standards are drafted and the level at which they are actually guaranteed is one reason why a minimum floor of standards attaching to the global sphere of competition is rendered difficult. Some have pressed for the inclusion of a social clause in the GATT (IMF, 1988), although there would seem to be little political will inclining toward this objective.
International codes of conduct	Voluntary codes of behaviour for multinational corporations were promulgated by both the ILO and the OECD in the 1970s. These remain important guides for conduct, and ones that reflect the will of the international community (ILO, 1989). As regulatory instruments, their impact is at the level of moral suasion (Pérez-López, 1991), and breaches of good conduct can expose the firm to adverse publicity.
Private agreements or unilateral actions	Cross-border coordination among trade unions, often facilitated by the regional or international labour organizations to which national unions may be affiliated, have either unilaterally or, in fewer instances, by agreement with multinational managements, influenced labour relations outcomes. At present, there are established structures of trade unions across national boundaries along industry, occupational, and even company lines. At the latter level, in a small number of multinational firms (e.g. BSN Gervais Danone, Thomson Grand Public, Volkswagen, among others), labour-management structures at the supra-national level have been created. It is to be noted as well that one effect of global strategies of firms may be to endow unions at the national level with cross-border significance in affecting production (e.g. a strike in the United Kingdom resulting in lost production in Belgium). Within the EC, supra-national labour-management structures appear to be evolving somewhat, with regional integration and public policy proposals supporting such new institutional forms being the primary motivating factors.

graphically widespread units of production within and between firms may be reducing the importance of purely national or local influences in the organization of work and production.

It is unrealistic to expect a globally coordinated trade unionism or a supranational system of industrial relations to emerge which is capable of matching the recent changes in the organization of production. Instead, representatives of workers, predominantly at local or national levels will respond to these new developments using their traditional methods or regulatory channels for attaining their objectives – via private agreements, and through the political/legislative system (see table 10.4).

5.2 Some potential issues for local industrial relations

It would be wrong to infer from the continuing importance of the national level in industrial relations that the emergence of trade-union style "strategic alliance" building, particularly at the level of the European Community, is out of the question. Indeed, one outcome of the firm's greater integration among its widespread activities may be to convey increased leverage to local bargaining agents. These two exceptions aside, however, the industrial relations regulation of globalization is a national and local matter. At those levels, then, several issues may arise:

(i) A more accentuated core-periphery distinction in internal labour markets

Assuming that a firm's globalization is directly linked to a growing dualism at the level of the firm's own labour force (and it remains a supposition at this stage), this tendency could reinforce gaps in trade union representation, particularly as "peripheral" workers, or those working under temporary or part-time contracts, are often difficult to organize. Are some groups more vulnerable to exclusion from the core (e.g. the older worker) or, in other words, internal work organization changes do have a segmenting effect to the detriment of those groups least able to be reabsorbed in the labour market? More fundamentally, do the intra-firm organizational changes associated with globalization inevitably lead to employment loss? Finally, is there "a" new model of work organization and is it superior in terms of employee satisfaction to previous model(s)? On this question, opinion is divided (see footnote 5).

(ii) The growing "company-centred" models of work organization, emphasizing greater employee commitment and closer ties to management objectives

Many would agree that cooperative labour-management relations are a prerequisite to "lean production". The degree to which cooperation is institutionalized in industrial relations systems varies, however, and it is not far-fetched to assume that cooperative production strategies raise the question of "systemic fit" across the various, historically distinctive locations in which multinationals operate. Where in the world do these new production strategies effectively exclude unions; or encounter resistance bred by the "mismatch" between the new, firm-based strategies and traditional patterns of industrial relations; or, finally, result in truly cooperative partnerships on the level of labour-management relations? Is, for example, the institution of enterprise unionism in Japan merely coincidental with the high incidence of labour/management cooperation frequently associated with Japanese firms?

(iii) The "externalization" of employment

One can optimistically view the trend toward the "vertical disintegration" of the large firm as a process creating entrepreneurially driven small firms: former employees of large firms may become independent, self-employed contractors. However, there is no guarantee of such a positive outcome on the labour market. In fact, the externalization of employment may result in a large measure of unemployment or, at least, a broader stratification of the labour market, since it is also the case that the terms and conditions of employment in large firms are most often superior to those prevailing in small firms. Former employees who become self-employed in the same industrial labour market may also be less inclined to join a trade union.

(iv) The shift from the "miniature replica" model of the subsidiary to its participation in a global network of activities

It would seem likely that, at the level of the subsidiary, competing or contradictory tendencies may be at work – toward greater decentralization in certain regards, but also toward the opposite. How this reconfiguration of decision-making levels affects industrial relations at the subsidiary level is not easy to predict. It would seem plausible, for example, that local-level employee representatives could experience a loss of autonomy or control as the subsidiary's production becomes more closely tied or coordinated to a global web. Conversely, the more integrated the subsidiary becomes within a global network, the more vulnerable it may become to leverage applied at the purely local level.

(v) The increasingly common experience of national unions dealing with foreign-owned firms

In itself, this general circumstance does not seem to matter much, as "foreign" need not imply "footloose" any more than it does for domestic capital. Nor are the foreign subsidiaries of multinational firms typically associated with substandard wages and working conditions. There are, however, two areas where foreign versus domestic ownership may matter. One is the now long-standing industrial relations concern over the locus of decision-making and access by employee representatives to the level at which decisions affecting the livelihood of local employees are made. The second, perhaps more recent issue relates to the multinational nature of the MNE: the plant's location on the value-added chain is certain to be of concern both to employees and to domestic policy-makers, given that the subsidiary as a miniature replica of the parent company may be of diminishing significance and that the concern of local economic actors ought to be not just employment, but the generation of high value-added jobs.

(vi) The unpredictable consequences of "horizontal" strategic alliances

If the employment consequences of horizontal alliances among firms remain difficult to pinpoint with any clarity, the industrial relations implications of inter-firm cooperation are equally unclear. Certainly, to the extent that strategic alliances may be prone to a high failure rate, the consequences for employment security are potentially worrying. Finally, it is likely that the quantity and quality of employment in a strategic alliance ultimately depend on the strategies of the partners themselves – specifically, whether these produce a good synergy or whether, as in one or two of the examples noted earlier, the costs and benefits of the alliance are unequally shared.

(vii) The blurring of organizational boundaries of formerly discrete internal labour markets

Company personnel practices and policies, whether determined bilaterally through employee representatives or not, have always constituted one of the main regulatory sources in internal labour markets, in addition to the regulatory influence of laws and extra-firm labour/management agreements. In cooperative networks involving firms in just-in-time production, one firm's production exigencies determine another's. Arguably, the terms and conditions of employment (work pace, hours of work, access to decision-makers and ability to influence decisions) become in a certain sense dependent upon decisions made in another firm. The consequences of this on the traditional patterns and content of employee representation are unknown, but it may be held as axiomatic that the adjustment of labour market institutions always lags behind changes in the organization of production.

(viii) The location of work in the global economy

The globalization of the firm appears related to a new economics in which location decisions are made on the basis of a particular site's competitive and comparative advantages. In addition to the need to know more about the quantity and quality of employment, of how industrial relations systems and actors, such as trade unions, are adjusting to the new international organization of production, there are shifts in the location of globally linked production. What are the causes and penalties of exclusion, and what could be the strategies of inclusion ?

6. Concluding remarks

Although its full effects are still to become apparent, the tendency towards globalization is none the less changing the setting for local industrial relations. These changes are complex, but are by no means uniformly negative nor do they pose insurmountable challenges to employment, wages and working conditions, or established patterns of employee representation. On the contrary, the globalization of the firm holds great potential for improving labour standards in the sort of intra-firm work organization changes described. But however great the promise of intra-firm and inter-firm organizational changes for meaningful, well-remunerated work, there are several potentially negative consequences of the transition. This is because globalization refers not just to the cross-border integration of major economic actors, but to the greater integration and openness of whole economies, whether national or subnational. As more jobs are affected by international competition, more of us are in greater competition with each other for employment – and for well-paying, satisfying employment.

This chapter has looked at globalization as an organizational phenomenon, but it may be the extra-firm consequences (e.g. possible employment loss, possible increases in labour market segmentation, erosion or adjustment lags in labour institutions) that ought to be of the greatest concern to policy-makers and trade unions. Although there will be disagreement over how much of this is rhetoric and how much is reality, one cannot fail to be struck by how central the notion of cooperation is in present tendencies of industrial organization – cooperation among employees formerly isolated in the division of labour, among units of the same global firm, among major competitors unrelated by ownership, among large and small firms in long-term supply relations, etc. These may be the intra- and inter-firm tendencies, however, and firms cannot be expected to act as extra-firm regulators of the consequences of economic activity, however much they may increasingly be called upon to "internalize" such extra-firm challenges as the environment, child care, etc. Finding new ways to involve the State and labour organizations in these cooperative networks, perhaps at relatively novel levels of organization such as the region or the community, might aid in balancing the benefits and costs of globalization.

Bibliography

Amin, Ash. 1991. "Giant shapers and shakers of the world economy leave British hopes behind as wishful thinking", in *The Guardian*, 7 Jan. 1991.

—; Dietrich, M. 1991. "From hierarchy to 'hierarchy': The dynamics of contemporary corporate restructuring in Europe", in Ash Amin and M. Dietrich (eds.): *Towards a New Europe*, Aldershot, Edward Elgar.

Atkinson, J. S. 1984. "Flexibility, uncertainty and manpower management", in *IMS Report*, No. 89, Institute for Manpower Studies, Brighton, Sussex.

Berggren, Christian; Bjorkman, Torsten; Hollander, Ernst. 1991. "Are they unbeatable?", Royal Institute of Technology, Department of Work Science, Stockholm, mimeo.

Canadian Council of Professional Engineers (CCPE). 1983. *Brief on research and development in Canada*, Ottawa, CCPE, Feb., p. 8.

de Granrut, Charles, 1990. "La mondialisation de l'économie: Eléments de synthèse", Forecasting and Assessment in Science and Technology, Working Paper, Brussels, Commission of the European Communities.

Dore, Ronald. 1989. "Where we are now: Musings of an evolutionist", in *Work, Employment and Society*, Vol. 3, No. 4, Dec.

Doz, Yves. 1987. "International industries: Fragmentation versus globalization", in B.R. Guile and H. Brooks (eds.): *Technology and global industry*, Washington, DC, National Academy Press.

Evans, Paul; Doz, Yves; Laurent, André (eds.). 1990. *Human resource management in international firms: Change, globalization, innovation*. New York, St. Martin's Press.

Frenkel, Steve. 1991. "Patterns of workplace relations in the global corporation: Towards convergence?", University of New South Wales, Sydney, mimeo.

Hoffman, Kurt. 1990. *New approaches to best-practice manufacturing: Multinational corporations and implications for developing countries*, United Nations Centre on Transnational Corporations Current Series No. 12, New York, United Nations.

ILO. 1989. *The ILO Tripartite Declaration of Principles concerning Multinational Enterprises and Social Policy: Ten years after*, Geneva.

International Metalworkers' Federation (IMF). 1988. *Trade and workers' rights: Time for a link*, Geneva, International Metalworkers' Federation.

Kanter, Rosabeth. 1991. "Transcending business boundaries: 12,000 world managers view change", in *Harvard Business Review*, Vol. 69, No. 3, May-June.

Kerr, C., et al. 1960. *Industrialism and industrial man: The problems of labor and management in economic growth*, Cambridge, Massachussetts, Harvard University Press.

Kern, Horst; Sabel, Charles. 1991. "Trade unions and decentralized production: Strategic problems in the West German labour movement", Discussion Paper No. 45, Geneva, International Institute for Labour Studies.

Lazerson, Mark. 1990. "Subcontracting as an alternative organizational form to vertically-integrated production", Discussion Paper No. 20, Geneva, International Institute for Labour Studies.

Lei, David; Slocum, John. 1991. "Global strategic alliances: Payoffs and pitfalls", in *Organizational Dynamics*, Vol. 19, No. 3, Winter.

Mendelowitz, Allen. 1988. *Foreign investment: Growing Japanese presence in the US auto industry*, GAO/NSIAD 88-111, Washington, DC, US General Accounting Office.

Morrison, Allen. 1990: *Strategies in global industries: How US businesses compete*, Westport, Connecticut, Quorum Books.

Morrison, Allen; Ricks, David; Roth, Kendall. 1991. "Globalization versus regionalization: Which way for the multinational?", in *Organizational Dynamics*, Vol. 19, No. 3, Winter.

OECD, Directorate for Science, Technology and Industry (DSTI). 1990. *Globalization in the computer industry*, Background Paper prepared by John Hagedoorn for an experts meeting held in Paris on 17 December.

Ohmae, Kenichi. 1990. *The borderless world: Power and strategy in the interlinked economy*, New York, Harper Perennial.

Pérez-López, Jorge. 1991. "Promoting international respect for worker rights through business codes of conduct", Washington, DC, US Department of Labor, mimeo.

Petrella, Riccardo. 1990. "La mondialisation de l'économie: Impacts sur le contrat social", Presentation at the annual congress of the Institut d'Administration Publique du Canada, Quebec, 27 August 1990, mimeo.

—. 1991. "Three analyses of globalization of technology and economy", Background Paper for a European meeting: *A new Europe: Visions and actions,* Namur, 10-12 April.

Piore, Michael and Sabel, Charles. 1984. *The second industrial divide: Possibilities for prosperity*, New York, Basic Books.

Porter, Michael. 1990. *The competitive advantage of nations*, London, Macmillan.

Reich, Robert. 1991. *The work of nations: Preparing ourselves for 21st-century capitalism*, New York, Alfred A. Knopf.

—; Mankin, Eric. 1986. "Joint ventures with Japan give away our future", in *Harvard Business Review*, Mar.-Apr.

Robins, Kevin. 1989: "Global times", in *Marxism Today*, Dec.

Roth, Kendall; Morrison, Allen. 1990. "An empirical analysis of the integration-responsiveness framework in global industries", in *Journal of International Business Studies*, Vol. 21, No. 4, Fourth Quarter.

Streeck, Wolfgang. 1991. "On the institutional conditions of diversified quality production", in Egon Matzner and Wolfgang Streeck (eds.): *Beyond Keynesianism: The socio-economics of production and full employment*, Aldershot, Edward Elgar.

Thomsen, Stephen. 1992. "We are all 'Us'", in *Columbia Journal of World Business*, Winter.

Tyson, Laura d'Andrea. 1991. "They are not us: Why American ownership still matters," in *The American Prospect*, Winter.

United Nations Centre on Transnational Corporations. 1988. *Transnational corporations in world development: Trends and prospects*, New York, United Nations.

Van Houten, George. 1990. "The implications of globalism: New management realities at Philips", in Evans, Doz and Laurent, 1990.

Van Liemt, Gijsbert. 1989. "Minimum labour standards and international trade: Would a social clause work?", in *International Labour Review*, Vol. 128, No. 41.

Womack, J.P.; Jones, D.; Roos, D. 1990. *The machine that changed the world*, New York, Rawson Associates.

11

Overview and conclusions

Geoffrey Renshaw

1. Trends in foreign direct investment in the 1980s

Chapter 1, by Jungnickel, gives an overall perspective of trends in FDI in the 1980s and its distribution between countries and regions. The first salient feature of the data he presents is that FDI "is essentially a First World business directed largely to First World locations". Thus in the latter 1980s the industrialized countries were the source of more than 95 per cent of FDI outflows and the host to more than 80 per cent of the inflows. Within the industrialized countries, moreover, FDI is heavily concentrated on only nine countries: the US, Canada, Germany, the UK, the Netherlands, France, Italy, Switzerland and Japan. In 1990 these nine were the source of almost nine-tenths of the world's outward stock of FDI, and the host to more than two-thirds of the inward stock (see Chapter 1, Appendix table 1).

The second feature of the data is the enormous expansion in FDI in the 1980s. The annual outflow grew from US$ 57 billion in 1980 to $ 222 billion in 1990. Growth was particularly rapid from 1985 to 1990, when the world FDI outflows grew at 33 per cent per annum. In the decade as a whole, outward FDI from the developed countries totalled $ 1,083 billion, of which 18 per cent was sourced from the United Kingdom, 18 per cent from the United States and 17 per cent from Japan. The US was overwhelmingly the largest host to inward FDI in the 1980s, accounting for 44 per cent of recorded inflows (compared with 26 per cent in 1971-79). The next largest host was the UK, with 15 per cent. Inflows to Japan were negligible in world terms (see Chapter 1, Appendix table 2).

The third feature is that since the mid-1970s there have been very substantial changes in country and regional shares in both outward and inward FDI flows, consisting principally in the decline in the relative importance of the US as a source and an increase in its importance as a host, a rise in the importance of Western Europe as both a source and a host, and the rapid rise of Japan as a source. Because flow data on FDI are subject to quite pronounced pro-cyclical variation (reflecting similar variation in total investment), the cumulative effects within the regional "triad" composed of Japan, North America and Western Europe are perhaps better assessed by looking at FDI stock data. Between 1980 and 1990 the US share of the world's *outward* stock fell from 43 per cent to 26 per cent, while its share of the world's *inward* stock rose from 17 to 27 per cent. Japan's outward share rose from 4 to

12 per cent, with its inward share constant at 1 per cent. In Europe, the outward share of the "big six" in FDI (the UK, Netherlands, France, Germany, Italy and Switzerland) rose from 40 to 44 per cent and their combined inward share from 32 to 34 per cent. Regarding inward stocks, it is worth noting that, although large in absolute terms, the inward stock of the US was only 7 per cent of US GDP in 1990, and relative to GDP the largest hosts were the Netherlands (24 per cent), the UK (21 per cent), and Canada (19 per cent). In several smaller industrialized countries the inward stock of FDI relative to GDP more than doubled in the 1980s.

A fourth feature was the declining relative importance of the developing countries in the 1980s as *hosts* to FDI. Between 1960 and 1985, their share of the world's inward stock of FDI remained remarkably constant at around 25 per cent, but by 1990 this share had fallen to 18 per cent. In dollar values the consequence of this declining share was that inward FDI flows into the industrialized countries increased fourfold between 1983-85 and 1988-89 to $140 billion, while inflows into the developing countries increased by only 50 per cent to $20 billion. The major factor in this relative decline was a pronounced shift of Japanese FDI away from developing countries. There were similar, though smaller, shifts by the UK, Germany and France. Notwithstanding the decline in the developing countries' share of world FDI, however, foreign affiliates of MNEs became more important in many developing countries, particularly in Asia, where both inward and outward FDI registered significant increases in the second half of the decade.

A fifth development is the rapid growth of FDI sourced from the newly industrialized economies (NIEs) of East Asia in the 1980s – Hong Kong, the Republic of Korea, Singapore and Taiwan (China). Available data are scanty, but Chapter 1 estimates that the outward stocks of FDI of Hong Kong and Taiwan (China) were around $20 billion in 1991, and those of the Republic of Korea and Singapore about $3 billion in 1990. In relation to the global stock of FDI of perhaps $1,500 billion, these numbers may appear small. But it is significant that most of this FDI has been concentrated in the Asian-Pacific region, where in Malaysia, Indonesia and the Philippines the Asian NIEs have supplanted Japan as the main source of FDI. FDI by these countries in other developing regions has been negligible, and only the Republic of Korea has so far invested significantly in industrialized countries – mainly in North America. As shown in Chapter 1, this FDI is contributing to rapid economic integration of the Asian-Pacific region, discussed further in section 6 below.

2. MNEs and employment

Chapter 2, by Parisotto, complements the data on FDI presented in Chapter 1 by examining the associated employment effects. Given that the employment data are seriously incomplete, the chapter is remarkably successful not only in assembling a coherent picture using data from many sources but in wringing the maximum information from it. Beginning with global employment by MNEs, the best available estimate, furnished by an ILO study,[1] suggests that their worldwide employment in the middle 1980s was (as a lower limit) around 70 million workers, of whom about three-quarters were employed in the home countries of their MNE employers, while the remainder were employed abroad, predominantly in industrialized countries.

Any attempt to go beyond these bald global employment totals immediately runs into data difficulties, and it is possible to proceed only with the aid of sample data for sub-sets of enterprises and countries, the choice of which is almost entirely dictated by data availability. Perhaps the most important data limitation is the almost complete absence of time series, which makes the detection of trends almost impossible. Subject to these limitations, Parisotto is able to paint the following picture. First, and notwithstanding the long-standing role of MNEs in mining, and the rapid growth of MNEs in the service sector, 70-80 per cent or more of MNE employment is in manufacturing. Second, and confirming the aggregate figures cited above, the partial data suggest that roughly two-thirds of MNE employees are located in the home countries of their employing MNEs. Thus, virtually all MNEs are strongly home-based in terms of employment (and presumably in terms of assets). Notwithstanding the trend to "globalization" (discussed further below) and indeed the very term "multinational enterprise", almost every MNE has a clearly identifiable home country and the truly "stateless" MNE is even now very rare.

Third, perhaps the most important question of all concerns the "weight" of MNEs in the world economy. Judged by their worldwide direct employment, the figure of 70 million cited above is of course almost infinitesimal in relation to total world employment. On the other hand, MNEs employ about 50 million workers in industrialized countries, roughly one-sixth of total employment there. Such broad ratios, however, are not very illuminating. A better perspective of the importance of MNEs, whether in terms of employment or assets, is found when we look at their weight in individual source and host economies, and their weight in particular industrial sectors.

One index of this is provided by the *total* (home plus foreign) employment of home-based MNEs. Parisotto shows that for some countries this is quite large in relation to the size of the domestic economy. For example, in the 1980s worldwide employment by MNEs based in the Netherlands, Switzerland and Sweden was in the range 28-33 per cent of total domestic paid employment in those countries, and for the US was 23 per cent (table 2.1). However, perhaps the best synopsis of the weight of MNE employment in individual industrialized countries is provided by figure 2.1b. This shows for example that in the US in 1988, non-MNEs were responsible for only

---

[1] O. Kreye, et al.: *Multinational enterprises and employment*, Multinational Enterprises Programme Working Paper No. 55 (Geneva, ILO, 1988).

38 per cent of total paid manufacturing employment, the remaining 62 per cent of employment in the US being divided between US-parent MNEs (52 per cent) and foreign-parent MNEs (10 per cent). In several other countries in the sample, the share of MNEs in domestic manufacturing employment exceeded 50 per cent.

In the 16 developing countries for which data are available, employment by foreign-owned affiliates in manufacturing ranged from 14 to 58 per cent of total manufacturing paid employment, with an unweighted average of 22 per cent (see table 2.10). As Parisotto points out, a better measure of foreign MNE presence in developing countries would be obtained by relating their employment not to total employment but to employment in the formal sector, or perhaps to private employment in the formal sector. Measured in such ways, the weight of MNE employment would doubtless increase substantially, as is indeed illustrated by Chapter 7, on MNEs in Indonesia (discussed in section 5 below). Unfortunately the broader data relevant to this question do not exist.

It is also important to recall that these employment data relate to direct employment, and thus neglect a variety of indirect employment effects. The best known of these is the employment generated in the local economy through MNE purchases of inputs and employees' expenditure on consumption, measurement of which has always been difficult and methodologically controversial. However two sub-types of indirect employment effect are worthy of comment. One is employment abroad that arises through subcontracting by MNEs, which is known to have increased rapidly in recent years but cannot be quantified. A second is employment in national (non-MNE) enterprises which may be dependent on strategic alliances with MNEs, which has also been increasing but which can be quantified. Given the paucity of data and the methodological difficulties, Parisotto's decision to steer clear of these indirect employment effects is probably wise.

A fourth inference concerns the importance of very large enterprises in MNE employment. The data are provided by the UNCTC's data bank on the so-called "Billion Dollar Club" – enterprises with annual world sales exceeding $1 billion. The club's members are dominant contributors to MNE employment. The 534 largest members of the BDC in 1989 employed over 26 million workers worldwide, or about 40 per cent of total MNE employees. Of these, US-based firms employed almost 10 million workers, UK-based MNEs (3.5 million workers), followed by German MNEs 3 million and Japanese MNEs 2.5 million (see table 2.2). Other sources cited in Chapter 2 also confirm that FDI is carried out predominantly by very large enterprises situated in oligopolistic markets.

In addition to this partial "snapshot" picture, *trends* in employment are clearly of great interest. Unfortunately data deficiencies permit few firm inferences. It is reasonably certain that total MNE employment grew rapidly until the late 1970s, followed by a decline which lasted until the early or middle 1980s. This decline was associated with massive retrenchment by MNEs in response to world recession and to structural changes which Parisotto aptly encapsulates as "rationalization, automation and subcontracting". What has happened since the mid-1980s is less clear. As Parisotto points out, and is developed in greater detail by Hamill in Chapters 3 and 4 (discussed in section 3 below), all the structural factors at work since the mid-1980s have been inimical to growth of direct MNE employment. This is borne out by the finding that although total employment by 343 leading industrial MNEs rose after 1983, the level nevertheless remained lower in 1990 than in 1980. Data for industrialized host countries also show that employment by foreign-based MNEs did not increase in many cases in the 1980s, although employment by foreign-based MNEs in the US was an important exception.

Trends in MNE employment in developing economies are even harder to assess, and time series data on MNE employment exist for only a few of them. These data show increases in Singapore, Hong Kong, the Republic of Korea, Mexico, Jamaica and Panama. Employment in developing countries by US MNEs certainly declined in the 1982-89 period, and affected all developing regions except Asia and Central America. The Asian developing region also benefited from increased FDI inflows from Japan and the Asian NIEs noted in Chapter 1, which for the most part created new jobs rather than taking over existing ones.

Growth of employment in export processing zones was also substantial, averaging 9 per cent a year from 1975 to 1986 and 14 per cent a year from 1986 to 1990. By the end of the 1980s there were about 4 million workers in over 200 EPZs worldwide (including an estimated 2.2 million in China (see table 2.11). However by no means all of this employment is directly attributable to MNE activity; the proportion of EPZ employment accounted for by foreign-owned firms has been found to range from 30 per cent to more than 80 per cent according to location. But clearly additional, though unquantified, EPZ employment is attributable to MNEs indirectly via minority joint ventures or subcontracting.

Chapter 2 also contains a valuable overview of the broader impact of MNEs on host countries' labour markets. In the present chapter this question is taken up in sections 3 and 4 (for the industrialized countries) and in sections 5 and 6 (for the developing countries).

Regarding the purely quantitative impact of MNEs on employment, on balance we may conclude from Chapter 2 that despite the massive increase in FDI documented in Chapter 1, the growth of total direct MNE employment in the 1980s was, at best, modest. Clearly, MNEs pursued (and continue to pursue in the 1990s) a labour-saving strategy, at least in respect of the number of workers directly employed. However since this stagnation in direct employment was at least partly offset by a growth in subcontracted and other forms of indirect employment – which we are unable to quantify – we should be wary of drawing any firm conclusions about the overall employment impact of MNEs. This argument is strengthened when we take into account the broader general equilibrium effects of MNEs, such as their effects on employment via their contribution to overall productivity growth. The data surveyed by Jungnickel and Parisotto identify an agenda for further inquiry. There are two major questions. First, how to explain the enormous surge in FDI which began in the second half of the 1980s. Second, to explain why global employment by MNEs stagnated, or possibly declined, despite this surge in FDI. Arising from these two, a number of subsidiary questions are also identifiable. In the context of the industrialized countries, these questions concern the changing regional and country shares in global FDI, the trend towards "globalization" by MNEs, their response to the prospect of the Single European Market after 1992, and the spate of mergers and acquisitions in recent years. These questions are addressed in Chapters 3, 4 and 5, to which we now turn. For the developing countries the questions raised concern the declining relative attractiveness of developing countries as hosts to FDI from the industrialized countries; and the growth of FDI from the NIEs in developing countries. These questions are examined in Part 2 of the book and in sections 5 and 6 below.

3. Changing MNE strategies

In Hamill's first contribution (Chapter 3), the core of the explanation of stagnating employment by MNEs is to be found in the "globalization" strategies pursued by MNEs in the 1980s. These strategies have had massive implications for employment in all its dimensions, and their effects are continuing in the 1990s. Hamill fleshes out the details of this somewhat nebulous term. In general, globalization involves the closer coordination, specialization and integration of geographically dispersed activities, but Hamill makes it clear that globalization is not a unique formula; rather, it encompasses a range of outcomes according to the degree of geographical dispersion and the intensity of coordination of the enterprise's activities. At the national level, foreign-owned subsidiaries which were previously "miniature replicas" of their parent must take on a new role, and the long-run employment effects depend critically on the role assigned, within the global strategy, to the MNE's operations in that country. The most unfavourable case is when the local operation is assigned the role of "rationalized manufacturer" – also described more graphically as a "screwdriver operation". This role is mainly, but not exclusively, assigned to MNE subsidiaries in developing countries. The volume of employment is then restricted by the low value added and high import content of production, and skill content and training are also low, for workers, engineers and managers. The most favourable case is when the subsidiary is a "product specialist" – the polar opposite of the "screwdriver operation" – where workers' skills and powers of management initiative are high, and potential employment growth is limited only by the subsidiary's own efforts and success.

Although globalization may thus have favourable long-run effects on direct employment in subsidiaries which become "product specialists", Hamill argues that the *transition* to globalized operations involves employment effects which are almost entirely unfavourable. As a consequence of rationalization by the MNE across the whole range of its activities, major reductions in employment levels will almost certainly ensue, with the only compensating benefit being the enhanced quality of employment in subsidiaries chosen as product specialists. Globalization also has a major adverse impact on job security at all levels because of the scope it creates for transferring production and other activities elsewhere. In addition, it implies a hostility towards trade unions because of their potential for disrupting the finely tuned global production system. These three factors combine to reinforce management's power to introduce new working practices designed to maximize the benefits of international integration. Finally, globalization is likely to exacerbate existing regional and international inequalities by sharpening the polarization of activity between low-wage "assemblers" and high-wage, high-skill activities which will tend to be carried on in already prosperous countries and regions due to market size and availability of

skills. Thus globalization not only brings workers in different countries into intensified competition with one another; it also brings national governments (and regional
authorities in the EC case) into similarly intensified competition as they struggle to
present themselves favourably as candidates for location of MNE plants. (This pessimistic picture may require modification in the 1990s if, as is discussed by Hamill,
globalization strategies themselves undergo further evolutionary change.)

Hamill's second contribution (Chapter 4) provides a behavioural explanation of the surge in FDI, particularly between industrialized countries, which the data
of Chapter 1 highlight. The most important characteristic of this surge is that since
about 1984 it has predominantly taken the form of mergers and acquisitions (M&A)
rather than investment in new facilities as was the norm in earlier years. A further
feature has been the growth of cross-border strategic alliances between partners who
remained formally independent. Thus we have to explain three forms of cross-border
activity: mergers, acquisitions and alliances (MAA). The scale and direction of these
activities are documented, supplementing the FDI data provided by Jungnickel
(Chapter 1) as well as the detail on Japanese FDI furnished by Watanabe (Chapter 5).
It is clear that in the late 1980s mergers and acquisitions became the predominant vehicle of FDI; for example, Hamill reports cross-border mergers and acquisitions to the
value of $130 billion in 1989 – a figure which may be compared with the $185 billion
of global FDI from industrialized countries reported by Jungnickel for the same year.
Initially, M&A activity was focused on the US as host, with acquirers predominantly
in Europe but also Japan. In the 1984-88 period acquisitions of US enterprises by foreign enterprises totalled $126 billion, or three-quarters of total foreign investment in
the US in that period. Companies based in the UK accounted for $84 billion of this.
Towards the end of the decade the focus shifted towards Europe; in 1989-90 there
were over 3,000 cross-border mergers and acquisitions in Europe with a value
exceeding $63 billion, almost half of them involving acquisitions of companies in the
UK. As to inter-enterprise alliances, the data are fragmentary, but it is clear that they
have increased enormously, particularly in the telecommunications, automotive and
semiconductor branches, as Hamill illustrates.

Although, as noted in Chapter 1, both FDI and MAA declined in the early
1990s, the surge in cross-border MAA activity in the late 1980s was so large that it
seems likely to have a significant influence on the evolution of the international economy; in particular, it may have profound implications for employment, both quanti-
tatively and qualitatively. It is clearly necessary to understand the motivation underlying it but, as Hamill notes, no comprehensive theory has yet been developed.
Drawing on and extending existing literature on domestic mergers and acquisitions,
he argues that there have been three exogenous or "environmental" groups of forces
acting upon enterprises: the increasing international integration of product and capital markets and the intensified global competition resulting from this; accelerated
technological change; and government policies – in particular deregulation and, in
Europe, the Single European Market or "1992". All of these have exerted strong
pressures on the enterprise to increase its size, to strengthen and broaden its product
portfolio and geographical market coverage, and to fund larger R&D programmes.
Enterprises which failed to respond in these ways became exposed to increasing risk
of loss of market share and/or takeover from larger and more aggressive global com-

petitors. Mergers, acquisitions and alliances offered the enterprise a rapid and relatively low-risk means of response to these pressures. Moreover the whole process became self-reinforcing since as more and more enterprises became active in MAA the threat to inactive enterprises increased, intensifying the pressure on them to follow suit.

The dominant motives to engage in MAA essentially fall into two categories, labelled by Hamill as "strategic" and "economic". Among strategic motives are the desire to achieve an instantaneous increase in market share, to achieve geographical or product diversification, or to threaten a competitor or respond to a competitor's threat. The economic motivation is to reduce costs via economies of scale and rationalization of overlapping production, research and marketing activities. M&A also permit the enterprise to deploy its own intangible assets more fully, to acquire additional intangible assets (technology, products, brand-names and management skills) and to achieve "internalization" or synergy gains resulting from the fact that the two enterprises involved now contribute to, and draw upon, a common pool of resources. The motivation of strategic alliances is basically the same, the essential distinction being merely that an alliance (which may in fact involve assets, in the case of a joint venture, or an exchange of equity) is more easily reversed and less comprehensive than a merger or acquisition.

It may be worth pausing for a moment to consider the relationship between the two behavioural phenomena under discussion: the globalization strategies of MNEs, and their MAA activities. Although Hamill does not explicitly make the point, it is clear from reading his two chapters that the motivation of both has been largely the same. Thus we may see the two phenomena as a sequential but partly overlapping response by MNEs to the environmental or exogenous changes enumerated above. First, in the early 1980s, they embarked upon the globalization of their existing activities; then, when this process was complete or at least well under way, they sought to achieve the further benefits of increased size and scope by engaging in MAA. The self-reinforcing character of these processes, in the sense that as they gather momentum it becomes increasingly risky for any one enterprise to remain aloof, is also noteworthy.

Given this common motivation for both globalization and MAA activity, the most important question for the purposes of this book concerns their implications for employment. Hamill's view is that whatever the relative strengths of the strategic and economic motives, both globalization and MAA activity have had, and will continue to have, negative effects on direct employment by the enterprises concerned in the short and medium term, due to the effects of rationalization. This is borne out by his case examples. In the longer term (perhaps by the middle 1990s), and to the extent that MAA leads to increased competitiveness (and hence increased market share) for the enterprises concerned, positive effects on their employment levels, job security and wages may result. But Hamill is not able to draw any general conclusions regarding employment effects in MNEs which engage in MAA. The employment outcomes are very specific to particular cases depending on the form of MAA, the sector and enterprises involved, and the geographical dimension. There is also the problem of specifying the counterfactual – that is, what would otherwise have happened. At the level of the individual enterprise (and its country of location), MAAs motivated by cost and efficiency considerations may be particularly adverse for employment because the enterprise may be reduced to "branch" status. We return to these crucial questions at the end of this chapter.

4. The growth of FDI from Japan

To complete the book's picture of the major developments in MNE activity in the industrialized countries in the 1980s, Chapter 5, by Watanabe, provides us with a comprehensive picture of the growth, motivation and effects of Japanese FDI. Average annual Japanese FDI increased fivefold from the 1981-85 to the 1986-90 period as Japan emerged as the world's largest source of FDI. Within this rapid expansion, the regional composition shifted strongly in favour of the industrialized countries, particularly the United States. With the exception of FDI in the United States, the sectoral composition shifted strongly towards services; in the latter 1980s finance, insurance and real estate accounted for over 40 per cent of total Japanese FDI, and the share of manufacturing had declined to only 25 per cent. There was also a shift in ownership mode in favour of M&A, especially in the US. As recently as 1986, only 4 per cent of Japanese affiliates abroad had, historically, been established in this way, although the proportion was higher in developing countries. In 1988, however, Watanabe shows that no less than 88 per cent of Japanese FDI in the US was used for M&A purposes – thus providing further confirmation of Hamill's analysis.

It should be borne in mind however that the rapid increase in Japanese FDI in the 1980s, and its shift towards the industrialized countries, was from very low base values. The data in Chapter 1 show that the share of inward FDI stocks owned by Japanese enterprises in Europe and North America have increased rapidly in the 1980s but that their levels remain quite low. In the US, Japanese enterprises pushed up their share of the inward FDI stock from 6 per cent to 22 per cent between 1980 and 1991, but this placed them only just ahead of the Netherlands and well behind the UK, which remained by a large margin the biggest foreign investor in the US, with a share of 27 per cent of the inward stock (see table 1.3). In the EC, Japan's largest shares of inward stocks were 7 per cent in Germany and 4 per cent in the UK, compared with US shares in these two countries of 33 per cent and 47 per cent respectively (see table 1.6).

Watanabe estimates that Japanese affiliates abroad employed about 1.6 million workers in 1989, of whom four-fifths were in manufacturing, about one-half in Asia, 20 per cent in North America and 10 per cent in the EC.[2] Relative to total employment in host countries, the direct employment contribution of Japanese FDI is, not surprisingly, negligible. Its contribution becomes somewhat larger if we focus on manufacturing, but even then exceeds 1 per cent in only eight economies: the four

---

[2] That such a large proportion of employment should be in manufacturing is surprising in view of the fact that since 1951 FDI in manufacturing has averaged scarcely more than 25 per cent of total FDI (table 5.1). It implies that investment in manufacturing has been far more labour-intensive than investment in the tertiary sector, which as we have seen has been the dominant vehicle for FDI. But there may be other explanations relating to classification of affiliates to their parents' principal activity, and the omission of locally financed investment from the data.

Asian NIEs, Thailand, Malaysia, the Philippines and Australia.[3] Echoing Chapter 2, Watanabe also argues that a more appropriate index of the "weight" of employment creation by Japanese FDI would be obtained by expressing it as a proportion of private, formal-sector employment; but the necessary data are lacking. He argues that weight should also be given to the quality of employment created and the fact that it is often located in areas of high unemployment (e.g. in the UK and US). Finally, employment indirectly created is probably as large, or larger, than direct employment.

A number of factors are cited in explanation of this explosion in FDI from Japan. First, from 1985 to 1989 Japan became increasingly unattractive as a location for physical investment, as labour shortages intensified and the yen almost doubled its dollar value. The resulting pressure on the international competitiveness of domestic production encouraged relocation in lower cost countries in Asia, where in some countries inward FDI was also encouraged by more liberal host government policies. Second, increased Japanese investment in the US, Europe, and other industrialized countries was motivated, at least partly, by increasing "trade frictions" which shifted the balance of argument in favour of supplying these markets by local production rather than exports. Third, the high savings ratio in Japan, in conjunction with low domestic interest rates and high land and property values there, encouraged investment in the tertiary sector abroad (including real estate), as well as in foreign financial assets. From this standpoint, FDI in real estate could be viewed as being an alternative to portfolio investment abroad rather than as an alternative to direct investment at home.[4] A further motivation which is implicit in Watanabe's argument is that Japanese manufacturing enterprises became increasingly persuaded that their ownership-specific assets (in particular, organizational and technological advantages) could be deployed successfully abroad.

From both an economic and political standpoint, a crucial question concerns the relative strength of these varied motives; and more specifically, whether the growth in FDI in this period is to be explained primarily as a spontaneous development reflecting Japan's industrial maturity, or as a strategic response to a combination of "trade frictions" and investment incentives offered by host governments. Watanabe reports some survey data which suggest that the role of trade frictions in motivating FDI by Japanese enterprises has been minor, with the dominant motive being the globalization of operations. That Japanese MNEs are indeed highly globalized is also indicated by the fact that in a large sample of major manufacturing companies, four-fifths operated an internationally consolidated accounting system, while more than 40 per cent had a global R&D programme to which affiliates contributed.

One source of controversy in host countries has been the suggestion that production by Japanese affiliates has a relatively high import content, at the expense of local content (i.e., that they tend to be "screwdriver operations"), and also that their export ratio is low. As Watanabe notes, the aggregate data on this question are

---

[3] The weighted average is 3.3 per cent (table 5.4).

[4] In Japan both real estate and share prices dropped sharply in the early 1990s, and by mid-1992 Japanese share prices were more than 50 per cent below their all-time peak. In reflection of this, and also because of profit reversals experienced by many Japanese firms consequent upon the world recession, FDI by Japanese companies fell by 27 per cent in the year ending April 1992. (See *The Economist*, 13 June 1992.)

ambiguous, but it is clear that Japanese FDI in North America and Western Europe is almost entirely oriented towards production for local markets, while in Asia it is much more export-oriented. Regarding the import ratio, he endorses the view of Graham and Krugman that in so far as Japanese affiliates in the US have a high propensity to import (especially from Japan) this is explained by their comparative youth, and the fact that their competitive advantage tends to lie in sectors and markets which make disproportionate use of imported inputs.[5] Survey data show clearly that the import ratio falls steadily with the age of the affiliate, but also tends to rise with the degree of sophistication of the product.[6]

However, in an analysis which constitutes a significant analytical contribution to this important debate, Watanabe argues that there are more fundamental reasons for Japanese affiliates' inhibitions regarding local procurement. His point of departure is that Japanese affiliates are predisposed towards local procurement, reflecting their parents' production methods in Japan which rely more heavily on subcontractors than do their European or North American counterparts. Yet in both Europe and North America, Japanese affiliates are frustrated in their desire to increase procurement from locally owned firms by these firms' inability both to meet Japanese quality standards and to engage in the continuous and relentless search for productivity improvements which is the Japanese norm. Moreover, local subcontractors are not always responsive to the attempts of Japanese affiliate customers to advise and assist in meeting the standards demanded of them. (In Asia the lack of local supply capability is being tackled more systematically by cooperation between Japanese affiliates and governments.)

The underlying cause of this problem in the West, Watanabe argues, is the difference between Japanese and established local managerial practices and industrial relations systems. These methods call for workers who are highly motivated and who possess diverse skills and knowledge developed through frequent retraining and job rotation, to which Japanese firms devote enormous resources. The resulting technological and organizational efficiency endows Japanese enterprises with a firm-specific asset or "ownership advantage" which has led them to become multinational in order to deploy this advantage more widely.

The core of Watanabe's argument is that although these organizational characteristics are often explained in the West as stemming from Japan's distinctively different socio-cultural heritage (an explanation which readily excuses any lack of success in emulating them in the West), the true explanation is that these characteristics flow quite straightforwardly from "the economic incentives provided by the lifetime employment system, a pay and promotion system largely but not entirely based on seniority, and the egalitarian remuneration structure". The success of Japanese affiliates abroad – in both Asia and the West – results from the replication of this incentive structure, reinforced by careful recruitment policies and extensive training. This success corroborates the view that the role of socio-cultural factors in the Japanese system is minor.

[5] E.M. Graham and P.R. Krugman: *Foreign direct investment in the United States* (Washington, DC, Institute for International Economics, 1989).

[6] A fall in the import ratio may result from increased in-house production and purchases from other local Japanese affiliates, as well as from increased purchases from local domestically owned firms.

Western companies have attempted to emulate Japanese methods. The "lean production system" has become highly fashionable as an organizational concept; and a number of companies have succeeded in restructuring their industrial relations systems along Japanese lines. Significantly though, Watanabe suggests that Western firms have failed to realize that the Japanese organizational and industrial relations philosophy cannot be adapted successfully without also adopting the incentive structure which makes it work. In particular, worker commitment, flexibility and cooperation cannot be achieved in the absence of a reciprocal commitment from the employer to security of employment, an egalitarian seniority-based pay structure, and minimization of status demarcation lines between workers and managers. Western enterprises are reluctant to make such a commitment. They are also reluctant to make the necessary commitment to training, partly because of shorter horizons but also because training will not pay off for the employer in the absence of a corresponding long-term commitment from workers, which in turn is inhibited by the absence of a lifetime commitment by the employer. A vicious circle is thus completed, and explains not only why local suppliers fail to meet Japanese affiliates' purchasing standards, but also more broadly helps to explain the comparatively poor productivity and competitiveness of European and North American enterprises. We return to this in the conclusions.

5.   MNEs in developing countries

Chapter 6, by James et al., is concerned with Mexico and serves as a case study on the role of export processing zones in development, a question also touched upon by Parisotto in Chapter 2. Mexico's EPZs, which are known as *maquilas,* were first established in 1965 and provided a model which many other countries quickly emulated. As indicated in Chapter 2, Mexican EPZs are now second only to their counterparts in China in the number of jobs provided, and employment grew very rapidly in the late 1980s – from 270,000 in 1986 to 440,000 in 1989.[7]

While the issue of wages and working conditions in EPZs has excited much controversy, it is arguable that the dynamic role of EPZs in promoting the development of the national economy is more important from a long-run perspective. Chapter 6 indicates that the circumstances in Mexico appear in some important respects at least to be particularly favourable for promoting interaction between the *maquila* and the local economy. The fact that the *maquila* programme is long-established, that since the early 1970s *maquila* zones have been permitted virtually anywhere in the country, and that the Mexican economy is large and its manufacturing capability has become increasingly sophisticated are all factors apparently conducive to favourable interaction. However, James et al.'s evidence is somewhat mixed. On the positive side, there has been a substantial increase in the variety of products manufactured or assembled in the *maquila*. Production has become more capital-intensive, and equipment has become more sophisticated. This has led to a substantial increase in the proportion of technically qualified workers and engineers in the *maquila* labour force,

[7] Table 6.1.

and, according to some studies, to productivity levels matching or surpassing corresponding levels in the US.

What is unfortunately uncertain is whether there has been any systematic tendency towards skill acquisition among operatives, who account for four-fifths of employment. One clear fact is that whereas in 1982 females comprised almost 80 per cent of the labour force, this proportion had fallen to one-third by 1987. James et al.'s explanation of this is quite subtle. They argue that in the *maquila*, employers were reluctant to pay more than the government-determined minimum wage, and this wage fell by one-half in its domestic purchasing power in the 1980s as the result of the Government's counter-inflation policy. This fall reduced the attractiveness to workers of *maquila* employment, forcing employers, whose labour requirements were expanding rapidly, to accept more males (who were not their first choice), to lower their hiring standards in other respects as well, and to move to other parts of the country in search of untapped reservoirs of labour. Thus rather than paying relatively high wages in order to recruit relatively high quality operatives, *maquila* employers seem to have done the opposite. A question which we cannot settle here is whether, as James et al. suggest, this was the result of conscious policy by employers, or whether it simply reflected the dictates of the relevant product markets and a labour market characterized by chronic excess supply. In any event, it was certainly facilitated by the willingness of the Government to allow new *maquilas* almost anywhere in the country; a willingness which may have reflected a conscious choice to promote the quantity rather than the quality of employment.

The main thrust of the chapter, however, is towards the question of local procurement by *maquila* producers, which is presumably one of the main channels whereby impulses favourable to development should be expected to be transmitted from EPZs to the local economy. During the 1980s less than 2 per cent of material inputs purchased by *maquila* firms were produced in Mexico, despite the fact that most of these inputs required very little technological sophistication and were low in value added.[8] In explaining this very low proportion of Mexican-supplied material inputs, reference is frequently made to high prices, together with poor quality and unreliable delivery. As James et al. point out, this merely raises the question why competitive processes, and Mexico's progress towards industrial maturity, have apparently not eliminated or at least diminished these shortcomings. Although the level and structure of taxes and import tariffs may be partly responsible, research by James et al. suggests that purchasing policies of MNEs operating in the *maquila* are important; in particular the degree of autonomy enjoyed by local affiliates' purchasing officers.

Reflecting disquiet at this situation, the Mexican authorities in 1989 and 1990 took a number of steps to promote better integration of *maquila* firms into the economy. The broader programme of liberalization and privatization of the Mexican economy has also been highly relevant; in particular, trade liberalization following

---

[8] A comparison is furnished by the EPZ sector in Mauritius, where in 1982 local suppliers provided 28 per cent of material inputs (i.e. inputs other than services). See C. Hein: *Multinational enterprises and employment in the Mauritian export processing zone*, Multinational Enterprises Programme Working Paper No. 52 (Geneva, ILO, 1988), table 3.9.

accession to the GATT, and the more liberal approach to foreign investment which resulted in a big increase in FDI inflows in the latter 1980s. The view of James et al. is that these and other policy measures can contribute significantly to the impetus to development which EPZs are capable of imparting to their host economies.[9]

Chapter 7, by Hill, provides a case study of MNEs in Indonesia, a developing country which, in contrast to Mexico, has not relied on EPZs; indeed for much of the period since 1945 it discouraged FDI of any kind. Although policies became more liberal in the 1980s, the estimated FDI stock remains relatively small. Foreign investment has been predominantly in oil and gas exploitation, of which four-fifths was sourced in the US.[10]

Of non-oil FDI up to 1989, about 40 per cent of the cumulative total was sourced from Japan and a further 10 per cent from the four Asian NIEs, principally Hong Kong. However these shares changed dramatically in the late 1980s, and Hill suggests that the four Asian NIEs may have collectively overtaken Japan. Other, though much smaller, sources of non-oil FDI were Belgium (in steel making) and the US (in metal products). Hill estimates that, excluding oil and gas, foreign-owned firms accounted for about 24 per cent of manufacturing value added and about 12 per cent of GDP in the late 1980s.[11]

In assessing the role of foreign capital in the economy there are many problems not only in unscrambling equity shares in joint ventures but also in relation to the question of where effective control resides. However, Hill shows that there are three broad loci of ownership and control. First, and reflecting government policy of controlling the "commanding heights" of the economy, government-owned or government-related firms are dominant in basic metals, fertilizers and machinery; and significant in cement, food processing (sugar) and paper products. Second, MNEs have tended to congregate, when permitted, in activities where their enterprise-specific advantages – principally brand names and technology – confer a decisive benefit. This explains their above-average shares in glass products, plastics, electronics, chemicals other than fertilizers, beverages and textiles. Within these branches, brand names are important to cigarettes, beer, pharmaceuticals, pesticides, batteries and dairy products; while technology is important in the spinning of synthetic fibres, sheet glass, agricultural equipment and motorcycles. Historically, knowledge of export markets has been an important source of advantage to MNEs only in the case of electrical equipment, though this picture began to change at the end of the 1980s with a wave of export-oriented activity by both foreign and domestic investors. Finally, domestic private enterprises may be viewed as having played something of a

---

[9] However, James et al. note that potentially the most important policy question concerns NAFTA, the Free Trade Agreement between the US, Mexico and Canada (which was signed after their manuscript was finalized). The authors point out that if trade between these three were to become duty-free, and they harmonized their tariffs vis-à-vis third countries, the rationale for the existence of the *maquilas* would almost entirely disappear.

[10] See Chapter 7, note 4. It should be emphasized that these are estimates, due to the difficulty of unscrambling joint ventures which involve all combinations of foreign, domestic government and domestic private equity participation. Since no data are published on FDI in the oil and gas subsector, Hill's discussion relates almost entirely to non-oil FDI, and within this concentrates on manufacturing.

[11] See tables 7.3 and 7.4.

residual role, taking up areas of activity other than those pre-empted by government or those where MNEs enjoyed a decisive advantage.

As already noted in the present chapter, the degree of multinational "presence" in the economy in terms of employment depends very much on the measure chosen. Hill estimates the manufacturing labour force in Indonesia in 1986 at about 6 million (or 10 per cent of the total labour force), of whom about 1.87 million were employed in enterprises with 20 or more employees, which he calls the "factory sector" and which includes all foreign firms.[12] We then have a choice of measures of MNE presence. Foreign-owned firms in 1985 employed roughly 9 per cent of the "factory sector" workforce, which equates to 3 per cent of the total manufacturing workforce and to 0.3 per cent of the total workforce. Given this latter figure, it is clear that the contribution of MNEs to *total* employment in Indonesia is insignificant and is likely to remain so for the foreseeable future.[13]

The question whether MNEs use inappropriately capital-intensive techniques in developing countries has, of course, been debated for many years. In Indonesia, Hill indeed finds that, excluding oil and gas, foreign firms were on average far more capital-intensive than private or government firms. However, we should perhaps treat this finding cautiously. In the absence of capital stock data, Hill uses value added per worker as a proxy for capital per worker, which introduces a crucial ambiguity since a high level of value added per worker may be the result of high efficiency in the use of all inputs rather than (or in addition to) the use of highly capital-intensive methods.

Other possible impacts of MNEs may be of greater importance than their quantitative contribution to employment. Hill looks in some detail at wage levels and training. He finds that for Indonesian manufacturing as a whole, wage levels in enterprises which are partly or wholly foreign owned are two to three times as high as wages in domestic private or government enterprises. As he points out, this may be explained by factors other than ownership, such as enterprise size and industrial branch location. More reliable evidence is to be found in comparisons between individual pairs of firms of the same size in the same branch, but here the outcome is arguably inconclusive.

On the question of training provided by MNEs, Hill reports a number of detailed studies which show that MNEs' training of local employees by expatriate managers and technical experts is more extensive than that of comparable domestic enterprises; and that the productivity of Indonesian workers, which initially was 50-60 per cent of that of Japanese or Korean workers, rose to 80-90 per cent after 12-18 months of work experience and closely supervised training. Taking all the evidence into account, he feels justified in concluding that MNEs "emerge as good employers of labour: they pay more, train more, and have lower labour turnover ...". However, he points out that the shortage of skilled workers in the Indonesian economy (notwithstanding the vast improvement in education in the past few decades) is far

[12] The remaining manufacturing employment was in small enterprises, often of a seasonal or casual nature, which Hill argues was in no meaningful sense related to the activities of MNEs.

[13] Although foreign-owned firms employ up to 30 per cent of the workforce in some branches (other chemicals, glass products and electrical equipment) none of these branches are large (see table 7.6).

greater than could conceivably be met by training by MNE employers. Indeed, low educational attainment limits the opportunities for workers to benefit from such training. It is also one factor limiting technology transfer to local enterprises.

This last point leads to consideration once again of the important issue of spin-offs to the local economy via local procurement by MNEs. As in the case of Mexico, in general subcontracting networks are underdeveloped and hence spin-offs are disappointingly small. In Indonesia, this is because suppliers have limited technological capability, poor quality control and little commercial expertise. This has remained true even in the automotive industry where there is an official programme to increase local content.

On this question Hill makes some important points which may be of relevance to other developing countries. A factor which has handicapped local suppliers is the structure of effective import protection, which gives low or even negative effective protection to intermediate stages in for example electrical and automotive components. The structure of protection is also biased in favour of capital-intensive activities such as steel and automobiles, while clothing, for example, enjoys very low or negative protection. This structure draws resources out of labour-intensive branches and makes the task of providing jobs for a rapidly expanding labour force more difficult.

High protection also has the effect that some MNE-intensive branches exhibit negative value added at world prices, which involves real resource losses to the economy. In addition, it also inhibits competition and encourages "rent-seeking" (lobbying for preferential treatment), a feature which has been exacerbated by the unpredictability of the policy regime. Such unpredictability also deters inward investment, adds to risk and thereby increases the required rate of return, and encourages excessively short-term investment horizons.

---

6. FDI from the newly industrialized economies

Chapter 7 remarks on the growing importance to Indonesia of FDI from the East Asian NIEs, a question also considered in a more general context in Chapter 1. The emergence of these new sources of FDI clearly has important portents and deserves closer examination, though there are some problems in collecting accurate information.[14] However it seems clear that the four NIEs collectively supplanted Japan in the 1980s as the largest investor in developing Asia.[15] None of the four

[14] Neither Hong Kong nor Singapore have any controls on capital outflows and hence do not publish official data on FDI, while in the case of Taiwan, China, there is strong evidence that the true magnitude of outward FDI is larger, possibly by a long way, than the official data reveal. Data must therefore be compiled for the most part from host countries, but these relate in many cases to official approvals rather than realized inflows, and the difference may be large.

[15] One study (World Bank, 1989) indicates that the four East Asian NIEs invested at least $16 billion in developing countries in Asia in the 1980s, accounting for 37 per cent of host country approvals. Notably, more than half of this was investment by Hong Kong in China. The largest investor was Hong Kong ($12 billion), followed by Taiwan, China ($2.5 billion, but almost certainly heavily under-recorded), Singapore ($1.8 billion), and the Republic of Korea ($0.4 billion). The next largest source of FDI was Japan, with $12 billion. According to the data of Chapter 5 of this book, within the rapidly growing total of Japan's FDI the share of developing countries fell from more than 50 per cent in the mid-1970s to less than 20 per cent in the mid-1980s.

invested large amounts in each other's economies, and their FDI in developing countries outside Asia was mostly negligible. As noted in Chapter 2, Section 3.3, Taiwan (China) and the Republic of Korea also began to invest in industrialized countries, though on a small scale. Brazil, Mexico and Colombia also emerged as significant sources of FDI.

Whereas in the 1960s and 1970s FDI from the four Asian NIEs, like Japan's, was almost exclusively attracted by import-substitution policies pursued by neighbouring countries in developing Asia, the motivation of the "new wave" of FDI from the Asian NIEs since the early 1980s has been somewhat different. Although access to raw material supplies continues to be relevant, the new wave has been primarily a response to rising domestic wage costs (measured in dollars), increased protectionism, and in some cases loss of preferential export status in industrialized countries' markets under the Generalized System of Preferences. Such FDI in industrialized countries as has occurred has probably been motivated by the desire to acquire brand names and technology.

The largest investor of the four was Hong Kong, with a stock estimated in Chapter 1 at over $20 billion in 1991. Uncertainty about the colony's economic and political future has been a strong motivating factor in recent years, but there has also developed a strong tendency towards a *de facto* economic integration between Hong Kong and China – reflected in FDI flows in both directions – which anticipates political integration in 1997. One study estimates that between 1983 and 1986 FDI flows from Hong Kong to China constituted over one-half of all FDI by NIEs in Asia, mostly in labour-intensive assembly in EPZs.[16] Chapter 1 estimates that investors from Hong Kong now employ up to 3 million workers in the neighbouring Guangdong Province of China. However, Hong Kong enterprises have also invested substantially in Indonesia, Thailand, and the other East Asian NIEs – principally Singapore and Taiwan, China. In the cases of Sri Lanka and Bangladesh, FDI from Hong Kong has constituted a large proportion of total FDI inflows. Most FDI has been in the production of export-oriented light manufactures such as toys and apparel, but in Indonesia and Thailand electrical and electronic products have also figured.[17]

Taiwan, China, has been the next largest investor and the growth of FDI was so rapid in 1989-90 that its stock may well have overtaken Hong Kong's. Official policy has been strongly influenced by huge balance-of-payments surpluses, which have been the second largest in the world after Japan. Data on FDI approvals show that over two-thirds of investment was in industrialized countries; mainly in the US, and mainly in electrical appliances, services, chemicals and plastics. However Jungnickel estimates that up to $3.5 billion has been invested in China and is either unrecorded or routed via Hong Kong. The industrialized countries and China aside, FDI from Taiwan (China) is predominantly in import-substituting capital-intensive sectors, the main hosts being the Philippines, Thailand and Indonesia.

[16] World Bank: *Foreign direct investment from the newly industrialized economies*, Industry Series Paper No. 22 (Washington, DC, World Bank, 1989), table 3.

[17] World Bank, op. cit., table 8. It should be noted that an unknown proportion of FDI from both Hong Kong and Singapore is attributable to affiliates of Western MNEs. A large but unknown volume of FDI in China is also routed via Hong Kong, from Taiwan, China.

Singapore, with a stock of outward FDI of about $3 billion in 1989, has invested primarily in China, Thailand, Indonesia and Malaysia. In manufacturing, FDI by Singapore enterprises has tended to concentrate on export-oriented labour-intensive products, but capital-intensive branches have also figured, as well as (increasingly) tourism, trade and financial services. A significant proportion of FDI from Singapore is probably attributable to local subsidiaries of MNEs based in industrialized countries.

Korea's FDI stock is comparable with Hong Kong's in size, but has been expanding very rapidly. According to a recent study undertaken for the ILO by Hong, in 1990 the outflow was close to $1 billion.[18] FDI by Korean enterprises has been determined more straightforwardly by economic factors rather than particular political or ethnic factors. Among these were the rise in domestic unit labour costs measured in dollars, increasing labour shortages, and labour disputes. As in Taiwan (China), the upsurge in FDI was also closely correlated with the emergence of substantial surpluses in the Korean balance of payments, which led the Government to encourage outward FDI as an alternative to exchange rate appreciation which would have damaged the competitiveness of exports. The increase in Korean FDI was strongly biased towards South-East Asia and North America; their respective shares in FDI outflows rose to 52 per cent and 34 per cent in 1990. FDI was also strongly oriented towards manufacturing, which increased its share in total outflows from 20 per cent in the early 1980s to 60 per cent in 1990.

Hong argues that the bi-polarization of investment between South-East Asia and North America reflects to a certain extent the industrial structure of the Republic of Korea, which is unbalanced as a result of very rapid and selective growth. Manufacturing branches which are intensive in their requirements of unskilled labour and which produce unsophisticated products are still strongly represented in the domestic production structure and have been heavily penalized by declining international competitiveness and growing protectionism in their principal export markets. These have increasingly relocated in South-East Asia (and to a certain extent, in the Caribbean area) in order to take advantage of lower unit labour costs and to sidestep import restrictions imposed on direct exports from the Republic of Korea.

FDI in the industrialized countries (principally in the US but increasingly in Europe) has been motivated by the same factors – declining international competitiveness and growing protectionism – but its character has been different. This FDI has emanated from branches of manufacturing such as cars and consumer electronics where labour costs are less important than sensitivity to local market trends and access to more technologically sophisticated labour. As Chapter 1 notes, this investment has been heavily concentrated on a small number of very large enterprises. According to Hong's study, the ten largest enterprises account for 43 per cent of cumulative FDI and the five largest – Samsung, Hyundai, Lucky-Goldstar, Daewoo and Ssangyong – for 36 per cent. These large enterprises frequently invest simultaneously in a new market. Such behaviour clearly reflects an awareness of oligopolistic interdependence, but it is of course impossible to say *a priori* whether this is the

---

[18] S. W. Hong: *MNEs from the Third World: The case of the Republic of Korea*, Multinational Enterprises Programme Working Paper (Geneva, ILO, forthcoming).

result of conscious collusion to achieve synergy gains, or merely reflects "follow my leader" behaviour.

A further regional trend which will be prominent on the policy agenda in the 1990s concerns the role of FDI in the newly liberalizing economies of Central and Eastern Europe (including the former USSR). This is examined in Chapter 8, by Welge and Holtbrügge. They note that regulations have been greatly liberalized and FDI is now warmly welcomed in all the countries concerned; but despite this, the volume remains disappointing and the major MNEs from Japan, the United Kingdom and the United States are for the most part conspicuous by their absence. The chief beneficiaries of FDI have been Poland, Hungary and the former Czechoslovakia, and the main source countries have been their neighbours – Germany, Austria, Finland and Sweden. Especially in the former USSR, FDI has taken the form of small-scale joint ventures, many of which are inactive and hence are described as "wait and see JVs". The authors suggest that uncertainty regarding the political environment, and associated uncertainty regarding whether the necessary policies for macroeconomic stabilization, "marketization" and structural reform will be put in place and maintained on a consistent basis, are the main factors which in the short run are holding back the realization of this potential. However they conclude that there is enormous potential for FDI, given the potential size of the market, that the region as a whole is abundant in natural resources, and has a well-educated and relatively skilled labour force, and that governments are extremely eager to attract FDI to provide the two ingredients – capital resources and managerial and technological skills – which are most lacking. They suggest that the role of the industrialized countries in providing financial support, technical assistance and opening up trade opportunities "will probably be decisive in putting the transition process on the right track".

7. New developments

Chapter 10, by Romero, focuses on another increasingly important area of MNE activity, international trade and FDI in services. The growth in the share of services in GDP in the industrialized economies in the past two decades, which is generally recognized as characteristic of the mature stage of industrialization, is of course well known and documented. In some developing regions too, Romero notes that services have grown faster then industry in the past decade or two, though the share of services in GDP remains low.

The growth of services has been given added impetus by changes in both technology and market structure. The revolution in information technology, and associated and almost equally breathtaking technological change in telecommunications, have led to rapid growth in the provision of sophisticated and high value added services in the fields of banking, other financial services, and insurance, as well as in telecommunications and data processing themselves. These technological changes have also encouraged changes in market structure. Business services which had previously been supplied "in-house" (or not at all) have been increasingly supplied from outside specialist firms.

In turn, these changes have had important implications for international trade and investment, and for the role of MNEs. The technological changes made it possible for many of the services noted above to be supplied from a distance, with the effect that international trade in these services began to expand rapidly. This was also true of other services such as hotel and tourism services, design and consultancy services, legal services, advertising and publishing. MNEs have played an important role in these trends, both as suppliers and customers for services, reflecting the symbiotic relationship between MNEs. As suppliers, large and mature MNEs were attracted by the opportunity to diversify into these new markets where their technological and managerial capabilities gave them firm-specific advantages. MNEs have had a particular advantage in providing these services on a worldwide scale because they enjoyed an established reputation, the ability to deliver across the globe services which were standardized and predictable in their quality, and other economies of scale and scope. However, there are few services which can be supplied entirely from a distance, and consequently there was a notable shift towards services in the sectoral composition of FDI flows – as is noted in several chapters in this book.

The growth of international trade and investment in services has raised a number of issues for international policy which have been an important focus of the Uruguay Round. First, from the early 1970s MNEs in industrialized countries became increasingly frustrated by the regulatory barriers which they found in both industrialized and developing countries and which restricted their ability to compete with local firms or public utilities in supplying services. The initial focus was on public telecommunications administration but soon extended to other services such as postal services, banking and insurance, and land and air transport, which were either provided by public enterprises or by local firms in which foreign participation was restricted or prohibited. By the early 1980s, MNEs' complaints on this score were evoking a sympathetic response from governments of several of the advanced industrialized countries – most importantly, the United States – which had become increasingly persuaded that privatization and deregulation were necessary to promote greater efficiency and economic growth.

In practice the attitude of governments in industrialized countries towards liberalization of trade and investment in services has proved to be ambivalent – reflecting a corresponding ambivalence towards these questions when goods rather than services are concerned. The attitude of developing countries has been even more ambivalent, reflecting an acute underlying dilemma. On the one hand, they were concerned that their indigenous fledgling enterprises in service sectors (in banking and insurance for example) might be overwhelmed by the greater sophistication and market power of service-providing MNEs from the industrialized countries. The fact that many services such as telecommunications, transport, banking, insurance, and finance are subject to strong economies of scale reinforced this danger. From this standpoint there seemed a good case for some form of "infant industry" protection of services in LDCs. But on the other hand, developing countries were also anxious not to be left behind by the very rapid technological and commercial developments in many services. Arguably, the best way to avoid this would be to encourage competition and to welcome the presence of MNEs subject to satisfactory arrangements regarding technology transfer.

An issue quite distinct from those just considered concerns the regulation of cross-border labour mobility and its role in the internationalization of the service sector. This has concerned some developing countries which have experienced obstacles in their attempts to provide labour-intensive service activities, particularly in civil engineering and construction, to other wealthier countries. For others, easier cross-border labour mobility is important in permitting skilled workers, such as computer professionals, to sell their services in the world market. Initially there was a tendency for some countries to view this as an immigration issue rather that one which concerned trade in services. As the result of negotiations in the Uruguay Round, the need to regulate cross-border movement of workers in a way which distinguishes the two types of situation has now been perceived, as well as its importance to the acquisition of technological and organizational skills by workers from developing countries. But as Romero points out, there are many unresolved questions concerning the social protection of such workers. Moreover, there is a large discontinuity in the spectrum of skills between the small numbers of skilled professionals and the large numbers of unskilled workers who could potentially find employment abroad in the service sector.

Romero outlines the draft General Agreement on Trade in Services which at the time of writing is close to agreement in the Uruguay Round. The agreement reflects two underlying principles. First, since for the most part services cannot be supplied directly from abroad, the liberalization of international trade in services must encompass a "right of access" of foreign capital and personnel in order to supply services locally. Second, to supply services in a particular market requires a "commercial presence" or right of establishment for this purpose, which includes any activity connected with the production, distribution, marketing or delivery of the service in question. This right of access encompasses joint ventures and acquisitions, as well as wholly owned subsidiaries of foreign firms. Regarding service activities which in many countries are state-owned or controlled and which are often considered to be of national strategic significance and/or to be natural monopolies (such as telecommunications, rail and air transport), the behaviour of these enterprises is constrained by the draft agreement. They are required to offer their services to all-comers on cost-related and non-discriminatory terms, and the scope for subsidies and cross-subsidization limited. Finally, there is a requirement for transparency in order that observance of the agreement may be monitored and enforced.

If agreed and implemented, it seems clear that the GATT agreement on trade in services will accelerate the current trend of rapid growth of FDI in the service sectors and intensify the pressures for privatization and deregulation throughout the world. In her final section, Romero considers some of the social and labour issues which are entailed. While new employment opportunities will be opened up (particularly in LDCs), there are likely to be many adverse effects in the areas of wages, working conditions and social protection. For example the tendency for the service sector to become polarized between low-paid, low-skilled and insecure jobs and well-paid professional jobs, which is evident at the national level, may become replicated and intensified at the international level. These questions, which Romero is able to survey only briefly in the space available to her, deserve higher political priority than they are commonly given and are worthy of more detailed research.

Chapter 10, by Campbell, is concerned with the implications of globalization for "the world of work". Earlier in the book, Hamill's two chapters analyse the motivations of globalization – as a worldwide phenomenon and also as an anticipatory response to the creation of the Single European Market – and its likely employment consequences. Campbell's thoughtful and thought-provoking contribution in a sense takes as its point of departure Hamill's work, together with the trends in FDI and MNE employment elaborated by Jungnickel and Parisotto. It then builds on this to explore across a broad front the long-term implications for almost the entire range of industrial relations and labour market issues.

Campbell argues that the tendency towards globalization entails a growing disparity between an increasingly *global* economic system and political, social and cultural systems and institutions which remain *national* in their character. For labour, this implies a "regulatory deficit" in the sense that national labour market legislation and institutions are becoming increasingly emasculated. At the same time, globalization entails massive organizational changes which affect both intra and inter-firm relationships. The regulatory deficit and the nature of these organizational changes – and their consequences for labour – form the focus of the chapter.

Dealing first with intra-firm changes, Campbell identifies four tendencies. First, new relationships are evolving between parent and subsidiary (as examined by Hamill in Chapter 3). Second, multinational firms are becoming increasingly stateless, in the sense of a blurring of the distinction between "domestic" and "foreign" firms (whether in terms of the national identity of their managers or of their owners). Third, and of the utmost significance for labour, a "new economics of location" is developing. Echoing Hamill's arguments on this score, global strategies can lead either to true operational decentralization and hence autonomy of subsidiaries, or to the "extended workbench" model of global organization. Which of these two outcomes occurs depends in part on the local prices and availability of inputs, both direct and indirect. This has clear implications for national policy-makers anxious to attract high value added activities, since availability of highly skilled labour, the quality of national universities and other infrastructure, and other factors amenable to policy may be decisive.

A further question here relates to trade union power. Like Hamill, Campbell takes the view that a high degree of cross-border integration of the multinational firm's activities confers great powers of disruption on national trade unions. But while Hamill concludes that this is likely to lead to an anti-union bias by the firm, Campbell argues that another strategic response, of institutionalizing labour-management cooperation, is also possible. He also implies that this is a more likely strategem by MNEs, and one which may well meet with a favourable trade union response when its overall benefits to the organization and its employees are recognized.[19]

Whether such a response occurs depends also on a fourth feature of globalization, changes in the intra-firm organization of work. Recent years have seen major

[19] We might however question the validity of both authors' argument that the global integration of the firm confers greater power on national trade unions. While it is true that trade union power to disrupt production in the short run is increased, the exercise of this power is likely to be inhibited by the fact that the firm can respond to union pressure in the longer run by reorganizing production and/or relocating elsewhere.

changes in work organization, changes characterized by flattened hierarchies, broader job descriptions, decentralization or devolution of authority, incentive-based and firm-specific payments systems, and policies to build worker motivation and commitment. The link between these changes and globalization derives from the fact that intensified international competition (which, as we have seen already in this book, is both a cause and a consequence of globalization) dictates the rapid adoption of "global best practice" methods, with respect to both technology and organization; while current best practice in both respects is heavily influenced, for obvious reasons, by Japanese models. These changes in work organization have two main implications, according to Campbell. First, the likelihood of pressure towards "social convergence" between countries as their forms of work organization become more similar. Second, a more "closed" internal labour market with higher standards for core workers but a sharper divide between core and periphery, with an increasing tendency to marginalize or exclude older, less skilled or otherwise less attractive workers.

Globalization has also been accompanied by important changes in inter-firm relationships, as discussed already in the context of Chapter 4. In recent years there has been a sharp increase in the number of strategic alliances, affecting the "horizontal" relationships between firms which are actually or potentially competing in the same markets. However, the more traditional "vertical" inter-firm relationships between customers and suppliers have also been undergoing change. Although its extent is hard to assess, there has been a clear tendency in large MNEs towards externalization or vertical disintegration, whereby they buy-in goods and services previously produced in-house. More generally, there has also been a trend towards greater cooperation between customer firms and their suppliers, a clear emulation of the Japanese model; though it is notable that Campbell, like Watanabe, records doubts on the question of how close these new relationships really are.

These changes in inter-firm relationships are likely to have many effects on employment and labour markets and it is very difficult to assess the overall balance. Regarding strategic alliances (horizontal relationships), Campbell's argument is broadly the same as Hamill's: that there may be employment losses due to rationalization by allying firms in the short and medium run, but also a possibility at least of increased employment in the longer term due to increased competitiveness. At the industry level, his approach is to argue that the employment effects are positive or negative according to whether the alliances concluded increase or reduce competition in the industry. We shall comment on this in the concluding section of this chapter.

Regarding vertical relationships between firms, Campbell is pessimistic about the quantitative employment effects of "externalization". He argues that the same pressures towards cost reduction which led to externalization itself will tend to be transferred in due course to the firm's suppliers via the stronger ties and influence which the new inter-firm relationships entail. At the same time however the quality of employment in subcontracting firms may be enhanced as the result of transfer to them of their customers' technology and organizational methods. But there are many uncertainties here.

All of these tendencies constitute a challenge to industrial relations systems, especially in industrialized countries. Campbell's final section considers the possible modes of response. Concerning the "regulatory deficit", or disparity between national industrial relations systems and the increasingly globalized organization of production, he argues that it would be unrealistic to expect any dramatic leap in international cooperation either between trade unions or between governments, except possibly within the EC. Rather, at the global level we should look for incremental improvements in these directions through established channels (not the least of which is the ILO itself).

However the "regulatory deficit" is only one consequence of globalization. There are many consequences at the purely national and sub-national level which have to be tackled there. Chief among these are the intensified competition between national and sub-national economies to attract internationally mobile plants; new methods of work organization which increase the distinction between core and peripheral workers; and the loss of autonomy of local plants consequent upon their increased integration into a global network of intra-firm and inter-firm activities. These fundamental changes will have both positive and negative effects on employment and working conditions, and the balance is impossible to predict. However, Campbell concludes by calling for a broadening of the emerging system of industrial organization, which is characterized by increasing cooperation both within and between firms, so as to involve state and labour organizations and in order to address the wider social consequences of globalization. The potential value of such institutional innovations, he believes, is especially great at the local level.

8. Conclusions

Industrialized countries

For the industrialized countries, and indirectly for developing countries too, the single most important question raised in this book concerns the long-run employment implications of the globalization strategies pursued by MNEs in the 1980s and the spate of mergers, acquisitions and strategic alliances which followed. Hamill's view (Chapters 3 and 4) is that these strategies have had, and are continuing to have, negative effects on direct employment by the MNEs concerned as the opportunities for cost-saving rationalization are exploited. However, for certain enterprises there may be employment gains in the medium to long term through increased competitiveness, the result of acquiring new assets (broadly defined to include brand names, R&D results, etc.) which can be exploited more effectively. To this we might also add the argument that such exploitation may in turn, through greater competition and faster dissemination of improved technologies and organizational methods, have favourable general equilibrium effects on productivity and employment. Incidentally, it is worth commenting that strategic alliances would appear likely to have particularly unfavourable employment effects since they open up the possibility of "rationalization" *between* enterprises which remain independent in their ownership and control, as well as *within* enterprises. This would appear to be only one step away from cartelization.

Unfortunately it might be argued that there are even greater grounds for pessimism regarding employment than Hamill suggests. His argument effectively treats "increased competitiveness" and "increased market share" as synonyms, thereby begging the crucial question whether enterprises will in fact use their increased competitiveness to pursue the objective of increased market share, and whether such pursuit will succeed. Scepticism on these questions may be based on the argument that the growth of multinational operations, particularly in the form of mergers, acquisitions and alliances (MAAs), increases oligopolistic interdependence among enterprises.[20] This arises not merely from the fact that MAAs definitionally increase producer concentration, but also because enterprises which are larger and more highly diversified in terms of their product range and geographical ambit have stronger and more wide-ranging powers of retaliation against aggressive actions by their rivals. Some economists argue that this stronger retaliatory capability among rivals has the effect of inhibiting aggressive behaviour aimed at increasing market share.[21]

If so, the evident shift towards more globalized strategies in the 1980s, and the wave of MAA activity associated with it, are likely to cause enterprise behaviour to become more defensive. This tendency has probably been intensified by the recession of the early 1990s, even though the FDI and the number of new mergers and acquisitions has declined sharply (see Chapter 1). In particular, increased defensiveness explains the current emphasis of MNEs on cutting costs, since this increases profits without damaging rivals. By increasing profit margins, cost-cutting also compensates for declining sales consequent upon world recession, and provides scope for future price-cutting in response to aggressive behaviour by others. The resulting intensification of work effort and downward pressure on real wages would be justified, by the individual enterprise, by the argument that these sacrifices by workers were necessary in order to remain competitive in the market-place. The outcome could be little or no change in the relative competitive positions of enterprises, but a shift in income distribution in favour of profits. In tandem with the pursuit of cost-cutting, enterprises are also encouraged towards still further product and geographical diversification, and yet more MAAs, in order to deter attack by rivals.

Against this viewpoint it may be argued that, historically, the balance of forces among oligopolists has almost invariably proved to be unstable. Typically there are at least some enterprises which may be relied upon to behave aggressively because they are confident that they have a decisive advantage. Rapid technological change and the integration of national markets are also conventionally viewed as factors which promote competition by disturbing the balance among oligopolists. It is

---

[20] The essence of oligopolistic interdependence is that the behaviour of each enterprise is modified by an awareness that its own behaviour (the pursuit of sales, profits or other objectives) will influence its rivals and therefore induce some retaliatory reaction from them, a reaction which the enterprise will rationally attempt to foresee and allow for in formulating its own plans (and for the same reason will try to forecast rivals' initiatives). Where the degree of oligopolistic interdependence is pronounced, enterprise behaviour is perhaps better described as "rivalrous" than "competitive"; and it may be just this terminological difference which is important in understanding the problem at hand.

[21] See K. Cowling and R. Sugden: *Transnational monopoly capitalism* (Brighton, Sussex, Wheatsheaf Books, 1987).

also pointed out that large, globalized and diversified MNEs have a stronger capacity to enter new markets as well as a stronger capacity to resist new entrants to their own, and that there is therefore no presumption that increased concentration of assets among the largest MNEs will inhibit competitive behaviour.

While a full examination of the issues raised in the last few paragraphs would require a book in itself, enough has been said to justify two broad conclusions. First, we cannot simply assume that the growth of FDI and the globalization strategies underlying it will lead to increased competition and thence to increased employment. The second conclusion is that this question is an issue for public policy. As international economic integration has increased in recent years, competition policy at the national level has become eclipsed. Within Europe, this has been offset by the development of competition policy at the EC level; but there is as yet little recognition that a truly global approach to anti-trust issues will sooner or later be required.

There is a second problem we might raise in connection with the argument that increased competitiveness leads to increased employment. Hamill is careful to advance this argument only at the enterprise level. The problem is to establish its implications for employment at higher levels of aggregation. Clearly one enterprise, country, or region may experience employment gains due to increased competitiveness vis-à-vis a second enterprise, country or region – which thereby experiences employment losses.[22] Taking a cosmopolitan view, however, the interesting question is whether it is possible for the world as a whole to experience a gain in employment due to increased competitiveness.

Since the term "competitiveness" refers to the position of one economic agent relative to another, it is of course logically impossible for the world as a whole to increase its competitiveness. Economists of the neoclassical school, however, argue that the attempts of economic agents to increase their competitiveness lead to increased productivity, and in this way the world as a whole gains. In particular, the gains for workers arise in two ways. First, higher productivity increases profitability in real terms; this stimulates investment, thereby increasing the demand for labour and thus increasing both employment and the real wage. Second, to the extent that faster productivity growth is an ongoing process rather than a one-off jump, the resulting faster growth of real incomes reduces inflationary pressure and thus permits a relaxation of monetary and fiscal restraints. The national economies in question can thus operate with smaller margins of excess capacity, resulting in additional employment gains.[23]

However there are other economists who in varying degrees are sceptical of these benign mechanisms. As noted earlier, increased competitiveness at the enterprise level need not be synonymous with higher productivity, but may also result from a shift in bargaining power against workers in the labour market. In one version

---

[22] The gainers may well choose to disregard these losses to others; indeed this is normal not only for enterprises but for countries and also for regional groups such as the European Community.

[23] It is by means of an argument along these lines that the Cecchini Report is able to argue that the Single European Market will, after the transition, lead to increased employment and real incomes throughout the EC; and that these gains will be in large part gains to the world as a whole, rather than at the expense of countries or regions outside of the EC. See P. Cecchini, et al.: *The European challenge 1992 – The benefits of a Single Market* (Aldershot, Hampshire, Wildwood House, 1988).

of this, there is a fall in real wages which increases profitability, investment and employment. In the stronger, more Marxist version, it is doubted whether increased profitability leads to increased investment, because the shift in income distribution in favour of profits serves to dampen aggregate demand. Thus the real wage reduction brings no benefit in increased employment.

In sum, it is clear that the question of whether the globalization of markets and of MNE operations will bring gains to the world as a whole in terms of employment and real wages hinges upon some difficult questions in the realms of industrial economics and macroeconomic theory, questions which are in urgent need of further research.

A second conclusion is that, whatever the overall and long-term employment effects may prove to be, there are important implications for society and government in the short-term national and local impact of globalization strategies. There is much food for thought in Campbell's suggestion that there are pressures towards "social convergence" among national economies as forms of work organization and the structure of labour markets become increasingly similar; and in the parallel tendency towards greater inequality within national economies resulting from greater labour market segmentation. For governments, there are important implications in what Campbell calls "the new economics of location", whereby national and local economies are brought into increasing competition with one another to attract high quality investment by MNEs. This has a positive side, in the sense that this exerts strong pressure on governments to invest in education and training, and physical infrastructure and the environment, with benefits to society as a whole. The negative side derives from the loss of national autonomy over wages and working conditions – the "regulatory deficit". We may well share Campbell's pessimism regarding the extent to which international action, whether through the ILO or other institutions, will be able to bridge this gap – though the Social Chapter of the Maastricht Treaty gives grounds for optimism.

A third and related conclusion of interest which may be derived from the book concerns the competitive economic struggle between the "triad powers" – Japan, North America and Western Europe. The expectation of adherents to the Western liberal or social-democratic consensus concerning this competition is that there will in the long run be no overall winners or losers, but that the improvements in technology and efficiency which result from the struggle itself will make all of us (including non-participants) better off. FDI from Japan may be expected to speed up this process of convergence in economic performance.

In Chapter 5, however, Watanabe raises something of a question mark against this comforting thesis. Whereas in the past it has been argued that the Japanese industrial system is embedded in a particular culture and society, and hence cannot be successfully transplanted, Watanabe effectively turns this argument on its head. Thus he suggests that the fundamental factor inhibiting Western adoption of Japanese organizational philosophy is a reluctance on the part of management to "buy the whole package" because its egalitarian implications would overturn the existing social and economic hierarchy. However, he also explores more fundamental socio-cultural inhibitions in the West which cut across social classes. These relate to power and individual liberty rather than income or status.

On the distributional issues discussed earlier in this section, Watanabe suggests that appeal to the "Japanese threat" has been used to enforce the adoption of practices which Western firms in any case have wished to introduce for many years – such as flexible working practices – but have been unable to introduce due to worker resistance. Thus Japanese competition is made the scapegoat for changes which in fact are a travesty of the Japanese system because they lack elements of the Japanese package which would be attractive to workers and which are essential to its success; that is job security, abundant training opportunities and egalitarian remuneration. Lacking these elements, attempts to transplant the Japanese system are likely to yield disappointing and socially divisive results.

From the point of view of the Western liberal consensus, there is much that is disturbing in Watanabe's chapter, and for that we should thank him. We are reminded that the economic models of Western Europe and North America are, like Japan's, embedded in a particular culture and society; that distributional and efficiency considerations can seldom be separated from one another; and that sociocultural features may well impede economic progress.

Central and Eastern Europe

Regarding the prospects for FDI in the newly liberalizing economies of Central and Eastern Europe, at first sight there is something of a puzzle to be explained. The new governments are all eager to attract FDI which they rightly see as simultaneously providing the real resources and the know-how which they conspicuously lack. Reflecting the resulting liberalization of foreign investment laws, there have been many thousands of very small-scale joint ventures, most of which are concerned with trading and distribution. Yet there has been relatively little FDI by established MNEs despite the willingness of would-be host governments to allow them to acquire existing state-owned assets at knock-down prices, either by joint venture or by outright sale. From the data in Welge and Holtbrügge's chapter it is clear that only a few dozen projects involving MNEs have occurred (though there are some in the pipeline).

While lack of interest by MNEs in the former USSR is understandable given the high degree of political uncertainty, we might have expected any alert MNE to take advantage of the situation in countries such as Poland, the CSFR and Hungary where the opportunity exists to acquire physical assets, market share, etc., at low prices, in economies where the local competition is weak. The fact that there have so far been only a small number of instances of MNE entry into these countries is therefore puzzling. One explanation may be that in most other cases the assets in question, and the market shares which go with them, are viewed by the relevant MNEs as worth so little that it is not attractive to buy them even at very low prices; but it seems rather unlikely that this should be so generally true across the board. Another type of explanation is that MNEs are engaged in a "wait and see" game in which they are waiting not only to see what transpires in Central and Eastern Europe in terms of political stability and growth, but also perhaps more importantly to see what their rivals do. The desire to "wait and see" may reflect not only oligopolistic interdependence, but also the interdependence of investment decisions. Clearly if a number of large MNEs simultaneously invested in, say, Hungary, then the growth of the economy would be stimulated and the profitability of each investment would be greater than if it alone had been undertaken.[24]

If this correctly explains MNEs' "wait and see" behaviour, it provides an additional argument in favour of a "New Marshall Plan" for Central and Eastern Europe. In Chapter 8 it is suggested that assistance from the industrialized countries is desirable to provide the necessary impetus to the transition process in Eastern Europe and the former USSR. Of course, such official assistance would encourage FDI by restoring credibility to transition programmes which in some countries is conspicuously lacking at present. But an additional role which might be fulfilled by such a programme would be that of coordinating private investment decisions, thereby overcoming the impasse which may result if each independent private agent is waiting for others to move first on the grounds that only if they do will his or her plan become profitable.[25] Once this deadlock is broken, we could envisage a flood of FDI by MNEs in the region, in part reflecting the "follow my leader" behaviour which is so characteristic of oligopolistic firms.

Developing countries

Part 1 of the book furnishes insights into the motivation of FDI strategies in the 1980s which help to explain why FDI in this period was so heavily biased against the developing countries. On the other hand, it is also clear from Part 2 that the global perspective of MNEs and their continued search for cost-minimization can make developing countries attractive locations for FDI under the right circumstances. Furthermore, there are some clues to be found as to how all parties may benefit from MNE presence in a developing country.

First, concerning the role of EPZs, some observers regard EPZs as being little more than a form of licensed exploitation of their workers. Chapter 2 confirms that unionization rates are generally low, and in some countries there are restrictions on the right to organize. However, it is arguable that the key questions concern not current wages and working conditions in EPZs but their dynamic role, in host countries, in promoting social and economic development in their hosts countries and integration into the global economy. There is an optimistic scenario which postulates that EPZs will, in the long run, prove to be a transitional arrangement, serving as an initial inducement to MNEs necessary to offset the additional costs and risks of establishing production in developing countries. In due course, according to this scenario, these costs and risks will diminish as on the one hand MNEs acquire local experience and on the other hand indigenous production capabilities, labour force

---

[24] This in fact is an echo of a very old argument to be found in the development economics literature. There is a case for state intervention where private investment projects are necessarily large scale and "lumpy", and also interdependent in the sense that the profitability of each is affected by whether the others are undertaken. The case for "indicative planning" is founded on similar reasoning.

[25] The importance of improving access for exporters to Western European markets should also be emphasized.

quality, etc., improve. This convergence should make it possible to phase out the concessions which EPZs enjoy in respect of taxation and social obligations (which give rise to the charge of exploitation) and also cause MNEs to reduce their initial heavy reliance on imported inputs. In this way EPZs should become gradually integrated into the national economies of their host countries.[26]

If this is correct, we may see the tax privileges and other special treatment which EPZs enjoy as a form of "infant industry" protection which should be strictly time-limited. In the same vein, we could argue that governments have an obligation to promote better wages and working conditions in EPZs as a way of exerting pressure on local enterprises and MNE affiliates to invest in labour skills and generally to promote productivity growth. The only policy issue would then concern not the principle of such policy measures but merely their time profile and intensity. However, a crucial qualification to this analysis is that in policy towards EPZs there is a severe problem of "regulatory deficit", in the sense that the autonomy of national policy is undermined by intense international competition. The case for international policy measures is thus very strong.

As a broader issue, the problems of integrating MNE activities into their host economy is in fact touched on by many chapters and from many different points of view in the book. Chapters 6 and 7 show that in both Mexico and Indonesia there are considerable problems in achieving the full potential benefit from MNE presence through local subcontracting, and the nature of the underlying problems and the ways in which they might be overcome are extensively discussed. It is intriguing to note how closely these discussions echo the problems of Japanese enterprises seeking to increase local procurement in both industrialized and developing countries, as reported in Chapter 5. The general conclusion, applicable perhaps across many countries, may be that where inward investors bring with them technological and managerial skills which give them an advantage over local producers sufficient to outweigh the additional costs associated with "foreignness", this logically implies that potential local suppliers are at a competitive disadvantage. Given this, it is perhaps unrealistic to imagine that local procurement on a significant scale will occur. The challenge for policy is to assist the competitive process to close this gap, but in the interim it is inevitably a source of frustration to both sides.[27]

In Chapter 6, three concrete suggestions are made regarding policy initiatives in Mexico to promote suppliers' performance, which appear relevant in other countries too. First, there is a case for government action to identify and remedy the underlying reasons for unreliable delivery on the part of Mexican suppliers – a factor which is becoming increasingly important as purchasers adopt "just-in-time" production methods. Second, for a number of reasons, technology transfer might be speeded up by government promotion of joint ventures between Mexican partners and small and medium-sized MNEs (rather than large multinationals). More generally, the

---

[26] UNCTC: *The challenge of free economic zones in Central and Eastern Europe* (New York, United Nations, 1989), Ch. I.

[27] That competition will in time close this gap is not, of course, inevitable; indeed there is a school of thought (and a number of economic models) which predict precisely the reverse. Space does not permit this question to be pursued here.

Government could use its powers of moral suasion to encourage MNEs to cultivate and assist domestic suppliers, citing examples from several countries (including Mexico itself) where this has been found to be mutually beneficial after initial reticence had been overcome. The authors conjecture that MNEs from Japan are more inclined to support domestic suppliers in this way, and this is indeed confirmed by Chapter 5 of this book.[28]

There is a further insight in Chapter 6 which is of broader relevance. In general terms the point made is that, while increased local purchasing by MNEs cannot be expected to have a very large quantitative employment impact, it has a very important role to play in the fostering of the host country's technological capabilities. Such fostering is all the more necessary because low wage costs cannot be relied upon indefinitely as the source competitiveness in world markets. In this sense, the authors imply that the apparent policy choice between targeting the *quantity* of employment via low wages, and targeting the *quality* of employment via technological upgrading, is in practice an illusion in the long run – a proposition with important implications for policy in industrialized and developing countries alike.

In Chapter 7 too there are several points which relate to Indonesia but which are of general relevance. First, although the training record of MNEs in Indonesia is good, the primary responsibility for education and training must necessarily lie with the Government, and inadequacies in the education system may prevent the full potential benefits of MNE presence from being achieved. Second, where the structure of domestic prices is highly distorted, labour-intensive activities may be discriminated against and employment growth handicapped. MNEs' activities which are attracted by high levels of tariff protection may be particularly damaging and may lead to net losses of real income for the country concerned. The remedy for this of course lies in the reform of trade policy.

There is a further argument for trade liberalization in Chapter 7. It is noted that, in Indonesia, local spin-offs do not only arise from equity participation by MNEs. Foreign buying groups, and other arms' length yet close business ties, serve to set standards and provide information conduits from which local producers can benefit significantly. This point reinforces the widely held view that export-orientation is at least as important as MNE presence in promoting development. This view is also reflected in the remarks in Chapter 1 concerning the rapid economic integration of the countries of the Pacific Rim, associated with the "new wave" of FDI from the NIEs.

This FDI from the NIEs has important implications for developing host countries. It seems likely that the factors motivating this investment will strengthen over time, and therefore its volume increase. Because this investment is primarily export-oriented, it is less dependent on the size of the host country; hence many developing countries could in due course become attractive as hosts to MNE from NIEs in Asia and elsewhere. Among the most important factors influencing the loca-

---

[28] There are also some insights to be found in Halbach's study of inter-industry linkages, which is based on a questionnaire (to which 112 MNEs responded) and on interviews with a smaller number. See A. J. Halbach: *Multinational enterprises and subcontracting in the Third World: A study of inter-industrial linkages*, Multinational Enterprises Programme Working Paper No. 58 (Geneva, ILO, 1989).

tion of these FDI decisions are likely to be the economic and political stability of the potential host country, the efficiency, simplicity and transparency of its administrative system, the presence of adequate infrastructure such as ports, roads, power and telecommunications; and above all, the quality of the labour force at all levels. Ethnic and geographical factors to a substantial degree explain why FDI from the East Asian NIEs has so far been heavily focused on developing Asia – leading, as is described in Chapter 1, to a high degree of *de facto* economic integration of the countries of the Pacific Rim. But it does not follow that developing Africa and Latin America are inevitably excluded. From an economic standpoint the value of both ethnic ties and geographical proximity lies in the fact that they facilitate information flows, which have an important bearing on FDI location decisions, especially in the early stages.[29] The lesson for other developing countries wishing to attract FDI from the NIEs (or from elsewhere) is that they could greatly improve their prospects by policy measures to facilitate information flows.

The future outlook for FDI from the NIEs in industrialized countries is also a question of interest. Of the NIEs, only the Republic of Korea and Taiwan, China, have so far invested in industrialized countries to a significant extent, principally in the US. As in the case of Japanese FDI, this may have been motivated in part by actual and prospective protectionism in industrialized countries. At the same time however the study by Hong cited in section 6 of this chapter suggests that Korean enterprises are investing abroad as part of a conscious globalization strategy in which they seek to supply world markets from least-cost locations. FDI in industrialized countries is then motivated by the desire to acquire as rapidly as possible the advantages which they currently lack, by joint ventures, by technological collaboration with enterprises in industrialized countries and by setting up their own R&D activities. It is also clear that some Korean enterprises have acquired technological, organizational and marketing skills, and established market outlets and brands; all of which are enterprise-specific or ownership advantages which can be deployed globally through FDI. While the sheer size of the largest Korean enterprises is in itself sufficient qualification for them to seek multinational status, there is also evidence of a long-term globalization strategy in the study's suggestion that Korean enterprises are establishing themselves in some markets (e.g. in Central and Eastern Europe) in order to gain "first mover" advantages. In sum, we may expect enterprises from both the Republic of Korea and Taiwan, China, to become increasingly evident as "global players" in FDI.

Finally, a broad and inevitably somewhat speculative conclusion is suggested by Chapter 9 on trade and MNE activity in services. Assuming that the Uruguay Round is concluded successfully (which at the time of writing is in doubt), then it seems clear that national markets for many important services, which have hitherto enjoyed a high degree of natural protection from international competition, will become increasingly internationally integrated through the activities of MNEs – though this may well prove to be a long drawn out process. A further important long-term outcome may prove to be a significant reduction in barriers to international

---

[29] The same argument helps to explain why Japan's FDI in Europe has concentrated on the UK, where the language barrier is at its lowest.

labour mobility, though this is more questionable in view of its obvious conflict with immigration controls, where the trend is in the opposite direction. These two developments would imply a gradual but highly significant movement towards a single world market for labour. Such a movement is of course already under way as the integration of national markets for goods and capital proceeds apace, and is the subject-matter of Chapter 10 in particular. However, the implications for the international distribution of employment and income of a further intensification of this trend are momentous.